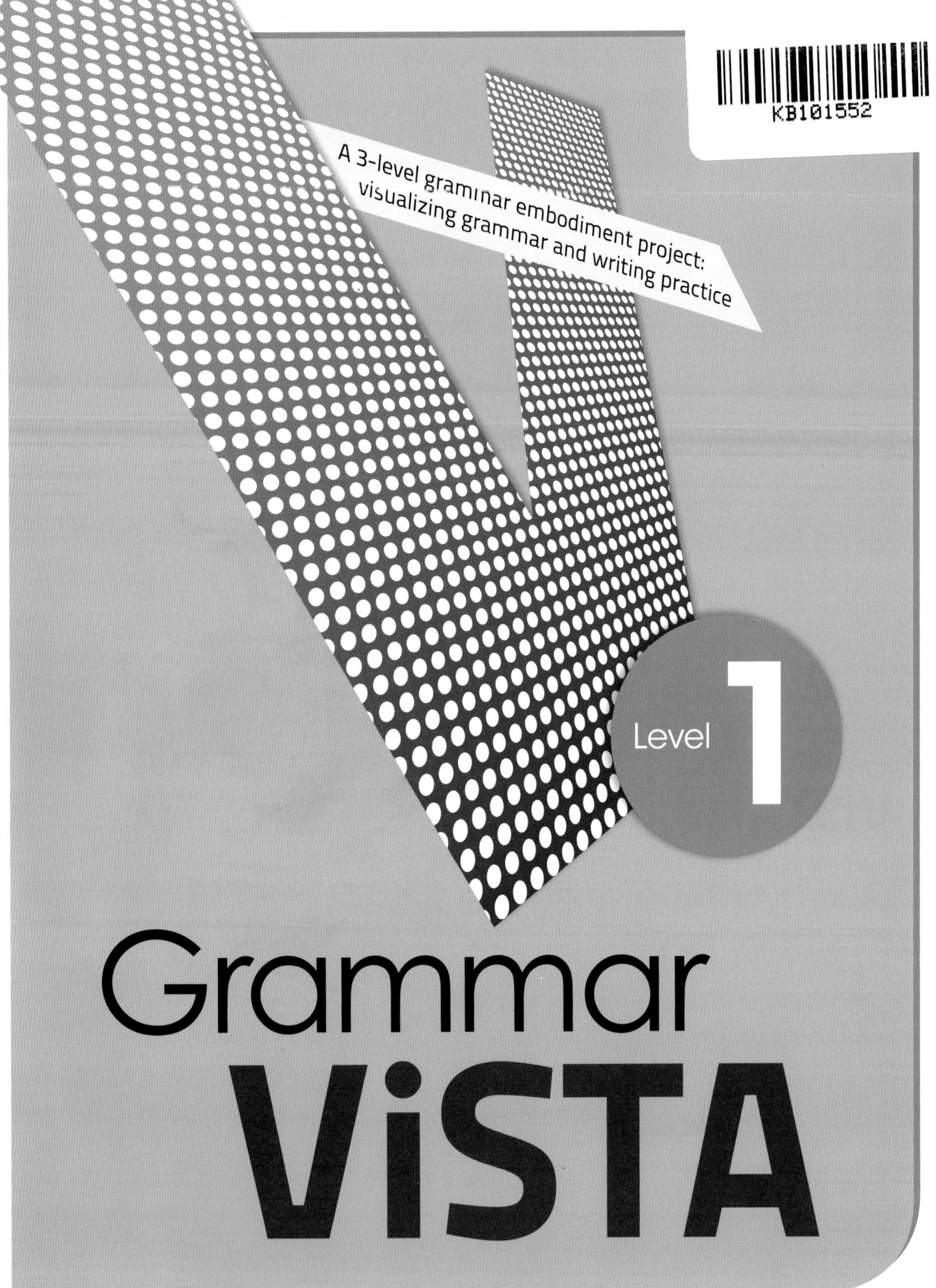

Grammar ViSTA

DARAKWON

지은이 김해자, 손의웅, 최현진
펴낸이 정규도
펴낸곳 (주)다락원

초판 1쇄 발행 2018년 4월 5일
초판 8쇄 발행 2024년 2월 20일

편집 이희경
디자인 조수정, 박은비, 김나경
일러스트 이경
영문 감수 Amy L. Redding, Michael A. Putlack

다락원 경기도 파주시 문발로 211
내용문의 (02)736-2031 내선 503
구입문의 (02)736-2031 내선 250~252
Fax (02)732-2037
출판등록 1977년 9월 16일 제 406-2008-000007호

ISBN 978-89-277-0825-4 54740
978-89-277-0824-7 54740(set)

http://www.darakwon.co.kr
다락원 홈페이지를 방문하시면 상세한 출판정보와 함께
동영상강좌, MP3자료 등 다양한 어학 정보를 얻으실 수 있습니다.

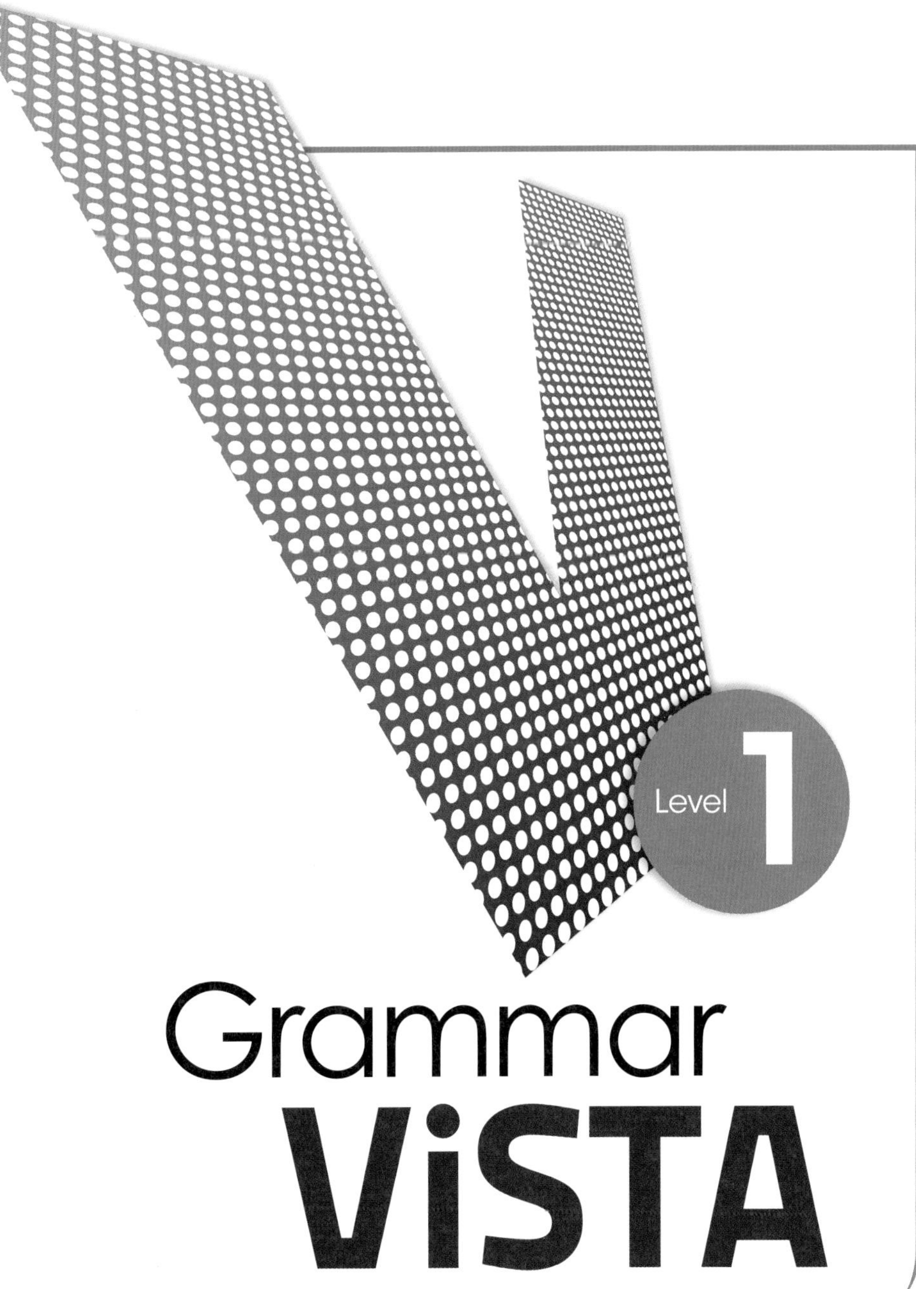

Grammar ViSTA

Grammar ViSTA Series

STRUCTURE

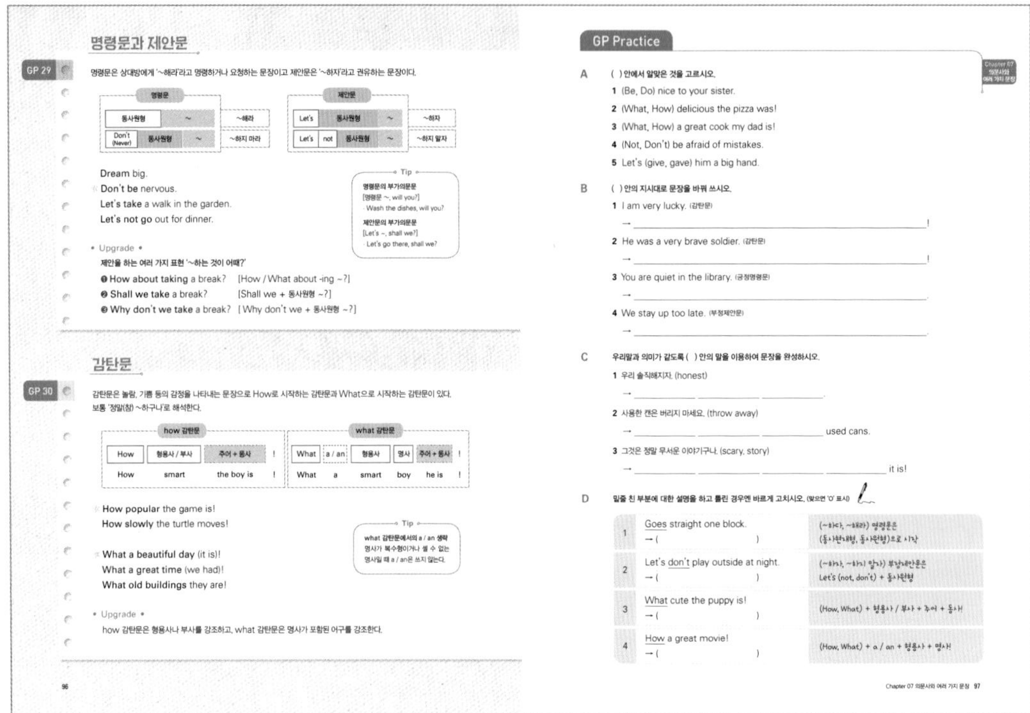

1 Grammar Point

• **문법패턴 도식화**

총 177개의 핵심 문법을 도식화하여
시각적 학습 효과를 극대화시켰습니다.

• **대표 예문 선정**

GP마다 대표 예문(☆)을 선정하여 문법 내용과
실전 예문을 동시에 학습할 수 있습니다.

• **Tip과 Upgrade**

주의해야 할 내용은 Tip으로,
심화 문법 내용은 Upgrade로 정리하였습니다.

2 GP Practice

• **선택형·단답형·서술형 문제**

선택형, 단답형, 서술형 영작으로
단계적이고 반복적인 학습이 되도록 하였습니다.

• **오답 찾고 설명하기 문제**

오답 찾기 방식으로 핵심 문법을 스스로 정리하고
자기 주도적 학습이 되도록 하였습니다.

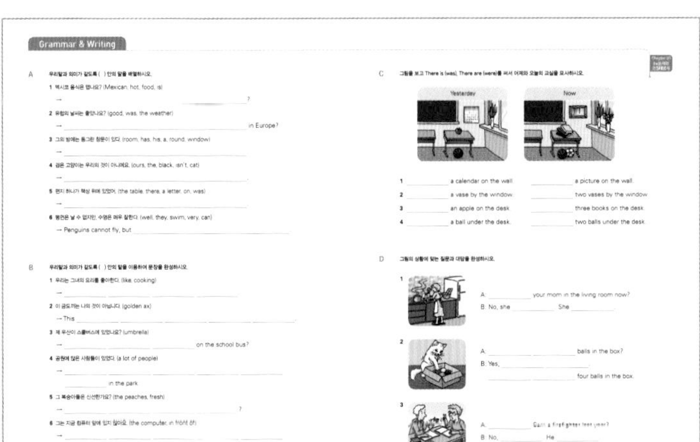

3 Grammar & Writing

- **단어 배열·문장 완성형 문제**

  학습한 문법 내용을 토대로 단어 배열 및 문장 완성을 통해 실질적인 쓰기 연습이 되도록 하였습니다.

- **구문 및 표현력 평가 문제**

  실생활을 소재로 한 대화나 삽화 문제를 구성함으로써 수행평가에 필요한 구문 작성 능력과 표현 능력을 키울 수 있도록 하였습니다.

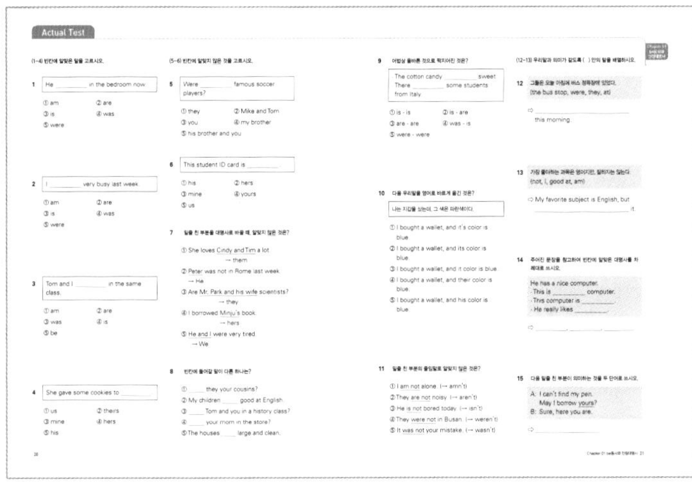

4 Actual Test

- **실전 문제**

  학습한 내용을 다양한 실전 문제를 통해서 다시 한 번 정리할 수 있도록 하였습니다.

- **내신 대비 서술형 문제**

  최신 내신 유형을 반영한 문제로 구성하여 서술형 내신을 완벽하게 대비할 수 있도록 하였습니다.

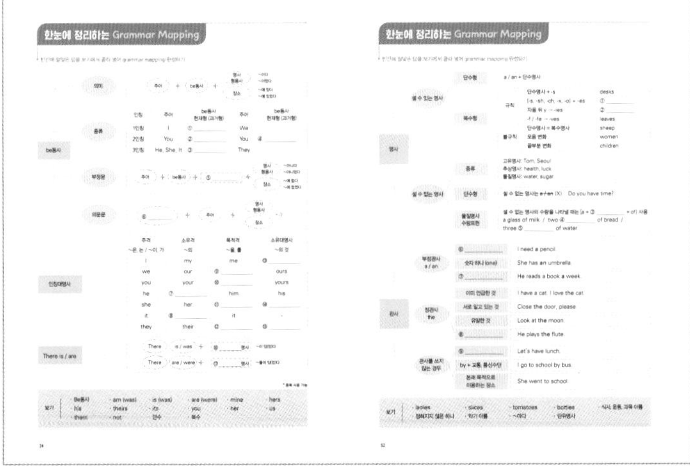

5 한눈에 정리하는 Grammar Mapping

- **문법 맵핑**

  학습한 문법 내용 전체를 한눈에 파악하고 핵심개념을 맵핑 이미지로 다시 한 번 정리할 수 있도록 하였습니다.

Workbook

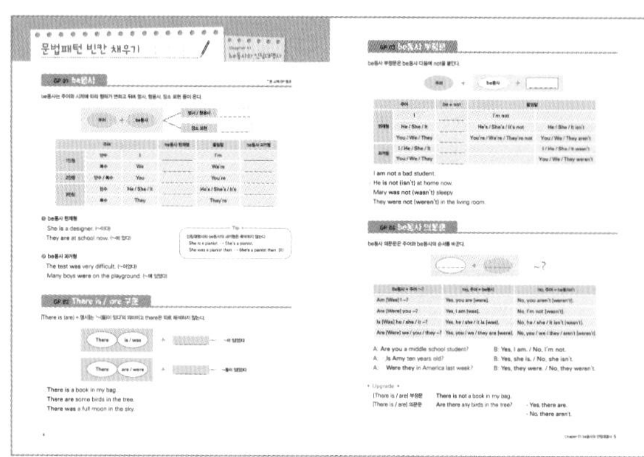

1 문법패턴 빈칸 채우기

• **노트 완성형 문제**

노트 형태로 제시한 핵심 문법 사항의 빈칸을 채워 나가면서 자기 주도적으로 학습할 수 있도록 하였습니다.

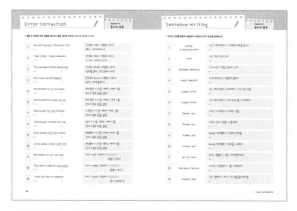

2 Workbook 연습문제

• **단계별 반복학습 문제**

풍부하고 다양한 연습문제를 통해 문법과 쓰기 연습을 극대화시켰습니다.

3 Error Correction & Sentence Writing

• **오답 찾고 설명하기 문제**

학습한 문법 개념을 정확하게 이해하고 있는지 시험해 볼 수 있는 자기 주도적 학습 방법입니다.

• **구문 영작 문제**

학습한 문법 지식을 바탕으로 구문 단위로 영작을 능숙하게 할 수 있는지 검증해 볼 수 있는 문제 유형입니다.

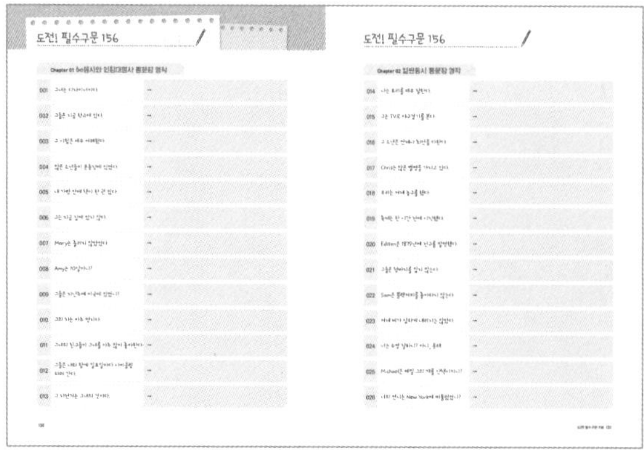

4 도전! 필수구문 156

• **대표 예문 영작 문제**

GP마다 선정한 대표 예문을 통문장으로 영작하고 암기할 수 있도록 구성하였습니다.

* 본 교재는 대등한 쓰임의 단어들의 경우 ( )나 /로 구분 표기합니다. (일반적 용도로도 사용)

ex which (that): which 또는 that 사용가능
which / that: which 또는 that 사용가능

* 본 교재는 문법 설명 파트에서 학습 요소의 강조를 위해 굵은 서체나 이탤릭체를 사용합니다.

Grammar ViSTA Contents

Contents

Contents

Chapter

01

be동사와 인칭대명사

be동사

GP 01

be동사는 주어와 시제에 따라 형태가 변하고 뒤에 명사, 형용사, 장소 표현 등이 온다.

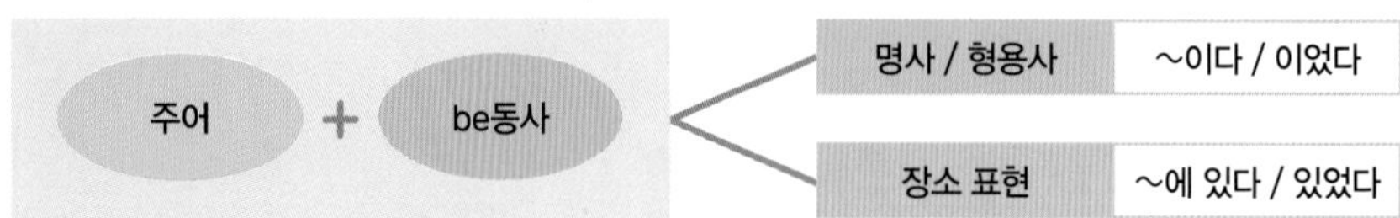

주어			be동사 현재형	줄임말	be동사 과거형
1인칭	단수	I	am	I'm	was
	복수	We	are	We're	were
2인칭	단수 / 복수	You	are	You're	were
3인칭	단수	He / She / It	is	He's / She's / It's	was
	복수	They	are	They're	were

❶ be동사 현재형

☆ She **is** a designer. (~이다)

☆ They **are** at school now. (~에 있다)

❷ be동사 과거형

☆ The test **was** very difficult. (~이었다)

☆ Many boys **were** on the playground. (~에 있었다)

Tip

인칭대명사와 be동사의 과거형은 축약하지 않는다.

· She is a pianist. → She's a pianist.

· She was a pianist then. → ~~She's~~ a pianist then. (X)

There is / are 구문

GP 02

[There is (are) + 명사]는 '~(들)이 있다'의 의미이고 there은 따로 해석하지 않는다.

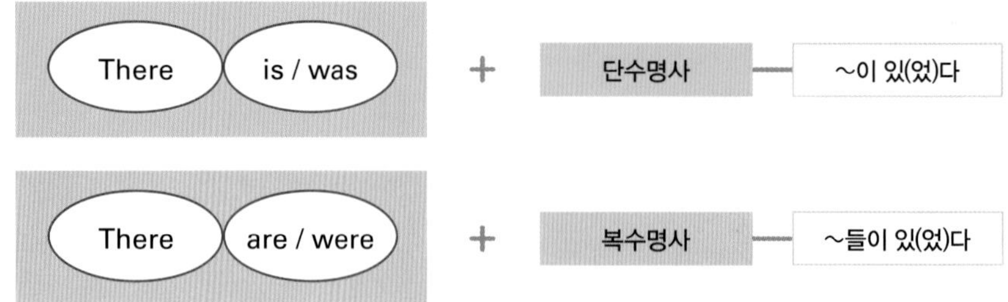

☆ **There is** a book in my bag.

There are some birds in the tree.

There was a full moon in the sky.

GP Practice

A ( ) 안에서 알맞은 것을 고르시오.

1 The spaceship (is, are) very small.

2 The pizza (was, were) delicious.

3 William and Peter (was, are) brothers.

4 There (is, are) a swimming pool at his house.

5 The students (was, were) on a field trip.

B 보기의 말을 골라 빈칸을 채우고 알맞은 뜻을 고르시오.

보기	am	are	is	were	was

1 It ______________ very hot today. (~에 있다, ~이다)

2 I ______________ 14 years old last year. (~에 있었다, ~이었다)

3 The actors ______________ behind the stage now. (~에 있다, ~이다)

4 The girls ______________ at the store yesterday. (~에 있었다, ~이었다)

C 우리말과 의미가 같도록 ( ) 안의 말을 이용하여 문장을 완성하시오.

1 그 아이는 매우 영리하다. (the child)

→ __________ __________ __________ very smart.

2 그들은 어젯밤에 피곤했다. (tired)

→ __________ __________ __________ last night.

3 벽에 시계가 있었다. (a clock)

→ __________ __________ __________ __________ on the wall.

D 밑줄 친 부분에 대한 설명을 하고 틀린 경우엔 바르게 고치시오. (맞으면 'O' 표시)

1	You am a great singer. → (are)	주어 (1인칭, 2인칭) + be동사 현재형 (am, are, is)
2	He were at the library yesterday. → ( )	주어 3인칭 (단수, 복수) + be동사 과거형 (was, were)
3	There is three schools near here. → ( )	There (is, are) + (단수명사, 복수명사)
4	They're at the shopping mall. → ( )	They are의 줄임말은 (They're, They's)

be동사 부정문

GP 03

be동사 부정문은 be동사 다음에 not을 붙인다.

주어 + be동사 + not

	주어	be + not	줄임말	
현재형	I	am not	I'm not	
	He / She / It	is not	He's / She's / It's not	He / She / It isn't
	You / We / They	are not	You're / We're / They're not	You / We / They aren't
과거형	I / He / She / It	was not		I / He / She / It wasn't
	You / We / They	were not		You / We / They weren't

I **am not** a bad student.

He **is not (isn't)** at home now.

Mary **was not (wasn't)** sleepy.

They **were not (weren't)** in the living room.

be동사 의문문

GP 04

be동사 의문문은 주어와 be동사의 순서를 바꾼다.

~?

Be동사 + 주어 ~?	Yes, 주어 + be동사	No, 주어 + be동사n't
Am [Was] I ~?	Yes, you are [were].	No, you aren't [weren't].
Are [Were] you ~?	Yes, I am [was].	No, I'm not [wasn't].
Is [Was] he / she / it ~?	Yes, he / she / it is [was].	No, he / she / it isn't [wasn't].
Are [Were] we / you / they ~?	Yes, you / we / they are [were].	No, you / we / they / aren't [weren't].

A: **Are you** a middle school student? B: **Yes, I am. / No, I'm not.**

A: **Is Amy** ten years old? B: **Yes, she is. / No, she isn't.**

A: **Were they** in America last week? B: **Yes, they were. / No, they weren't.**

• Upgrade •

[There is / are] 부정문 — **There is not** a book in my bag.

[There is / are] 의문문 — **Are there** any birds in the tree? - Yes, there are.
- No, there aren't.

GP Practice

A ( ) 안에서 알맞은 것을 고르시오.

1 (Is, Are) math your favorite subject?

2 Those (isn't, aren't) sunflowers.

3 (Are, Were) you in Seoul last month?

4 (I'm not, I amn't) a high school student.

5 (Is, Was) it sunny yesterday?

B 주어진 문장을 부정문으로 바꾸시오. (줄일 수 있으면 줄임말 사용)

1 I am at school now. → I ____________ at school now.

2 Mike is from Canada. → Mike ____________ from Canada.

3 Your friends are in the same class. → Your friends ____________ in the same class.

4 Kevin was busy. → Kevin ____________ busy.

5 Your socks were wet. → Your socks ____________ wet.

C 우리말과 의미가 같도록 ( ) 안의 말을 이용하여 문장을 완성하시오.

1 그 새끼 고양이는 조심스럽지 않아. (the kitten)

→ ________ ________ ________ ________ careful.

2 내 지갑이 침대 아래 있었니? (my wallet)

→ ________ ________ ________ under the bed?

3 A: 네 방은 깨끗하니? (your room) B: 아니, 그렇지 않아.

→ A: ________ ________ ________ clean? B: No, it ____________.

D 밑줄 친 부분에 대한 설명을 하고 틀린 경우엔 바르게 고치시오. (맞으면 'O' 표시)

1	They <u>not are</u> famous in Korea. → ( )	be동사 부정문은 주어 + (not + be동사, be동사 + not)
2	<u>It was</u> rainy this morning? No, it wasn't. → ( )	be동사 의문문은 (주어 + be동사 ~?, Be동사 + 주어 ~?)
3	Is Jack your best friend? Yes, <u>Jack</u> is. → ( )	be동사 의문문의 대답은 Yes / No, 주어(명사, 대명사) + be동사
4	<u>Are</u> fast food good for you? → ( )	be동사 의문문은 (Am, Are, Is) + 3인칭 단수 주어 ~?

인칭대명사

GP 05

인칭대명사는 사람이나 사물을 대신 가리키는 말로 인칭, 수, 격에 따라 형태가 달라진다.

인칭	수	주격 ~은, 는 / ~이, 가	소유격 ~의	목적격 ~을 / 를	소유대명사 ~의 것
1인칭	단수	I	my	me	mine
	복수	we	our	us	ours
2인칭	단수 (복수)	you	your	you	yours
3인칭	단수	he	his	him	his
		she	her	her	hers
		it	its	it	-
	복수	they	their	them	theirs

❶ **주격:** '~은, 는 / ~이, 가'로 해석하며, 문장에서 주어 역할을 한다.

She is an only daughter.

They are interested in cooking.

❷ **소유격:** '~의'로 해석하며, [소유격 + 명사] 형태로 쓴다.

☆ **His** car is very fancy.

Their shoes are very cheap.

Tip

it's vs. its

· It's cute. (It is의 줄임말)

· We like its color. (it의 소유격)

❸ **목적격:** '~을, ~를, ~에게'로 해석하며, 문장에서 동사 또는 전치사의 목적어 역할을 한다.

☆ Her friends like **her** very much. (동사의 목적어)

☆ They go cycling with **me** every Sunday. (전치사의 목적어)

❹ **소유대명사:** '~의 것'이라고 해석하며, [소유격 + 명사]를 대신한다.

This cell phone is **mine**. (mine = my cell phone)

☆ The bike is **hers**. (hers = her bike)

• Upgrade •

명사의 소유격과 소유대명사는 형태가 같으며 [명사's]로 나타낸다.

This is Jane's pen. (소유격)

This pen is Jane's. (소유대명사)

GP Practice

A ( ) 안에서 알맞은 것을 고르시오.

1 The car is very nice. Is it (you, yours)?

2 I have a little dog. (Its, It's) color is white.

3 The police always help (we, us).

4 Tiffany likes (hers, her) new jacket.

5 (Her, She) plays the guitar well.

B 밑줄 친 부분을 대신하는 알맞은 대명사를 ( ) 안에 쓰시오.

1 I read stories, but I can't remember (   ).

2 The dog is very big, but I am not afraid of (   ).

3 Sam and I went to Seoul. (   ) had a wonderful time.

4 Mr. Smith is an artist. (   ) pictures are perfect.

C 우리말과 의미가 같도록 ( ) 안의 말을 이용하여 문장을 완성하시오.

1 그 운동화는 나의 것이다. (be)

→ The sneakers ______________ ______________.

2 그의 휴대폰이 꺼졌어. (cell phone)

→ ______________ ______________ ______________ is dead.

3 새들은 그들의 둥지에 알을 낳았다. (nests)

→ The birds laid eggs in ______________ ______________.

D 밑줄 친 부분에 대한 설명을 하고 틀린 경우엔 바르게 고치시오. (맞으면 'O' 표시)

1	Me love Mexican food. → ( )	'(나는, 나를) + 사랑한다'이므로 (주격, 목적격)인 (I, Me)
2	Jisu ate hers apple pie. → ( )	(그녀의, 그녀의 것)이므로 (소유격, 소유대명사)인 (her, hers)
3	The big chair is me. → ( )	(나를, 나의 것)이므로 (목적격, 소유대명사)인 (me, mine)
4	I go to church with them. → ( )	전치사 + (주격, 목적격)이므로 with + (they, them)

A 우리말과 의미가 같도록 ( ) 안의 말을 배열하시오.

1 멕시코 음식은 맵나요? (Mexican, hot, food, is)

→ ______________________________?

2 유럽의 날씨는 좋았나요? (good, was, the weather)

→ ______________________________ in Europe?

3 그의 방에는 동그란 창문이 있다. (room, has, his, a, round, window)

→ ______________________________.

4 검은 고양이는 우리의 것이 아니에요. (ours, the, black, isn't, cat)

→ ______________________________.

5 편지 하나가 책상 위에 있었어. (the table, there, a letter, on, was)

→ ______________________________.

6 펭귄은 날 수 없지만, 수영은 매우 잘한다. (well, they, swim, very, can)

→ Penguins cannot fly, but ______________________________.

B 우리말과 의미가 같도록 ( ) 안의 말을 이용하여 문장을 완성하시오.

1 우리는 그녀의 요리를 좋아한다. (like, cooking)

→ ________ ________ ________ ________.

2 이 금도끼는 나의 것이 아닙니다. (golden ax)

→ This ________ ________ ________ ________ ________.

3 제 우산이 스쿨버스에 있었나요? (umbrella)

→ ________ ________ ________ on the school bus?

4 공원에 많은 사람들이 있었다. (a lot of people)

→ ________ ________ ________ ________ ________

________ in the park.

5 그 복숭아들은 신선한가요? (the peaches, fresh)

→ ________ ________ ________ ________?

6 그는 지금 컴퓨터 앞에 있지 않아요. (the computer, in front of)

→ ________ ________ ________ ________ ________

________ ________ now.

C 그림을 보고 There is (was), There are (were)를 써서 어제와 오늘의 교실을 묘사하시오.

1 ______________ a calendar on the wall. ______________ a picture on the wall.

2 ______________ a vase by the window. ______________ two vases by the window.

3 ______________ an apple on the desk. ______________ three books on the desk.

4 ______________ a ball under the desk. ______________ two balls under the desk.

D 그림의 상황에 맞는 질문과 대답을 완성하시오.

1 

A: ______________ your mom in the living room now?

B: No, she ______________. She ______________.

2 

A: ______________ ______________ balls in the box?

B: Yes, ______________ ______________.

______________ ______________ four balls in the box.

3 

A: ______________ Sam a firefighter last year?

B: No, ______________. He ______________.

Actual Test

(1-4) 빈칸에 알맞은 말을 고르시오.

1

He ________ in the bedroom now.

① am ② are
③ is ④ was
⑤ were

2

I ________ very busy last week.

① am ② are
③ is ④ was
⑤ were

3

Tom and I ________ in the same class.

① am ② are
③ was ④ is
⑤ be

4

She gave some cookies to ________.

① us ② theirs
③ mine ④ hers
⑤ his

(5-6) 빈칸에 알맞지 않은 것을 고르시오.

5

Were ________ famous soccer players?

① they ② Mike and Tom
③ you ④ my brother
⑤ his brother and you

6

This student ID card is ________.

① his ② hers
③ mine ④ yours
⑤ us

7 밑줄 친 부분을 대명사로 바꿀 때, 알맞지 않은 것은?

① She loves Cindy and Tim a lot.
→ them
② Peter was not in Rome last week.
→ He
③ Are Mr. Park and his wife scientists?
→ they
④ I borrowed Minju's book.
→ hers
⑤ He and I were very tired.
→ We

8 빈칸에 들어갈 말이 다른 하나는?

① _____ they your cousins?
② My children _____ good at English.
③ _____ Tom and you in a history class?
④ _____ your mom in the store?
⑤ The houses_____ large and clean.

9 어법상 올바른 것으로 짝지어진 것은?

· The cotton candy ___________ sweet.
· There ___________ some students from Italy.

① is - is
② is - are
③ are - are
④ was - is
⑤ were - were

10 다음 우리말을 영어로 바르게 옮긴 것은?

나는 지갑을 샀는데, 그 색은 파란색이다.

① I bought a wallet, and it's color is blue.
② I bought a wallet, and its color is blue.
③ I bought a wallet, and it color is blue.
④ I bought a wallet, and their color is blue.
⑤ I bought a wallet, and his color is blue.

11 밑줄 친 부분의 줄임말로 알맞지 않은 것은?

① I am not alone. (→ amn't)
② They are not noisy. (→ aren't)
③ He is not bored today. (→ isn't)
④ They were not in Busan. (→ weren't)
⑤ It was not your mistake. (→ wasn't)

(12-13) 우리말과 의미가 같도록 ( ) 안의 말을 배열하시오.

12 그들은 오늘 아침에 버스 정류장에 있었다.
(the bus stop, were, they, at)

⇨ ______________________________ this morning.

13 가장 좋아하는 과목은 영어지만, 잘하지는 않는다.
(not, I, good at, am)

⇨ My favorite subject is English, but ______________________________ it.

14 주어진 문장을 참고하여 빈칸에 알맞은 대명사를 차례대로 쓰시오.

He has a nice computer.
· This is ___________ computer.
· This computer is ___________.
· He really likes ___________.

⇨ ___________, ___________, ___________

15 다음 밑줄 친 부분이 의미하는 것을 두 단어로 쓰시오.

A: I can't find my pen.
May I borrow yours?
B: Sure, here you are.

⇨ ____________________

16 밑줄 친 부분 중 어법상 어색한 것을 고르시오.

① We're not thirsty now.

② He is not a famous comedian.

③ Brian was on the news last week.

④ The singers weren't late for the concert.

⑤ Sam and Suji was lovely kids.

17 다음 중 어법상 알맞은 것을 고르시오.

① Was you interested in sports?

② A: Is Ann in the room?
B: No, Ann isn't.

③ Are his classmates kind to him?

④ Were he in America last week?

⑤ Is the paintings yours?

18 과거형으로 고친 문장 중 잘못된 것은?

① His hair is brown now.
→ His hair was brown then.

② You and I are late for school.
→ You and I was late for school yesterday.

③ Are the fans loud?
→ Were the fans loud last week?

④ The reporters aren't busy.
→ The reporters weren't busy last year.

⑤ Am I rude now?
→ Was I rude last night?

19 다음 문장을 부정문으로 알맞게 고친 것은?

The fish in the tank are alive.

① The fish not in the tank are alive.

② The fish in the tank not are alive.

③ The fish in the tank are not alive.

④ The fish in the tank are alive not.

⑤ Not the fish in the tank are alive.

(20–21) 빈칸에 알맞은 be동사를 써서 대화를 완성하시오.

20 A: ________ I late for the flight to Paris?
B: No, you aren't. But hurry up.

⇨ ____________

21 A: Were the kids noisy last night?
B: No, they ________.

⇨ ____________

(22–23) 우리말과 의미가 같도록 ( ) 안의 말을 이용하여 문장을 완성하시오.

22 너의 사촌들은 그때 파티에 있었니?
(your cousins, at the party)

⇨ ______________________________ then?

23 이 도시에는 큰 동물원이 없다.
(a big zoo)

⇨ ______________________ in this city.

24 다음 대화 중 어색한 것을 모두 고르시오.

ⓐ Q: Are you twins?
A: No, we aren't.
ⓑ Q: Were the soldiers brave?
A: Yes, he was.
ⓒ Q: Are Paul and you the same age?
A: Yes, they are.
ⓓ Q: Is Mary kind to everyone?
A: No, she isn't.
ⓔ Q: Are you in the bathroom?
A: No, I'm not.

⇨ __________

(25-27) 주어진 문장을 ( ) 안의 지시대로 바꿔 쓰시오.

25 The chicken salad is delicious. (의문문)

⇨ ______________________?

26 Minji and I were in Seoul last week. (부정문)

⇨ ______________________
______________________.

27 There are two cushions on the sofa. (의문문)

⇨ ______________________?

28 다음 문장에 공통으로 들어갈 be동사는?

· That eraser ________ not yours.
· He ________ in the parking lot now.
· My teacher ________ not in the classroom.

⇨ __________

(29-30) 다음 문장에서 어색한 부분을 찾아 바르게 고치고 알맞은 이유를 고르시오.

29 Is David your English teacher last year?

고치기: __________ ⇨ __________
이유: last year은 (현재, 과거)를 나타내므로 be동사의 (현재형, 과거형)을 사용

30 Mary invited you and I to the party.

고치기: __________ ⇨ __________
이유: '너와 나를'은 (주격, 목적격)을 사용하므로 (you and I, you and me)

31 다음 조건을 이용하여 알맞게 영작하시오.

그 요리사는 그때 인기 있지 않았다.
조건 1: the cook, popular, then
조건 2: 5단어, 줄임말 사용

⇨ ______________________.

한눈에 정리하는 Grammar Mapping

빈칸에 알맞은 답을 보기에서 골라 넣어 grammar mapping 완성하기

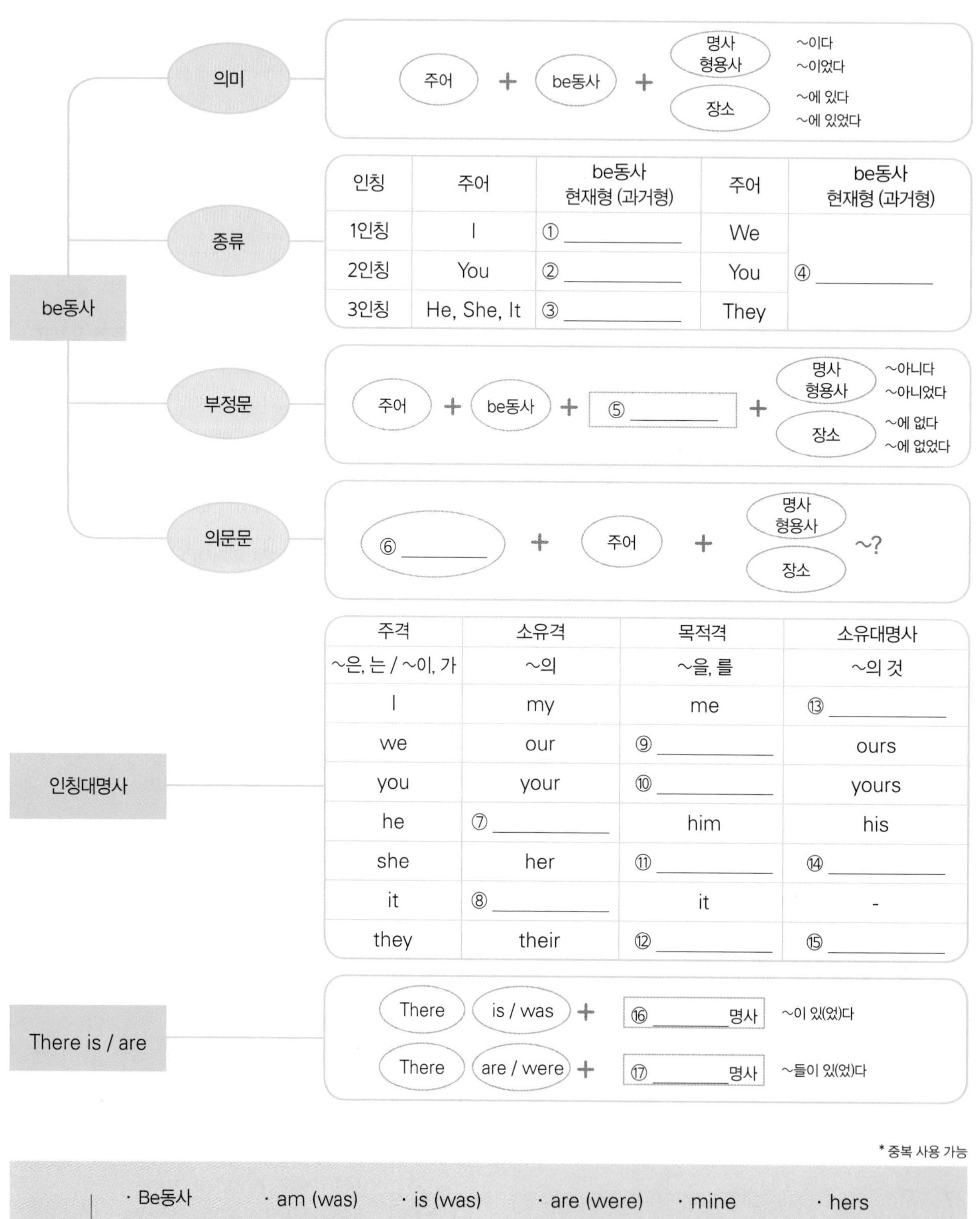

인칭	주어	be동사 현재형 (과거형)	주어	be동사 현재형 (과거형)
1인칭	I	① ______	We	④ ______
2인칭	You	② ______	You	
3인칭	He, She, It	③ ______	They	

주격	소유격	목적격	소유대명사
~은, 는 / ~이, 가	~의	~을, 를	~의 것
I	my	me	⑬ ______
we	our	⑨ ______	ours
you	your	⑩ ______	yours
he	⑦ ______	him	his
she	her	⑪ ______	⑭ ______
it	⑧ ______	it	-
they	their	⑫ ______	⑮ ______

* 중복 사용 가능

보기					
· Be동사	· am (was)	· is (was)	· are (were)	· mine	· hers
· his	· theirs	· its	· you	· her	· us
· them	· not	· 단수	· 복수		

Chapter

02

일반동사

일반동사

GP 06

일반동사는 be동사와 조동사를 제외한 모든 동사로 주어의 동작이나 상태를 나타낸다.

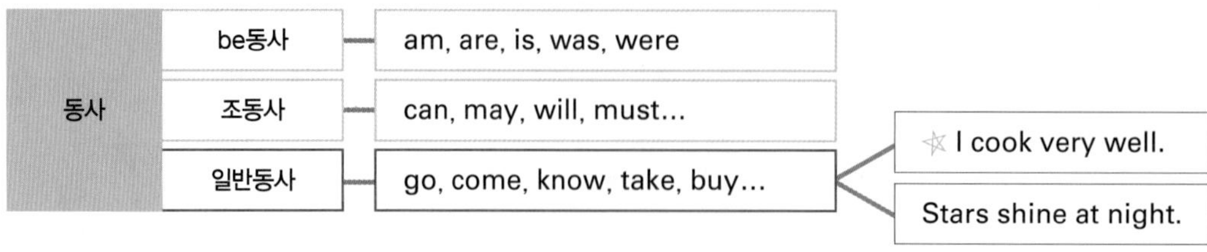

일반동사 현재형

GP 07

❶ 일반동사 현재형

3인칭 단수 주어를 제외하고는 동사원형을 쓰고 3인칭 단수 주어는 [동사원형 + -(e)s] 등의 형태로 쓴다.

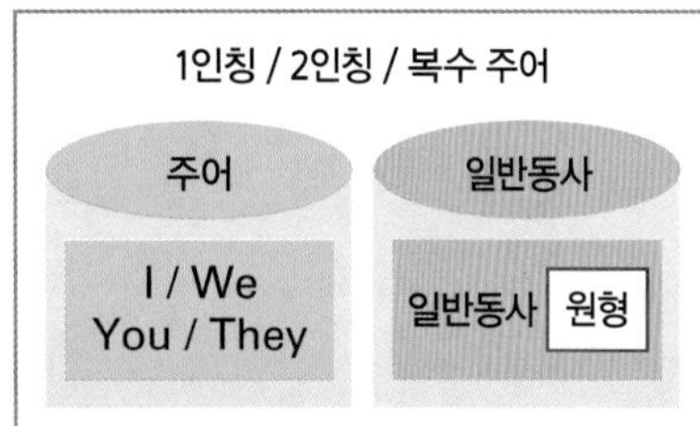

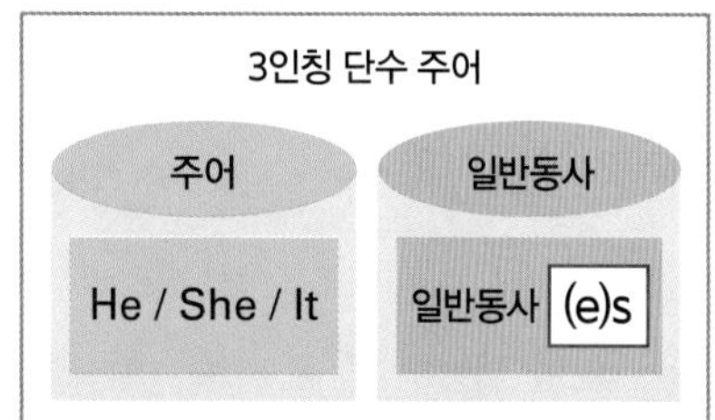

❷ 3인칭 단수 현재형 만드는 방법

규칙 변화	대부분의 동사	동사원형 + -s	walk → walks love → loves	know → knows make → makes
	-s, -ch, -sh, -o, -x로 끝나는 동사	동사원형 + -es	pass → passes wash → washes	teach → teaches go → goes
	[자음 + y]로 끝나는 동사	y를 i로 바꾸고 + -es	study → studies cry → cries	try → tries copy → copies
불규칙 변화	have → has			

We **study** computer science at college.

He **watches** baseball games on TV.

The boy always **tries** his best.

Chris **has** many nicknames.

❸ 일반동사 현재형의 쓰임

현재의 사실, 반복적 습관, 일반적 사실 등을 나타낸다.

My uncle **designs** cars. (현재의 사실)

I usually **go** to bed after eleven. (습관)

The sun **rises** in the east. (일반적 사실)

Tip

현재형과 주로 쓰이는 부사(구)

now, today, every day, every Sunday, on Sundays, once a week...

GP Practice

A ( ) 안에서 알맞은 것을 고르시오.

1 Bears (sleep, sleeps) in winter.

2 The school bus always (come, comes) on time.

3 He (buys, buies) some chocolate for them.

4 The woman (do, does) aerobics three times a week.

5 My parents (get, gets) up early in the morning.

B ( ) 안에 주어진 동사의 현재형을 써서 빈칸을 채우시오.

1 Horses ____________ grass. (eat)

2 Jennifer ____________ a bad cold. (have)

3 My grandfather ____________ his teeth gently. (brush)

4 He ____________ his children after school. (pick up)

5 Austin ____________ a tree every year. (plant)

C 우리말과 의미가 같도록 ( ) 안의 말을 이용하여 문장을 완성하시오.

1 시드니는 많은 해변을 가지고 있다. (have many beaches)

→ Sydney ________ ________ ________.

2 그녀는 매일 조깅하러 간다. (go jogging)

→ She ________ ________ every morning.

3 그 로봇은 사람과 체스를 둔다. (play chess)

→ The robot ________ ________ with people.

D 밑줄 친 부분에 대한 설명을 하고 틀린 경우엔 바르게 고치시오. (맞으면 'O' 표시)

1	My aunt often <u>visit</u> us. → ( )	주어가 3인칭 + 일반동사 현재형 (단수, 복수) (동사원형, 동사원형(e)s)
2	Koreans usually <u>use</u> chopsticks. → ( )	주어가 3인칭 + 일반동사 현재형 (단수, 복수) (동사원형, 동사원형(e)s)
3	The class <u>finishs</u> at 5 o'clock. → ( )	3인칭 단수 주어 + -sh로 끝나는 현재형 동사 (동사원형s, 동사원형es)
4	The bird <u>crys</u> at night. → ( )	3인칭 단수 주어 + [자음 + y]로 끝나는 현재형 동사 (y 뒤에 es, y 대신 ies)

일반동사 과거형

GP 08

❶ 일반동사 과거형

주어의 인칭이나 수에 상관없이 동일한 형태로 쓰고 규칙 변화 동사(-ed)와 불규칙 변화 동사가 있다.

❷ 과거형 만드는 방법

ⓐ 규칙 변화

규칙 변화	대부분의 동사	동사원형 + -ed	walk → walk**ed**	help → help**ed**
	e로 끝나는 동사	동사원형 + -d	love → love**d**	live → live**d**
	[자음 + y]로 끝나는 동사	y를 i로 바꾸고 + -ed	study → stud**ied** cry → cr**ied**	try → tr**ied** worry → worr**ied**
	[단모음 + 단자음]으로 끝나는 동사	자음을 한 번 더 쓰고 + -ed	stop → stop**ped** drop → drop**ped**	plan → plan**ned** clap → clap**ped**

Mammoths **lived** a long time ago.

☆ We **played** basketball yesterday.

ⓑ 불규칙 변화

불규칙 변화	형태가 다른 경우	begin → **began** find → **found** grow → **grew** make → **made** speak → **spoke**	come → **came** get → **got** have → **had** say → **said** tell → **told**	do → **did** give → **gave** hear → **heard** sleep → **slept** think → **thought**
	형태가 같은 경우	cut → **cut**	put → **put**	read → **read**

☆ The festival **began** an hour ago.

We **heard** the news on the radio.

❸ 일반동사 과거형의 쓰임

과거의 동작이나 상태, 과거의 습관, 역사적 사실 등을 나타낸다.

She **knew** David very well. (과거의 상태)

I **helped** Dad in the garden this morning. (과거의 동작)

☆ Edison **invented** the light bulb in 1879. (역사적 사실)

> **Tip**
> 과거형과 주로 쓰이는 부사(구)
> yesterday, at that time, last night (week, year), [~ ago], [in + 과거 연도]...

GP Practice

A ( ) 안에서 알맞은 것을 고르시오.

1 My father (readed, read) my report.

2 He (thinked, thought) about his future.

3 She (put, putted) a plate on the table.

4 In 2000, he (leaves, left) San Francisco.

5 I (see, saw) a famous tower in France last year.

B ( ) 안에 주어진 동사의 과거형을 써서 빈칸을 채우시오.

1 It ____________________ a lot last month. (rain)

2 She ____________________ an email to her boss. (send)

3 My son ____________________ the piano hard. (practice)

4 I ____________________ a coin on the beach. (lose)

5 We ____________________ a great summer vacation this year. (have)

C 우리말과 의미가 같도록 ( ) 안의 말을 이용하여 문장을 완성하시오.

1 그는 신호등에서 멈추었다. (stop)

→ He ____________________ at a traffic light.

2 Mike는 소파에서 잠을 잤다. (sleep)

→ Mike ____________________ on the sofa.

3 곡식들이 작년에 잘 자랐다. (grow)

→ Crops ____________________ well last year.

D 밑줄 친 부분에 대한 설명을 하고 틀린 경우엔 바르게 고치시오. (맞으면 'O' 표시)

1	We buyed some gifts for him. → ( )	buy의 과거형은 (동사원형 + -ed, 불규칙 변화)
2	I live in an apartment two years ago. → ( )	과거 표현과 쓰면 동사 (현재형, 과거형)을 쓰고 live의 과거형은 (동사원형 + -d, 불규칙 변화)
3	Chris cuts the melon in half yesterday. → ( )	과거 표현과 쓰면 동사 (현재형, 과거형)을 쓰고 cut의 과거형은 (동사원형 + -ed, 불규칙 변화)
4	He studyed Chinese last year. → ( )	study의 과거형은 (규칙, 불규칙) 변화하고 (y 뒤에 ed, y 대신 ied)

일반동사 부정문

GP 09

일반동사 부정문은 [주어 + do / does / did + not + 동사원형] 형태이다.

❶ 일반동사 현재형 부정문

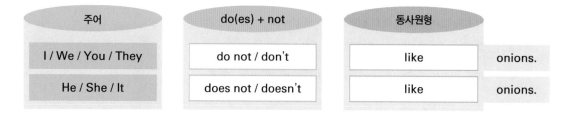

주어	do(es) + not	동사원형	
I / We / You / They	do not / don't	like	onions.
He / She / It	does not / doesn't	like	onions.

I **do not study** on weekends.
Penguins **don't live** at the North Pole.
☆ They **don't wear** blue jeans.

He **does not come** from Canada.
This plant **doesn't need** much sunlight.
☆ Sam **doesn't like** black coffee.

❷ 일반동사 과거형 부정문

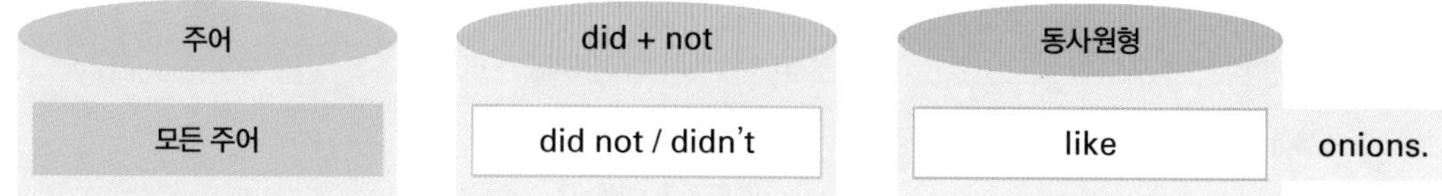

주어	did + not	동사원형	
모든 주어	did not / didn't	like	onions.

I **did not go** to his concert.
Olivia **did not take** the school bus.
☆ It **didn't rain** heavily yesterday.
They **didn't use** a compass.
The boys **did not arrive** late.

• Upgrade •

동사 do의 부정문은 [주어 + do / does / did + not + do] 형태이다.
She **does** the dishes after dinner.
→ She **doesn't** the dishes after dinner. (X)
→ She **doesn't do** the dishes after dinner. (O)

GP Practice

A ( ) 안에서 알맞은 것을 고르시오.

1 He (don't doesn't) listen to me.

2 They (don't, doesn't) watch TV.

3 Sarah (doesn't, didn't) cook dinner yesterday.

4 We (don't, didn't) visit the museum last week.

5 Tom and Jerry didn't (like, liked) each other.

B ( ) 안의 말을 이용하여 빈칸을 채우시오.

1 Kathy likes fruit. But she ____________ apples. (not, like)

2 It was rainy. Daniel ____________ sunglasses. (not, wear)

3 Paul was sick. So he ____________ outside. (not, play)

4 Bats hunt at night. They ____________ at night. (not, sleep)

5 He has a bike. But he ____________ it. (not, ride)

C 우리말과 의미가 같도록 ( ) 안의 말을 이용하여 문장을 완성하시오.

1 나는 크게 웃지 않는다. (laugh)

→ I ____________ ____________ loudly.

2 Betty는 콩을 먹지 않는다. (eat)

→ Betty ____________ ____________ beans.

3 그들은 놀이공원에 가지 않았다. (go)

→ They ____________ ____________ to the amusement park.

D 밑줄 친 부분에 대한 설명을 하고 틀린 경우엔 바르게 고치시오. (맞으면 'O' 표시)

1	I <u>not write</u> in my diary every day. → ( )	1인칭 주어 + 현재형 부정문 (not, don't) + 동사원형
2	My father <u>don't drink</u> wine. → ( )	3인칭 단수 주어 + 현재형 부정문 (don't, doesn't) + 동사원형
3	She <u>doesn't drive</u> yesterday. → ( )	모든 인칭 주어 + 과거형 부정문 (do(es)n't, didn't) + 동사원형
4	He <u>didn't got</u> any pocket money. → ( )	모든 인칭 주어 + 과거형 부정문 didn't + (과거형, 동사원형)

일반동사 의문문

GP 10

일반동사 의문문은 [Do / Does / Did + 주어 + 동사원형 ~?] 형태이다.

❶ 일반동사 현재형 의문문

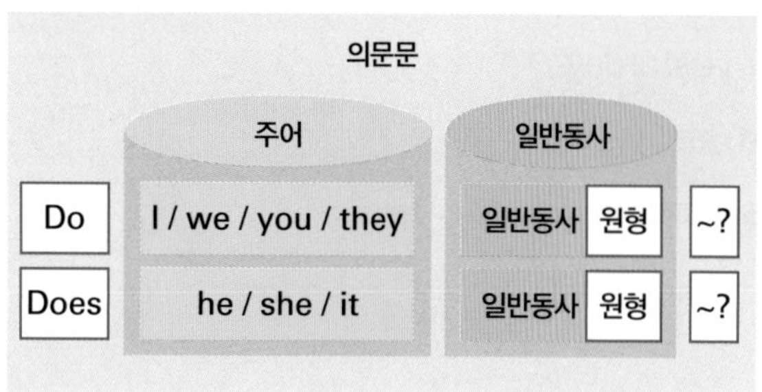

대답			
긍정 대답		부정 대답	
Yes,	주어 + do.	No,	주어 + don't.
Yes,	주어 + does.	No,	주어 + doesn't.

A: ☆ **Do you swim** well?
B: **Yes, I do.** / ☆ **No, I don't.**
A: **Do the stores close** on Sundays?
B: **Yes, they do.** / **No, they don't.**
A: ☆ **Does Michael walk** his dog every day?
B: **Yes, he does.** / **No, he doesn't.**

❷ 일반동사 과거형 의문문

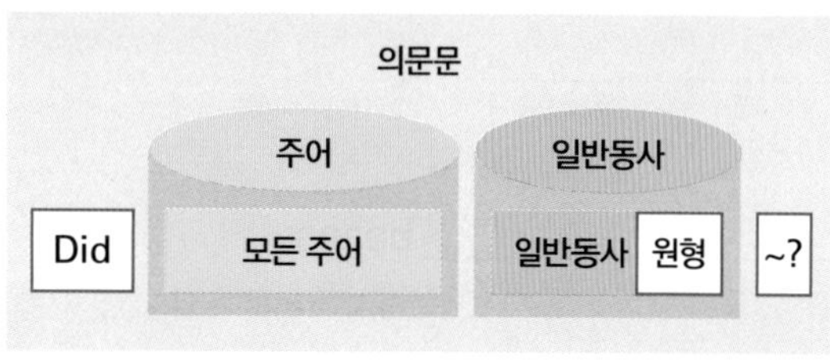

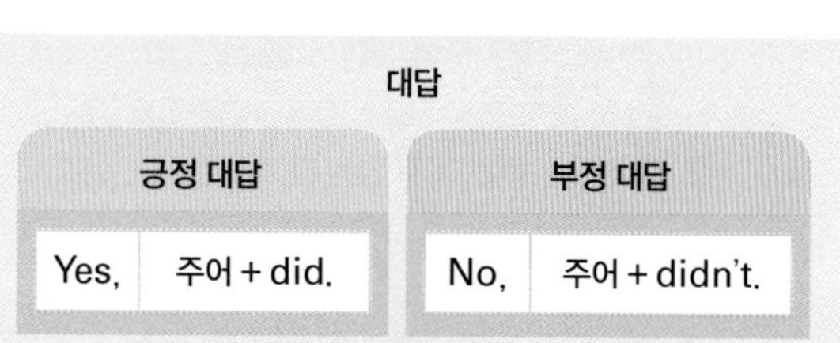

A: ☆ **Did your sister stay** in New York?
B: **Yes, she did.** / **No, she didn't.**
A: **Did Alex and you catch** a big fish?
B: **Yes, we did.** / **No, we didn't.**

• Upgrade •

[Do you ~?], [Do I ~?], [Do we ~?] 의문문의 대답은 주어의 형태가 바뀐다.

A: Do you have a pet? B: Yes, I (we) do. / No, I (we) don't.
A: Do I (we) walk to school? B: Yes, you (we) do. / No, you (we) don't.

GP Practice

A ( ) 안에서 알맞은 것을 고르시오.

1 (Do, Does) your friend wear sunglasses?

2 (Do, Does) the children take a nap?

3 (Does, Did) you hear the news?

4 (Do, Does) your parents exercise?

5 Does the woman (like, likes) ice cream?

B 다음 문장을 의문문으로 바꾸고 주어진 대답을 완성하시오.

1 The dolphin made bubbles.

→ A: ________ the dolphin ________ bubbles? B: Yes, ________ ________.

2 She reads the magazine.

→ A: ________ she ________ the magazine? B: Yes, ________ ________.

3 They play computer games.

→ A: ________ they ________ computer games? B: No, ________ ________.

C 우리말과 의미가 같도록 ( ) 안의 말을 이용하여 문장을 완성하시오.

1 그는 밤에 코를 고나요? (snore)

→ ________ ________ ________ at night?

2 그것들은 물속에서 사나요? (live)

→ ________ ________ ________ underwater?

3 그 기차는 정시에 도착했나요? (the train, arrive)

→ ________ ________ ________ ________ on time?

D 밑줄 친 부분에 대한 설명을 하고 틀린 경우엔 바르게 고치시오. (맞으면 'O' 표시)

1	Know you the secret? → ( )	현재형 의문문은 (일반동사 + 주어 ~?, Do(es) + 주어 + 동사원형 ~?)
2	Do he always wake up at seven? → ( )	3인칭 단수 주어 현재형 의문문은 (Do, Does) + 주어 + 동사원형 ~?
3	Does she enjoy the film yesterday? → ( )	과거형 의문문은 (Does, Did) + 주어 + 동사원형 ~?
4	Did they needed water? → ( )	과거형 의문문은 Did + 주어 + 동사(과거형, 원형) ~?

Grammar & Writing

A **우리말과 의미가 같도록 ( ) 안의 말을 배열하시오.**

1 Daniel은 나를 위해 샌드위치를 만들었다. (sandwiches, Daniel, made)

→ ______________________________ for me.

2 너는 나의 그림을 보았니? (see, painting, you, my, did)

→ ______________________________?

3 나는 LA로 가는 비행기를 놓치지 않았다. (for, miss, I, the plane, didn't)

→ ______________________________ L.A.

4 그녀는 매일 바이올린을 연습하나요? (does, the violin, practice, she)

→ ______________________________ every day?

5 상어는 바다 바닥에 알들을 낳는다. (her eggs, lays, a shark)

→ ______________________________ on the ocean floor.

6 마라톤 선수는 차가운 물을 마시지 않는다. (drink, water, doesn't, cold)

→ The marathon runner ______________________________.

B **우리말과 의미가 같도록 ( ) 안의 말을 이용하여 문장을 완성하시오.**

1 그녀는 당근을 먹지 않는다. (eat carrots)

→ She ________ ________ ________.

2 그들은 학교에서 요가를 배웠나요? (learn yoga)

→ ________ ________ ________ ________ at school?

3 나는 부모님을 위해 파티를 준비했었다. (prepare a party)

→ ________ ________ ________ ________ for my parents.

4 내 동생은 하루에 한 번 이를 닦는다. (brush his teeth)

→ My brother ________ ________ ________ once a day.

5 그는 Mary를 파트너로 선택하지 않았다. (choose)

→ ________ ________ ________ ________ as his partner.

6 너의 어머님은 직업이 있으시니? (have a job)

→ ________ ________ ________ ________ ________ ________?

C 그림에 맞게 주어진 말을 이용하여 문장을 완성하시오.

know, not

breathe, not

wear, not

1 He liked the girl, but he ____________________ her name.

2 Whales live in water, but they ____________________ underwater.

3 My grandmother is very old. But she ____________________ glasses.

D Cathy의 지난해 Taiwan 여행 스케줄을 참고하여 대화를 완성하시오.

Trip schedule (for three days)

First day	Arrive in Taiwan & take a taxi to Taipei
	Visit the National Taiwan Museum
Second day	Catch the bus to Yehliu Geopark
	Go to the night market
Third day	Visit the Taipei 101 Tower & eat dim sum
	Leave Taipei & arrive in Seoul

1 A: ___________ Cathy ___________ the National Taiwan Museum on the first day?

B: Yes, she did.

2 A: Did Cathy take a taxi to Yehliu Geopark?

B: No, she ___________. She ___________ a bus to the park.

3 A: Did Cathy ___________ to the night market on the third day?

B: No, she ___________. She ___________ there on the second day.

4 A: Did Cathy eat dim sum on the first day?

B: ___________, she ___________. She ___________ dim sum on the third day.

5 A: Did Cathy leave Taipei on the third day?

B: ___________, she ___________. She also ___________ in Seoul on the third day.

Actual Test

1 동사의 3인칭 단수 현재형이 잘못 연결된 것은?

① run - runs
② play - plays
③ study - studies
④ pay - pays
⑤ drink - drinkes

2 동사의 과거형이 잘못 연결된 것은?

① read - readed
② drop - dropped
③ put - put
④ carry - carried
⑤ write - wrote

(3-5) 빈칸에 들어갈 알맞은 말을 고르시오.

3

__________ takes a shower every morning.

① I ② You
③ Kate ④ We
⑤ John and Sam

4

Andrew __________ old chairs yesterday.

① doesn't fix ② doesn't fixes
③ didn't fixes ④ didn't fix
⑤ didn't fixed

5

__________ your dad go on vacation in the summer?

① Is ② Do
③ Does ④ Did
⑤ Were

6 빈칸에 들어갈 말로 알맞지 않은 것은?

Do __________ learn Korean from him?

① you ② your friend
③ they ④ the students
⑤ Minji and her sister

(7-8) 다음 대화의 빈칸에 알맞은 것은?

7

A: __________ this book? B: No, he didn't. I wrote it.

① Did he write ② Do he write
③ Does he write ④ Is he write
⑤ Was he write

8

A: Do Peter and Jack often meet? B: __________

① Yes, we do. ② No, they doesn't.
③ Yes, they do. ④ No, he doesn't.
⑤ Yes, he does.

9 빈칸에 들어갈 말이 나머지와 다른 것은?

① ________ the kids know the toys?

② ________ the animals help each other?

③ ________ his friends like the city?

④ ________ your house have a garden?

⑤ ________ you do your homework after school?

10 빈칸에 들어갈 말로 알맞게 짝지어진 것은?

· Judy __________ some cookies an hour ago.
· Judy __________ breakfast every day.

① bake - eat　② bakes - eats

③ baked - eats　④ baked - eat

⑤ baked - ate

(11–12) 질문에 대한 대답을 알맞게 쓰시오.

11 A: Do your aunt and you live together?

B: Yes, __________ __________.

12 A: Did you go out last weekend?

B: No, __________ __________.
I stayed at home.

(13–14) 다음 우리말을 영어로 바르게 옮긴 것은?

13 그는 내 얼굴을 기억하지 못한다.

① He didn't remembered my face.

② He doesn't remembers my face.

③ He isn't remember my face.

④ He remember not my face.

⑤ He doesn't remember my face.

14 그녀는 모든 시험에 통과했나요?

① Was she pass all the exams?

② Did she passes all the exams?

③ Did she pass all the exams?

④ Passed she all the exams?

⑤ Did she passed all the exam?

15 우리말을 영어로 잘못 옮긴 것은?

① 그녀는 부모님을 방문하지 않았어.
→ She didn't visit her parents.

② 군인들은 Amy의 집에 머물렀다.
→ The soldiers stayed at Amy's house.

③ 우리는 차를 빌려서 캠핑을 갔다.
→ We rented a car and went camping.

④ 그는 월요일에 회사에 가지 않는다.
→ He doesn't goes to work on Monday.

⑤ Jason은 영국에서 왔니?
→ Does Jason come from England?

(16-17) ( ) 안의 말을 이용하여 빈칸을 채우시오.

16 __________ your parents __________ a big meal every Sunday? (cook)

⇨ __________, __________

17 We usually take a nap after lunch, but we __________ a nap yesterday. (take, not)

⇨ __________

18 빈칸에 공통으로 들어갈 말을 쓰시오. (대문자와 소문자 적용)

· __________ it snow a lot last winter?
· Wilson __________ not join the soccer club.

⇨ __________, __________

(19-20) 우리말과 의미가 같도록 ( ) 안의 말을 이용하여 문장을 완성하시오.

19 지구는 태양 주변을 돈다. (go around)

⇨ The Earth __________ the sun.

20 나는 어젯밤에 그 TV 쇼를 보지 않았다. (watch the TV show

⇨ I __________ last night.

21 밑줄 친 부분이 어색한 것을 고르시오.

① I didn't work late last week.
② Does she know the answer?
③ She cut the cake into pieces.
④ Did Gary like my present?
⑤ Does the restaurant close yesterday?

22 다음 중 어법상 올바른 문장을 고르시오.

① He didn't went to class.
② Did you meet interesting people?
③ The baby bird wasn't fly away.
④ The pizza didn't warm.
⑤ William swim well.

23 "do"의 쓰임이 나머지 넷과 다른 것은?

① Do you have a big dinner?
② They don't drive at night.
③ He does the dishes every day.
④ We don't live together.
⑤ Do you like Internet shopping?

(24-25) 우리말과 의미가 같도록 ( ) 안의 말을 배열하시오.

24 여름에는 비가 많이 내리지만 겨울에는 비가 내리지 않는다.
(in, doesn't, winter, rain, it)

⇨ It rains a lot in summer, but ________
________________________.

25 너는 핼러윈 의상을 구입했니?
(Halloween, you, a, did, costume, buy)

⇨ ________________________?

(26-27) ( ) 안의 말을 이용하여 빈칸을 채우시오.

26 The baby often cries at night, but she ________ last night. (cry, not)

⇨ ________________

27 My father ________ for his office late this morning, but he usually ________ at 8 o'clock. (leave)

⇨ ____________, ____________

28 어법상 올바른 것으로 짝지어진 것은?

ⓐ We chat online last week.
ⓑ She doesn't asks any questions.
ⓒ He didn't say a word.
ⓓ Young people loses their job.
ⓔ Did the Korean War end in 1953?

① ⓐ, ⓔ
② ⓒ, ⓔ
③ ⓒ, ⓓ
④ ⓑ, ⓒ
⑤ ⓐ, ⓒ

(29-30) 다음 문장에서 어색한 부분을 찾아 바르게 고치고 알맞은 이유를 고르시오.

29 Suji usually read a book after dinner.

고치기: ____________ ⇨ ____________

이유: 주어가 3인칭 (단수, 복수)이므로 일반동사 현재형 (동사원형, 동사원형(e)s)을 사용

30 The ant saved food for the future, but the grasshopper didn't saved food.

고치기: ____________ ⇨ ____________

이유: 일반동사 과거형 부정문은 didn't + (동사 과거형, 동사원형)

31 다음 조건을 이용하여 알맞게 영작하시오.

Sam은 우유를 매일 아침 마시나요?
조건 1: drink, every morning
조건 2: 6단어

⇨ ________________________
________________________?

한눈에 정리하는 Grammar Mapping

빈칸에 알맞은 답을 보기에서 골라 넣어 grammar mapping 완성하기

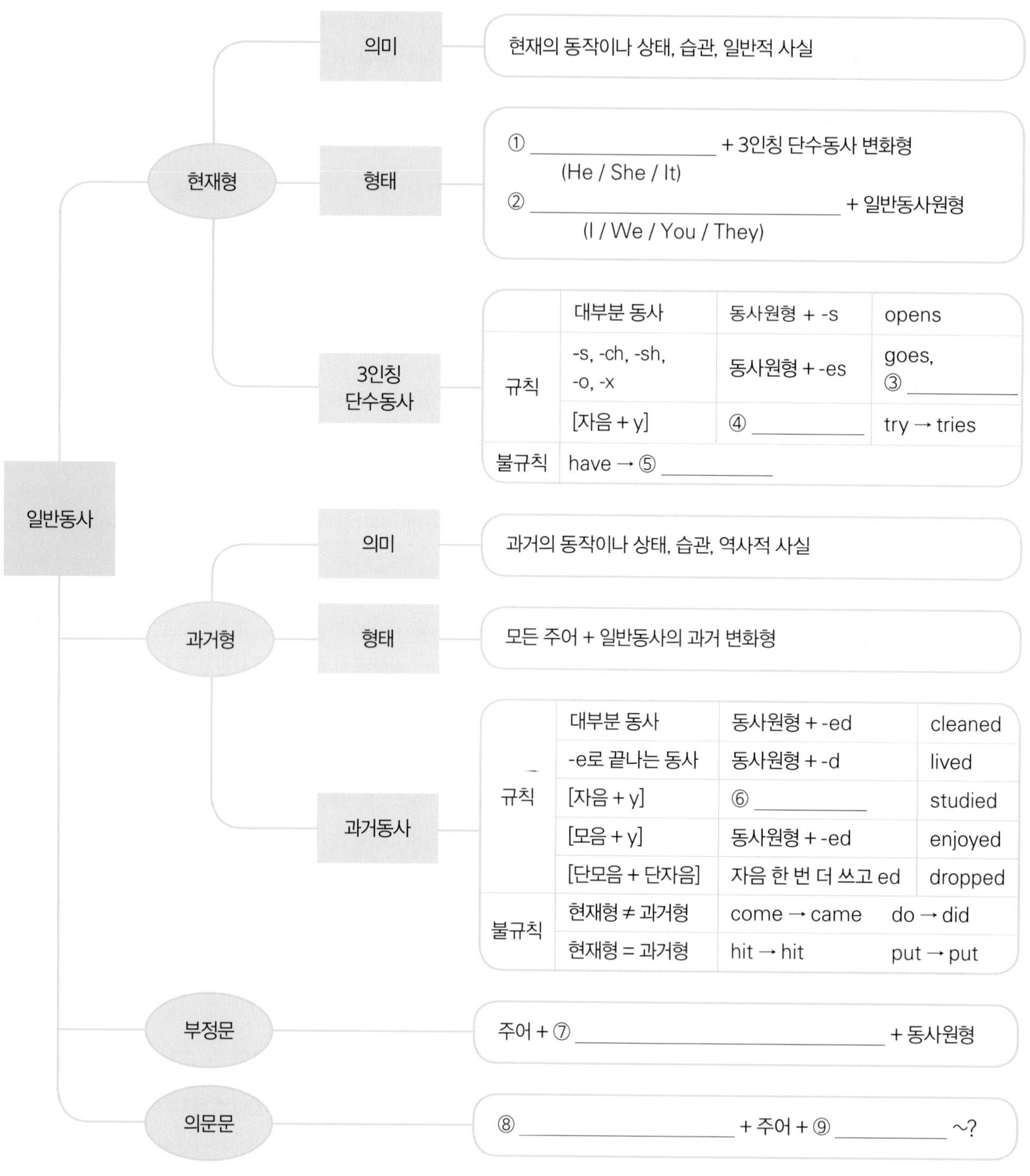

보기			
	· 복수 주어 / 1, 2인칭 단수 주어	· 3인칭 단수 주어	· do / does / did + not
	· Do / Does / Did	· 동사원형	· y대신 ied
	· y 대신 ies	· has	· washes

Chapter

03

명사와 관사

셀 수 있는 명사

GP 11

❶ **셀 수 있는 명사:** 단수형과 복수형이 있고, 단수형 앞에는 부정관사 a / an을 쓴다.

셀 수 있는 명사	단수형	a / an을 쓴다	a boy
	복수형	(e)s를 붙인다	boys

☆ She wants **a** new **bag**. ☆ She wants ten **bags**.

❷ **셀 수 있는 명사의 복수형**

규칙 변화	대부분의 명사	명사 + -s	desks trees hours apples
	-s, -sh, -ch, -x, -o로 끝나는 명사	명사 + -es	bus**es** bench**es** box**es** potato**es** tomato**es** (예외) *photo**s** *piano**s**
	[자음 + y]로 끝나는 명사	y를 i로 바꾸고 + -es	city → cit**ies** baby → bab**ies** lady → lad**ies** party → part**ies**
	-f, -fe로 끝나는 명사	f(e)를 v로 바꾸고 + -es	leaf → lea**ves** knife → kni**ves** wolf → wol**ves** (예외) *roof → roof**s**
불규칙 변화	단수와 복수가 같은 경우	sheep → **sheep**	deer → **deer** fish → **fish**
	모음이 달라지는 경우	man → **men**	foot → **feet** woman → **women**
	그 외의 경우	child → **children**	mouse → **mice**

셀 수 없는 명사

GP 12

❶ **셀 수 없는 명사:** 단수형만 있고 부정관사 a / an을 쓰지 않는다.

셀 수 없는 명사	단수형	a / an을 쓰지 않는다	~~a~~ sugar

She has very long **hair**. ☆ We had a lot of **fun** at the party.

❷ **물질명사의 수량 표현:** 물질명사는 단위 명사를 이용하여 양을 나타내고, 단위 명사는 복수형으로 쓸 수 있다.

	단위명사		
a	glass	of	water, juice, milk
a	piece	of	paper, cake, pizza
a	bottle	of	water, juice, ink

	단위명사		
a	cup	of	coffee, tea
a	slice	of	cheese, bread
a	loaf	of	bread

☆ Can you bring me **a glass of water**?

☆ They ordered **three cups of coffee**.

• Upgrade •

한 쌍을 이루는 명사(pants, shoes...)는 항상 복수형으로 쓰고, [a pair of] 형태로 수를 나타낸다.

I bought **a pair of / two pairs of shoes** yesterday.

GP Practice

A 다음 주어진 명사의 복수형을 쓰시오.

1	dish	→	________	6	potato	→	________
2	knife	→	________	7	party	→	________
3	orange	→	________	8	tooth	→	________
4	roof	→	________	9	photo	→	________
5	piano	→	________	10	deer	→	________

B ( ) 안에서 알맞은 것을 고르시오.

1 I have six (class, classes) today.

2 There is (photo, a photo) on his desk.

3 Two (babies, babys) are sleeping on the bed.

4 We can't buy (happiness, a happiness) with money.

5 She drinks (two cup of tea, two cups of tea) every day.

C 우리말과 의미가 같도록 ( ) 안의 말을 이용하여 문장을 완성하시오.

1 내 음식에 설탕을 넣지 마세요. (sugar)

→ Please don't put ________ on my food.

2 감자는 최고의 식품이다. (potato)

→ ________ are super foods.

3 그녀는 물 세 병을 샀다. (water)

→ She bought ________ ________ ________ ________.

D 밑줄 친 부분에 대한 설명을 하고 틀린 경우엔 바르게 고치시오. (맞으면 'O' 표시)

1	Many leaf are in the backyard. → ( )	셀 수 있는 명사는 복수형이 (있고, 없고) leaf의 복수형은 (leafs, leaves)
2	There is box in front of the door. → ( )	box는 셀 수 (있는, 없는) 명사이고 앞에 a / an을 (쓴다, 쓰지 않는다)
3	An air is important to us. → ( )	air는 셀 수 (있는, 없는) 명사이고 앞에 a / an을 (쓴다, 쓰지 않는다)
4	He needs a paper. → ( )	물질명사인 paper는 셀 수 (있고, 없고) 수량 표현은 (a, a piece of) + paper

관사

GP 13

관사는 명사 앞에서 명사의 의미와 성격을 나타내는 말로 부정관사와 정관사가 있다.

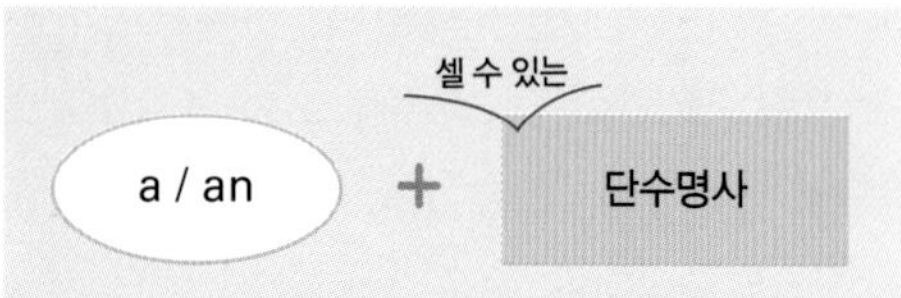

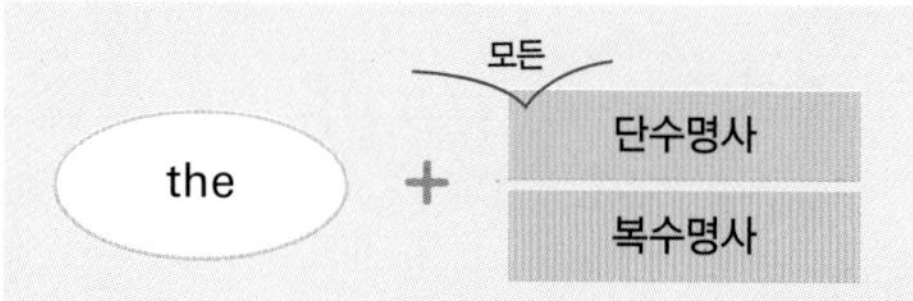

❶ 부정관사 a / an

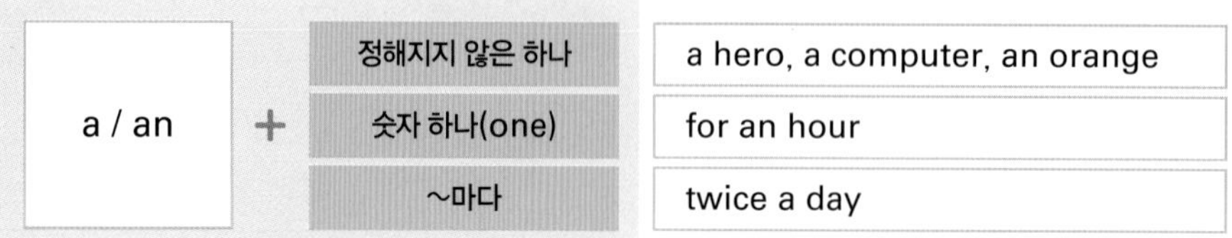

a / an	+	정해지지 않은 하나	a hero, a computer, an orange
		숫자 하나(one)	for an hour
		~마다	twice a day

☆ I usually eat **an apple** in the morning.
☆ My sister reads two books **a week**.

Tip

a vs. an
a는 자음으로 발음되는 단어 앞에 쓰고
an은 모음으로 발음되는 단어 앞에 쓴다.
· a university · an hour

❷ 정관사 the

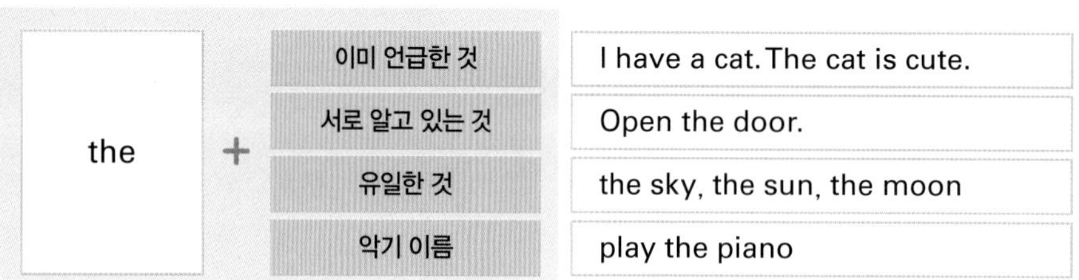

the	+	이미 언급한 것	I have a cat. The cat is cute.
		서로 알고 있는 것	Open the door.
		유일한 것	the sky, the sun, the moon
		악기 이름	play the piano

☆ She has a pen. **The pen** is very useful.
☆ Can you pass me **the salt**?
☆ **The Earth** is not a star but a planet.
☆ I usually play **the violin** after school.

❸ 관사를 쓰지 않는 경우

관사 없음	+	식사, 운동경기, 과목	breakfast, soccer, math
		by + 교통, 통신수단	by car, by bus, by email
		본래 목적의 장소	go to school, go to bed

☆ John's favorite sport is **soccer**.
☆ I traveled across Europe **by bus**.
My brother **goes to bed** before midnight.

GP Practice

A ( ) 안에서 알맞은 것을 고르시오.

1 Is there (a, the) zoo near here?

2 Please pass me (a, the) chilli sauce.

3 Henry plays (a, the) violin every day.

4 The shop is closed for (a, the) month.

5 Tom is (a, an) honest boy.

B ( ) 안에 a, an, the 중에 알맞은 것을 쓰시오. (필요 없는 경우 'X' 표시)

1 (   ) sun is the hottest at noon.

2 My dad goes to work by (   ) subway.

3 (   ) pet shop over there isn't open today.

4 I bought (   ) orange at the supermarket.

5 She usually has cereal for (   ) breakfast.

C 우리말과 의미가 같도록 ( ) 안의 말을 이용하여 문장을 완성하시오.

1 엄마는 주말마다 첼로를 연주한다. (cello)

→ My mom plays ____________ ____________ every weekend.

2 우산 하나가 하늘에서 날고 있었다. (umbrella)

→ ____________ ____________ was flying in the sky.

3 Tony는 일주일에 4일 일한다. (week)

→ Tony works four days ____________ ____________.

D 밑줄 친 부분에 대한 설명을 하고 틀린 경우엔 바르게 고치시오. (맞으면 'O', 불필요하면 '삭제' 표시)

1	Turn off <u>a</u> computer. → ( )	관사 + 명사 (a, the) (정해지지 않은 것, 서로 알고 있는 것)
2	I bought a sofa. <u>The</u> sofa was too big. → ( )	관사 + 명사 (a, the) (정해지지 않은 것, 이미 언급된 것)
3	He goes camping once <u>the</u> month. → ( )	관사 + 명사 (a, the) (~마다, 유일한 것)
4	They played <u>the</u> baseball. → ( )	관사 + 명사 (없음, the) (운동 경기)

A **우리말과 의미가 같도록 ( ) 안의 말을 배열하시오.**

1 저는 의자가 필요합니다. (chair, need, I, a)

→ ______________________________.

2 그는 밥 두 공기를 먹었다. (rice, ate, he, two, of, bowls)

→ ______________________________.

3 나의 형은 바지 한 벌을 샀다. (a, my, of, pants, pair, bought, brother)

→ ______________________________.

4 너의 어머니에게 하루에 한 번 전화 드리렴. (your mom, a, call, day, once)

→ ______________________________.

5 그 학생들은 버스를 타고 학교에 간다. (go, by, to, the, bus, school, students)

→ ______________________________.

6 그녀의 정원에는 두 개의 벤치가 있었다. (were, two, garden, benches, her, in, there)

→ ______________________________.

B **우리말과 의미가 같도록 ( ) 안의 말을 이용하여 문장을 완성하시오.**

1 엄마는 훌륭한 요리사이다. (great cook)

→ My mom is ________ ________ ________.

2 두 명의 여자들이 드레스를 입어보고 있다. (woman)

→ ________ ________ are trying on dresses.

3 그는 아침에 주스 한 잔을 마신다. (juice, glass)

→ He drinks ________ ________ ________ ________ in the morning.

4 Jacob은 학교에서 유니폼을 입는다. (uniform)

→ Jacob wears ________ ________ at school.

5 모든 집의 지붕들이 파랗다. (roof)

→ ________ ________ of all the houses are blue.

6 치즈 세 장을 빵에 올리세요. (cheese, slice)

→ Put ________ ________ ________ ________ on the bread.

C 다음은 세 사람이 주문한 음식이다. 보기의 말을 이용하여 문장을 완성하시오. (중복 사용 가능)

보기 | cup glass piece bottle

1 Mike
2 Jin
3 Chris

1 Mike ordered ______________ milk and ______________ pizza.

2 Jin ordered ______________ cheesecake and ______________ water.

3 Chris ordered ______________ coffee and ______________ apple pie.

D ( ) 안에 a, an, the 중에 알맞은 것을 쓰고 필요 없는 경우에는 'X' 표시 하시오.

1

A: What did you do during summer vacation?

B: I visited my cousins in (   ) Busan.

2

A: Did you go there by car?

B: No, I didn't. I went by (   ) train.

3

A: Did it take two hours?

B: No. It isn't far from here. It took about (   ) hour.

4

A: Did you eat a lot of fish there?

B: Yes, I did. We ate fish once (   ) day.

5

A: Did you go to the beach with your cousins?

B: Yes, we did. We sang and played (   ) guitar there.

(1–2) 명사의 복수형이 잘못 연결된 것을 고르시오.

1 ① bus - buses
② day - days
③ knife - knives
④ piano - pianoes
⑤ body - bodies

2 ① foot - foots
② sheep - sheep
③ roof - roofs
④ mouse - mice
⑤ tomato - tomatoes

(3–5) 빈칸에 들어갈 알맞은 말을 고르시오.

3 There are ________ in the woods.

① deer ② childs
③ leafs ④ tree
⑤ two man

4 My brother has a lot of ________.

① funs ② photos
③ waters ④ breads
⑤ knowledges

5 She drinks two ________ of juice every day.

① cup ② glass
③ glasses ④ pieces
⑤ loaves

(6–7) 빈칸에 알맞지 않은 것을 고르시오.

6 My mother bought ________ at the grocery store.

① bananas ② an apple
③ a salt ④ a bottle of milk
⑤ sugar

7 ________ is looking in the mirror.

① My sister ② The actress
③ A little girl ④ The tall women
⑤ Your daughter

8 보기의 밑줄 친 것과 쓰임이 같은 것은?

보기 | They traveled abroad once a year.

① I drank a glass of juice.
② He is a hero to many people.
③ There are seven days in a week.
④ She calls me twice a day.
⑤ They took a trip to Africa.

9 **빈칸에 들어갈 말이 바르게 짝지어진 것을 고르시오.**

> · My cousin is ________ university student.
> · We had some noodles for ________ lunch today.

① an - a ② the - a
③ the - the ④ a - 관사 없음
⑤ an - 관사 없음

(10–11) 빈칸에 들어갈 말이 다른 하나는?

10 ① ________ building is very tall.
② ________ moon is beautiful tonight.
③ Look at ________ sky! There is a UFO.
④ He plays ________ violin in his free time.
⑤ I sent the pictures by ________ e-mail.

11 ① He always carries ________ umbrella.
② This is ________ elementary school.
③ Jack has ________ wallet in his backpack.
④ He is ________ honest boy.
⑤ My family had ________ unusual experience.

(12–13) 다음 우리말을 영어로 바르게 옮긴 것은?

12

> 그 치과 의사는 이를 두 개 뽑았다.

① The dentist took out two tooth.
② The dentist took out two teeth.
③ The dentist took out two tooths.
④ The dentist took out two teeths.
⑤ The dentist took out two toothes.

13

> 그녀는 커피 두 잔을 쟁반에 놓았다.

① She put two coffee on the tray.
② She put two cup of coffee on the tray.
③ She put two cups of coffee on the tray.
④ She put two cups of coffees on the tray.
⑤ She put two cup of coffees on the tray.

(14–15) 우리말과 의미가 같도록 ( ) 안의 말을 배열하시오.

14

> 우리는 밤하늘에서 그 별을 찾았다.
> (the, sky, in, found, the, we, night, star)

⇨ ________________________________.

15

> David는 그의 친구들과 드럼을 쳤다.
> (his, the, David, drum, played, friends, with)

⇨ ________________________________.

(16–19) 빈칸에 보기의 관사를 넣어 문장을 완성하시오.

보기	a	an	the	x(관사 없음)

16 나는 자기 전에 물을 마신다.

⇨ I drink ___________ water before ___________ bed.

17 나는 공룡에 관한 영화를 보았는데, 그 영화는 대단했다.

⇨ I watched a movie about dinosaurs, and ___________ movie was great.

18 어떤 꽃들은 일 년에 두 번 핀다.

⇨ Some flowers bloom two times ___________ year.

19 어떤 노신사가 그녀를 기다리고 있다.

⇨ ___________ old gentleman is waiting for her.

(20–21) 빈칸에 공통으로 들어갈 말을 고르시오.

20

· Can I eat two ___________ of bread?
· I put two___________ of cheese on my sandwich.

① bottles ② slices ③ sheets
④ glasses ⑤ spoonfuls

21

· Turn off ___________ light.
· Is there water on ___________ moon?

① a ② an ③ the
④ that ⑤ 관사 없음

22 다음 중 어법상 올바른 문장을 고르시오.

① Would you like more teas?
② I have a lot of homeworks.
③ She got many advices.
④ Mouses are afraid of cats.
⑤ The player smiled with joy.

23 다음 중 어법상 어색한 문장을 고르시오.

① My mom went to bed late.
② Could you fix a window?
③ We all need love.
④ William went to England by ship.
⑤ Look at the little puppy.

24 밑줄 친 부분이 어색한 것을 고르시오.

① He needs two pieces of papers.
② She brought three glasses of juice.
③ A bottle of wine is two dollars.
④ He ate two pieces of chocolate cake.
⑤ A slice of pizza is on the table.

(25-28) 우리말과 의미가 같도록 ( ) 안의 말을 이용하여 문장을 완성하시오.

25 접시들을 잘 말려 주세요. (dish)

⇨ Please dry the ____________ well.

26 당신이 부엌에 있는 식탁을 바꿨나요? (table)

⇨ Did you change ____________ in the kitchen?

27 잎들은 가을에 노랗게 변한다. (leaf)

⇨ The ____________ turn yellow in autumn.

28 두 마리의 생쥐가 구멍으로 달려 들어갔다. (mouse)

⇨ ____________ ran into the hole.

(29-30) 다음 문장에서 어색한 부분을 찾아 바르게 고치고 알맞은 이유를 고르시오.

29 Twenty sheeps were on the farm.

고치기: ____________ ⇨ ____________
이유: sheep은 단수형과 복수형이 (같음, 다름)

30 Potatos grow in the ground.

고치기: ____________ ⇨ ____________
이유: -o로 끝나는 명사의 복수형은 -o + (s, es)

(31-32) 다음 조건을 이용하여 알맞게 영작하시오.

31 나는 두 덩어리의 빵이 필요합니다.
조건 1: loaf, bread
조건 2: 6단어

⇨ ______________________________.

32 그녀는 파란 눈과 긴 머리를 가지고 있다.
조건 1: blue, long, and
조건 2: 7단어

⇨ ______________________________.

한눈에 정리하는 Grammar Mapping

빈칸에 알맞은 답을 보기에서 골라 넣어 grammar mapping 완성하기

보기

· ladies · slices · tomatoes · bottles · 식사, 운동, 과목 이름
· 정해지지 않은 하나 · 악기 이름 · ~마다 · 단위명사

Chapter

04

대명사

this (these), that (those)

GP 14

❶ **this**: 상대적으로 가까이 있는 사람이나 사물을 가리키고 복수형은 these이다.

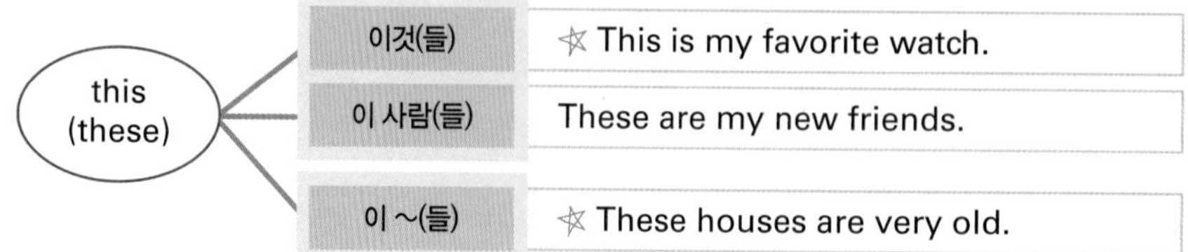

this (these)
이것(들)
✫ This is my favorite watch.
이 사람(들)
These are my new friends.
이 ~(들)
✫ These houses are very old.

❷ **that**: 상대적으로 멀리 있는 사람이나 사물을 가리키고 복수형은 those이다.

that (those)		
	저것(들)	✫ That is your birthday gift.
	저 사람(들)	Are those your children?
	저 ~(들)	✫ Those trees don't have leaves.

• Upgrade •

this의 다른 쓰임

❶ 사람을 소개할 때

A: Allen, **this** is my sister Cathy.　　B: Nice to meet you, Cathy.

❷ 전화를 건 사람을 가리킬 때

Hi. **This** is Allen. Can I speak to Cathy?

비인칭 주어 it

GP 15

❶ **비인칭 주어 it**: 시간, 요일, 날짜, 날씨, 거리, 명암 등을 나타낼 때 쓰는 it을 가리키고 '그것'이라고 해석하지 않는다.

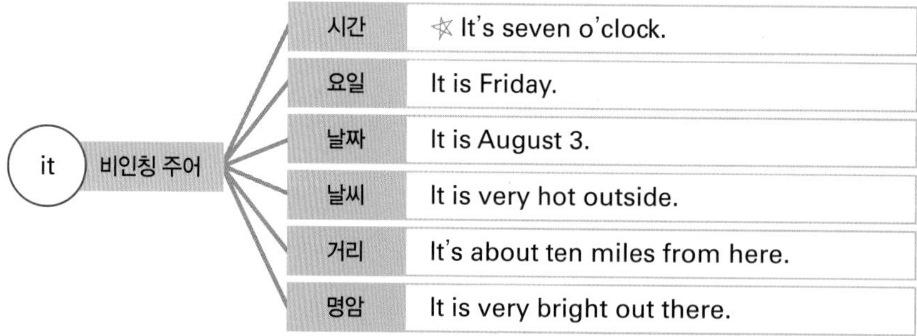

it
비인칭 주어
시간
✫ It's seven o'clock.
요일
It is Friday.
날짜
It is August 3.
날씨
It is very hot outside.
거리
It's about ten miles from here.
명암
It is very bright out there.

❷ **대명사 it**: 앞에 언급한 특정한 명사를 가리키며, '그것'으로 해석한다.

• Upgrade •

대명사 one: 앞에 언급한 명사와 같은 종류의 어떤 것을 가리킨다.

I need an eraser. Do you have **one**?

GP Practice

A ( ) 안에서 알맞은 것을 고르시오.

1 (This, These) lemon is too sour.

2 Are (that, those) your shoes?

3 (This, These) are Tom's dogs.

4 She drew (that, those) paintings.

5 (That, It) is Saturday today. (This, It) is very cold.

B 밑줄 친 it의 알맞은 해석에 'O' 표시하시오.

		해석 안 함	그것
1	It is March 3.	해석 안 함 ( )	그것 ( )
2	It is 2km to the beach.	해석 안 함 ( )	그것 ( )
3	I opened it carefully.	해석 안 함 ( )	그것 ( )
4	It is raining outside.	해석 안 함 ( )	그것 ( )
5	He has a backpack. It is very light.	해석 안 함 ( )	그것 ( )

C 우리말과 의미가 같도록 ( ) 안의 말을 이용하여 문장을 완성하시오.

1 저 모자는 너에게 잘 어울려. (hat)

→ ____________ ____________ looks good on you.

2 호주는 지금 여름이다. (summer)

→ ____________ ____________ ____________ in Australia now.

3 이 판다들은 중국에서 왔다. (panda)

→ ____________ ____________ are from China.

D 밑줄 친 부분에 대한 설명을 하고 틀린 경우엔 바르게 고치시오. (맞으면 'O' 표시)

1	Those is my sister's bag. → ( )	멀리 있는 (단수, 복수)명사를 가리키며 (That, Those) + 단수동사
2	This are Paula's storybooks. → ( )	가까이 있는 (단수, 복수)명사를 가리키며 (This, These) + 복수동사
3	I like this cake. It looks delicious. → ( )	앞에 언급한 (특정한, 불특정한) 단수명사를 가리키는 대명사 (it, one)
4	This was very cold yesterday. → ( )	(이것, 날씨)을·를 나타내는 (비인칭 주어, 대명사)

some, any

GP 16

some과 any는 '약간, 조금'의 의미로 사람이나 사물의 수와 양을 나타낸다.

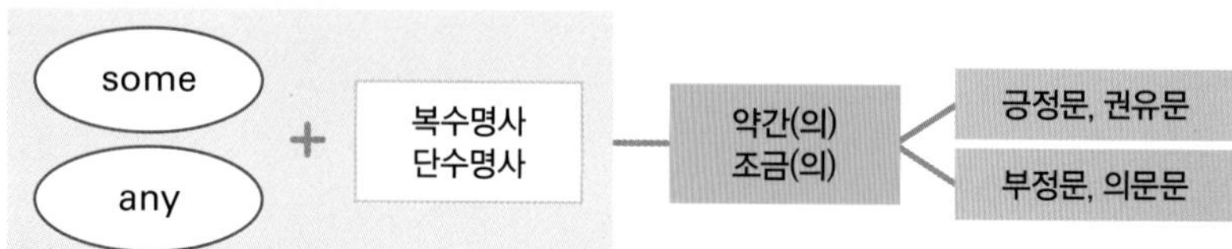

❶ some

☆ I have **some** questions. (긍정문)

☆ Will you have **some** chocolate? (권유문)

❷ any

☆ I don't have **any** questions. (부정문)

Do you have **any** idea? (의문문)

all, every, each

GP 17

all과 every는 '모든'을 each는 '각각의'를 의미하고 막연한 전체를 대상으로 한다.

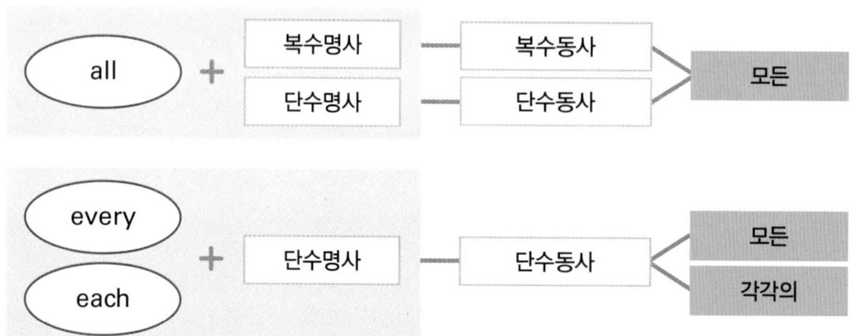

❶ all

☆ **All the boys** *are* standing in the hall.

☆ **All the money** *is* in a safe place.

❷ each

☆ **Each boy** *has* his own cell phone.

❸ every

☆ **Every student** *is* wearing shorts.

GP Practice

A ( ) 안에서 알맞은 것을 고르시오.

1 (Every, All) the guests arrived on time.

2 Do you need (some, any) help?

3 I walk my dog every (day, days).

4 There weren't (some, any) empty seats.

5 There are (some, any) gift boxes on the table.

B 빈칸에 some 또는 any 중 알맞은 것을 쓰시오.

1 Is there ____________ milk in the freezer?

2 You need to get ____________ rest.

3 Jack doesn't have ____________ brothers.

4 I found ____________ coins under the bed.

5 Would you like ____________ tea?

C 우리말과 의미가 같도록 ( ) 안의 말을 이용하여 문장을 완성하시오.

1 모든 아이들은 보살핌이 필요하다. (child)

→ ____________ ____________ needs care.

2 화성에 공기가 있나요? (air)

→ Is there ____________ ____________ on Mars?

3 모든 선수들이 열심히 연습하고 있다. (the players)

→ ____________ ____________ ____________ are practicing hard.

D 밑줄 친 부분에 대한 설명을 하고 틀린 경우엔 바르게 고치시오. (맞으면 'O' 표시)

1	We don't have <u>some</u> problems. → ( )	(any, some)은·는 (긍정문, 부정문)에 사용
2	All <u>the apple</u> are sweet. → ( )	all + (단수, 복수)명사 + 복수동사
3	Every <u>students</u> wears a uniform. → ( )	every + (단수명사, 복수명사)
4	Would you like <u>any</u> mango juice? → ( )	(any, some)은·는 (권유문, 의문문)에 사용

A **우리말과 의미가 같도록 ( ) 안의 말을 알맞게 배열하시오.**

1 나는 내 모든 돈을 저축했다. (all, I, my, money, saved)

→ ______________________________.

2 이것은 우리 집에서 멀지 않다. (it, is, my house, far, not, from)

→ ______________________________.

3 이 사람들은 나에게 정말 친절했다. (very, kind, these, were, people)

→ ______________________________ to me.

4 그녀는 몇 가지 조언을 위해 나에게 전화했었어. (me, she, for, some, called, advice)

→ ______________________________.

5 저쪽에 있는 저 여자를 너는 아니? (that, you, do, know, woman)

→ ______________________________ over there?

6 그는 저녁 이후에 어떤 간식도 먹지 않았다. (he, eat, any, didn't, snacks)

→ ______________________________ after dinner.

B **우리말과 의미가 같도록 ( ) 안의 말을 이용하여 문장을 완성하시오.**

1 이들은 나의 반 친구들이다. (classmates)

→ ________ ________ ________ ________.

2 제 음료수에는 얼음을 넣지 말아 주세요. (put, ice)

→ Please don't ________ ________ ________ in my drink.

3 지난주에 비가 많이 내렸다. (rain a lot)

→ ________ ________ ________ ________ last week.

4 저 소리들에 귀 기울여 보렴. (listen to, sounds)

→ ________ ________ ________ ________.

5 모든 학생은 특별한 재능을 가지고 있다. (special talents)

→ ________ ________ ________ ________ ________.

6 안녕하세요. 저는 Mary예요. Tom과 통화할 수 있을까요? (Mary)

→ Hello. ________ ________ ________. Can I speak to Tom?

C 그림에 맞게 대명사를 이용하여 대화를 완성하시오.

1

A: Which one do you like?

B: I like ___________ bag.

2

A: What day is this?

B: ___________ is December 24.

3

A: Jessie, ___________ is my brother Sam.

B: Nice to meet you, Sam.

D 보기의 말을 이용하여 그림에 맞게 문장을 완성하시오.

보기 |	each	all	some	any

1 ___________ table has a red tablecloth.

2 There are ___________ flowers and dishes on ___________ the tables.

3 There isn't ___________ cake or bread.

4 The wall has ___________ pictures on it.

(1-4) 빈칸에 들어갈 알맞은 말을 고르시오.

1

Look at the kids over there.
__________ are my children.

① That ② These
③ Those ④ This
⑤ Some

2

__________ is already 7 p.m. Let's eat something for dinner.

① It ② This
③ Time ④ That
⑤ Today

3

Hello. __________ is David. May I speak to Tom?

① He ② It
③ These ④ This
⑤ That

4

My mom bought a new washing machine. __________ works well.

① It ② One
③ They ④ Some
⑤ Any

(5-6) 다음 대화의 빈칸에 알맞은 것은?

5

A: What date is __________ today?
B: July 10.

① this ② that
③ you ④ it
⑤ they

6

A: Are these candles yours?
B: Yes, __________ are.

① these ② those
③ it ④ candles
⑤ they

(7-8) 밑줄 친 부분이 나머지와 쓰임이 다른 것을 고르시오.

7

① This is Tony's glove.
② This is not my USB.
③ Is this a new app?
④ Is this doll your sister's?
⑤ This is his classmate.

8

① What date is it today?
② It is my favorite program.
③ It is snowing a lot.
④ It takes about an hour.
⑤ It is Saturday today.

(9–11) 우리말과 의미가 같도록 빈칸에 알맞은 말을 쓰시오.

9 저 사람이 네 쌍둥이 동생이니?
→ Is ________ your twin brother?

⇨ ____________

10 모든 학생은 이름표를 착용한다.
→ ________ student wears a name tag.

⇨ ____________

11 팬케이크를 만들기 위해 버터가 좀 필요하다.
→ I need ________ butter to make pancakes.

⇨ ____________

12 밑줄 친 말을 복수형으로 바르게 고친 문장은?

That is a brand-new cell phone.

① That is a brand-new cell phones.
② Those are a brand-new cell phones.
③ Those are brand-new cell phones.
④ These is a brand-new cell phones.
⑤ These are brand-new cell phones.

(13–15) 빈칸에 공통으로 들어갈 말을 쓰시오.
(대문자와 소문자 적용)

13
· I lost my key, and I can't find ________.
· ________ takes 30 minutes by car.

⇨ ____________, ____________

14
· Mom, ________ is my teacher Ms. Kim.
· ________ boy in the photo is Dylan.

⇨ ____________, ____________

15
· Do you have ________ questions?
· The carrots are not fresh. So we didn't buy ________.

⇨ ____________

16 빈칸에 any가 들어갈 수 없는 것은?

① I don't know ________ of them.
② Can I have ________ milk?
③ Does she have ________ puppies?
④ Are there ________ banks around here?
⑤ There aren't ________ chairs in the room.

(17–18) 다음 대화의 빈칸에 알맞은 말을 쓰시오.

17

A: Would you like ________ tea?
B: Yes, please.

⇨ ____________

18

A: How was the weather in Dubai?
B: ________ was hot and dry.

⇨ ____________

(19–20) 다음 우리말을 영어로 바르게 옮긴 것은?

19

이 경찰들이 나를 집에 데려다 줬어요.

① This police officers took me home.
② That police officers took me home.
③ Those police officers took me home.
④ This police officers took me home.
⑤ These police officers took me home.

20

병원까지는 10킬로미터 거리이다.

① This is ten kilometers to the hospital.
② Those are ten kilometers to the hospital.
③ That is ten kilometers to the hospital.
④ Those are ten kilometers to the hospital.
⑤ It is ten kilometers to the hospital.

21 다음 중 어법상 어색한 문장을 고르시오.

① Are these art books?
② It was very foggy yesterday.
③ Those man is my neighbor.
④ All birds have wings.
⑤ He added some sugar to his coffee.

(22–24) 우리말과 의미가 같도록 ( ) 안의 말을 배열하시오.

22

녹차에는 약간의 카페인이 있다.
(green tea, some, in, caffeine)

⇨ There is ____________
____________.

23

이제 밖이 어두워.
(dark, is, it)

⇨ Now ____________ outside.

24

그들은 나의 모든 말에 귀 기울였다.
(every, word, my)

⇨ They listened to ____________
____________.

25 다음 중 어법상 어색한 대화를 고르시오.

① A: Do you have any money?
B: Yes, I have some.
② A: How is the weather?
B: It is windy.
③ A: Are these things yours?
B: No, they are my brother's.
④ A: Do you want some coffee?
B: Yes, please.
⑤ A: Alex, that is my roommate Bill.
B: Good to meet you.

(26-28) 빈칸에 들어갈 말이 바르게 짝지어진 것을 고르시오.

26

> A: Is there __________ cheese in the refrigerator?
> B: Yes. there is __________.

① this - it　② that - it
③ some - any　④ any - some
⑤ some - some

27

> · He gave a chocolate bar to __________ kid.
> · __________ the children are waiting for you.

① each - All　② every - Each
③ all - Every　④ all - Each
⑤ each - Each

28

> A: Can I help you?
> B: Yes, I'm looking for a blue skirt.
> A: How about __________ skirt?
> B: __________ looks nice.

① these - It　② this - It
③ that - One　④ those - One
⑤ this - These

(29-30) 다음 문장에서 어색한 부분을 찾아 바르게 고치고 알맞은 이유를 고르시오.

29

> He doesn't have some plans for his vacation.

고치기: __________ ⇨ __________
이유: '약간'을 의미하는 (any, some)은·는 부정문에 사용

30

> This letters are from Spain.

고치기: __________ ⇨ __________
이유: (this, these) + 복수명사

31 다음 조건을 이용하여 알맞게 영작하시오.

> 각 팀은 다섯 명의 선수를 갖고 있다.
> 조건 1: team, player
> 조건 2: 5단어

⇨ ______________________________.

한눈에 정리하는 Grammar Mapping

빈칸에 알맞은 답을 보기에서 골라 넣어 grammar mapping 완성하기

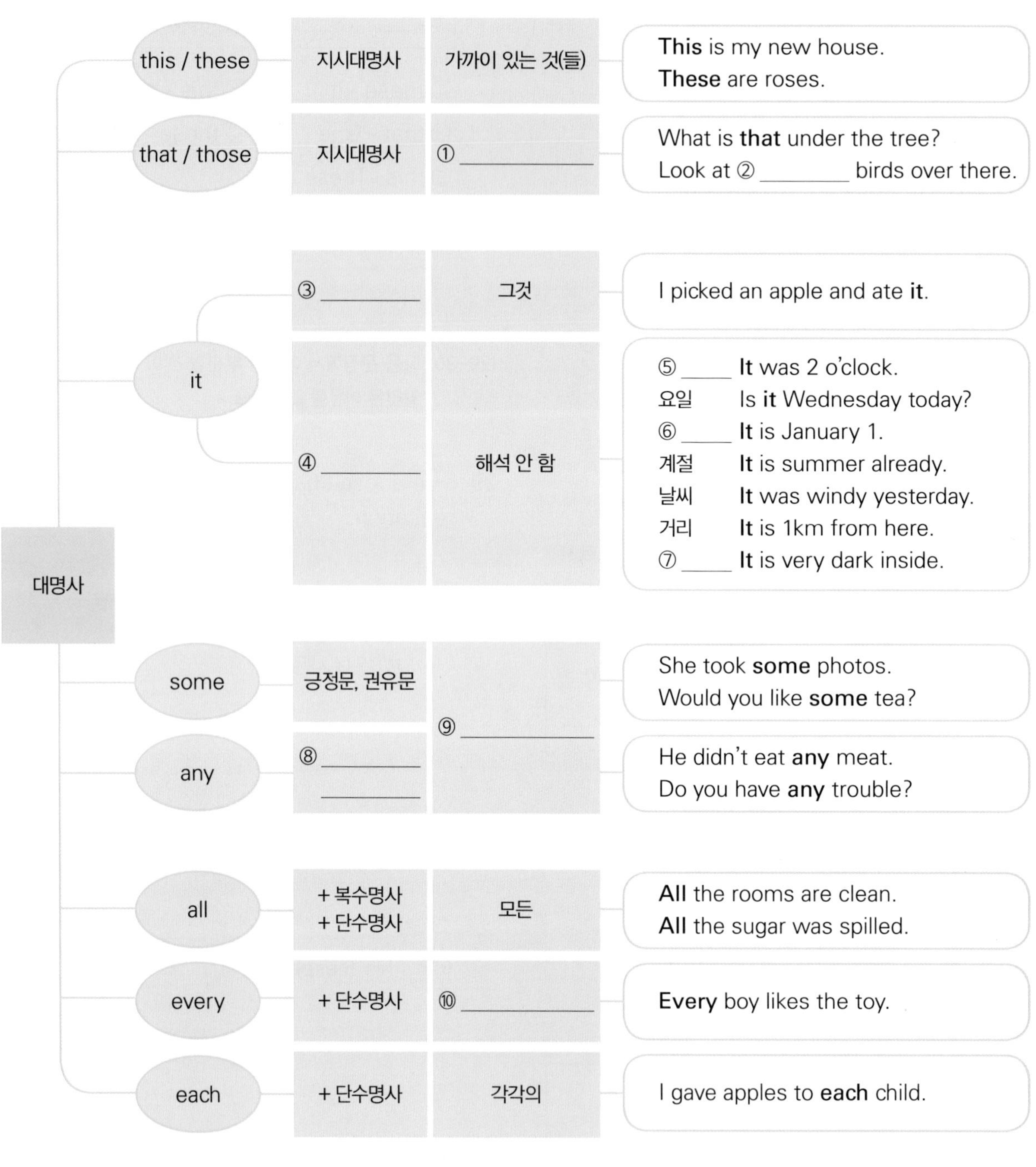

보기				
	· 날짜	· 모든	· 시간	· 대명사
	· 명암	· 비인칭 주어	· 약간의, 조금의	· 부정문, 의문문
	· 멀리 있는 것(들)	· those		

Chapter

05

진행형과 미래시제

진행형

GP 18

❶ **현재진행형**: 지금 진행 중인 일을 나타낸다.

He **is surfing** the Internet.

We **are studying** English grammar.

❷ **과거진행형**: 과거의 특정 시점에 진행 중인 일을 나타낸다.

They **were watching** a baseball game then.

• [동사원형 + -ing] 만들기

대부분의 동사	동사원형 + -ing	walk → walk**ing**	help → help**ing**
-e로 끝나는 동사	e를 빼고 + -ing	live → liv**ing** come → com**ing**	have → hav**ing** make → mak**ing**
-ie로 끝나는 동사	ie를 y로 바꾸고 + -ing	die → d**ying**	lie → l**ying**
[단모음 + 단자음]으로 끝나는 동사	자음을 한 번 더 쓰고 + -ing	stop → stop**ping** plan → plan**ning**	sit → sit**ting** put → put**ting**

진행형 부정문과 의문문

GP 19

❶ 진행형 부정문

I **am not joking**.

Andrew **was not listening** to the teacher.

❷ 진행형 의문문

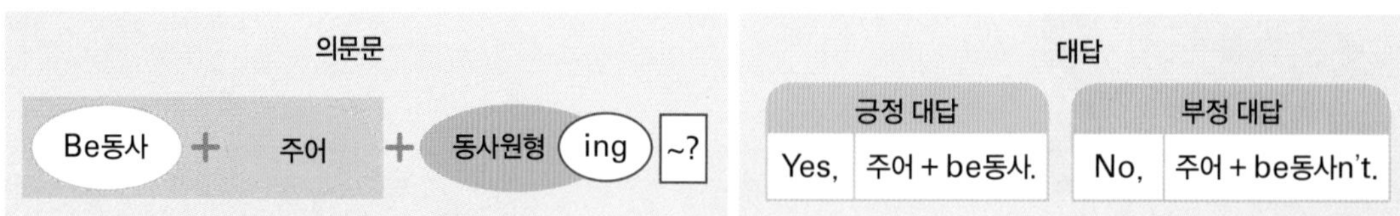

A: **Are you wearing** glasses? B: **Yes, I am. / No, I'm not.**

A: **Was Ann having** lunch then? B: **Yes, she was. / No, she wasn't.**

GP Practice

A ( ) 안에서 알맞은 것을 고르시오.

1 I (walking, am walking) to school.

2 The models are (wait, waiting) behind the stage.

3 She (is not, not is) talking on the phone.

4 Is Jason (clean, cleaning) his room now?

5 A: (Are, Do) you listening to me? B: Yes, I (am, do).

B ( ) 안의 말을 이용하여 진행형 문장을 완성하시오. (부정문은 축약형으로 쓰기)

1 I ________________ to the library now. (go)

2 ________________ Tom ________________ a comic book now? (read)

3 Janet ________________ the Internet now. (not, use)

4 ________________ Alex ________________ the fence then? (paint)

5 They ________________ at me at that time. (not, look)

C 우리말과 의미가 같도록 ( ) 안의 말을 이용하여 문장을 완성하시오.

1 Ryan은 인터넷을 검색하고 있는 중이다. (search)

→ ____________ ____________ ____________ for information on the Internet.

2 누군가가 문을 두드리고 있나요? (someone, knock)

→ ____________ ____________ ____________ on the door?

3 그는 그때 저녁 뉴스를 보고 있지 않았다. (watch)

→ ____________ ____________ ____________ the evening news then.

D 밑줄 친 부분에 대한 설명을 하고 틀린 경우엔 바르게 고치시오. (맞으면 'O' 표시)

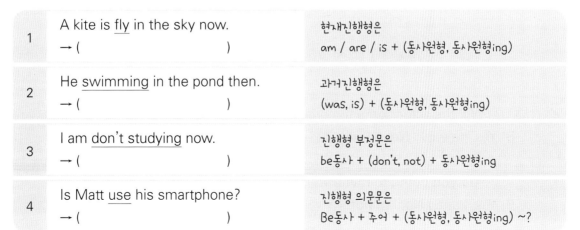

1	A kite is <u>fly</u> in the sky now. → ( )	현재진행형은 am / are / is + (동사원형, 동사원형ing)
2	He <u>swimming</u> in the pond then. → ( )	과거진행형은 (was, is) + (동사원형, 동사원형ing)
3	I am <u>don't studying</u> now. → ( )	진행형 부정문은 be동사 + (don't, not) + 동사원형ing
4	Is Matt <u>use</u> his smartphone? → ( )	진행형 의문문은 Be동사 + 주어 + (동사원형, 동사원형ing) ~?

미래시제

GP 20

미래시제는 아직 일어나지 않은 미래의 동작이나 상태를 나타낸다.

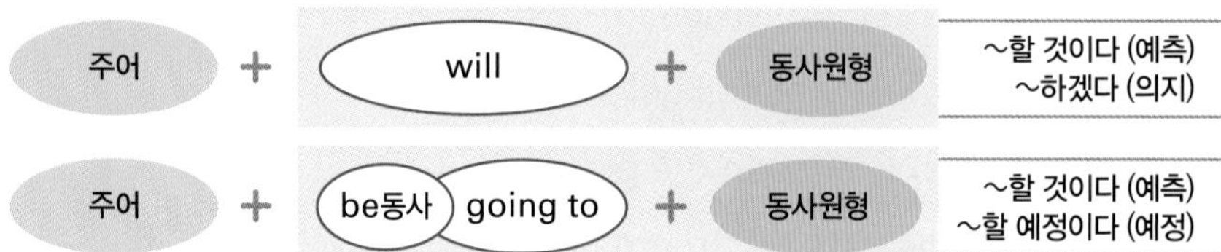

The game **will be** popular.
Mr. Johnson **will stay** at my house.
It **is going to rain** soon.
We **are going to have** a party.

Tip
미래시제와 주로 쓰는 부사(구)
tomorrow, soon, next week, next month, this Sunday, this weekend...

미래시제 부정문과 의문문

GP 21

❶ 미래시제 부정문

We **won't (will not) fight** again.
I **am not going to run** in the classroom.

❷ 미래시제 의문문

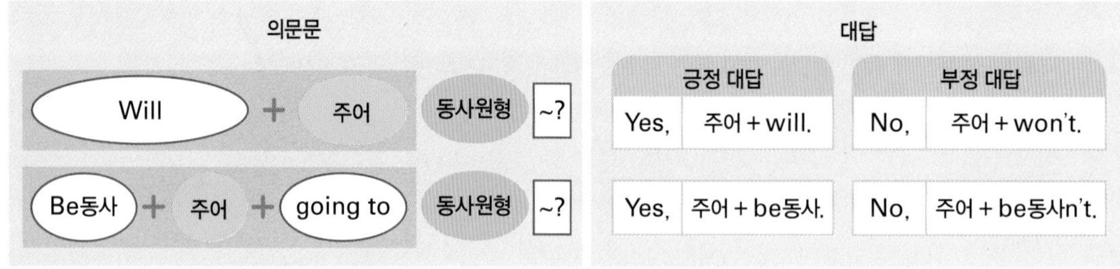

A: **Will the actor come** to Korea?
B: **Yes, he will. / No, he won't.**

A: **Are you going to invite** your friends?
B: **Yes, I am. / No, I'm not.**

GP Practice

A ( ) 안에서 알맞은 것을 고르시오.

1 Tom will (give, gives) me a call.

2 Is she going (join, to join) the club?

3 I (am not, don't) going to take a nap.

4 (Is he, Will he be) twenty years old next year?

5 (Is, Are) they going to come back?

B ( ) 안의 말을 이용하여 문장을 완성하시오. (부정문은 축약형으로 쓰기)

1 Mary ____________ her homework by nine. (finish, will)

2 I ____________ any trouble. (make, will, not)

3 ____________ they ____________ a job interview today? (have, will)

4 He ____________ soup. (have, be going to, not)

5 ____________ you ____________ money? (borrow, be going to)

C 우리말과 의미가 같도록 ( ) 안의 말을 이용하여 문장을 완성하시오.

1 나는 약속을 깨지 않을 것이다. (break, will)

→ ________ ________ ________ ________ my promise.

2 아빠는 고장 난 문을 고치실 예정이다. (fix, be going to)

→ My dad ________ ________ ________ ________ the broken door.

3 Nick이 파티에 올까? (come, will)

→ ________ ________ ________ to the party?

D 밑줄 친 부분에 대한 설명을 하고 틀린 경우엔 바르게 고치시오. (맞으면 'O' 표시)

1	I going to meet her soon. → ( )	주어 + (going to, be going to) + 동사원형
2	Will he moves to a new house? → ( )	will 포함한 의문문은 Will + 주어 + (동사, 동사원형) ~?
3	Does she going to wear a raincoat? → ( )	be동사 going to 포함한 의문문은 (Does, Be동사) + 주어 + going to + 동사원형 ~?
4	Rosa not will take a taxi. → ( )	will 포함한 부정문은 주어 + (not will, will not) + 동사원형

A 우리말과 의미가 같도록 ( ) 안의 말을 배열하시오.

1 내 남동생이 기타를 연주하고 있는 중이야. (is, brother, the guitar, playing, my)

→ ______________________________.

2 그 학생들은 신문을 읽고 있나요? (newspapers, are, reading, the students)

→ ______________________________?

3 그 아이는 손을 씻을 것이다. (is, to, her hands, wash, the child, going)

→ ______________________________.

4 학교 축제는 아주 재미있을 거야. (fun, the school festival, be, very, will)

→ ______________________________.

5 Bill은 지금 침대를 정리하고 있지 않아. (Bill, is, his bed, making, not)

→ ______________________________ now.

6 그들은 오늘밤에 서울을 떠나지 않을 거야. (to, Seoul, aren't, they, leave, going)

→ ______________________________ tonight.

B 우리말과 의미가 같도록 ( ) 안의 말을 이용하여 문장을 완성하시오.

1 그 새들이 체리를 먹을까? (eat, birds)

→ ________ ________ ________ ________ the cherries?

2 그들은 그때 풍선을 잡고 있었다. (hold)

→ ________ ________ ________ the balloons then.

3 우리는 다시 늦지 않을 거야. (late, will)

→ We ________ ________ ________ ________ again.

4 그녀는 마루를 닦고 있나요? (mop)

→ ________ ________ ________ the floor?

5 나는 그 초록색 바지를 입지 않을 거야. (wear, going)

→ ________ ________ ________ ________ ________ ________

the green pants.

6 너는 그때 쓰레기를 내놓는 중이었니? (take out)

→ ________ ________ ________ ________ the garbage then?

C 그림 상황에 맞도록 주어진 말을 이용하여 대화를 완성하시오.

1 be going to, play

A: Is he going to play with his friends?

B: Yes, ________ ________. He ________ ________ ________ ________ soccer with them.

2 will, water

A: ________ ________ ________ the plants in the garden?

B: Yes, he will.

3 be going to, get

A: Are ________ ________ ________ ________ a cat soon?

B: No, I already have three pets.

D ( ) 안의 동사를 진행형으로 써서 대화를 완성하시오.

1 A: Is Jimmy listening to his teacher?

B: No, he ________ ________ ________ the window. (look out)

2 A: Are you cleaning up your desk?

B: No, ________ ________. I ________ ________ on the bed. (rest)

3 A: Are your brothers writing in their journals?

B: No, ________ ________. They ________ ________ comic books. (read)

4 A: Was your sister reading a book on the sofa?

B: No, ________ ________. She ________ ________ TV. (watch)

5 A: Were the two students working hard?

B: No, they ________ ________ ________ ________ ________.

(talk, on the phone)

1 동사와 진행형이 잘못 연결된 것은?

① live - living
② tie - tying
③ walk - walking
④ plan - planing
⑤ cut - cutting

(2–4) 빈칸에 들어갈 알맞은 말을 고르시오.

2

She ________ her friend tomorrow.

① will meet ② meets
③ met ④ going to meet
⑤ will going to meet

3

She is not ________ in London.

① live ② lives
③ lived ④ going to live
⑤ going live

4

A cat is ________ on the ground.

① sleep ② sleeps
③ will sleep ④ slept
⑤ sleeping

(5–6) 빈칸에 공통으로 들어갈 말을 고르시오. (대문자와 소문자 적용)

5

· ________ he traveling in Africa now? · Lucy ________ going to buy a new ring.

① Is, is ② Was, was
③ Are, are ④ Were, were
⑤ Will, will

6

· Is Jun ________ to sing here? · He was ________ to work then.

① will ② go
③ going ④ will go
⑤ went

(7–8) 빈칸에 알맞지 않은 것을 고르시오.

7

The men ________ the mountain.

① climbed ② will climb
③ are climbing ④ was climbing
⑤ are going to climb

8

He will cook dinner ________.

① tonight ② this weekend
③ yesterday ④ tomorrow
⑤ soon

(9-10) 다음 대화를 완성할 때 알맞은 것을 고르시오.

9

A: Is your father driving now?
B: ________

① Yes, he is.
② No, you aren't.
③ Yes, you do.
④ No, he is.
⑤ Yes, he isn't.

10

A: Did James wash his sneakers?
B: Not yet. He ________ them later.

① is not washing
② is going to washing
③ be going to wash
④ will going to wash
⑤ is going to wash

11 빈칸에 들어갈 말이 바르게 짝지어진 것을 고르시오.

· ______ Emily going to cook tonight?
· ______ you go shopping with me?

① Are - Are
② Is - Are
③ Are - Will
④ Is - Will
⑤ Will - Will

(12-13) 다음 중 어법상 어색한 문장을 고르시오.

12 ① Is she buying flowers?
② She won't oversleep.
③ They aren't swim now.
④ Are they playing badminton?
⑤ They are not planning a trip now.

13 ① It is not snow now.
② Was she wearing a cap?
③ He was lying on the beach.
④ Andy is not writing a report.
⑤ Are you going to eat out?

(14-15) ( ) 안의 말을 이용하여 빈칸을 채우시오.

14 I feel terrible. I am going to ________ soon. (sick)

⇨ ________________

15 The puppies are ________ now. (not, sleep)

⇨ ________________

(16–18) 우리말과 의미가 같도록 ( ) 안의 말을 배열하시오.

16 그 스웨터는 너무 끼여서 그녀는 그것을 입지 않을 거야.
(is, it, she, not, wear, to, going)

⇨ The sweater is too tight, so ________ ________________________________.

17 너 지금 내 말 듣고 있니?
(to, now, you, are, me, listening)

⇨ ________________________________?

18 나는 거짓말을 하지 않을 거야.
(not, will, tell a lie)

⇨ I ________________________________.

19 빈칸에 들어갈 말이 다른 하나는?

① __________ the sky getting dark soon?

② Jessy __________ telling a joke now.

③ __________ he working on the computer now?

④ She __________ going to take the subway.

⑤ My friend __________ move to London soon.

(20–21) 우리말과 의미가 같도록 ( ) 안의 말을 이용하여 문장을 완성하시오.

20 그들은 인터넷에서 채팅 중인가요?
(chat)

⇨ __________ they __________ on the Internet?

21 뮤지컬이 곧 시작할 예정이야.
(start, is)

⇨ The musical ______________________ soon.

(22–23) 다음 질문에 대한 대답을 알맞게 쓰시오.

22 A: Will he be a high school student next year?
B: No, __________. He will be a middle school student.

⇨ ________________

23 A: Was Jack riding his bike then?
B: Yes, __________. It is his favorite hobby.

⇨ ________________

24 다음 우리말을 영어로 바르게 옮긴 것은?

그들은 축구 경기를 보고 있었어.

① They were watch a soccer game.
② They did watch a soccer game.
③ They were watched a soccer game.
④ They are watching a soccer game.
⑤ They were watching a soccer game.

25 어법상 어색한 것으로 짝지어진 것은?

ⓐ He was lieing on the beach.
ⓑ I am going to eat out tonight.
ⓒ Will you helped me with my homework?
ⓓ Jack not was using the computer.
ⓔ It won't be cold tomorrow.

① ⓐ, ⓑ ② ⓐ, ⓓ
③ ⓐ, ⓒ, ⓓ ④ ⓒ, ⓔ
⑤ ⓒ, ⓓ, ⓔ

(26–27) 다음 문장에서 어색한 부분을 찾아 바르게 고치고 알맞은 이유를 고르시오.

26 Is your English get better?

고치기: ______________ ⇨ ______________
이유: 진행형 의문문은
Be동사 + 주어 + (동사원형, 동사원형ing) ~?

27 He does not going to grow apple trees next year.

고치기. ______________ ⇨ ______________
이유: 미래시제 부정문은
(is not, not is) + going to + 동사원형

(28–29) 주어진 문장과 의미가 같도록 빈칸을 채우시오.

28 Will she rent a car?

⇨ ______________ ______________
______________ ______________ rent
a car?

29 We aren't going to join the speech club.

⇨ ______________ ______________
______________ ______________
the speech club.

30 다음 조건을 이용하여 알맞게 영작하시오.

그는 그의 마음을 바꾸지 않을 것이다.
조건 1: mind, change
조건 2: 5단어, 축약형

⇨ ______________________________.

한눈에 정리하는 Grammar Mapping

빈칸에 알맞은 답을 보기에서 골라 넣어 grammar mapping 완성하기

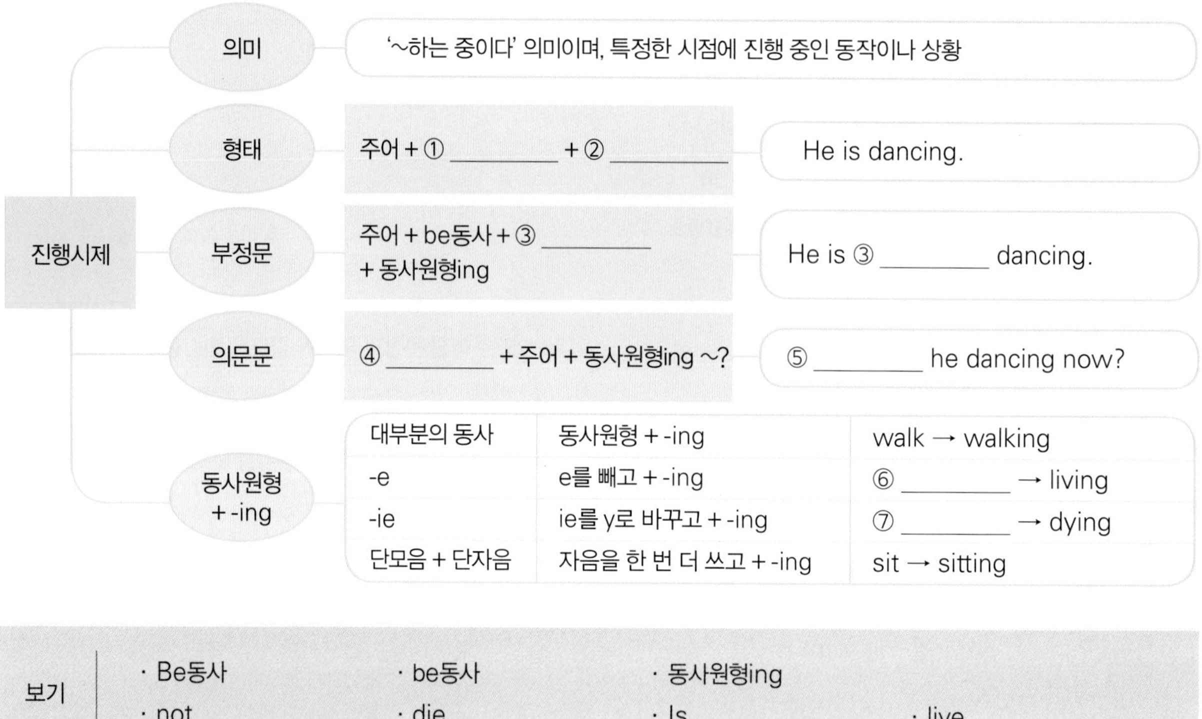

보기			
· Be동사	· be동사	· 동사원형ing	
· not	· die	· Is	· live

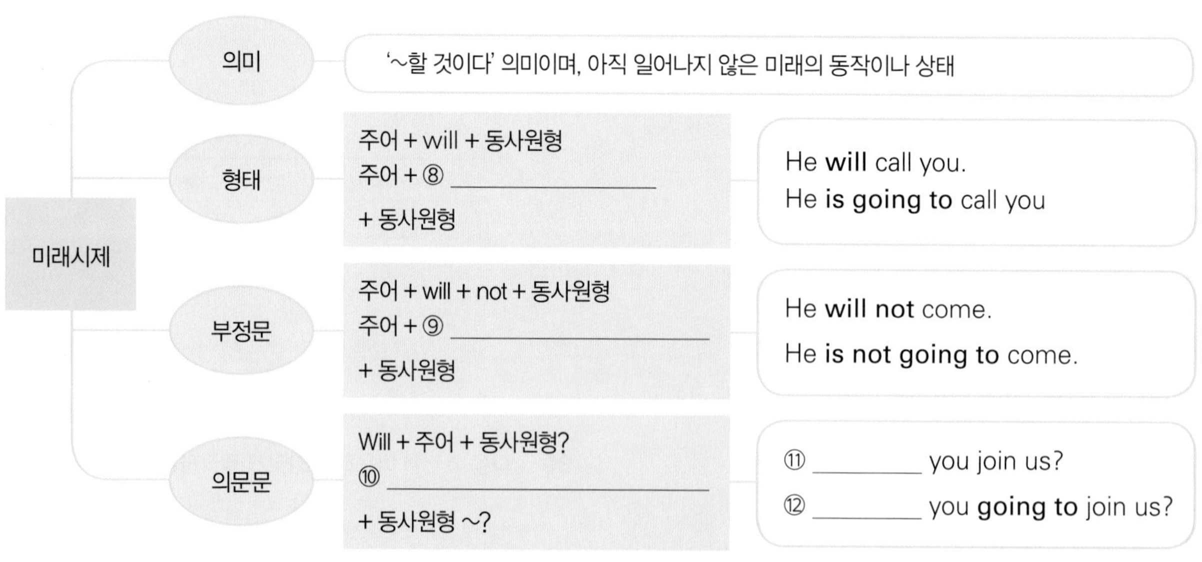

보기		
· be동사 + going to	· Be동사 + 주어 + going to	
· be동사 + not + going to	· Are	· Will

Chapter

06

조동사

GP 22 can, may

GP 23 must, have to, should

- Grammar & Writing
- Actual Test
- 한눈에 정리하는 Grammar Mapping

can, may

GP 22

❶ can + 동사원형

	can	
능력, 가능	~할 수 있다 (am / are / is able to)	She can play the violin. = She is able to play the violin.
허락	~해도 된다	You can sit next to me.

(1) 능력·가능: ~할 수 있다 (= be able to)

☆ The robot **can** talk. (= is able to)

☆ He **can't** ride a bicycle. (= is not able to)

The child **could** use chopsticks. (= was able to)

A: ☆ **Can** you fix the computer? B: Yes, I **can**. / No, I **can't**.

(2) 허락: ~해도 된다

You **can** come in.

Can (= Could) I use your pen?

• Upgrade •

조동사의 부정문과 의문문

평서문: 주어 + 조동사 + 동사원형	She **can read** Chinese.
부정문: 주어 + 조동사 + not + 동사원형	She **cannot read** Chinese.
의문문: 조동사 + 주어 + 동사원형 ~?	**Can** she **read** Chinese?

❷ may + 동사원형

	may	
허락	~해도 된다	☆You may go home now.
불확실한 추측	~일지도 모른다	She may know you.

(1) 허락: ~해도 된다

You **may** leave your bag in the room.

You **may not** go out alone.

A: ☆ **May** (Can) I ask a question? B: Yes, you **may**. / No, you **may not**.

(2) 추측: ~일지도 모른다

☆ She **may** be hungry.

Alex **may not** like the plan.

GP Practice

A 밑줄 친 부분의 쓰임을 보기에서 고르고 해석을 쓰시오. (중복 사용 가능)

보기 | ⓐ 능력 ⓑ 허락 ⓒ 추측	쓰임	해석
1 I can solve the puzzle.	______	______________
2 You may eat a snack now.	______	______________
3 It may rain this afternoon.	______	______________
4 You can call me any time.	______	______________

B 빈칸에 can 또는 can't 중 알맞은 것을 쓰시오.

1 This box is too heavy. I __________ carry it.

2 The pool is closed. You __________ swim here.

3 I like the soup. __________ I have more?

4 Bats __________ sleep upside down.

C 우리말과 의미가 같도록 ( ) 안의 말을 이용하여 문장을 완성하시오.

1 고래는 물 아래에서 숨 쉴 수 없다. (breathe)

→ Whales __________ __________ underwater.

2 제가 창가 자리에 앉아도 될까요? (take)

→ __________ __________ __________ the window seat?

3 나는 그 작은 글씨들을 읽을 수 있었어. (read)

→ I was __________ __________ __________ the small print.

4 그 전화번호가 틀릴 수도 있어. (be)

→ The phone numbers __________ __________ wrong.

D 밑줄 친 부분에 대한 설명을 하고 틀린 경우엔 바르게 고치시오. (맞으면 'O' 표시)

1	You can sat next to me. → ( )	(허락, 능력) 의미 조동사 + (동사, 동사원형)
2	He can buy the ticket yesterday. → ( )	(할 수 있다, 할 수 있었다)이므로 조동사 (현재형, 과거형)
3	Your answer may is correct. → ( )	(약한 추측, 허락) 의미 조동사 + (동사, 동사원형)
4	Do you will marry me? → ( )	조동사 의문문 어순은 (Do + 주어 + 조동사, 조동사 + 주어) + 동사원형 ~?

must, have to, should

GP 23

❶ must + 동사원형

	must	
의무	~해야 한다	You must wear a seatbelt.
강한 추측	~임에 틀림없다	He must be tired.

(1) **의무:** (반드시) ~해야 한다 (= have to)

☆We **must (have to)** stop at red lights.

부정문: ☆You **must not** give dogs ice cream.

의문문: A: **Must** I wear a seatbelt? B: Yes, you **must**. / No, you **don't have to**.

(2) **강한 추측:** ~임에 틀림없다

☆The cheesecake **must be** delicious. It is popular.

Anna always asks about you. She **must** like you.

❷ have to + 동사원형

	have to	
의무	~해야 한다	You have to wait here.

☆She **has to** get some rest. She has a cold.

부정문: ☆Phillip **doesn't have to** lose weight.

의문문: ☆A: **Do** I **have to** wait? B: Yes, you **do**. / No, you **don't have to**.

• Upgrade •

평서문	He **must** go.	~해야 한다	He **has to** go.	~해야 한다
부정문	He **must not** go.	~해서는 안 된다	He **doesn't have to** go.	~할 필요가 없다
의문문	**Must** he go?	~해야 합니까?	**Does** he **have to** go?	~해야 합니까?

❸ should + 동사원형

	should	
충고, 조언	~해야 한다	You should learn table manners.

☆Tom **should** eat more vegetables.

부정문: You **should not** tell a lie.

의문문: A: **Should** I call her tonight? B: Yes, you **should**. / No, you **don't have to**.

GP Practice

A ( ) 안에서 알맞은 것을 고르시오.

1 She (have to, must) be Jack's mother.

2 We (not must, must not) make any noise here.

3 She should (get, gets) more sunlight.

4 I (don't have to, must not) swim here. It is dangerous.

5 (Must, Have to) I wear the uniform?

B 빈칸에 must 또는 have to 중 알맞은 것을 쓰시오.

1 This tree ____________ be around ten years old.

2 He doesn't ____________ get up early on Sundays.

3 They ____________ not run on the escalator.

4 Did you ____________ work late?

C 보기의 조동사와 ( ) 안의 말을 이용하여 문장을 완성하시오. (한 번씩만 사용)

보기 |	should	must	have to

1 너는 운동을 너무 많이 하면 안 돼. (exercise)

→ You ____________ ____________ ____________ too much.

2 나는 안경을 쓸 필요가 없어. (wear)

→ I ____________ ____________ ____________ ____________ glasses.

3 Tom의 휴대폰이 꺼져 있는 것이 분명해. (be)

→ Tom's cell phone ____________ ____________ dead.

D 밑줄 친 부분에 대한 설명을 하고 틀린 경우엔 바르게 고치시오. (맞으면 'O' 표시) 

1	You <u>must be</u> tired after work. → ( )	(~해야 한다, ~가 틀림없다) 의미 조동사 + (동사, 동사원형)
2	I <u>must</u> go to the hospital yesterday. → ( )	(~해야 한다, ~해야 했다) 의미 (must, had to) + 동사원형
3	You <u>don't should</u> waste water. → ( )	조동사의 부정형은 (don't + 조동사, 조동사 + not)
4	I <u>not</u> have to take a taxi. → ( )	(~하면 안 된다, ~할 필요 없다) 의미 (don't, not) + have to

Grammar & Writing

A **우리말과 의미가 같도록 ( ) 안의 말을 알맞게 배열하시오.**

1 나는 알람을 맞춰야 해. (the alarm, set, have to)

→ I ______________________________.

2 이름과 전화번호를 알려 주시겠어요? (I, may, have, your name)

→ ______________________________ and phone number?

3 너는 선인장에 물을 자주 주면 안 돼. (water, must, the cactus, not)

→ You ______________________________ often.

4 Janet은 그녀의 오빠 흉내를 낼 수 있어. (is, to, her, able, imitate, brother)

→ Janet ______________________________.

5 Joan은 배고픈 것이 분명해. 이건 그녀의 두 번째 샌드위치야. (be, hungry, must)

→ Joan ______________________________. This is her second sandwich.

6 여러분은 캥거루를 호주에서 발견할 수 있습니다. (kangaroos, can, find, Australia, in)

→ You ______________________________.

B **우리말과 의미가 같도록 ( ) 안의 말을 이용하여 문장을 완성하시오.**

1 그 두 소녀는 쌍둥이임이 분명해. (be, twins)

→ The two girls ________ ________ ________.

2 너는 나를 기억 못할지도 몰라. (remember)

→ You ________ ________ ________ ________.

3 고양이들은 밖에 나갈 필요가 없어. (go outside)

→ Cats ________ ________ ________ ________ ________.

4 그 곤충은 물 위를 걸을 수 있어. (walk, on)

→ The insect ________ ________ ________ ________.

5 타조는 일 년에 60개의 알을 낳을 수 있어. (lay, eggs, a)

→ An ostrich ________ ________ ________ ________ ________ ________.

6 고마워요. 잔돈은 가지셔도 됩니다. (keep, the change)

→ Thank you. You ________ ________ ________ ________.

C 조동사 can 또는 cannot을 이용하여 각 표지판에 맞는 설명을 완성하시오.

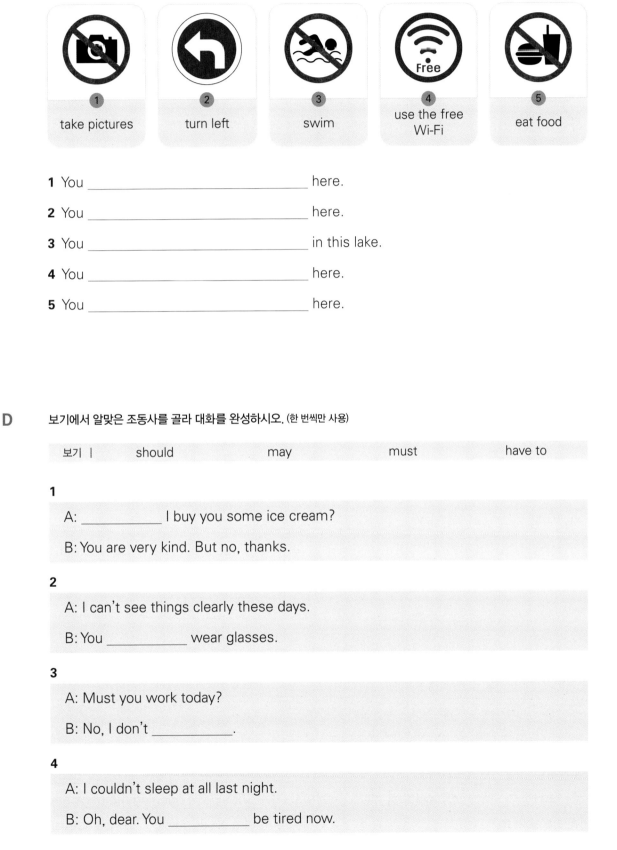

1	2	3	4	5
take pictures	turn left	swim	use the free Wi-Fi	eat food

1 You ______________________ here.

2 You ______________________ here.

3 You ______________________ in this lake.

4 You ______________________ here.

5 You ______________________ here.

D 보기에서 알맞은 조동사를 골라 대화를 완성하시오. (한 번씩만 사용)

보기	should	may	must	have to

1

A: __________ I buy you some ice cream?

B: You are very kind. But no, thanks.

2

A: I can't see things clearly these days.

B: You __________ wear glasses.

3

A: Must you work today?

B: No, I don't __________.

4

A: I couldn't sleep at all last night.

B: Oh, dear. You __________ be tired now.

Actual Test

(1-3) 빈칸에 들어갈 알맞은 말을 고르시오.

1

We are sorry, but you __________ bring your pet inside.

① can ② may
③ should ④ have to
⑤ can't

2

He __________ like sweets. He always has candy.

① must ② has to
③ is able to ④ should
⑤ may not

3

__________ I see your ticket, please?

① Must ② May
③ Should ④ Have to
⑤ Will

(4-5) 밑줄 친 부분과 같은 의미의 말을 고르시오.

4

You must change your password.

① can ② may
③ had to ④ have to
⑤ are able to

5

I was able to get a free ticket.

① must ② can
③ may ④ could
⑤ had to

(6-7) 빈칸에 공통으로 들어갈 말을 고르시오.
(대문자와 소문자 적용)

6

· The tree __________ be over 100 years old.
· You __________ dry your hair.

① should ② have to
③ must ④ are able to
⑤ don't

7

· __________ I ask you some questions?
· The phone is ringing. It __________ be John.

① Must, must ② Have to, have to
③ Do, do ④ May, may
⑤ Can't, can't

8 밑줄 친 부분이 어법상 어색한 것을 고르시오.

① He must look after his brother.
② May I speak to Clara?
③ You have to speak nicely to people.
④ Should we opening the book now?
⑤ Jim must be sick. He has a fever.

(9–10) 밑줄 친 부분이 보기와 의미가 같은 것은?

9 You should listen to your parents.

① Jack can swim across the river.
② The girl must be Jack's sister.
③ You must bring your own water.
④ We were able to catch a taxi.
⑤ The little bird may be sick.

10 Can we give carrots to the horse?

① Must we stay at home today?
② Can turtles live longer than humans?
③ May I sit next you?
④ Should I wear a raincoat?
⑤ Does she have to clean the room?

11 다음 중 어법상 알맞은 것을 고르시오.

① She be able to drive a truck.
② He can plays the violin well.
③ Do you must follow the rules?
④ You don't should shout loudly.
⑤ Are you able to read the sign?

(12–14) 보기에서 알맞은 말을 골라 빈칸을 채우시오.

보기 | must not have to can

12 I am not cold. I don't ____________ turn on the heater.

13 We have an extra bed.
You ____________ use it.

14 This is a no-parking zone.
We ____________ park here.

(15–16) 우리말과 의미가 같도록 알맞은 조동사를 쓰시오.

15 Tiffany는 한국 문화를 좋아하는 것이 분명해.

⇨ Tiffany ____________ like Korean culture.

16 학생들은 특별 할인을 받을 수 있었다.

⇨ Students ____________ get a special discount.

17 어법상 올바른 것으로 짝지어진 것은?

ⓐ Can you helped me?
ⓑ Do you must move to New York?
ⓒ Tim may not be from Canada.
ⓓ I have to finish the report yesterday.
ⓔ You should not be late again.

① ⓐ, ⓑ ② ⓐ ⓓ
③ ⓑ ⓒ ⓓ ④ ⓒ ⓔ
⑤ ⓓ ⓔ

(18–19) 밑줄 친 부분의 의미가 나머지와 다른 것은?

18 ① She must wear a helmet.
② He must not be at school now.
③ You must not open this box.
④ Must I wait for you?
⑤ We must save the children.

19 ① Can you understand me?
② He can jump very high.
③ You can use my umbrella.
④ Can Paula speak Spanish?
⑤ I can drive a car.

(20–22) 주어진 문장과 의미가 같도록 빈칸을 채우시오.

20 The boy is able to count to 100.

⇨ The boy ____________ count to 100.

21 Can I help you, sir?

⇨ ____________ I help you, sir?

22 He must cook his own meals.

⇨ He ____________ cook his own meals.

(23–24) 우리말과 의미가 같도록 ( ) 안의 말을 배열하시오.

23 나는 체중을 줄일 필요가 없어.
(have to, don't, lose, weight)

⇨ I ______________________________.

24 너는 눈을 비비면 안 돼.
(not, rub, should, your, eyes)

⇨ You ______________________________.

25 다음 중 의도하는 바가 나머지와 <u>다른</u> 것은?

① You must not touch the painting.
② You should not touch the painting.
③ Don't touch the painting.
④ You can't touch the painting.
⑤ You don't have to touch the painting.

26 다음 우리말을 영어로 바르게 옮긴 것은?

이 신발은 분명히 그의 것이야.

① These shoes must his.
② These shoes has to be his.
③ These shoes are able to be his.
④ These shoes should be his.
⑤ These shoes must be his.

27 다음 대화 중 <u>어색한</u> 것을 고르시오.

① A: May I leave a message for Luna?
B: Sure, what is it about?
② A: Must I write a report?
B: Yes, you must.
③ A: Can I pay now?
B: Sure, it is seven dollars.
④ A: Are you able to win the game?
B: Yes, I am.
⑤ A: Do we have to take tests?
B: No, you must not.

(28–29) 우리말과 의미가 같도록 ( ) 안의 말을 이용하여 문장을 완성하시오

28 그녀는 약속을 지킬 수 있었어.
(be able to, keep)

⇨ She ______________________
her promise.

29 그는 너의 계획을 좋아하지 않을지도 몰라.
(may, like)

⇨ He ______________________
your plan.

(30–31) 다음 문장에서 어색한 부분을 찾아 바르게 고치고 알맞은 이유를 고르시오.

30 You must are quiet in the library.
This is a rule.

고치기: ____________ ⇨ ____________
이유: (~해야 한다, ~임이 틀림없다) 의미는
조동사 + (동사, 동사원형)

31 I don't can speak German.

고치기: ____________ ⇨ ____________
이유: '~할 수 없다'를 의미하는 부정형은
조동사 (앞, 뒤)에 (not, don't)

32 다음 조건을 이용하여 알맞게 영작하시오.

그는 새 차를 살 필요가 없어.
조건 1: have, buy, new
조건 2: 8단어, 축약형

⇨ ______________________.

한눈에 정리하는 Grammar Mapping

빈칸에 알맞은 답을 보기에서 골라 넣어 grammar mapping 완성하기

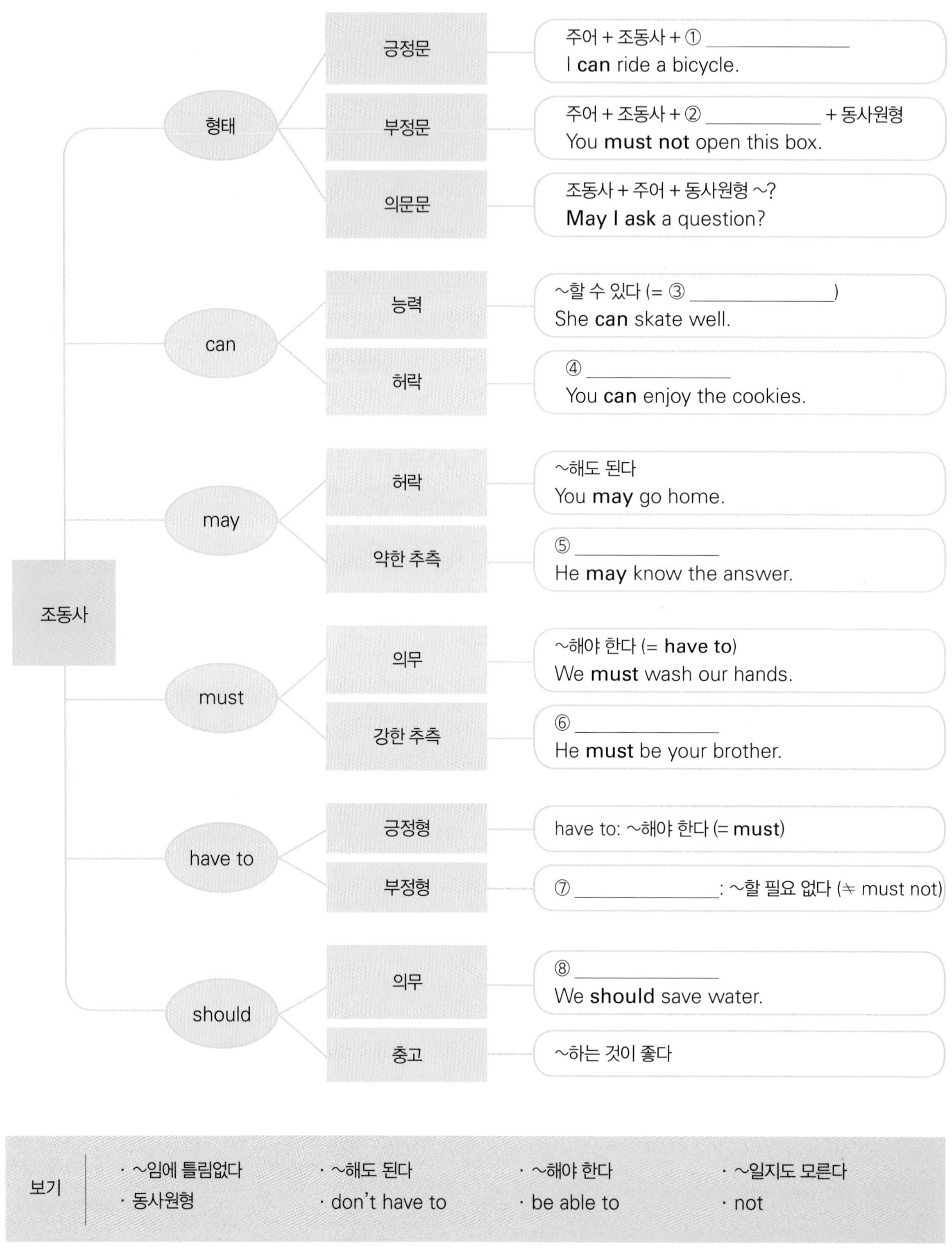

보기				
	· ~임에 틀림없다	· ~해도 된다	· ~해야 한다	· ~일지도 모른다
	· 동사원형	· don't have to	· be able to	· not

Chapter

07

의문사와 여러 가지 문장

who, what, which

GP 24

who, what, which는 각각 사람, 사물, 정해진 대상의 선택을 물을 때 사용한다.

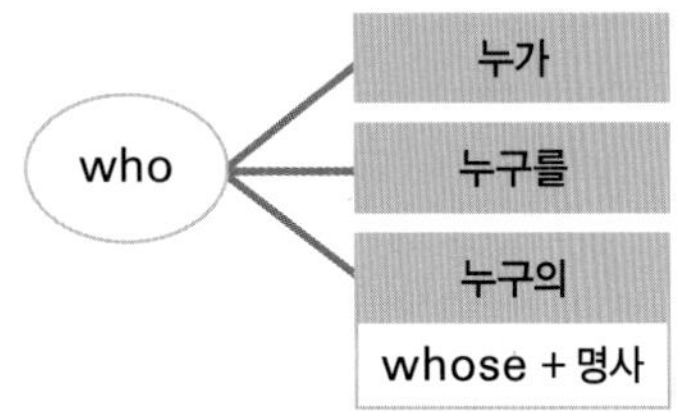

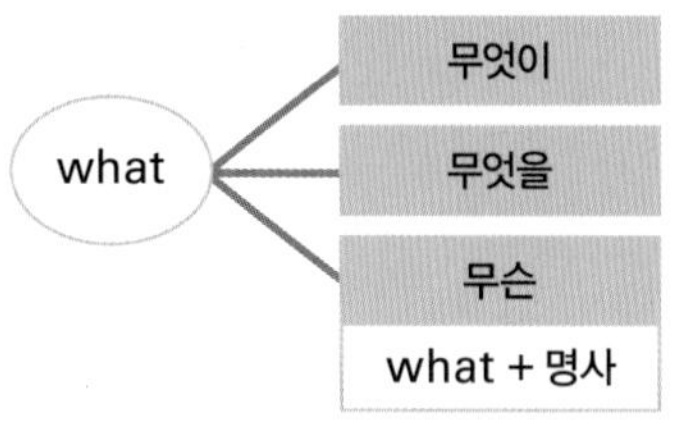

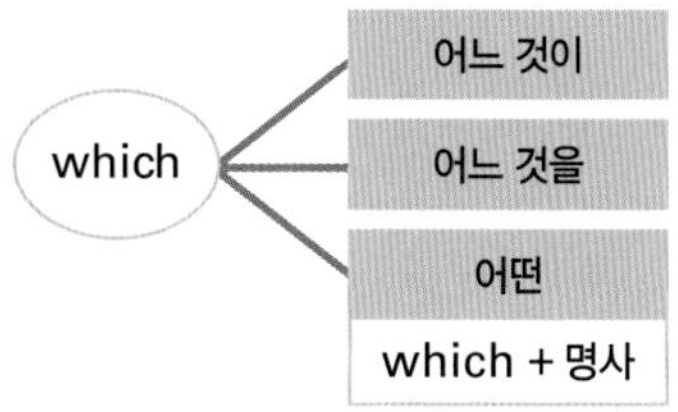

❶ **who(m), whose:** 사람에 대해(이름이나 관계 등) 물을 때 사용

☆ **Who** is your new teacher?
Who won the race?
Who(m) did you invite to the party?
Whose dog is barking outside?

> **Tip**
> 의문사가 주어일 때 어순
> [의문사 + 동사 ~?]
> · Who saw the accident?

❷ **what:** 사물에 대한 구체적인 정보를 물을 때 사용

☆ **What** is your favorite subject?
What did you buy for Jenny's birthday?
What time is it now?

> **Tip**
> what은 정해지지 않은 사물에 대한 정보를 묻는 말이고 which는 정해진 대상에 대한 선택을 묻는 말이다.

❸ **which:** 정해진 대상(A or B)에 대한 선택을 물을 때 사용

Which is cheaper, **pork or beef**?
☆ **Which** do you want, **an orange or a kiwi**?
Which sport do you like better, **baseball or volleyball**?

• Upgrade •

의문문의 대답 형태

❶ 의문사가 없는 의문문: Yes나 No로 대답한다.
Is your mom a teacher? - Yes, she is. / No, she isn't.

❷ 의문사가 없는 선택형 의문문: Yes나 No로 대답하지 않고 구체적인 정보로 대답한다.
Is it true or false? - It is true.

❸ 의문사가 있는 의문문: Yes나 No로 대답하지 않고 구체적인 정보로 대답한다.
What did you do yesterday? - I went to a concert.

GP Practice

A ( ) 안에서 알맞은 것을 고르시오.

1 (Whose, Who) made the cake?

2 (What, Who) did you eat for lunch?

3 (Who, What) was your mom doing?

4 (Who, What) do you live with?

5 (Which, What) do you like better, juice or soda?

B 자연스러운 대화가 되도록 두 문장을 연결하시오.

1 What day is it today? •	• ⓐ My English teacher's.
2 Who used this computer? •	• ⓑ He read a magazine.
3 Whose cell phone is this? •	• ⓒ Friday.
4 Which is better, summer or winter? •	• ⓓ David used it.
5 What did he read yesterday? •	• ⓔ Summer.

C 우리말과 의미가 같도록 ( ) 안의 말을 이용하여 문장을 완성하시오.

1 너는 파티에서 누구를 만났니? (meet)

→ ____________ ____________ ____________ ____________ at the party?

2 미국인들은 추수감사절에 무엇을 먹나요? (Americans, eat)

→ ____________ ____________ ____________ ____________ on Thanksgiving Day?

3 스파게티와 스테이크 중 어느 것이 더 맛있었니? (more delicious)

→ ____________ ____________ ____________ ____________, the spaghetti or the steak?

D 밑줄 친 부분에 대한 설명을 하고 틀린 경우엔 바르게 고치시오. (맞으면 'O' 표시)

1	Who did you eat? → ( )	(사람, 사물)에 대해 물을 때 (Who, What) 사용
2	Who umbrella is this? → ( )	(누구, 누구의) 의미일 때 (Who + 명사, Whose + 명사)
3	What is better, this one or that one? → ( )	정해진 범위 (없을 때, 있을 때) '어느 것이' 의미는 (What, Which)
4	What happened last night? → ( )	의문사가 (주어, 목적어)일 때 (의문사 + 동사, 의문사 + 동사 + 주어) ~? 어순

when, where, why, how

GP 25

when, where, why, how는 각각 시간, 장소, 이유, 방법을 물을 때 사용한다.

when	언제
where	어디서
why	왜
how	어떻게

❶ **when**: 시간, 요일, 날짜 등을 물을 때 사용
When is the next holiday?
☆ **When** does the movie start?

❷ **where**: 위치와 장소를 물을 때 사용
Where is the restroom?
☆ **Where** did you find this book?

❸ **why**: 원인을 물을 때 사용하고 because로 대답
A: **Why** is Henry popular?
B: **Because** he has a sense of humor.

❹ **how**: 상태, 수단, 방법 등을 물을 때 사용
How did you know that?
☆ **How** can I get to the airport?

Tip

why를 이용한 다양한 표현
① Why don't you ~?: 너 (너희들) ~하는 게 어때?
· Why don't you see a doctor?
② Why don't we ~?: 우리 ~하는 게 어때?
· Why don't we meet at the bookstore?

how + 형용사 / 부사

GP 26

[how + 형용사 / 부사]는 '얼마나 ~한, 얼마나 ~하게'라는 의미로 정도를 나타낸다.

how	tall	얼마나 키가 큰
how	old	몇 살의
how	often	얼마나 자주
how	long	얼마나 긴

how	far	얼마나 먼
how	much	얼마나 많이
how many	복수명사	얼마나 많은 수의 ~
how much	단수명사	얼마나 많은 양의 ~

How old is her baby?
☆ **How often** do you work out?
How many students are there in the classroom?

GP Practice

A 보기에서 알맞은 말을 골라 빈칸을 채우시오.

보기	how tall	when	why	where

1 A: ________________ is Jane from? B: She is from England.

2 A: ________________ is Mike's birthday? B: Next Tuesday.

3 A: ________________ do you like me? B: Because you are honest.

4 A: ________________ is the player? B: 200cm.

B 자연스러운 대화가 되도록 두 문장을 연결하시오.

1 When does he take a shower? •

2 How did you come here? •

3 Where were you born? •

4 How often do you work out? •

5 Why did you take a taxi? •

• ⓐ After breakfast.

• ⓑ Twice a week.

• ⓒ I was late.

• ⓓ In Jeju.

• ⓔ By subway.

C 우리말과 의미가 같도록 ( ) 안의 말을 이용하여 문장을 완성하시오.

1 그는 어린 시절에 어디에서 살았나요? (live)

→ ________ ________ ________ ________ in his childhood?

2 너는 그것을 어떻게 구했니? (get)

→ ________ ________ ________ ________ it?

3 그 커피숍은 언제 문을 닫나요? (close)

→ ________ ________ the coffee shop ________?

D 밑줄 친 부분에 대한 설명을 하고 틀린 경우엔 바르게 고치시오. (맞으면 'O' 표시)

1	<u>When</u> is the subway station? → ( )	(시간, 장소)를 물을 때 (When, Where)
2	<u>What</u> was the weather? → ( )	(상태, 사물)을 물을 때 (How, What)
3	<u>How age</u> is your brother? → ( )	'얼마나 ~한' 정도를 물을 때 (How + 명사, How + 형용사)
4	<u>Where</u> do you like me? → ( )	(원인, 장소)를 물을 때 (Why, Where)

부정의문문

GP 27

부정의문문은 동사의 부정형으로 시작하는 의문문으로 '~않니?'로 해석한다. 대답은, 질문이 긍정이든 부정이든 상관없이 대답하는 내용이 긍정이면 Yes로 부정이면 No로 쓴다.

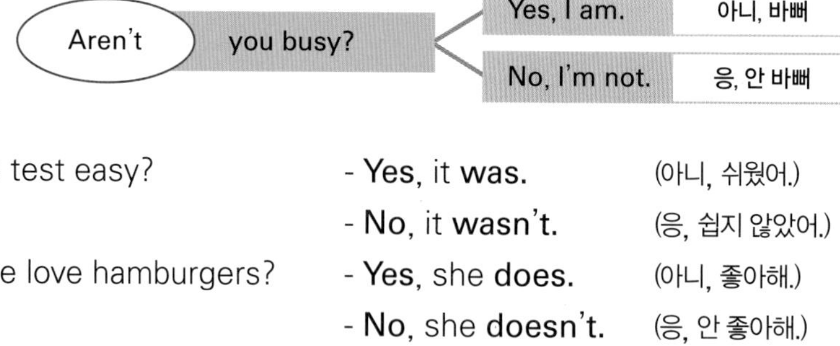

☆ **Wasn't** the test easy?	- **Yes**, it **was**.	(아니, 쉬웠어.)
	- **No**, it **wasn't**.	(응, 쉽지 않았어.)
Doesn't she love hamburgers?	- **Yes**, she **does**.	(아니, 좋아해.)
	- **No**, she **doesn't**.	(응, 안 좋아해.)
Can't we join the club?	- **Yes**, you **can**.	(아니, 할 수 있어.)
	- **No**, you **can't**.	(응, 할 수 없어.)

부가의문문

GP 28

부가의문문은 상대방에게 확인이나 동의를 구하기 위해 평서문 뒤에 짧게 덧붙이는 의문문으로 '그렇지?', '그렇지 않니?'로 해석한다.

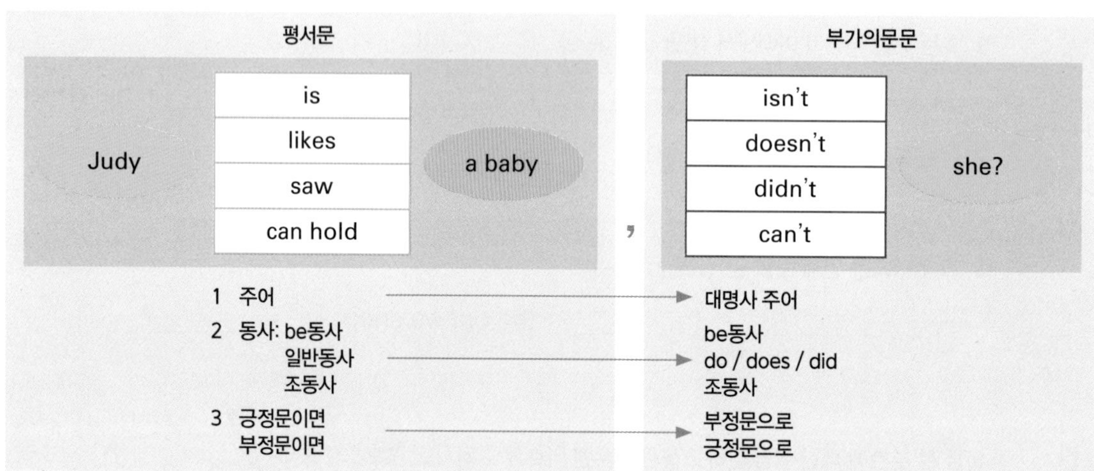

☆ *She has* breakfast every morning, **doesn't she**?
☆ *You didn't see* the polar bear, **did you**?
Cindy will move to the city, **won't she**?

• Upgrade •

부가의문문에 대한 대답은 부정의문문처럼 대답하는 내용이 긍정이면 Yes로, 부정이면 No로 한다.
이때 not은 항상 No 뒤에 써야 한다.

You have a pen, don't you?	- **Yes**, I **do**. (아니, 있어.)
You will go to the theater, won't you?	- **No**, I **won't**. (응, 안 갈 거야.)

GP Practice

A ( ) 안에서 알맞은 것을 고르시오.

1 (Isn't, Doesn't) she look great today?

2 (Don't, Didn't) he teach history?

3 (Wasn't, Weren't) it exciting?

4 A: Won't you buy a necklace? B: No, I (will, won't).

5 A: Aren't the boxes heavy? B: Yes, they (are, aren't).

B 빈칸에 알맞은 말을 써서 부가의문문을 완성하시오.

1 You like Vietnamese food, ____________ ____________?

2 The actors are twins, ____________ ____________?

3 Jun doesn't live in England, ____________ ____________?

4 She can speak French, ____________ ____________?

5 Jenny wrote a lot of poems, ____________ ____________?

C 우리말과 의미가 같도록 문장을 완성하시오.

1 알람 소리를 듣지 못했니? (hear)

→ ____________ ____________ ____________ the alarm?

2 그 영화 대단하다, 그렇지 않니?

→ The movie is amazing, ____________ ____________?

3 이 버스는 경주로 가, 그렇지 않니?

→ This bus goes to Gyeongju, ____________ ____________?

D 밑줄 친 부분에 대한 설명을 하고 틀린 경우엔 바르게 고치시오. (맞으면 'O' 표시) 

1	A. Didn't you use my spoon? B: No, I did. → ( )	부정의문문의 대답은 Yes, (긍정문, 부정문) / No, (긍정문, 부정문)
2	She isn't a famous singer, isn't she? → ( )	부정문의 부가의문문은 (긍정문, 부정문)
3	You need more time, aren't you? → ( )	긍정문의 부가의문문 (긍정문, 부정문) 일반동사의 부가의문문 (aren't, don't) you?
4	Jane can speak French, can't Jane? → ( )	부가의문문의 형태는 동사 + (명사, 대명사) 주어?

명령문과 제안문

GP 29

명령문은 상대방에게 '~해라'라고 명령하거나 요청하는 문장이고 제안문은 '~하자'라고 권유하는 문장이다.

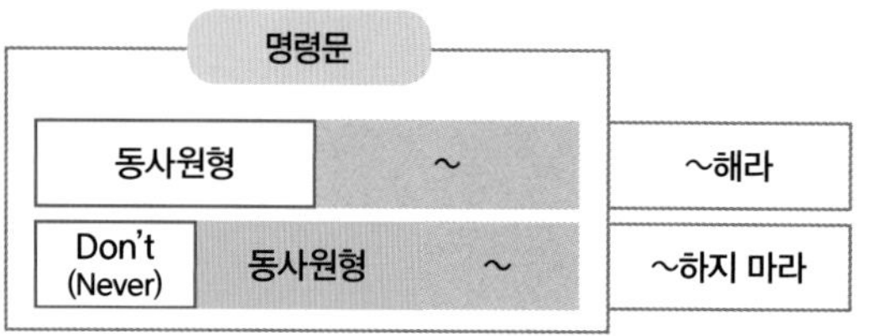

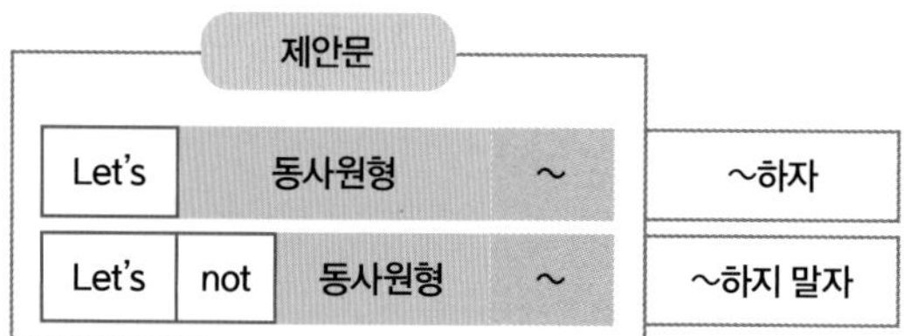

Dream big.
Don't be nervous.
Let's take a walk in the garden.
Let's not go out for dinner.

Tip

명령문의 부가의문문
[명령문 ~, will you?]
· Wash the dishes, will you?

제안문의 부가의문문
[Let's ~, shall we?]
· Let's go there, shall we?

• Upgrade •

제안을 하는 여러 가지 표현 '~하는 것이 어때?'

❶ **How about taking** a break? [How / What about -ing ~?]
❷ **Shall we take** a break? [Shall we + 동사원형 ~?]
❸ **Why don't we take** a break? [Why don't we + 동사원형 ~?]

감탄문

GP 30

감탄문은 놀람, 기쁨 등의 감정을 나타내는 문장으로 How로 시작하는 감탄문과 What으로 시작하는 감탄문이 있다. 보통 '정말(참) ~하구나'로 해석한다.

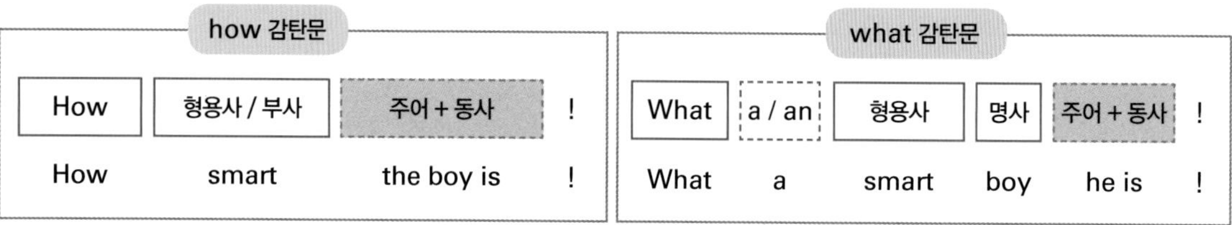

How popular the game is!
How slowly the turtle moves!

What a beautiful day (it is)!
What a great time (we had)!
What old buildings they are!

Tip

what 감탄문에서의 a / an 생략
명사가 복수형이거나 셀 수 없는 명사일 때 a / an은 쓰지 않는다.

• Upgrade •

how 감탄문은 형용사나 부사를 강조하고, what 감탄문은 명사가 포함된 어구를 강조한다.

GP Practice

A ( ) 안에서 알맞은 것을 고르시오.

1 (Be, Do) nice to your sister.

2 (What, How) delicious the pizza was!

3 (What, How) a great cook my dad is!

4 (Not, Don't) be afraid of mistakes.

5 Let's (give, gave) him a big hand.

B ( ) 안의 지시대로 문장을 바꿔 쓰시오.

1 I am very lucky. (감탄문)

→ ______________________________!

2 He was a very brave soldier. (감탄문)

→ ______________________________!

3 You are quiet in the library. (긍정명령문)

→ ______________________________.

4 We stay up too late. (부정제안문)

→ ______________________________.

C 우리말과 의미가 같도록 ( ) 안의 말을 이용하여 문장을 완성하시오.

1 우리 솔직해지자. (honest)

→ ________ ________ ________.

2 사용한 캔은 버리지 마세요. (throw away)

→ ________ ________ ________ used cans.

3 그것은 정말 무서운 이야기구나. (scary, story)

→ ________ ________ ________ ________ it is!

D 밑줄 친 부분에 대한 설명을 하고 틀린 경우엔 바르게 고치시오. (맞으면 'O' 표시)

1	Goes straight one block. → ( )	(~하다, ~해라) 명령문은 (동사현재형, 동사원형)으로 시작
2	Let's don't play outside at night. → ( )	(~하자, ~하지 말자) 부정제안문은 Let's (not, don't) + 동사원형
3	What cute the puppy is! → ( )	(How, What) + 형용사 / 부사 + 주어 + 동사!
4	How a great movie! → ( )	(How, What) + a / an + 형용사 + 명사!

A 우리말과 의미가 같도록 ( ) 안의 말을 배열하시오.

1 태양은 얼마나 큰가요? (is, the sun, big, how)

→ ______________________________?

2 언제 그들은 다시 만날까요? (meet, again, when, they, will)

→ ______________________________?

3 누가 이 상자를 열었나요? (opened, this, who, box)

→ ______________________________?

4 왜 그들은 북극으로 갔나요? (they, to, go, the North Pole, did, why)

→ ______________________________?

5 너의 오빠는 대학에서 무엇을 공부하니? (your brother, study, does, what)

→ ______________________________ at his university?

6 박물관에서는 사진을 찍지 마세요. (take, the museum, don't, photos, in)

→ ______________________________.

7 너는 새 자전거를 살 거야, 그렇지 않니? (won't, will, a, you, you, buy, new bicycle)

→ ______________________________?

B 우리말과 의미가 같도록 ( ) 안의 말을 이용하여 문장을 완성하시오.

1 누구의 전화기가 수업 시간에 울렸었니? (ring, phone)

→ ________ ________ ________ in class?

2 그녀는 여왕처럼 보이지 않나요? (look)

→ ________ ________ ________ like a queen?

3 당신은 어디에서 저의 개를 찾으셨나요? (find, dog)

→ ________ ________ ________ ________ ________ ________?

4 그 새끼 고양이들은 정말 사랑스러워! (lovely, the kittens)

→ ________ ________ ________ ________ are!

5 그는 하루에 얼마나 많은 우유를 마시나요? (drink, milk)

→ ________ ________ ________ ________ ________ ________ in a day?

6 한국 영화와 할리우드 영화 중 어느 것을 더 좋아하니? (like, better)

→ ________ ________ ________ ________ ________, Korean films or Hollywood films?

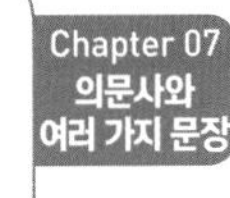

C B의 정보를 참고하여 A의 문장을 완성하시오.

1 A: __________ is his birthday?
B: It is on May 1.

2 A: __________ does he live?
B: He lives in Mok-Dong.

3 A: __________ is his phone number?
B: It's 010-1243-6578.

4 A: __________ was he born?
B: He was born in Seoul.

5 A: __________ is he?
B: He is 16 years old.

6 A: __________ is he?
B: He is 168cm tall.

7 A: __________ does he weigh?
B: He weighs 70kg.

D 다음 그림은 극장에서 지켜야 할 규칙에 관한 것이다. 보기의 단어를 이용하여 지켜야 할 규칙을 쓰시오.

①

②

③

④

보기 | walk around turn off leave lower

1 ________________ your cell phone.
2 ________________ during the show.
3 ________________ your trash on the floor.
4 ________________ your voice during the show.

Actual Test

(1–3) 빈칸에 들어갈 알맞은 말을 고르시오.

1

He asked a favor of you, __________?

① did he ② was he
③ wasn't he ④ didn't he
⑤ didn't you

2

Wow! __________ long river it is!

① How ② What
③ How a ④ What a
⑤ What an

3

Peter, __________ step on the grass.

① not ② no
③ don't ④ doesn't
⑤ not let's

(4–8) 다음 대화에 들어갈 알맞은 말을 고르시오.

4

A: __________ does he go to school?
B: On foot.

① How ② When
③ Why ④ Where
⑤ What

5

A: __________ made this wooden chair?
B: My dad.

① What ② Whose
③ Who ④ How
⑤ Why

6

A: Wasn't he a soldier?
B: No, he __________.
He was an artist.

① didn't ② wasn't
③ was ④ isn't
⑤ did

7

A: __________ shoes are these?
B: They are my father's shoes.

① Who ② What
③ Which ④ Who's
⑤ Whose

8

A: __________ is your blood type?
B: It's O.

① Who ② Which
③ Whose ④ What
⑤ How

9 다음 대화 중 어색한 것을 고르시오.

① A: What did you see yesterday?
B: My old friend.

② A: Where is my stapler?
B: It is in the drawer.

③ A: Whose USB is this?
B: It is Alice's.

④ A: Why do you have red eyes?
B: Because I feel tired.

⑤ A: When does the next train leave?
B: It leaves at six.

10 밑줄 친 부분이 어색한 것을 고르시오.

① You aren't tired, are you?

② Turn off the light, will you?

③ He can join us, can he?

④ Let's save energy, shall we?

⑤ There wasn't much snow, was there?

11 다음 중 어법상 어색한 문장을 고르시오.

① Doesn't she miss her hometown?

② Where did you put my pencil?

③ When will he finish the project?

④ What made her so happy?

⑤ How old the city is?

(12–14) 빈칸에 공통으로 들어갈 말을 쓰시오.

12
· ________ waste your time. Time is precious.
· ________ you want to succeed?

⇨ ____________

13
· ________ is your dream job?
· ________ date it is today?

⇨ ____________

14
· ________ long the water slide is!
· ________ will you spend your vacation?

⇨ ____________

15 두 문장의 의미가 서로 다른 것을 고르시오.

① Don't make a fire.
= You must not make a fire.

② What a difficult test!
= How difficult the test is!

③ Let's join the club.
= Why don't you join the club?

④ How often does she walk her dog?
= How many times does she walk her dog?

⑤ When do you wake up in the morning?
= What time do you wake up in the morning?

16 어법상 올바른 것으로 짝지어진 것은?

ⓐ Don't noisy. It's midnight.
ⓑ Warms up before swimming.
ⓒ Never dive into the lake.
ⓓ The panda is very cute, isn't it?
ⓔ Let's don't eat food on the subway.

① ⓐ, ⓑ
② ⓑ, ⓒ, ⓓ
③ ⓒ, ⓓ
④ ⓒ, ⓓ, ⓔ
⑤ ⓓ, ⓔ

(17–18) 우리말을 영어로 가장 바르게 옮긴 것은?

17 그가 모나리자를 그렸어, 안 그래?

① He painted the *Mona Lisa*, he did?
② He painted the *Mona Lisa*, did he?
③ He painted the *Mona Lisa*, didn't he?
④ He didn't paint the *Mona Lisa*, didn't he?
⑤ He didn't paint the *Mona Lisa*, did he?

18 얼마나 많은 종이가 필요한가요?

① How much do we need paper?
② How much paper do we need?
③ How much papers do we need?
④ How many paper do we need?
⑤ How many papers do we need?

(19–20) 다음 대화의 빈칸에 알맞은 말을 쓰시오.

19 A: __________ did you do last weekend?
B: We went swimming.

20 A: Can't you hear me?
B: __________, I can't. Could you use a microphone?

(21–23) 우리말과 의미가 같도록 ( ) 안의 말을 배열하시오.

21 누가 정답을 알고 있니?
(the, knows, who, answer)

⇨ ______________________________?

22 세상은 정말 좁구나!
(a, small, what, world)

⇨ ______________________________ it is!

23 그 빙하는 얼마나 크니?
(big, is, how, glacier, the)

⇨ ______________________________?

24 빈칸에 들어갈 말이 나머지와 다른 것은?

① ___________ a funny guy he is!

② ___________ smart kids they are!

③ ___________ a wonderful party!

④ ___________ pretty dolls she has!

⑤ ___________ amazing the adventure was!

(25-27) 우리말과 의미가 같도록 ( ) 안의 말을 이용하여 문장을 완성하시오.

25 우리의 계획을 Tom에게 얘기하지 말자.
(tell)

⇨ ______________________ our plan to Tom.

26 미술과 음악 중에서 어느 것을 더 좋아하니?
(like, better)

⇨ ______________________
______________, art or music?

27 어찌나 추웠던지!
(cold, it)

⇨ ______________________!

(28-29) 다음 문장에서 어색한 부분을 찾아 바르게 고치고 알맞은 이유를 고르시오.

28 Cindy likes pizza, doesn't Cindy?

고치기: ___________ ⇨ ___________

이유: 긍정문의 부가의문문은 (긍정문, 부정문) 어순은 동사 + (주어, 대명사 주어)?

29 Don't gives up your dream.

고치기: ___________ ⇨ ___________

이유: '~하지 마라' 부정명령문은 (Don't, Not) + (동사, 동사원형)

30 다음 조건을 이용하여 알맞게 영작하시오.

정말 놀라운 독수리구나!
조건 1: amazing, eagle, it
조건 2: 6단어, 감탄문

⇨ ______________________!

31 밑줄 친 우리말을 영어로 알맞게 옮기시오.

A: Your sisters like vegetables, don't they?
B: <u>응, 안 좋아해.</u>

⇨ ______________________.

한눈에 정리하는 Grammar Mapping

빈칸에 알맞은 답을 보기에서 골라 넣어 grammar mapping 완성하기

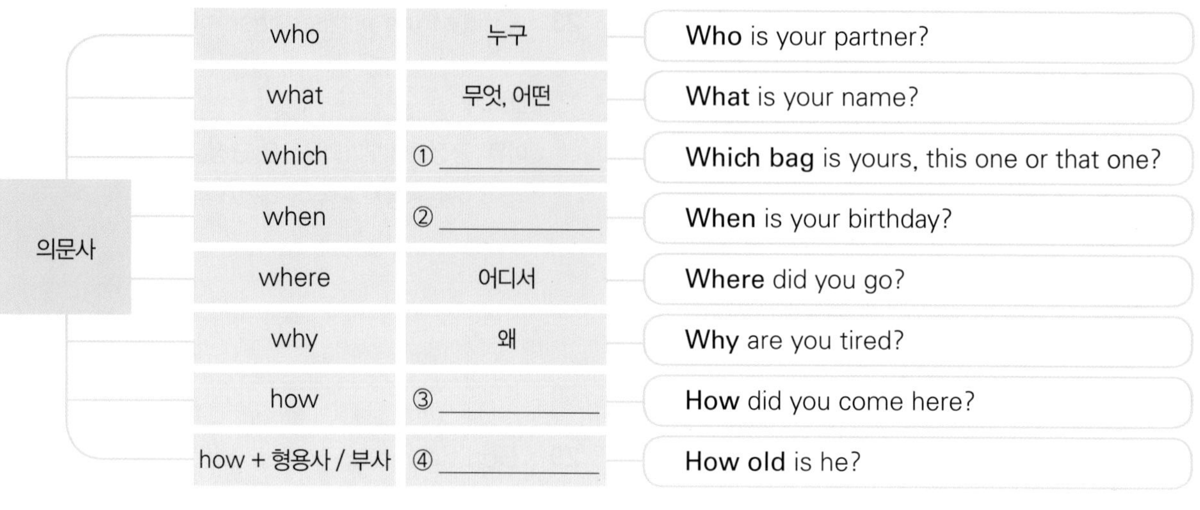

의문사	who	누구	**Who** is your partner?
	what	무엇, 어떤	**What** is your name?
	which	① ________	**Which bag** is yours, this one or that one?
	when	② ________	**When** is your birthday?
	where	어디서	**Where** did you go?
	why	왜	**Why** are you tired?
	how	③ ________	**How** did you come here?
	how + 형용사 / 부사	④ ________	**How old** is he?

보기 | · (~ 중에) 어떤 · 어떻게 · 언제 · 얼마나 ~한 / 하게

여러 가지 문장	부정의문문	의미	부정형으로 묻는 의문문이며, '~하지 않니?' 의미
		~이지 않니?	**Isn't** he cute?
		~하지 않니?	⑤ ________ he like chocolate?
	부가의문문	의미	상대의 확인, 동의를 구하기 위해 평서문 뒤에 붙인다.
		그렇지 않니?	She is strong, ⑥ ________?
		그렇지?	She didn't eat the carrots, ⑦ ________?
	명령문	~해라	(동사원형) **Tell** me the reason.
		~하지 마라	(⑧ ________ + 동사원형) ⑧ ________ tell a lie.
	제안문	~하자	(Let's+동사원형) **Let's eat** out tonight.
		~하지 말자	(Let's not+동사원형) ⑨ ________ out tonight.
	감탄문	how	**How** + ⑩ ________ + (주어 + 동사)!
		what	**What** + ⑪ ________ + (주어 + 동사)!

보기 | · Let's not eat · did she · isn't she · Doesn't · Don't · a / an + 형용사 + 명사 · 형용사 / 부사

Chapter

08

형용사와 부사

형용사의 쓰임

GP 31

❶ **명사 수식:** 대부분의 형용사는 명사 앞에서 명사를 수식하고 -thing, -one, -body로 끝나는 대명사는 형용사가 뒤에서 수식한다.

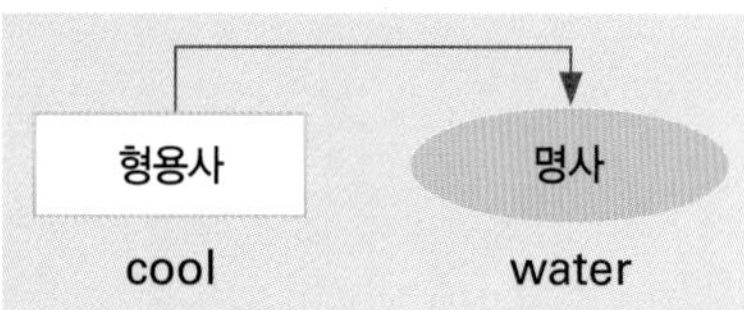

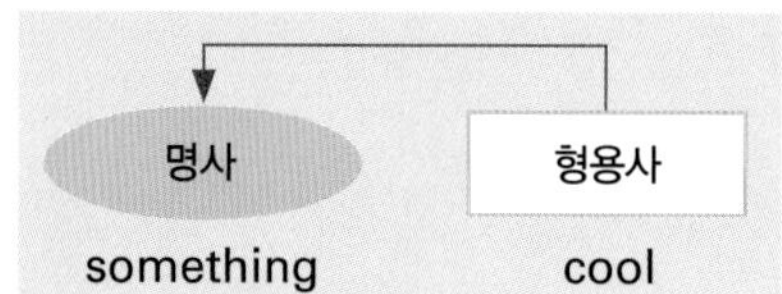

☆ We are **close** *friends*.
I heard *something* **strange**.

❷ **보어:** 동사 또는 목적어 뒤에서 주어나 목적어를 보충 설명한다.

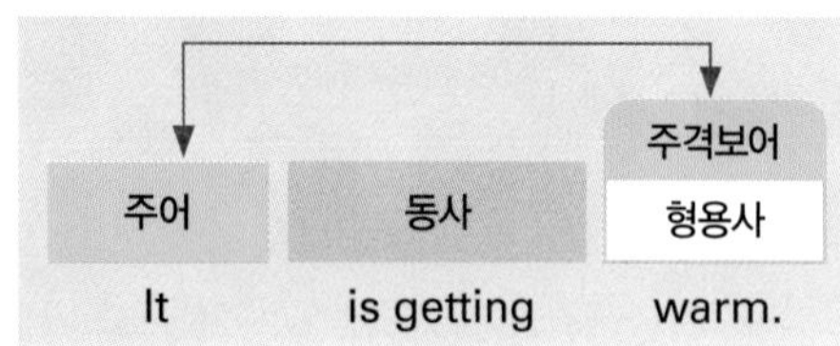

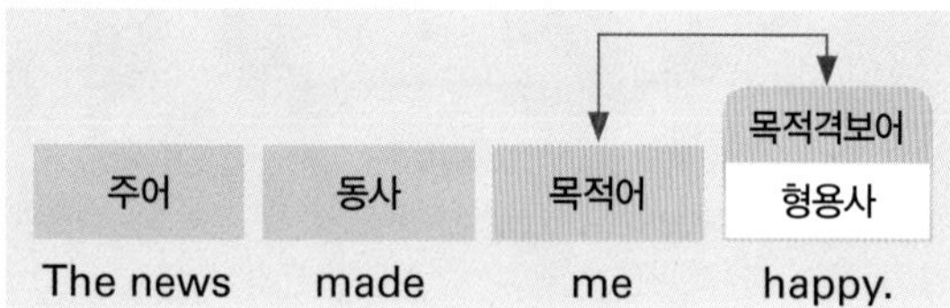

☆ *This movie* was **interesting**.
I found *him* **honest**.

수량 형용사

GP 32

많은	약간, 몇몇의	거의 없는		
many	a few	few	+	셀 수 있는 명사의 복수형
much	a little	little	+	셀 수 없는 명사
a lot of (lots of)			+	셀 수 있는 명사의 복수형 셀 수 없는 명사

☆ There are **many (= a lot of)** *holidays* in May.
Did you get **much (= a lot of)** *snow* last year?

☆ He met Julie **a few** *days* ago.
☆ She spread **a little** *jam* on the bread.
The actor is not famous. He has **few** *fans*.

GP Practice

A ( ) 안에서 알맞은 것을 고르시오.

1 The rose smells (sweet, sweetly).

2 May I ask (a few, a little) questions?

3 The song made the singer (famous, famously).

4 The chef doesn't use (much, many) sugar.

5 Look! I found (great something, something great).

B 보기에서 알맞은 말을 골라 문장을 완성하시오. (한 번씩만 사용)

보기 |	few	little	a little	a lot of

1 There were ____________ roses at the rose festival.

2 She was very busy. So she had ____________ time to cook.

3 The store was almost empty. There were ____________ people.

4 I had ____________ luck on the test. So I could pass it.

C 우리말과 의미가 같도록 ( ) 안의 말을 이용하여 문장을 완성하시오 .

1 그녀의 충고는 유용했어. (useful)

→ Her advice ____________ ____________.

2 그 소년은 낚시에 관심이 거의 없어. (interest)

→ The boy has ____________ ____________ in fishing.

3 뷔페에 맛있는 것이 하나도 없었어. (delicious, nothing)

→ There was ____________ ____________ at the buffet.

D 밑줄 친 부분에 대한 설명을 하고 틀린 경우엔 바르게 고치시오. (맞으면 'O' 표시) 

1	You have a <u>love</u> sister. → ( )	(명사 수식, 보어) 쓰임의 (형용사, 명사)
2	I will use <u>few</u> shampoo. → ( )	(few, little) + 셀 수 없는 명사 (거의 없는, 약간은 있는) 의미
3	He doesn't have <u>much</u> friends. → ( )	(many, much) + 셀 수 있는 명사의 복수형 (많은, 거의 없는) 의미
4	The water is <u>cleanly</u>. → ( )	(명사 수식, 보어) 쓰임의 (형용사, 부사)

부사의 쓰임과 형태

GP 33

❶ **부사의 쓰임:** 부사는 동사, 형용사, 다른 부사, 문장 전체를 수식하고 '~하게'로 해석한다.

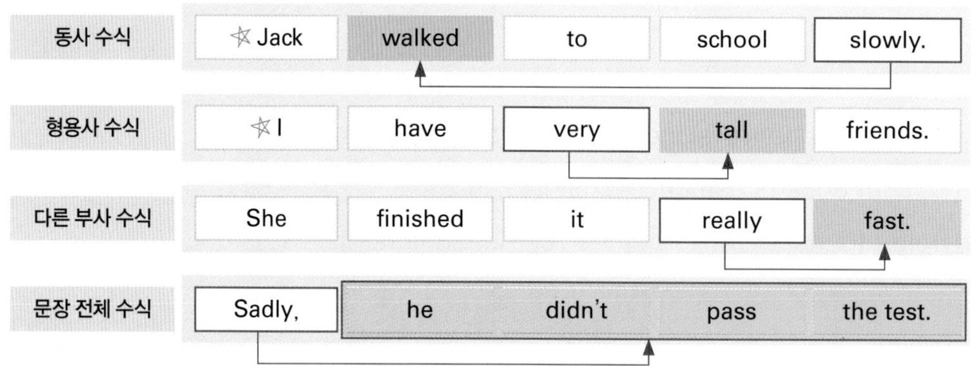

동사 수식
Jack
walked
to
school
slowly.
형용사 수식
I
have
very
tall
friends.
다른 부사 수식
She
finished
it
really
fast.
문장 전체 수식
Sadly,
he
didn't
pass
the test.

❷ **부사의 형태**

대부분 형용사	+ ly	slow → slow**ly** kind → kind**ly**	quick → quick**ly** nice → nice**ly**
자음 + -y로 끝나는 형용사	y를 i로 바꾸고 + -ly	happy → happ**ily** easy → eas**ily**	lucky → luck**ily** pretty → prett**ily**
-le, -ue로 끝나는 형용사	e를 지우고 + -(l)y	simple → simp**ly** possible → possib**ly**	terrible → terrib**ly** true → tru**ly**
형용사와 형태가 같은 부사	late 늦은 – **late** 늦게 fast 빠른 – **fast** 빨리	early 이른 – **early** 일찍 high 높은 – **high** 높게	pretty 예쁜 – **pretty** 매우
형용사와 형태가 같은 부사 + -ly	**hard** 열심히 – **hardly** 거의 ~않는 **near** 가까이에 – **nearly** 거의	**late** 늦게 – **lately** 최근에 **high** 높은 – **highly** 매우	

Isabel is a **fast** learner. (형용사)
She learns things very **fast**. (부사)

Tip
명사에 –ly를 붙이면 형용사가 된다.
friend + ly → friendly (친근한) love + ly → lovely (사랑스러운)

빈도부사

GP 34

빈도부사는 반복의 정도를 나타내는 말로 조동사와 be동사 뒤, 일반동사 앞에 위치한다.

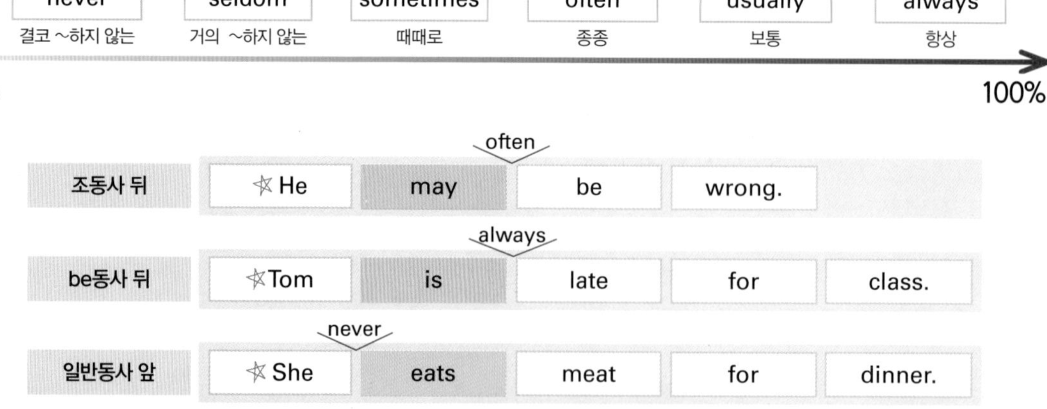

GP Practice

A ( ) 안에서 알맞은 것을 고르시오.

1 We practiced (hard, hardly) for the contest.

2 The boy walked on the ice (careful, carefully).

3 (Interesting, Interestingly), there is a fashion show for dogs.

4 She (rides usually, usually rides) her bike to school.

B ( ) 안에서 알맞은 말을 골라 문장을 완성하시오.

1 (good, well) Sophia is a ____________ dancer.
She dances very ____________.

2 (easy, easily) He found the answer ____________.
But the question was not ____________.

3 (slow, slowly) She does everything ____________.
But when she is busy, she is not ____________.

C 우리말과 의미가 같도록 ( ) 안의 말을 이용하여 문장을 완성하시오.

1 그는 공원으로 빨리 걸어갔어. (walk, fast)
→ He ____________ ____________ to the park.

2 어젯밤에 비가 거세게 내렸어. (rain, heavy)
→ It ____________ ____________ last night.

3 나는 너의 이번 도움을 절대 잊지 않을 거야. (forget, never)
→ I ____________ ____________ ____________ your help this time.

D 밑줄 친 부분에 대한 설명을 하고 틀린 경우엔 바르게 고치시오. (맞으면 'O' 표시) 

1	The boys talked quiet. → ( )	(조용한, 조용히) (동사, 명사)를 수식하는 (부사, 형용사)
2	Danny talks real fast. → ( )	(사실의, 정말로) (부사, 명사)를 수식하는 (부사, 형용사)
3	He often is late for school. → ( )	빈도부사의 위치는 be동사의 (앞, 뒤)
4	This bag is highly useful. → ( )	'(매우, 높이) 쓸모 있는' 의미의 부사는 (high, highly)

원급, 비교급, 최상급

GP 35

❶ **원급을 이용한 비교**: 두 개 대상을 비교하여 그 정도가 같음을 의미한다.

A	as	형용사 / 부사의 원급	as	B	A 가 B 만큼 ~한 (하게)

Sarah is **as busy as** a bee.
Chris can speak Korean **as well as** I.

❷ **비교급을 이용한 비교**: 두 개의 대상에 대한 정도를 비교한다.

A	형용사 / 부사의 비교급	than	B	A 가 B 보다 ~한 (하게)

Cold air is **heavier than** hot air.
Apples are **cheaper than** strawberries today.

❸ **최상급을 이용한 비교**: 셋 이상의 대상에 대한 정도를 비교한다.

A	the	형용사의 최상급	in / of	B	A 가 B 에서 가장 ~한 (하게)

This is **the biggest** orange **in** the store.
The whale is **the largest of** all animals.

❹ 비교급, 최상급 만드는 규칙

			원급	비교급	최상급
규칙 변화	대부분의 경우	+ -er / -est	long	long**er**	long**est**
	-e로 끝나는 경우	+ -r / -st	close	close**r**	close**st**
	[단모음 + 단자음]으로 끝나는 형용사 / 부사	자음 한 번 더 쓰고 + -er / -est	big	big**ger**	big**gest**
	자음 + -y로 끝나는 경우	y를 i로 고치고 + -er / -est	busy	bus**ier**	bus**iest**
	2, 3음절 이상 형용사 / 부사	more / most +	famous	**more** famous	**most** famous
	-ly로 끝나는 부사	more / most +	slowly	**more** slowly	**most** slowly
불규칙 변화			good / well	**better**	**best**
			bad / ill	**worse**	**worst**
			many / much	**more**	**most**
			little	**less**	**least**

GP Practice

A ( ) 안에서 알맞은 것을 고르시오.

1 The water is as (clear, clearer) as crystal.

2 He is the (popularest, most popular) player on the team.

3 Iron is (stronger, strong) than gold.

4 The Pacific Ocean is the (larger, largest) ocean on the Earth.

B ( ) 안의 말을 알맞게 고쳐 문장을 완성하시오.

1 Your hands are as ________________ as ice. (cold)

2 The bird flew ________________ than the helicopter. (high)

3 They chose the ________________ dresser of the year. (good)

4 The movie was ________________ than the book. (exciting)

C 우리말과 의미가 같도록 ( ) 안의 말을 이용하여 문장을 완성하시오.

1 이 젤리는 레몬만큼 시어. (sour)

→ This jelly is __________ __________ __________ a lemon.

2 독수리들은 인간보다 더 잘 볼 수 있어. (well)

→ Eagles can see __________ __________ humans.

3 보름달은 반달보다 더 밝아. (bright)

→ A full moon is __________ __________ a half moon.

4 세상에서 가장 큰 새는 무엇이지? (big)

→ What is __________ __________ __________ in the world?

D 밑줄 친 부분에 대한 설명을 하고 틀린 경우엔 바르게 고치시오. (맞으면 'O' 표시)

1	He is the taller man in the world. → ( )	~에서 (더 큰, 가장 큰) 남자 the + (비교급, 최상급) + in 장소
2	Its skin is as hardest as a rock. → ( )	~처럼 (딱딱한, 가장 딱딱한) as + (원급, 최상급) + as
3	Cheetahs are fast than tigers. → ( )	~ 보다 (빠른, 더 빠른) (원급, 비교급) + than
4	She is the famousest actress in Korea. → ( )	3음절 이상 단어의 최상급 the + (most + 원급, 원급 + est)

Grammar & Writing

A **우리말과 의미가 같도록 ( ) 안의 말을 배열하시오.**

1 신발에 모래가 조금 있어. (sand, in, a little, my shoes)

→ There is ______________________________.

2 그는 절대 기회를 놓치지 않아. (misses, chance, never, a)

→ He ______________________________.

3 그 조종사는 비행기를 안전하게 착륙시켰어. (the airplane, landed, safely)

→ The pilot ______________________________.

4 너는 언제나 내 컴퓨터를 쓸 수 있어. (always, use, can, my, computer)

→ You ______________________________.

5 암탉들이 요즘에 알을 거의 낳지를 않아. (laying, the hens, eggs, few, are)

→ ______________________________ these days.

6 우린 표지판을 거의 읽을 수가 없었어. (seldom, the road signs, read, could)

→ We ______________________________.

7 이 새로운 청소기는 예전 것보다 더 강력해. (more, than, powerful, old one, the, is)

→ This new cleaner ______________________________.

B **우리말과 의미가 같도록 ( ) 안의 말을 이용하여 문장을 완성하시오.**

1 그 귀여운 소년은 곱슬머리를 가지고 있었다. (curly)

→ The cute boy has __________ __________.

2 이것은 내 인생의 가장 위대한 순간이었어. (great, moment)

→ It was __________ __________ __________ of my life.

3 나는 달팽이처럼 느렸어. (slow)

→ I was __________ __________ __________ a snail.

4 그 도시에는 건물이 많이 있어. (buildings)

→ There are __________ __________ __________ __________ in the city.

5 Dave는 항상 밤에 일기를 써. (write)

→ Dave __________ __________ in his diary at night.

6 내 예전 신발이 새 신발보다 더 편안해. (comfortable)

→ My old shoes are __________ __________ __________ the new ones.

C 주어진 상황에 어울리는 문장을 연결하시오.

1 The road is almost empty. •
ⓐ There are few cars.
ⓑ There are many cars.

2 Put the plant outside. •
ⓐ It gets little sunlight here.
ⓑ It gets few sunlight here.

3 The juice is too sweet. •
ⓐ I put a little sugar in it.
ⓑ I put too much sugar in it.

4 Tylor is a popular singer. •
ⓐ He has many fans.
ⓑ He has few fans.

D 전시되어 있는 3개의 피규어를 비교하는 문장들이다. ( ) 안의 말을 이용하여 원급, 비교급, 최상급이 쓰인 문장을 완성하시오.

Taekwon V
Weight: 800g
Height: 33cm
Price: $20

Dragon
Weight: 600g
Height: 30cm
Price: $17

Gundam
Weight: 600g
Height: 27cm
Price: $20

1 The Taekwon V figure is ____________ the Dragon figure. (heavy)

2 The Dragon figure is ____________ the Gundam figure. (tall)

3 The Taekwon V figure is ____________ the Gundam figure. (expensive)

4 The Gundam figure is ____________ the three figures. (short)

Actual Test

(1-4) 빈칸에 들어갈 알맞은 말을 고르시오.

1

> James came to Korea last week.
> So he has __________ friends here.

① little ② a little
③ much ④ more
⑤ few

2

> He is the shortest __________ the five boys.

① in ② of
③ at ④ than
⑤ with

3

> This cup is __________ expensive than that one.

① very ② more
③ much ④ really
⑤ even

4

> The 3D printer built a house __________.

① easy ② fast
③ quick ④ slow
⑤ careful

(5-7) 빈칸에 들어갈 말로 알맞지 않은 것은?

5

> I put __________ ketchup on my hot dog.

① too much ② a lot of
③ many ④ little
⑤ a little

6

> Paula helped an old man __________.

① nicely ② carefully
③ kindly ④ friendly
⑤ quickly

7

> My hands are bigger than __________.

① Tom's ② his
③ your ④ hers
⑤ yours

8 다음 중 어법상 어색한 문장을 고르시오.

① I always take a shower in the evening.
② You sometimes can visit me.
③ Jane is often out of town.
④ He never tells lies.
⑤ We usually walk to school.

9 문장의 의미가 어색한 것을 두 개 고르시오.

① Jane is pretty kind.
→ Jane는 예쁘고 친절해.
② Tom ate faster than me.
→ Tom은 나보다 빨리 먹었어.
③ You are as smart as Paul.
→ 너는 Paul만큼 영리하구나.
④ He hardly helps his mom.
→ 그는 엄마를 열심히 돕는다.
⑤ I am the best in the world.
→ 내가 세상에서 최고야.

(10–11) 다음 중 어법상 알맞은 것을 고르시오.

10 ① There is few rain in the desert.
② We took much pictures.
③ The car uses a few gasoline.
④ Young kids have little homework.
⑤ James doesn't talk many.

11 ① He visited many countries than me.
② The tree is an oldest in town.
③ She is the most smart girl in the class.
④ James is as taller as Brian.
⑤ I am heavier than you.

(12–13) 주어진 문장과 의미가 같도록 빈칸을 채우시오.

12 Mr. Kelly works hard.

⇨ Mr. Kelly is a ____________ worker.

13 Eric is a good swimmer.

⇨ Eric swims ____________.

14 빈칸에 공통으로 들어갈 말로 알맞은 것은?

He has __________ books.
There was __________ dust on the books.

① many ② much
③ a few ④ a little
⑤ a lot of

15 밑줄 친 부분의 품사가 나머지와 다른 것을 고르시오.

① He drives slowly on snowy days.
② You have a really pretty smile.
③ Sadly, he failed the test.
④ She won the prize easily.
⑤ It is a lovely day today.

16 빈칸에 들어갈 말을 순서대로 연결한 것을 고르시오.

· He had a ________ lunch.
· It rained ________ this afternoon.

① heavy - heavy
② heavy - heavily
③ heavily - heavy
④ heavily - heavily
⑤ heavy - heavier

17 두 문장을 한 문장으로 쓸 때 빈칸에 알맞은 말은?

Emily is 16 years old. You are 16 years old, too.
= Emily is ________ you.

① older than ② as old as
③ as older as ④ as oldest as
⑤ the oldest of

(18-19) 우리말과 의미가 같도록 ( ) 안의 말을 이용하여 문장을 완성하시오.

18 내 백팩은 돌만큼 무거워.
(heavy)

⇨ My backpack is ________ a rock.

19 이것이 올해 최악의 영화야.
(bad)

⇨ This is ________ of the year.

20 밑줄 친 부분의 쓰임이 나머지와 다른 것은?

① The baby got up early this morning.
② Come home early and help me.
③ I didn't want to leave early.
④ We arrived at the airport too early.
⑤ The kid had an early lunch.

(21-23) 우리말과 의미가 같도록 ( ) 안의 말을 배열하시오.

21 우리는 너를 위해 무언가 특별한 것을 준비하고 있다.
(something, are, we, special, planning)

⇨ ________ ________ for you.

22 아빠는 우리를 위해 자주 저녁식사를 요리하셔.
(dinner, cooks, often, us, for)

⇨ My dad ________.

23 그의 사생활을 아는 사람은 거의 없었다.
(people, knew, his, about, few, private life)

⇨ ________ ________.

24 어법상 올바른 것으로 짝지어진 것은?

ⓐ I have a few books.
ⓑ You never should swim at night.
ⓒ He ate more pizza than her.
ⓓ Is the runner as faster as you?
ⓔ Adam likes sweet anything.

① ⓐ, ⓑ ② ⓐ, ⓒ
③ ⓑ, ⓓ ④ ⓒ, ⓓ
⑤ ⓓ, ⓔ

25 다음 우리말을 영어로 바르게 옮긴 것은?

그 아기는 그의 아빠보다 더 유명해.

① The baby is the most famous.
② The baby is as famous as his dad.
③ The baby is famouser than his dad.
④ The baby is more famous than his dad.
⑤ The baby is the more famous than his dad.

26 우리 반에서 애완동물을 기르는 친구들의 숫자이다. popular를 이용하여 문장을 완성하시오.

Our Favorite Pets

Dogs	Cats	Hamsters
5명	2명	2명

Ⓐ Cats are as ____________ as hamsters.
Ⓑ Dogs are ____________ of the three animals.

(27–28) ( ) 안의 말이 들어갈 알맞은 곳을 고르시오.

27 There ① is ② nothing ③ in ④ the kid's ⑤ room. (dangerous)

⇨ ____________

28 Jack ① goes ② to bed ③ at 10 p.m. ④ during vacation. (usually)

⇨ ____________

(29–30) 다음 문장에서 어색한 부분을 찾아 바르게 고치고 알맞은 이유를 고르시오.

29 Chris has a little nicknames.

고치기: ____________ ⇨ ____________
이유: '몇몇의' 의미의 수량형용사
(a little, a few) + (복수, 단수)명사

30 She got up lately this morning.

고치기: ____________ ⇨ ____________
이유: '(늦게, 최근에) 일어나다' 의미의 부사

31 다음 조건을 이용하여 알맞게 영작하시오.

시간이 돈보다 더 중요해.
조건 1: important, than
조건 2: 6단어

⇨ ____________.

한눈에 정리하는 Grammar Mapping

빈칸에 알맞은 답을 보기에서 골라 넣어 grammar mapping 완성하기

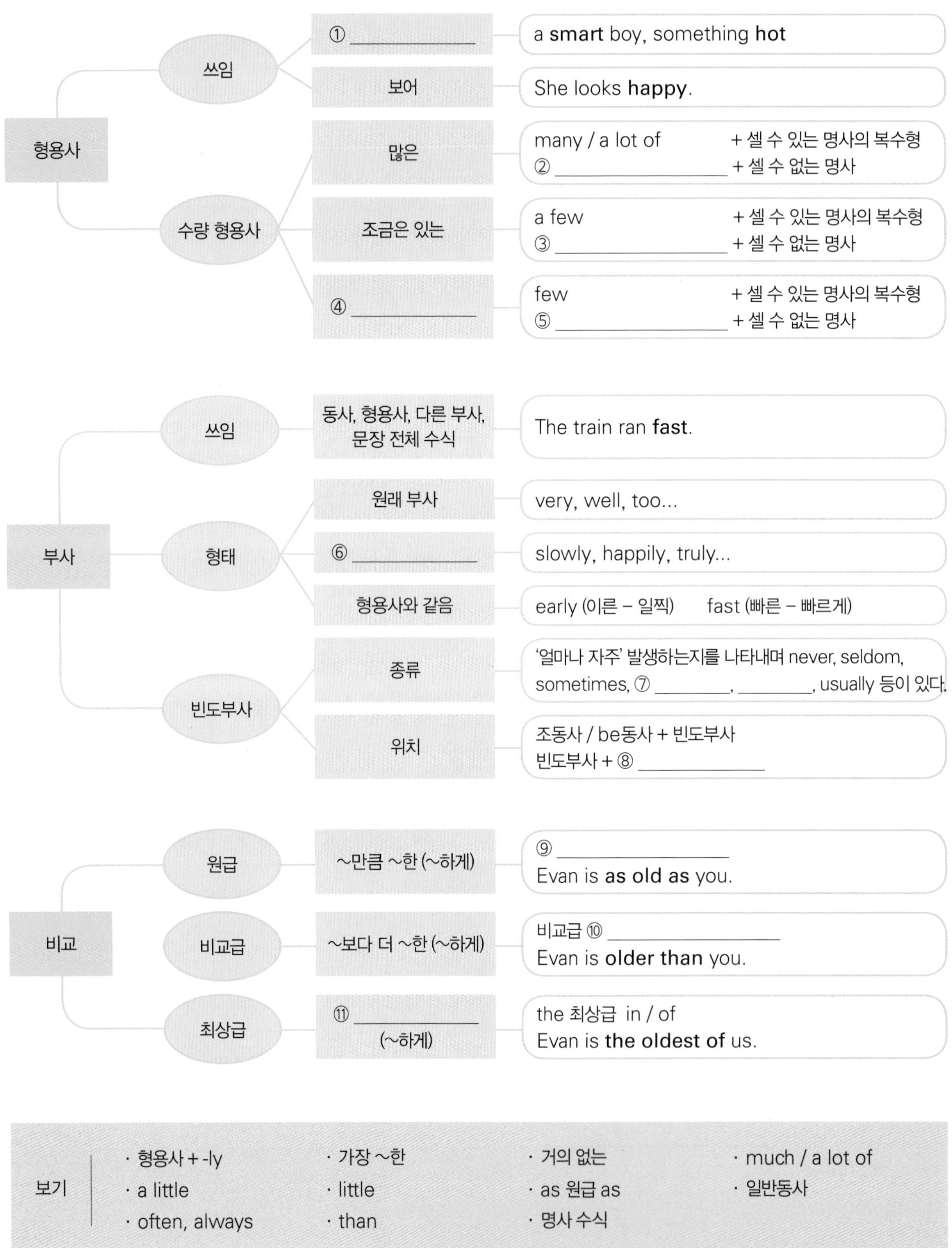

보기				
	· 형용사 + -ly	· 가장 ~한	· 거의 없는	· much / a lot of
	· a little	· little	· as 원급 as	· 일반동사
	· often, always	· than	· 명사 수식	

Chapter

09

부정사와 동명사

GP 36 to부정사의 명사적 쓰임

GP 37 to부정사의 형용사적 쓰임

GP 38 to부정사의 부사적 쓰임

GP 39 동명사의 명사적 쓰임

- Grammar & Writing
- Actual Test
- 한눈에 정리하는 Grammar Mapping

to부정사의 명사적 쓰임

GP 36

[to부정사의 의미]

to부정사는 [to + 동사원형]의 형태로 동사의 성질을 가지며 명사, 형용사, 부사 역할을 한다.

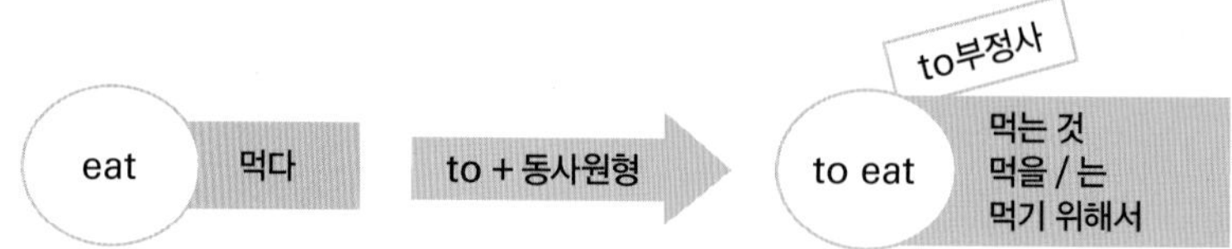

[to부정사의 명사적 쓰임]

to부정사가 '~하는 것'의 의미로 명사처럼 문장에서 주어, 목적어, 보어 역할을 한다.

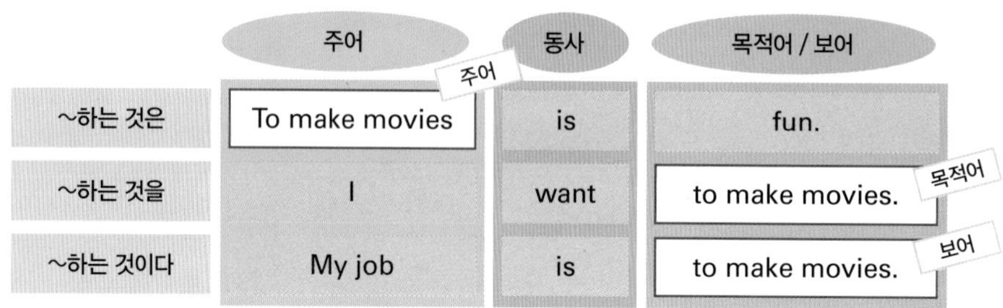

❶ **주어 역할**: to부정사가 주어인 경우 보통 주어 자리에 It을 사용하고 to부정사는 뒤로 보낸다.

To read webtoons *is* fun.

= **It** *is* fun **to read** webtoons. (가주어 It)

❷ **목적어 역할**: 동사 want, plan, promise, learn, decide, need, like 등의 목적어로 쓰인다.

We *decided* **to visit** the zoo.

Jane *plans* **to raise** a dog.

❸ **보어 역할**: 보통 be동사 뒤에서 주어의 상태, 성질 등을 나타낸다.

My dream *is* **to become** a game designer.

Their goal *was* **to find** gold.

> **Tip**
>
> **to부정사의 부정문**:
> not 또는 never를 to부정사 바로 앞에 쓴다.
> I promised **not to be** late again.

• Upgrade •

[의문사 + to부정사]는 명사처럼 문장에서 주어, 목적어, 보어 역할을 한다.

Do you know **what to bring** to camp?

Tell me **where to go** next.

who(m) + to부정사	what + to부정사	when + to부정사	where + to부정사	how + to부정사
누구를 ~할지	무엇을 ~할지	언제 ~할지	어디로 ~할지	어떻게 ~할지

GP Practice

A ( ) 안에서 알맞은 것을 고르시오.

1 (Watch, To watch) the stars is interesting.

2 His mission is (make, to make) robot soldiers.

3 (It, This) is exciting to ride roller coasters.

4 We plan (to climbs, to climb) the mountain this month.

B 보기의 말을 이용하여 문장을 완성하시오. (한 번씩만 사용)

보기	become	live	drive	wash

1 When did you learn ____________ a car?

2 My dream is ____________ a writer.

3 You need ____________ your hands first.

4 It is impossible ____________ without water.

C 우리말과 의미가 같도록 ( ) 안의 말을 이용하여 문장을 완성하시오.

1 나는 벽에 페인트칠하고 싶어. (want, paint)

→ I ________ ________ ________ the wall.

2 꿀벌의 일은 꿀을 만드는 것이다. (make honey)

→ The honeybee's job ________ ________ ________ ________.

3 그 다큐멘터리를 시청하는 것은 지루했어. (watch)

→ ________ was boring ________ ________ the documentary.

4 Leo가 이번에 우리를 도와주겠다고 약속했어. (promise, help)

→ Leo ________ ________ ________ us this time.

D 밑줄 친 부분에 대한 설명을 하고 틀린 경우엔 바르게 고치시오. (맞으면 'O' 표시)

1	This is not easy to make friends. → ( )	가주어 ~ 진주어 (This, It) (to부정사, 동사)
2	To sleep well is important. → ( )	주어 + 동사 ~ (to부정사, 동사원형)
3	Jane plans visit the museum. → ( )	주어 + plan + 목적어 (동사, to부정사)
4	His wish is to meets her again. → ( )	주어 + be동사 + 보어 (to + 동사원형, to + 동사)

to부정사의 형용사적 쓰임

GP 37

to부정사가 '~할, ~하는'의 의미로 형용사처럼 명사, 대명사를 수식한다. 이때 to부정사는 명사, 대명사 뒤에서 수식한다.

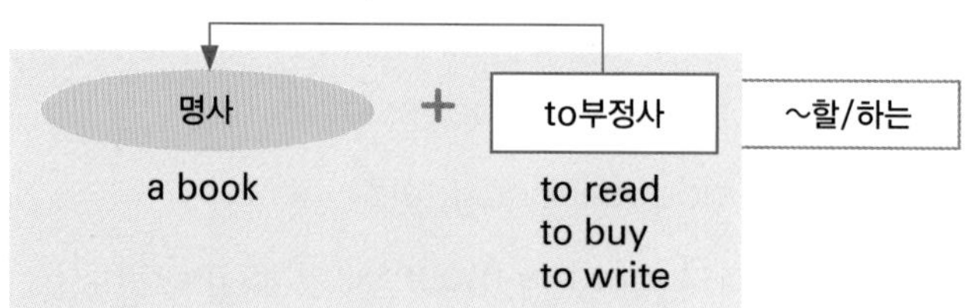

He knows a special *way* **to cook** noodles.
Please give me *something cold* **to drink**.

Tip
-thing, -body, -one으로 끝나는 대명사 수식 어순
[대명사 + 형용사 + to부정사]

to부정사의 부사적 쓰임

GP 38

to부정사가 '~하기 위해, ~해서, ~하기에' 등의 의미로 부사처럼 동사, 형용사 등을 수식한다.

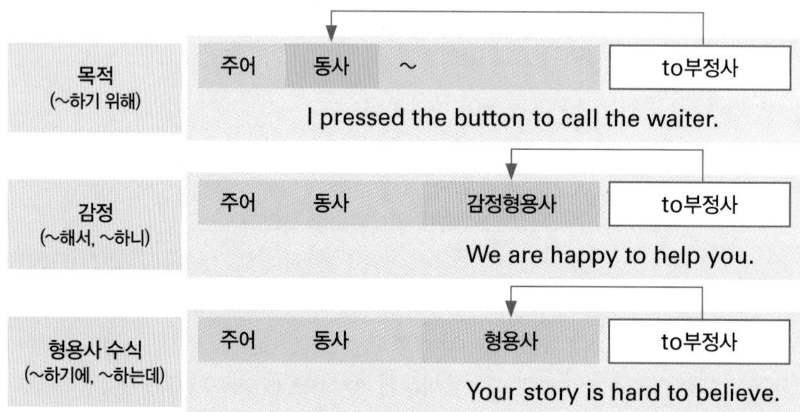

❶ 목적

They *used* robots **to make** ships.

❷ 감정의 원인

I am *sorry* **to hear** the news.

❸ 형용사 수식

His name is *easy* **to remember**.

Tip
여러 가지 감정을 나타내는 형용사
happy, glad, sorry, sad, surprised, shocked...

GP Practice

A 보기와 같이 명사를 수식하는 말에 밑줄을 치고, 해석을 쓰시오.

보기 | Do you have a book to read? — 읽을 책

1 Brandy needs something to drink. ____________ 무언가

2 It is time to go home. ____________ 시간

3 He gave us homework to do. ____________ 숙제

4 Write down the things to buy. ____________ 물건들

B 자연스러운 문장이 되도록 알맞게 연결하시오.

1 The singer is ready • • ⓐ to make jam.

2 The player was happy • • ⓑ to buy new pants.

3 I bought blueberries • • ⓒ to start the concert.

4 Daniel saved money • • ⓓ to win the game.

C 우리말과 의미가 같도록 ( ) 안의 말을 이용하여 문장을 완성하시오.

1 그 말을 듣게 되어 유감이야. (sorry, hear)

→ I am ________ ________ ________ that.

2 나는 입을 만한 멋진 스커트가 없어. (wear, fancy skirts)

→ I don't have any ________ ________ ________ ________.

3 그는 늙어 보이기 위해 특수 메이크업을 했어. (look old)

→ He wore special makeup ________ ________ ________.

4 오늘은 내가 설거지를 해야 할 차례야. (turn, do the dishes)

→ It is ________ ________ ________ ________ ________ ________ today.

D 밑줄 친 부분에 대한 설명을 하고 틀린 경우엔 바르게 고치시오. (맞으면 'O' 표시)

1	He came here meet you. → ( )	'(~ 만나기에, ~ 만나기 위해) 오다' 의미의 동사 + (to부정사, 동사)
2	My dog was happiness to see me. → ( )	'(~ 봐서, ~ 보기 위해) 기쁜' 의미의 (감정형용사, 감정명사) + to부정사
3	Eggs are easily to cook. → ( )	'(~ 요리해서, ~ 요리하기에) 쉬운' 의미의 (부사, 형용사) + to부정사
4	Do you have anything sell? → ( )	'(~ 판매하기 위해, ~ 판매할) 어떤 것' 의미의 명사 + (동사, to부정사)

동명사의 명사적 쓰임

GP 39

[동명사의 의미]

동명사는 [동사원형 + -ing]의 형태로 문장에서 동사의 성질을 가지면서 명사의 역할을 한다.

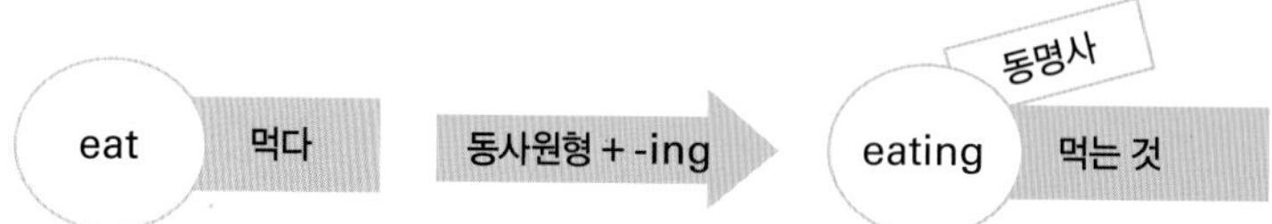

[동명사의 명사적 쓰임]

동명사가 '~하는 것'의 의미로 명사처럼 문장에서 주어, 목적어, 보어 역할을 한다.

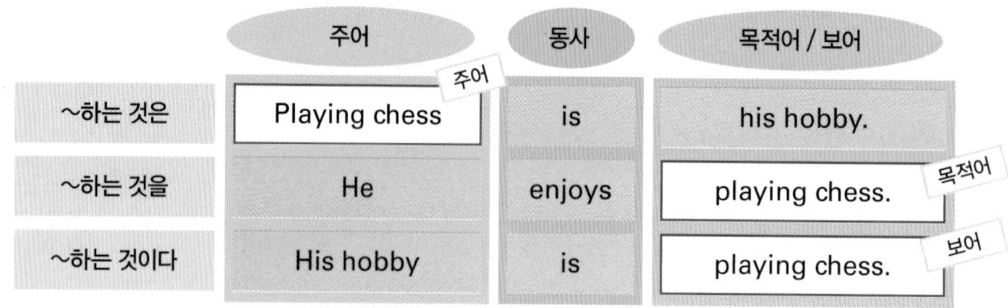

	주어	동사	목적어 / 보어
~하는 것은	Playing chess (주어)	is	his hobby.
~하는 것을	He	enjoys	playing chess. (목적어)
~하는 것이다	His hobby	is	playing chess. (보어)

❶ 주어 역할

☆ **Riding** a roller coaster *is* scary.
Making movies *is* not easy.

❷ 목적어 역할

동사의 목적어: enjoy, mind, finish, give up, keep, quit 등의 목적어로 쓰인다.
전치사의 목적어: in, about, for 등의 목적어로 쓰인다.

☆ Do you *mind* **opening** the door for me?
☆ Thank you *for* **listening**.

❸ 보어 역할

보통 be동사 뒤에서 주어의 상태, 성질 등을 나타낸다.

☆ Her good habit *is* **getting up** early.

• Upgrade •

동명사의 부정문

not 또는 never를 동명사 바로 앞에 쓴다.
We are sorry for **not coming** earlier.

GP Practice

A ( ) 안의 말을 이용하여 문장을 완성하시오.

1 ____________ this machine is simple. (use)

2 He gave up ____________ a dancer. (become)

3 My favorite activity is ____________ cartoons. (draw)

4 Tom is interested in ____________ ships. (build)

B 밑줄 친 부분의 쓰임을 보기에서 골라 쓰시오.

보기 | ⓐ 주어 ⓑ 동사의 목적어 ⓒ 전치사의 목적어 ⓓ 보어	쓰임
1 I am good at telling stories.	________
2 Collecting dolls is her hobby.	________
3 My hobby is taking pictures.	________
4 The boys kept talking for an hour.	________

C 우리말과 의미가 같도록 ( ) 안의 말을 이용하여 문장을 완성하시오.

1 그녀는 새로운 음식을 먹어 보는 것을 즐겨한다. (enjoy, try)

→ She ____________ ____________ new dishes.

2 첫 번째 단계는 계획을 만드는 것이다. (make a plan)

→ The first step ____________ ____________ ____________ ____________.

3 그는 계속 버스를 기다렸다. (keep, wait for)

→ He ____________ ____________ ____________ the bus.

4 행성을 발견하는 것이 그들의 목표이다. (find a planet)

→ ____________ ____________ ____________ ____________ their goal.

D 밑줄 친 부분에 대한 설명을 하고 틀린 경우엔 바르게 고치시오. (맞으면 'O' 표시)

1	His role is protect the singer. → ( )	주어 + 동사 + 보어 (동사, 동명사)
2	Do you mind to close the door? → ( )	주어 + mind + 목적어 (to부정사, 동명사)
3	Eat healthy food is important. → ( )	주어 + 동사 ~ (동사, 동명사)
4	He is interested in cook. → ( )	주어 + 동사 + 전치사 + 목적어 (동사, 동명사)

A 우리말과 의미가 같도록 ( ) 안의 말을 배열하시오.

1 욕실 청소하는 것을 끝냈나요? (cleaning, finish, bathroom, the)

→ Did you ______________________________?

2 그 사자는 공격할 기회를 잃었다. (lost, a, chance, attack, to)

→ The lion ______________________________.

3 그 소년들은 그 동굴에 들어가고 싶어 했어. (enter, wanted, the cave, to)

→ The boys ______________________________.

4 TV에는 볼 만한 재미있는 것이 아무것도 없다. (to, nothing, watch, interesting)

→ There is ______________________________ on TV.

5 그는 감기에 걸리는 것이 두려웠어. (catching, was afraid of, a, cold)

→ He ______________________________.

6 그들은 토마토를 던지는 것을 즐거워했다. (throwing, enjoyed, tomatoes)

→ They ______________________________.

7 내 꿈은 메이크업 아티스트가 되는 것이야. (become, makeup artist, a, is, to)

→ My dream ______________________________.

B 우리말과 의미가 같도록 ( ) 안의 말을 이용하여 문장을 완성하시오.

1 나는 연습을 더 할 필요가 있다. (need, practice)

→ I ________ ________ ________ more.

2 애완동물을 기르는 것은 쉽지 않아. (raise, a pet)

→ ________ ________ ________ ________ not easy.

3 그는 사과를 따기 위해 점프했다. (jump, pick)

→ He ________ ________ ________ an apple.

4 역할극을 하는 것은 흥미로웠어. (role-play)

→ ________ was interesting ________ ________.

5 그는 새 신발을 쇼핑하러 갔어. (buy, new shoes)

→ He went shopping ________ ________ ________ ________.

6 저녁으로 무엇을 먹을지를 결정하자. (eat, for)

→ Let's decide ________ ________ ________ ________ ________.

C to부정사를 이용하여 그림에 맞는 여러 가지 money를 표현하시오.

1 save
2 buy
3 burn
4 lend

1 Evan has money ____________________.

2 Evan has money ____________________ a pencil.

3 Evan has money ____________________. (*돈이 매우 많다는 관용표현)

4 Evan has money ____________________ you.

D 다음 그림의 상황에 맞도록 주어진 말을 이용하여 문장을 완성하시오.

1 become

2 order

3 surf

4 do the dishes

1 I want ______________________________.

2 She agrees ______________________________ for lunch.

3 He enjoys ______________________________ in the sea.

4 She finished ______________________________.

Actual Test

(1-4) 빈칸에 들어갈 알맞은 말을 고르시오.

1

Jane went to the library __________ a book.

① borrows ② borrowed
③ to borrows ④ to borrow
⑤ to borrowed

2

He has many friends __________.

① to invite ② to invites
③ invites ④ inviting
⑤ invited

3

Do you mind __________ for a minute?

① wait ② waited
③ to wait ④ waiting
⑤ to waiting

4

__________ was fun to meet new people at the party.

① This ② That
③ It ④ And
⑤ We

(5-6) 밑줄 친 부분의 쓰임이 어법상 어색한 것은?

5 ① It is boring to stay at home alone.
② He avoids talking to strangers.
③ Do you hope win a medal?
④ Recycling cans is a good habit.
⑤ I decided to save my money.

6 ① He was sad to move to another school.
② It is fun play in the pool.
③ We stayed in the shade to rest.
④ You need to call your mom now.
⑤ Walking up the stairs is good exercise.

7 밑줄 친 부분이 보기와 같은 쓰임인 것을 고르시오.

I expect to see you soon.

① Do you have anything to say?
② We are happy to see you again.
③ He wore his glasses to read the book.
④ She likes to play soccer.
⑤ The zoo is a great place to visit.

(8-9) 빈칸에 들어갈 말로 알맞지 않은 것은?

8

Ken ________ watching a horror movie.

① finishes ② keeps
③ decides ④ enjoys
⑤ doesn't mind

9

They ________ to ride on the space shuttle.

① hoped ② wanted
③ gave up ④ decided
⑤ expect

(10-11) 다음 우리말을 영어로 바르게 옮긴 것은?

10

음식을 장식하는 것이 내 직업이야.

① My job is decorate food.
② My job is to decorating food.
③ Decorating food is my job.
④ Decorate food is my job.
⑤ It is my job decorate food.

11

이 수수께끼는 풀기 쉬워.

① This riddle is easily to solve.
② This riddle is easily solving.
③ This riddle is easy to solve.
④ This riddle is easy solving.
⑤ This riddle is easy to solving.

(12-14) 보기에서 알맞은 말을 골라 형태를 바꿔 문장을 완성하시오.

보기	ask	do	swim

12

She is busy today. She has so many things ________.

⇨ ____________

13

We enjoyed ________ in the sea. We love summer.

⇨ ____________

14

Nicky raised his hand ________ a question.

⇨ ____________

15 빈칸에 들어갈 말이 순서대로 짝지어진 것을 고르시오.

I am sorry ________ late. = I am sorry for ________ late.

① to be - be ② to be - being
③ being - be ④ being - being
⑤ to am - be

(16–18) 밑줄 친 부분의 쓰임이 나머지와 다른 것은?

16 ① When do you plan to leave?

② His goal is to build his own house.

③ She wrote a book to tell her story.

④ Brian went to the theme park.

⑤ You need to wear glasses.

17 ① I have some photos to show you.

② You have four messages to check.

③ Why do you want to meet him?

④ He chose two places to visit.

⑤ Jim brought something to eat.

18 ① His hobby is drawing cartoons.

② I avoided going out at night.

③ Do you mind changing the channels?

④ Harry is interested in cooking.

⑤ We kept talking all night.

(19–20) 주어진 문장과 의미가 같도록 빈칸을 채우시오.

19 To walk underwater was exciting.

⇨ ____________ was exciting
____________ underwater.

20 To see is to believe.

⇨ Seeing is ____________.

(21–22) 우리말과 의미가 같도록 ( ) 안의 말을 배열하시오.

21 나는 너를 만나게 되어 기뻐.
(glad, am, I, you, meet, to)

⇨ ______________________________
______________________________.

22 그녀의 취미는 추리소설을 읽는 것이야.
(detective novels, hobby, reading, is, her)

⇨ ______________________________
______________________________.

23 어법상 올바른 것으로 짝지어진 것은?

ⓐ Do you have time to talks?
ⓑ Jane wanted having the soup.
ⓒ My dream is to become a writer.
ⓓ He is good at swimming.
ⓔ She finished to use the computer.

① ⓐ, ⓒ ② ⓐ, ⓔ
③ ⓑ, ⓓ ④ ⓒ, ⓓ
⑤ ⓓ, ⓔ

(24–26) 우리말과 의미가 같도록 ( ) 안의 말을 이용하여 문장을 완성하시오.

24 우리는 낭비할 시간이 없어.
(time, waste)

⇨ We don't have ________________.

25 Lucas는 아침 열 시까지 여기에 도착하기로 약속했어.
(promise, arrive)

⇨ Lucas ________________
here by 10 a.m.

26 당신은 왜 문법 배우는 것을 포기했나요?
(give up, learn)

⇨ Why did you ________________
grammar?

27 두 문장을 한 문장으로 알맞게 고쳐 쓰시오.

· Lucy wanted to succeed.
· So she worked hard.

⇨ Lucy worked hard ________________.

(28–29) 다음 문장에서 어색한 부분을 찾아 바르게 고치고 알맞은 이유를 고르시오.

28 The kids went to the stream catch small fish.

고치기: ____________ ⇨ ____________
이유: (~하는 것을, ~하기 위해) 의미의
(to + 동사원형, 동사원형)

29 Do you mind turn on the air conditioner?

고치기: ____________ ⇨ ____________
이유: 동사 mind 는 (주어, 목적어)로
(동사원형, 동사원형 + -ing)를 가짐.

30 다음 조건을 이용하여 알맞게 영작하시오.

너의 집을 찾는 것이 어려웠어.
조건 1: difficult, find, it
조건 2: 7단어

⇨ ________________________
________________________.

한눈에 정리하는 Grammar Mapping

빈칸에 알맞은 답을 보기에서 골라 넣어 grammar mapping 완성하기

to부정사

- 형태와 의미: [① ______________]의 형태로 문장 안에서 명사, 형용사, 부사 등 다양한 역할을 한다.
- 용법

용법	역할	의미 / 예문
명사 쓰임	② ______________	~하는 것은 **To make** plans is important.
	목적어	~하는 것을 She wants **to go** home.
	보어	~하는 것이다 His job is **to make** movies.
형용사 쓰임	③ ______________	~할 He has a book **to read**.
부사 쓰임	④ ______________	~하기 위해 Max came **to meet** you.
	⑤ ______________	~하게 되어 (~한 감정이 들다) I am ⑥ ______________ **to meet** you.
	형용사 수식	~하기에 (~한) This cake is ⑦ ______________ **to make**.

보기 | · 목적 · 명사 수식 · 주어 · 감정의 원인 · to + 동사원형 · difficult · happy

동명사

- 형태와 의미: [⑧ ______________]의 형태로, 명사처럼 '⑨ ______________'을 의미한다.
- 용법

용법	역할	의미 / 예문
⑩ ______ 쓰임	⑪ ______________	~하는 것은 **Catching** fish is not easy.
	⑫ ______________	~하는 것을 We enjoyed **swimming** in the lake. He is good at **singing**.
	보어	~하는 것이다 My hobby is **traveling**.

보기 | · ~하는 것 · 목적어 · 명사 · 주어 · 동사원형 + -ing

Chapter

10

동사의 종류

감각동사 + 형용사

GP 40

보고, 듣고, 느끼는 등 감각을 표현하는 동사를 감각동사라고 하며, 이 동사들 뒤에는 형용사를 쓴다.

주어
감각동사
형용사
S
look
feel
smell
sound
taste
happy
soft
nice
good
sweet
~하게 보이다
~한 느낌이 나다
~한 냄새가 나다
~하게 들리다
~한 맛이 나다

❶ look + 형용사

You **look** *young* in that blue shirt.

❷ feel + 형용사

I **feel** *cold*. I need a blanket.

❸ smell + 형용사

The sausage **smells** *delicious*.

❹ sound + 형용사

Her voice **sounds** *beautiful*.

❺ taste + 형용사

This juice **tastes** *sweet*.

Tip

감각동사 뒤에 부사를 쓰지 않는다.

· She looks happily. (X)

· She looks happy. (O)

• Upgrade •

[감각동사 + like + 명사]

감각동사 뒤에 명사가 오면 명사 앞에 like를 쓴다.

My dog looks a bear. (X)

My dog **looks like** *a bear*. (O)

GP Practice

A ( ) 안에서 알맞은 것을 고르시오.

1 The noodles taste (good, well).

2 The pie smells (sweet, sweetly).

3 You (look, look like) an actor.

4 The story (sounds, looks) strange.

5 He felt (safe, safely) with the police.

B 보기에서 알맞은 동사를 골라 현재시제로 문장을 완성하시오. (한 번씩만 사용)

보기	sound	taste	feel	look

1 Try this peach. It ____________ delicious.

2 Look at the puppy. It ____________ cute.

3 Put on this scarf! It ____________ soft.

4 Listen to the song. It ____________ beautiful.

C 우리말과 의미가 같도록 ( ) 안의 말을 이용하여 문장을 완성하시오.

1 그녀가 무대 위에서 멋져 보인다. (great)

→ She ________ ________ on the stage.

2 숲에서는 공기가 신선한 냄새가 난다. (fresh)

→ The air ________ ________ in the forest.

3 이 포도는 신맛이 난다. (sour)

→ These grapes ________ ________.

4 나는 집에서 편안한 기분이 들어. (comfortable)

→ I ________ ________ at home.

D 밑줄 친 부분에 대한 설명을 하고 틀린 경우엔 바르게 고치시오. (맞으면 'O' 표시) 

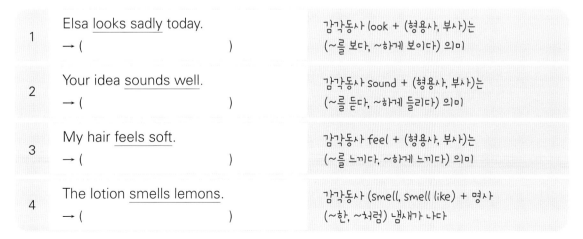

1	Elsa <u>looks sadly</u> today. → ( )	감각동사 look + (형용사, 부사)는 (~를 보다, ~하게 보이다) 의미
2	Your idea <u>sounds well</u>. → ( )	감각동사 sound + (형용사, 부사)는 (~를 듣다, ~하게 들리다) 의미
3	My hair <u>feels soft</u>. → ( )	감각동사 feel + (형용사, 부사)는 (~를 느끼다, ~하게 느끼다) 의미
4	The lotion <u>smells lemons</u>. → ( )	감각동사 (smell, smell like) + 명사 (~한, ~처럼) 냄새가 나다

수여동사 + 간접목적어 + 직접목적어

GP 41

수여동사는 두 개의 목적어를 필요로 하고 '~에게(간접목적어) ~를(직접목적어) 해 주다'는 의미의 동사이다.

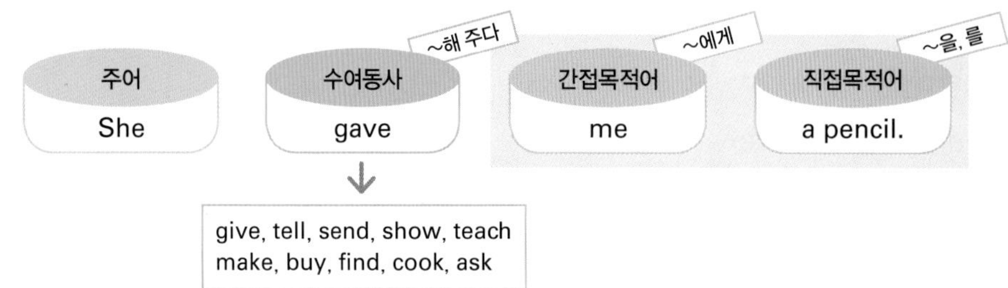

give, tell, send, show, teach
make, buy, find, cook, ask

I **told** *him the reason.*
Andrew **teaches** *us English.*
He **bought** *his cat a toy.*

• Upgrade •

[주어 + 동사 + 목적어] → He **made** *a chair.* (의자를 **만들었다**)
[주어 + 동사 + 간접목적어 + 직접목적어] → He **made** *me a chair.* (나에게 의자를 **만들어 주었다**)

수여동사 + 직접목적어 + 전치사 + 간접목적어

GP 42

[수여동사 + 간접목적어 + 직접목적어]는 [수여동사 + 직접목적어 + 전치사 + 간접목적어]로 바꿀 수 있다.
이때 전치사는 동사에 따라 전치사 to, for, of를 쓴다.

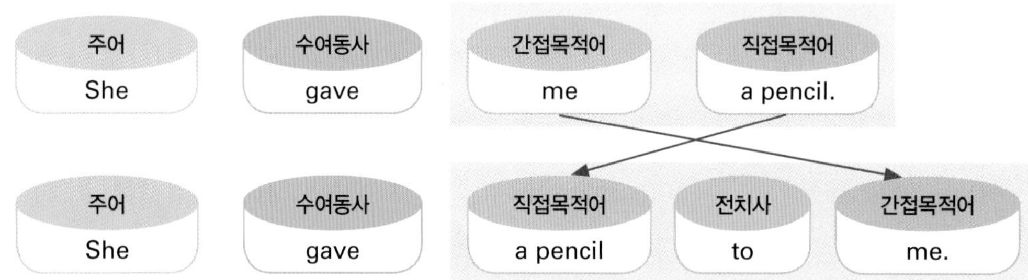

❶ **to를 사용하는 동사**: give, tell, send, show, teach, write, lend...
☆ He **showed** *us his puppy.*
→ ☆ He **showed** *his puppy* **to** *us.*

❷ **for를 사용하는 동사**: make, buy, cook, find, get...
☆ She **bought** *me a flower.*
→ ☆ She **bought** *a flower* **for** *me.*

❸ **of를 사용하는 동사**: ask...
☆ Anna **asked** *him a favor.*
→ ☆ Anna **asked** *a favor* **of** *him.*

GP Practice

A ( ) 안에서 알맞은 것을 고르시오.

1 I bought hand cream (for, of) my mom.

2 Could you pass (the salad me, me the salad)?

3 The chef cooked some Italian food (to, for) us.

4 James told (me his secret, his secret me).

5 Don't ask strange questions (her, of her).

B 두 문장이 같은 의미를 갖도록 문장을 완성하시오.

1 Isabel gave me some advice.
→ Isabel gave some advice ____________ me.

2 I bought my parents two movie tickets.
→ I bought two movie tickets ____________ my parents.

3 Can I ask you a favor?
→ Can I ask a favor ____________ you?

C 우리말과 의미가 같도록 ( ) 안의 말을 이용하여 문장을 완성하시오.

1 그는 우리에게 카드 묘기를 보여 줬다. (show, card tricks)
→ He ____________ ____________ ____________ ____________.

2 아빠는 우리에게 돈가스를 요리해 주었다. (cook, pork cutlets)
→ Dad ____________ ____________ ____________ ____________.

3 나는 그녀에게 문자 메시지를 보냈다. (send, a text message)
→ I ____________ ____________ ____________ ____________ ____________ ____________.

D 밑줄 친 부분에 대한 설명을 하고 틀린 경우엔 바르게 고치시오. (맞으면 'O' 표시)

1	Eric showed us a picture. → ( )	show + (~를 ~에게, ~에게 ~를) 전치사 필요 (있음, 없음)
2	Eric showed a picture us. → ( )	show + (~를 ~에게, ~에게 ~를) 전치사 필요 (있음, 없음)
3	I bought Joe a book. → ( )	buy + (~를 ~에게, ~에게 ~를) 전치사 필요 (있음, 없음)
4	He made a chair of me. → ( )	make + (~를 ~에게, ~에게 ~를) 전치사 필요 (있음, 없음)

목적격보어가 필요한 동사

GP 43

일부 동사들은 목적어와 목적격보어를 필요로 한다. 목적격보어는 목적어의 상태, 성질 등을 설명하는 말이다.

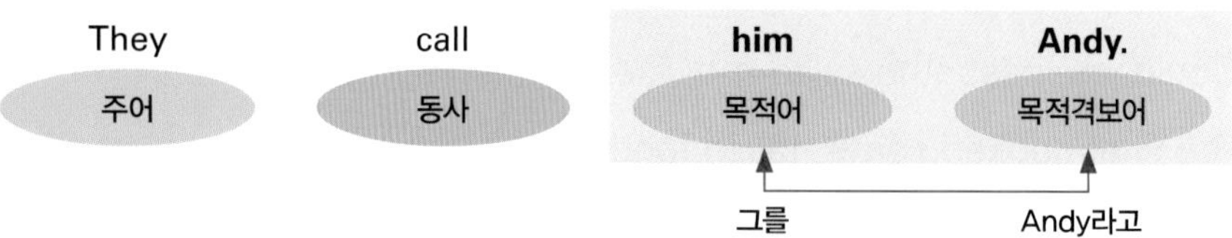

동사의 종류에 따라 명사, 형용사, to부정사 등이 목적격보어로 쓰인다.

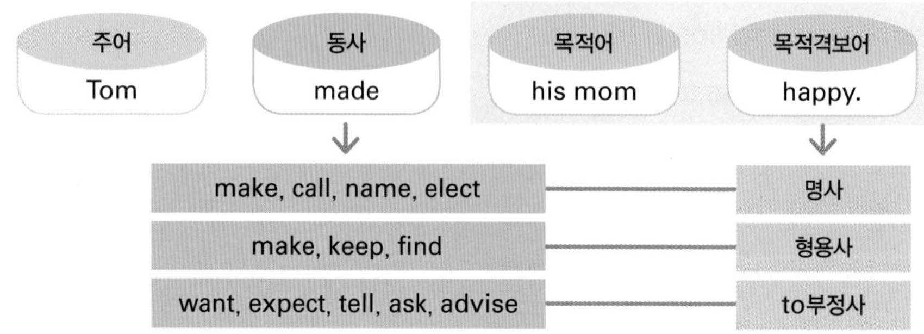

❶ **목적격보어로 명사를 쓰는 동사**: make, call, name, elect, choose…

★ We **called** him an *iron man*.

They **named** the young lion *Simba*.

❷ **목적격보어로 형용사를 쓰는 동사**: make, keep, find, leave…

★ The news **made** him *famous*.

I **found** Peter *smart*.

❸ **목적격 보어로 to부정사를 쓰는 동사**: want, expect, tell, ask, advise, allow…

★ I **want** you *to like* my present.

The police **told** him *to stop*.

He **asked** us *to be* quiet.

GP Practice

A ( ) 안에서 알맞은 것을 고르시오.

1 A refrigerator keeps vegetables (fresh, freshly).

2 The doctor advised me (get, to get) some rest.

3 A lady asked me (changed, to change) seats with her.

4 The music made us (sleepy, sleepily).

5 His hard training made him (a winner, to win).

B 보기에서 알맞은 동사를 골라 현재시제로 문장을 완성하시오. (한 번씩만 사용)

보기	baby	class president	helpful	to sit

1 We elected her ____________________.

2 My teacher told me ____________________ down.

3 Lily found the cleaning robot ____________________.

4 Don't call me ____________________. I am not a baby.

C 우리말과 의미가 같도록 ( ) 안의 말을 이용하여 문장을 완성하시오.

1 그냥 Leo라고 불러 줘. (call)

→ Just ____________ ____________ ____________.

2 구름은 지구를 따스하게 유지시켜 준다. (keep, warm)

→ Clouds ____________ ____________ ____________ ____________.

3 나는 엄마가 나를 이해해 주기를 원해. (want, understand)

→ I ____________ ____________ ____________ ____________ ____________ me.

D 밑줄 친 부분에 대한 설명을 하고 틀린 경우엔 바르게 고치시오. (맞으면 'O' 표시)

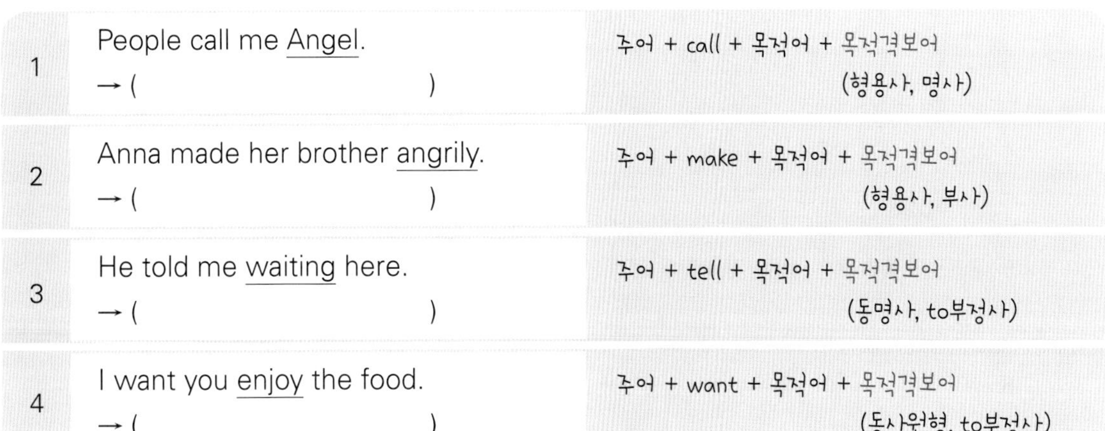

1	People call me <u>Angel</u>. → ( )	주어 + call + 목적어 + 목적격보어 (형용사, 명사)
2	Anna made her brother <u>angrily</u>. → ( )	주어 + make + 목적어 + 목적격보어 (형용사, 부사)
3	He told me <u>waiting</u> here. → ( )	주어 + tell + 목적어 + 목적격보어 (동명사, to부정사)
4	I want you <u>enjoy</u> the food. → ( )	주어 + want + 목적어 + 목적격보어 (동사원형, to부정사)

Grammar & Writing

A 우리말과 의미가 같도록 ( ) 안의 말을 배열하시오.

1 이 카펫은 새것처럼 보인다. (this, new, looks, carpet)

→ ______________________________.

2 간호사가 그에게 독감주사를 주었어. (him, a flu shot, gave)

→ The nurse ______________________________.

3 제게 호박파이를 만들어 주시겠어요? (me, a, pumpkin pie, make)

→ Could you ______________________________?

4 그 코치는 선수들에게 열심히 연습하라고 말했다. (told, the players, practice, to)

→ The coach ______________________________ hard.

5 그 예술가는 그의 작품을 우리에게 보여 주었어. (showed, to, us, his work)

→ The artist ______________________________.

6 태양은 사막을 뜨겁고 건조하게 유지시켜. (keeps, hot and dry, the desert)

→ The sun ______________________________.

B 우리말과 의미가 같도록 ( ) 안의 말을 이용하여 문장을 완성하시오.

1 너의 계획은 완벽하게 들린다. (perfect)

→ Your plan ________ ________.

2 그는 그 고양이를 가필드라고 이름 지었어. (Garfield)

→ He ________ ________ ________ ________.

3 그들은 그 가난한 나라에 식량을 보내 줬어. (the poor country)

→ They ________ ________ ________ ________ ________

________.

4 Austin은 내게 공을 패스해 줬어. (the ball)

→ Austin ________ ________ ________ ________.

5 우리는 진흙축제가 신나는 것을 알게 되었어. (exciting, the mud festival)

→ She ________ ________ ________ ________ ________.

6 눈이 이번 크리스마스를 특별하게 만들었어. (special, this Christmas)

→ The snow ________ ________ ________ ________.

C Emily가 어버이날 부모님께 해 드린 일이다. 보기에서 알맞은 동사를 골라 주어진 말과 함께 문장을 완성하시오.

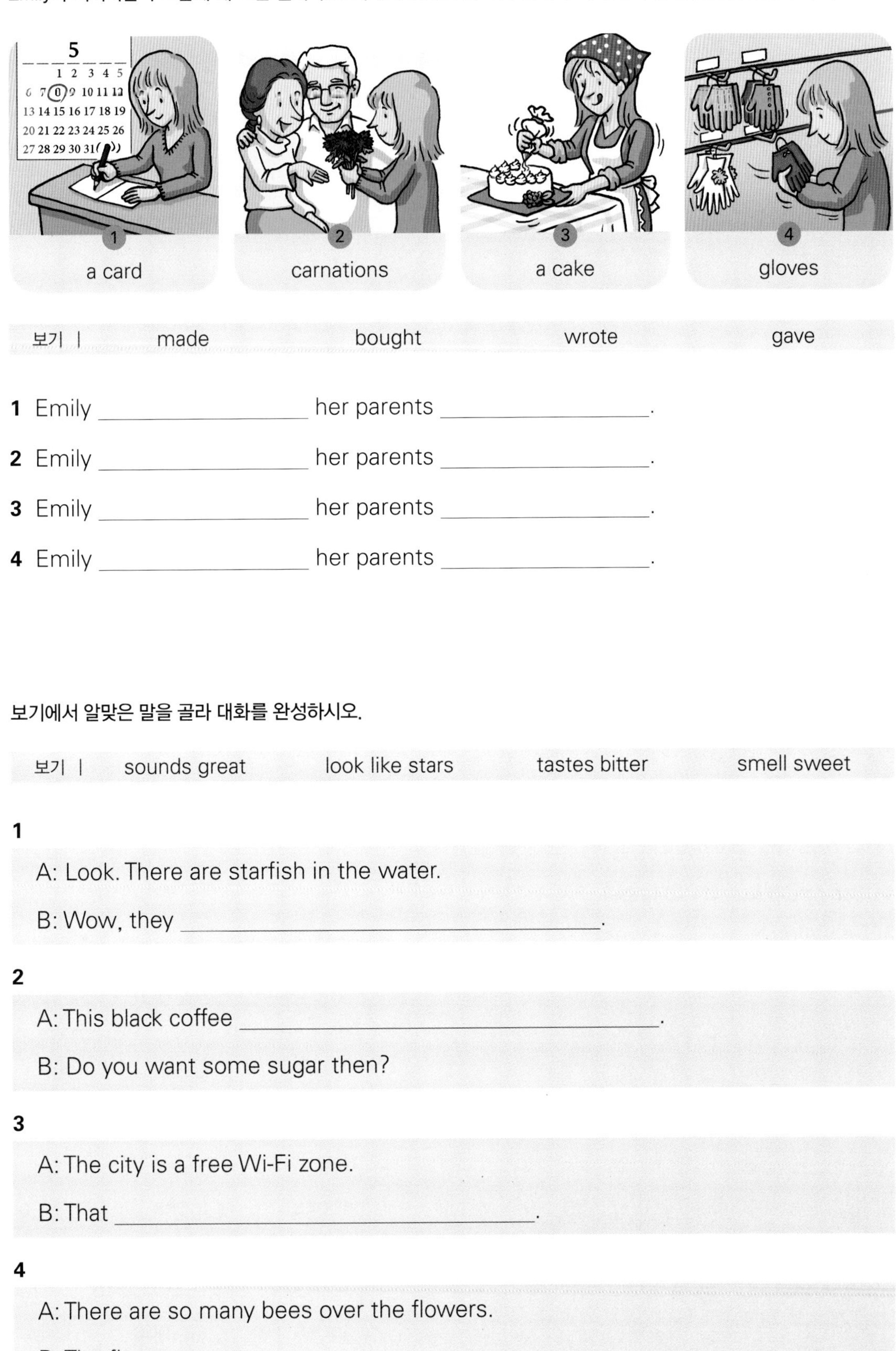

보기 | made bought wrote gave

1 Emily ________________ her parents ________________.

2 Emily ________________ her parents ________________.

3 Emily ________________ her parents ________________.

4 Emily ________________ her parents ________________.

D 보기에서 알맞은 말을 골라 대화를 완성하시오.

보기 | sounds great look like stars tastes bitter smell sweet

1

A: Look. There are starfish in the water.

B: Wow, they ________________________.

2

A: This black coffee ________________________.

B: Do you want some sugar then?

3

A: The city is a free Wi-Fi zone.

B: That ________________________.

4

A: There are so many bees over the flowers.

B: The flowers must ________________________.

(1-4) 빈칸에 알맞지 않은 것을 고르시오.

1

Daisy looked ________.

① excited ② smartly
③ sleepy ④ healthy
⑤ tired

2

She ________ a message to me.

① gave ② sent
③ wrote ④ made
⑤ brought

3

This jelly tastes like ________.

① an apple ② paper
③ a lemon ④ sweet
⑤ milk

4

He ________ me to speak slowly.

① wanted ② told
③ keep ④ asked
⑤ expected

(5-6) 다음 중 어법상 어색한 문장을 고르시오.

5 ① The rice cake tastes good.
② The music sounds sadly.
③ Brian looks sleepy.
④ The fish smells terrible.
⑤ I feel great this morning.

6 ① Did you send him a present?
② Please get me some hot chocolate.
③ Ann didn't lend me her bike.
④ I made a new house my dog.
⑤ She asked a favor of her teacher.

7 빈칸에 알맞은 말로 연결된 것은?

The bridge ⓐ________ strong. His voice ⓑ________ friendly. The pizza ⓒ________ delicious.

	ⓐ	ⓑ	ⓒ
①	looks	looks	tastes
②	looks	sounds	smells
③	looks	sounds like	feels
④	looks like	sounds	smells
⑤	looks	sounds like	smells

(8-10) 빈칸에 들어갈 알맞은 말을 고르시오.

8 He cooked Mexican food ________ us.

① to ② for
③ of ④ at
⑤ in

9 The full moon ________ beautiful.

① sounds ② tastes
③ looks ④ feels
⑤ smells

10 We will ________ the air clean.

① keep ② call
③ tell ④ look
⑤ give

11 빈칸에 들어갈 말이 나머지와 다른 것을 고르시오.

① She sent roses and a letter ________ Tom.
② They found a seat ________ the old lady.
③ Mia gave her favorite pencil ________ me.
④ He lent his book ________ us.
⑤ I teach history ________ college students.

(12-14) 주어진 문장과 의미가 같도록 빈칸을 채우시오.

12 Joe showed me his model airplane.

⇨ Joe showed his model airplane ________ ________.

13 I will get you some cookies.

⇨ I will get some cookies ________ ________.

14 May I ask you a question?

⇨ May I ask a question ________ ________?

15 밑줄 친 단어가 나머지와 다르게 해석되는 것을 고르시오.

① They bought <u>me</u> new shoes.
② Jean taught <u>me</u> French.
③ She sent <u>me</u> to school.
④ He gave <u>me</u> a hug.
⑤ Jim brought <u>me</u> a cup of juice.

16 빈칸에 사용되지 않는 것을 고르시오.

ⓐ Don't call him __________
ⓑ He made me __________.
ⓒ It smells like __________.
ⓓ She told me __________
ⓔ Keep your teeth __________.

① a liar
② cleanly
③ to run
④ an orange
⑤ cold noodles

(17–18) 다음 우리말을 영어로 바르게 옮긴 것은?

17 Peter는 그녀에게 기다리라고 부탁했다.

① Peter asked her wait.
② Peter asked she wait.
③ Peter asked to her to wait.
④ Peter asked her to wait.
⑤ Peter asked to wait to her.

18 조깅은 나를 건강하게 만들었다.

① Jogging made I healthy.
② Jogging made I healthily.
③ Jogging made me healthy.
④ Jogging made me health
⑤ Jogging made my healthy.

(19–20) 우리말과 의미가 같도록 ( ) 안의 말을 배열하시오.

19 눈이 담요 같이 보여.
(looks, a, blanket, like, the snow)

⇨ ______________________________
______________________________.

20 우리는 여러분이 파티를 즐기기를 원해요.
(want, you, we, to, enjoy)

⇨ ______________________________
____________________ the party.

(21–22) 빈칸에 공통으로 들어갈 말을 고르시오.

21
· She showed her pictures __________ us.
· Max asked us __________ hurry.

① to
② for
③ of
④ with
⑤ in

22
· Austin __________ some cookies for you.
· His smile __________ me happy.

① cooked
② bought
③ made
④ found
⑤ wanted

23 ( ) 안의 말을 알맞게 고친 것으로 짝지어진 것은?

My grandma told (I) a fairy tale. I cooked (she) a special dinner.

① I - she ② my - her
③ my - she ④ me - her
⑤ me - she

24 어법상 올바르지 않은 것으로 짝지어진 것은?

ⓐ I asked him open the door. ⓑ Your plan sounds like perfect. ⓒ She bought us lunch. ⓓ We felt sorry for Jimmy. ⓔ The exam gave too much stress for us.

① ⓐ, ⓑ ② ⓐ, ⓑ, ⓔ
③ ⓐ, ⓒ, ⓔ ④ ⓑ, ⓒ
⑤ ⓑ, ⓓ, ⓔ

(25–26) 우리말과 의미가 같도록 ( ) 안의 말을 이용하여 문장을 완성하시오.

25 이 샐러드는 신선한 맛이 난다. (fresh)

⇨ This salad ____________________.

26 Emma는 그의 이야기가 사실임을 알게 되었다. (find, true)

⇨ Emma ____________________.

(27–29) 다음 문장에서 어색한 부분을 찾아 바르게 고치고 알맞은 이유를 고르시오.

27 He made a nice dress of me.

고치기: __________ ⇨ __________

이유: '~를 ~에게 만들어 주다'는 make + 직접목적어 + (of, for) + 간접목적어

28 Your bag looks heavily.

고치기: __________ ⇨ __________

이유: 감각동사 look + (형용사, 부사)는 (~를 보다, ~하게 보이다) 의미

29 She advised me speak slowly.

고치기: __________ ⇨ __________

이유: '~에게 ~하라고 충고하다'는 advise + 목적어 + 목적격보어 (동사, to부정사)

30 다음 조건을 이용하여 알맞게 영작하시오.

나는 내 햄스터에게 약간의 씨앗을 주었다.
조건 1: some seeds, hamster
조건 2: 7단어, 전치사

⇨ ____________________.

한눈에 정리하는 Grammar Mapping

빈칸에 알맞은 답을 보기에서 골라 넣어 grammar mapping 완성하기

동사의 종류

감각동사 — 형식

주어 + 감각동사 + ① ____________
(주어를 보충 설명)

You **look** great today.

수여동사 — 형식

주어 + 동사 + ② ____________ + ③ ____________
(~해 주다) (____________) (____________)

She **sent** us a present.
I **bought** him a book.
He **asked** me a question.

형식

주어 + 동사 + 직접목적어 + ④ ____________ + 간접목적어
(~하다) (~을 / 를) (to / for / of) (~에게)

She sent a present ⑤ ____________ us.
I bought a book ⑥ ____________ him.
He asked a question ⑦ ____________ me.

목적격보어가 필요한 동사 — 형식

주어 + 동사 + ⑧ ____________ + ⑨ ____________
(⑩ ____________, 형용사, to부정사)

She **calls** me Andy.
It **made** us ⑪ ____________.
He **told** me ⑫ ____________ hard.

보기				
	· 간접목적어(~에게)	· 형용사	· 직접목적어(~을 /를)	· 목적어
	· 목적격보어	· 전치사	· 명사	· for
	· to study	· of	· excited	· to

Chapter

11

접속사

and, but, or, so

GP 44

등위접속사 and, but, or은 대등한 관계에 있는 두 대상을 연결하고, so는 원인과 결과를 나타내는 두 문장을 연결한다.

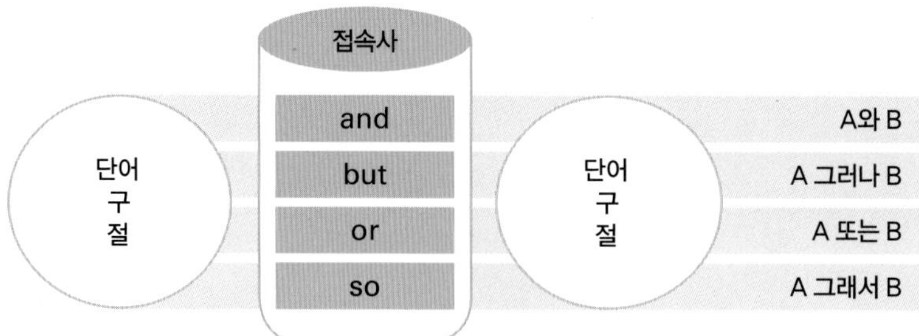

❶ and: 그리고, ~와

☆ I think of you night **and** day.

The actor is married **and** has five sons.

❷ but: 그러나, 그런데

☆ The soccer player is short **but** fast.

She heard the alarm, **but** she didn't get up.

❸ or: 또는, 혹은

☆ Which subject do you like better, math **or** English?

You can visit the island by airplane **or** by ship.

❹ so: 그래서, 그러므로

Pandas are lazy, **so** they don't move a lot.

☆ He missed the last bus, **so** he took a taxi.

Tip

접속사 so는 and, but, or과 달리 두 문장을 이어주는 역할만 할 수 있다.

Tom is kind so popular.(X)

Tom is kind, so **he is popular**.(O)

• Upgrade •

❶ [명령문, and ~]: ~해라, 그러면 ~할 것이다

☆ **Open** the window, **and** you will see the rainbow.

❷ [명령문, or ~]: ~해라, 그렇지 않으면 ~할 것이다

☆ **Open** the window, **or** you won't see the rainbow.

GP Practice

A ( ) 안에서 알맞은 것을 고르시오.

1 You can call me (or, so) send a message.

2 He cleaned his room, (or, but) it was still messy.

3 I was late for school, (so, but) I had to run.

4 The magic show was fun (but, and) interesting.

B 보기에서 알맞은 접속사를 골라 문장을 연결하시오. (한 번씩만 사용)

보기	and	but	so	or

1 The chef added too much salt, ____________ it was salty.

2 I will meet her ____________ tell her the truth.

3 Will you cook ____________ wash the dishes after dinner?

4 He called me many times, ____________ I didn't answer.

C 우리말과 의미가 같도록 ( ) 안의 말을 이용하여 문장을 완성하시오.

1 Jessy는 항상 많이 먹지만, 그녀는 날씬하다. (slim)

→ Jessy always eats a lot, ____________ ____________ ____________ ____________.

2 너는 이 계획에 찬성이니, 반대이니? (agree, disagree)

→ Do you ____________ ____________ ____________ with the plan?

3 그녀는 사과를 하나 따서 먹었어. (pick, eat)

→ She ____________ ____________ ____________ ____________ ____________ it.

4 그는 감기에 걸려서 병원에 갔다. (go)

→ He caught a cold, ____________ ____________ ____________ to see a doctor.

D 밑줄 친 부분에 대한 설명을 하고 틀린 경우엔 바르게 고치시오. (맞으면 'O' 표시)

1	He was tired, <u>but</u> he got some rest. → ( )	피곤하다 + (그래서, 그러나) 휴식을 취한다
2	She is young <u>or</u> wise. → ( )	어린 + (또는, 그러나) 현명한
3	He is tall <u>but</u> strong. → ( )	키가 큰 + (그리고, 그러나) 힘이 센
4	Eat more, <u>or</u> you will be hungry soon. → ( )	더 먹어라 (그러면, 그렇지 않으면) 배고파질 거다

when, before, after

GP 45

[주절과 부사절]

주절은 독립적으로 쓰일 수 있는 문장을 말하고 부사절은 [접속사 + 주어 + 동사]의 형태로 시간, 조건, 이유 등을 나타내며 주절의 앞뒤에서 주절 전체를 수식한다.

[when, before, after]

when, before, after는 시간을 나타내는 접속사이다.

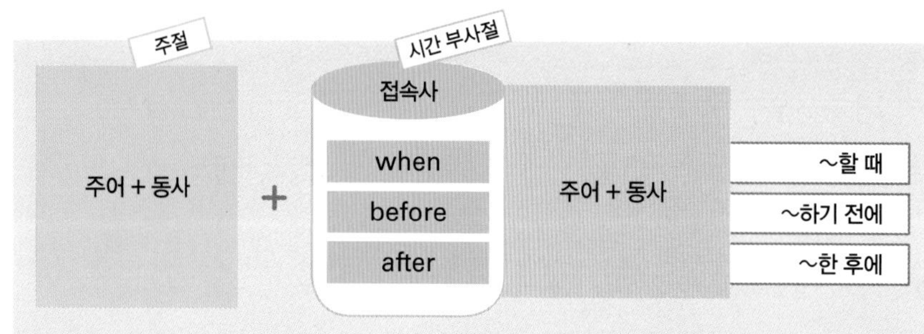

❶ when 주어 + 동사

Give me a call **when** *you have time.*

☆ **When** *Clara feels shy*, her face turns red.

❷ before 주어 + 동사

☆ **Before** *you pay for the candy*, you can't eat it.

Knock on the door **before** *you come in.*

❸ after 주어 + 동사

After *he saw me*, he ran away.

Dry the dishes **after** *you wash them.*

• Upgrade •

시간 부사절에서는 미래시제 대신에 현재시제를 사용한다.

☆ [I will bring a tent] [**when** ***I go*** (~~will go~~) *camping.*]
(주절) (부사절)

GP Practice

A ( ) 안에서 알맞은 것을 고르시오.

1 Don't talk (that, when) your mouth is full.

2 You have 5 minutes (before, after) the test starts.

3 Return the book to the library (after, before) you read it.

4 She will call me when she (will arrive, arrives) at the airport.

B 자연스러운 문장이 되도록 알맞게 연결하시오.

1 I look both ways •	• ⓐ after he makes his bed.
2 He always eats breakfast •	• ⓑ when it gets angry.
3 The fish gets bigger •	• ⓒ after you use it.
4 Turn off the gas •	• ⓓ before I cross the street.

C 우리말과 의미가 같도록 ( ) 안의 말을 이용하여 문장을 완성하시오.

1 비가 그친 후에는 무지개가 나와. (the rain, stop)

→ ______ ______ ______ ______, a rainbow appears.

2 그녀는 초조해지면, 손에 땀이 나. (be nervous)

→ ______ ______ ______ ______, her hands sweat.

3 그는 비가 올 때는 약간 우울해진다. (it, rain)

→ He feels a bit blue ______ ______ ______.

4 네가 저녁을 먹기 전에, 네 방 청소를 해라. (eat)

→ Clean your room ______ ______ ______ ______.

D 밑줄 친 부분에 대한 설명을 하고 틀린 경우엔 바르게 고치시오. (맞으면 'O' 표시) 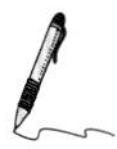

1	I put on lotion <u>before</u> I wash my face. → ( )	로션을 바른다 + 세수 (한 후, 하기 전)
2	I will buy the bike when it <u>is</u> on sale. → ( )	시간 부사절에서는 미래를 나타낼 때 (현재, 미래)시제 사용
3	<u>Before</u> she saw me, she smiled at me. → ( )	나를 (보기 전에, 봤을 때) + 내게 웃어 줬다
4	Pack your bag <u>after</u> you go to bed. → ( )	가방을 꾸려라 + 잠자기 (후에, 전에)

because, if

GP 46

because는 이유·원인을 나타내고, if는 조건을 나타내는 접속사이다.

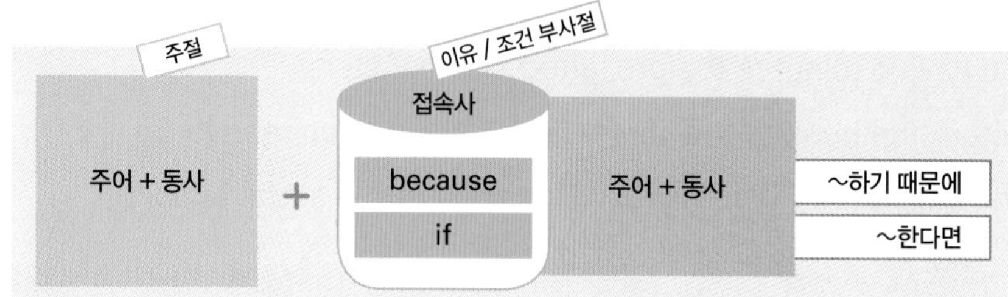

❶ **because 주어 + 동사**

☆ She likes the actor **because** *he is funny.*

Because *the movie is scary*, I won't watch it alone.

❷ **if 주어 + 동사**

☆ **If** *it snows tomorrow*, we will go skiing.

☆ Pass me the cake **if** *you don't want to eat it.*

• Upgrade •

조건 부사절에서는 미래시제 대신에 현재시제를 사용한다.

[If *she* ***wears*** (~~will wear~~) *jeans*], [she will look younger.]

(부사절) (주절)

that

GP 47

[that + 주어 + 동사]는 '~하는 것(을)'로 해석하고, 명사처럼 주어, 목적어, 보어로 쓰인다.
한 묶음으로 특정 동사의 목적어로 쓰이며, 이때 that은 생략할 수 있다.

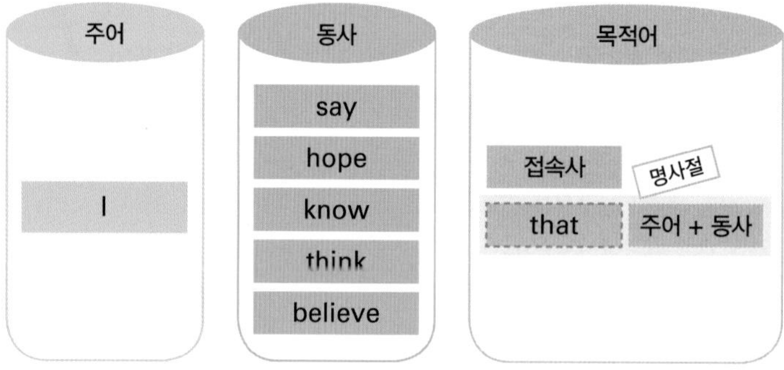

I can't believe **(that)** *my summer vacation is over.*

Some people say **(that)** *polar bears are left-handed.*

☆ Do you think **(that)** *Emily is an angel?*

GP Practice

A ( ) 안에서 알맞은 것을 고르시오.

1 (If, That) you are not busy, we can talk now.

2 I will visit you if you (will be, are) at home.

3 They married (if, because) they loved each other.

4 I hope (because, that) she likes the gift.

B 보기에서 알맞은 접속사를 골라 문장을 완성하시오.

보기 |	if	that	because

1 ____________ it is windy, we will go paragliding.

2 She said ____________ the jacket looked good on you.

3 We will be excited ____________ we see a UFO.

4 Brian had a cold ____________ he didn't wear warm clothes.

C 우리말과 의미가 같도록 ( ) 안의 말을 이용하여 문장을 완성하시오.

1 2와 3을 더하면, 5가 된다. (add)

→ ____________ ____________ ____________ two and three, you get five.

2 더웠기 때문에, Mike는 그늘에 앉았다. (it, hot)

→ ____________ ____________ ____________ ____________, Mike sat in the shade.

3 Olive는 우리가 그녀를 좋아한다는 것을 알고 있어. (like)

→ Olivia knows ____________ ____________ ____________ ____________.

4 네가 늦는다면, 우리는 너를 기다리지 않을 거야. (be late)

→ We won't wait for you ____________ ____________ ____________ ____________.

D 밑줄 친 부분에 대한 설명을 하고 틀린 경우엔 바르게 고치시오. (맞으면 'O' 표시)

1	Do you know <u>that</u> penguins are birds? → ( )	너는 아니 + 펭귄이 새라는 (것을, ~라면)
2	Jack is tall <u>if</u> his parents are tall. → ( )	Jack은 키가 크다 + 부모님 키가 (크다면, 커서)
3	We went swimming <u>if</u> it was hot. → ( )	우리는 수영하러 갔다 + 날씨가 (더웠기 때문에, 더웠다면)
4	His nose will become longer <u>that</u> he tells a lie. → ( )	코가 길어질 거다 + 거짓말을 (하는 것을, 한다면)

A 우리말과 의미가 같도록 ( ) 안의 말을 배열하시오.

1 그가 재킷을 빨았더니 그의 재킷은 줄어들었다. (he, it, after, washed)

→ His jacket shrank ______________________________.

2 의자가 젖어 있었기 때문에, 우리는 앉지 않았다. (wet, because, chair, was, the)

→ We didn't sit ______________________________.

3 그들은 소파에 앉아서 텔레비전을 켰다. (and, TV, turned on, the)

→ They sat on the sofa ______________________________.

4 내 여자 친구는 야구가 지루하다고 생각해. (boring, that, is, baseball)

→ My girlfriend thinks ______________________________.

5 내가 충분한 돈이 있다면 새로운 핸드폰을 살 거야. (have, enough, I, if, money)

→ I will buy a new cell phone ______________________________.

6 그 음악은 매우 인기 있어서 십대들이 많이 듣는다. (so, listen to, teenagers, it, a lot)

→ The music is very popular, ______________________________.

B 우리말과 의미가 같도록 ( ) 안의 말을 이용하여 문장을 완성하시오.

1 그가 좋아하는 계절은 겨울이지만, 그는 눈을 싫어한다. (hate, snow)

→ His favorite season is winter, ________ ________ ________ ________.

2 아빠는 운전하기 전에 언제나 브레이크를 점검하신다. (drive)

→ My father always tests the brakes ________ ________ ________.

3 나는 치통이 있어서 아이스크림을 먹지 않았다. (have a toothache)

→ I didn't eat ice cream ________ ________ ________ ________

________.

4 Susan은 영국을 방문할 때 fish and chips를 먹을 거다. (visit England)

→ Susan will eat fish and chips ________ ________ ________ ________.

5 비누로 손을 자주 씻어, 그렇지 않으면 너는 감기에 걸려. (catch a cold)

→ Wash your hands often with soap, ________ ________ ________

________ ________ ________.

6 선생님들은 영어 문법이 중요하다고 믿는다. (English grammar, important)

→ Teachers believe ________ ________ ________ ________ ________.

C 다음 짝지어진 그림을 보고, 보기의 접속사를 이용하여 문장을 완성하시오. (한 번씩만 사용)

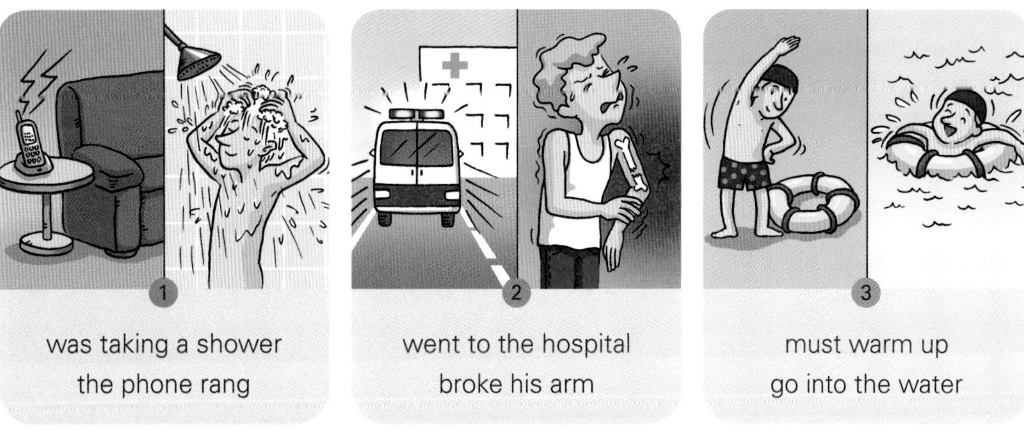

①	②	③
was taking a shower the phone rang	went to the hospital broke his arm	must warm up go into the water

보기 | because when before

1 He ______________________________.

2 He ______________________________.

3 You ______________________________.

D 보기 A와 보기 B를 연결하여 주어진 문장을 완성하시오.

A	B
so	I come back home
if	It gives us a lot of information
after	so I won't read it
when	after he talked with Paul
because	You wear the sunglasses

1 He changed his mind ______________________________.

2 My dog always wags its tail ______________________________.

3 This book is too difficult for me, ______________________________.

4 ______________________________, they will protect your eyes from the sun.

5 The Internet is very useful ______________________________.

Actual Test

(1–5) 빈칸에 들어갈 알맞은 말을 고르시오.

1 Alan heard the alarm, __________ he didn't get up.

① and ② but
③ so ④ that
⑤ or

2 Which cap did you choose, the blue one __________ the pink one?

① but ② so
③ when ④ or
⑤ if

3 Your brother is cute __________ funny.

① and ② if
③ after ④ but
⑤ so

4 He was hungry __________ he didn't have breakfast.

① and ② but
③ after ④ because
⑤ when

5 I will help you __________ I finish the report.

① when ② that
③ but ④ so
⑤ because

(6–8) 우리말과 일치하도록 빈칸에 알맞은 말을 쓰시오.

6 집에서 떠나기 전에 내게 전화해 줘.

⇨ Give me a call __________ you leave home.

7 우리는 할아버지 댁에 한 달에 한 번 또는 두 번 방문해.

⇨ We visit our grandfather one __________ two times a month.

8 게임 캐릭터들이 귀여워서 이 게임은 매우 인기가 있더라고.

⇨ The game is very popular __________ the characters are cute.

(9–11) 밑줄 친 부분이 어법상 어색한 것을 고르시오.

9 ① Bears are slow but strong.
② I forgot my password and ID again.
③ You can sleep on the bed or on the floor.
④ She loves animals, so she wants to be a chef.
⑤ Take this bus, and you will get to the park.

10 ① She thinks that you are clever.
② Because we stayed inside, it rained.
③ I hope that you will be healthy soon.
④ When I cleaned the room, I found a coin.
⑤ Raise your hand if you have a question.

11 ① If you will go, I will go, too.
② I think that it will rain soon.
③ I will eat lunch before I leave home.
④ Dry your hair after you take a shower.
⑤ She will join us when we go camping.

12 빈칸에 들어갈 말이 나머지와 다른 것을 고르시오.

① I hope _____ you visit us again.
② He thought _____ she was clever.
③ She heard _____ she won a prize.
④ I know him _____ I live near him.
⑤ Do you know _____ whales can sing?

(13–14) 다음 대화의 빈칸에 알맞은 것을 고르시오.

13

A: What do you think of the model?
B: I think __________ she is too skinny.

① and ② but
③ so ④ if
⑤ that

14

A: I am worried about the test tomorrow.
B: Don't worry. __________ you work hard, you can do well.

① Before ② After
③ Because ④ If
⑤ That

(15–16) 빈칸에 들어갈 말이 바르게 짝지어진 것을 고르시오.

15

· Olivia burned the cookies, __________ they tasted delicious.
· Take an umbrella, __________ you will get wet.

① and - but ② and - or
③ but - or ④ or - but
⑤ but - so

16

· I will wake you up __________ Santa comes tonight.
· __________ you read this book, you will find the answer.

① if - That ② when - If
③ before - And ④ but - When
⑤ or - That

(17–18) 빈칸에 들어갈 알맞은 말을 쓰시오.

17 He lost some weight, __________ his pants became too big for him.

⇨ __________

18 I know __________ Emily has a twin sister.

⇨ __________

19 어법상 올바른 것으로 짝지어진 것은?

ⓐ She will leave today and tomorrow.
ⓑ He will come if you will invite him.
ⓒ Let's go out after the rain stops.
ⓓ Bill is smart but lazy.
ⓔ I got upset because I said nothing.

① ⓐ, ⓑ ② ⓐ, ⓒ
③ ⓑ, ⓒ ④ ⓒ, ⓓ
⑤ ⓓ, ⓔ

(20–22) 보기의 접속사를 이용하여 주어진 문장을 연결하시오.

보기	and	when	that

20 She thinks.
William is a good singer.

⇨ She thinks __________
__________.

21 She drives slowly.
She drives in a school zone.

⇨ She drives slowly __________
__________.

22 Go to bed early every day.
You will grow tall.

⇨ Go to bed early every day, __________
__________.

(23-24) 다음 두 문장을 한 문장으로 쓸 때 알맞은 말을 고르시오.

23 He put on his pajamas. He went to bed.
⇨ He went to bed __________ he put on his pajamas.

① or ② so
③ if ④ after
⑤ because

24 She missed the bus. She had to wait for the next one.
⇨ __________she missed the bus, she had to wait for the next one.

① Because ② But
③ And ④ Before
⑤ That

(25-27) 우리말과 의미가 같도록 ( ) 안의 말을 배열하시오.

25 만약 이 버튼을 누른다면, 웨이터가 당신의 테이블로 올 것입니다.
(press, the, you, button, if)

⇨ ______________________________, a waiter will come to your table.

26 내가 컴퓨터로 일을 할 때, 내 고양이가 키보드 위에 앉아버려.
(on, work, when, I, the computer)

⇨ My cat sits on the keyboard __________ ______________________________.

27 호랑이는 화가 나서 이빨을 드러냈어.
(showed, it, so, its, teeth)

⇨ The tiger was angry, __________ ______________________________.

(28-29) 다음 문장에서 어색한 부분을 찾아 바르게 고치고 알맞은 이유를 고르시오.

28 When Jane will move to London next month, I will be sad.

고치기: __________ ⇨ __________
이유: 시간 부사절에서는 (미래, 현재)시제 대신 (미래, 현재)시제 사용

29 I can't sleep so it is noisy outside.

고치기: __________ ⇨ __________
이유: 잠을 잘 수 없는 (결과, 이유)를 이끄는 접속사는 (so, because)

30 다음 조건을 이용하여 알맞게 영작하시오.

나는 기름이 물과 잘 섞이지 않는다는 것을 알아.
조건 1: oil, mix with, that
조건 2: 8단어

⇨ ______________________________.

한눈에 정리하는 Grammar Mapping

빈칸에 알맞은 답을 보기에서 골라 넣어 grammar mapping 완성하기

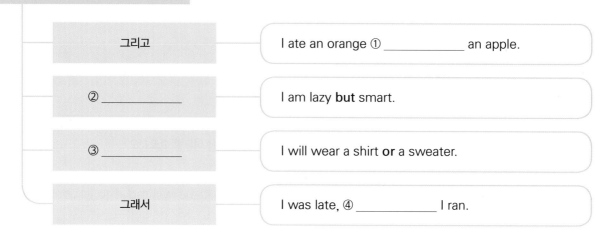

같은 대상을 연결해 주는 접속사

의미	예문
그리고	I ate an orange ① ____________ an apple.
② ____________	I am lazy **but** smart.
③ ____________	I will wear a shirt **or** a sweater.
그래서	I was late, ④ ____________ I ran.

문장과 문장을 연결해 주는 접속사

형태	의미	예문
⑤ __________ + 주어 + 동사	~ 때문에	I was happy ⑤ ____________ you came.
when + 주어 + 동사	⑥ ____________	I was happy **when** you came.
after + 주어 + 동사	⑦ ____________	I was happy **after** you came.
⑧ __________ + 주어 + 동사	~하기 전에	I was happy ⑧ ____________ you came.
if + 주어 + 동사	⑨ ____________	I will be happy **if** you come.
that + 주어 + 동사	~하는 것을	I hope **that** you will come.

보기

· 또는　· ~한 후에　· 그러나　· ~할 때　· ~한다면

· and　· before　· so　· because

Chapter

12

전치사

시간을 나타내는 전치사 I

GP 48

at	on	in
at 2 o'clock	on Sunday	in September
at noon	on June 2	in summer
at night	on Halloween	in 2018
at dawn	on my birthday	in the morning
구체적인 시각이나 특정 시점	요일, 날짜 및 특정한 날	월, 계절, 연도 등 비교적 긴 시간

- My school starts **at** 8:30 a.m.
- Alex was born **on** May 7.
- People enjoy skiing **in** the winter.

시간을 나타내는 전치사 II

GP 49

before	~ 전에	after	~ 후에
for	~ 동안	during	~ 동안
by	~까지 (동작 완료)	until	~까지 (동작의 계속)
between A and B	A와 B 사이에	from A to B	A부터 B까지

The actor became famous **after** the movie.
I don't eat snacks **before** dinner.

- Some koalas sleep **for** 17 hours a day.
- Hamsters are underground **during** the day.

• Upgrade •

for + 숫자를 포함한 구체적인 기간	during + 특정한 때(사건)를 나타내는 명사
for 20 minutes / five weeks	**during** class / vacation

I must finish the report **by** tomorrow.
You can download the file **until** next month.

The beach is open **from** June **to** August.
He works **from** Monday **to** Friday.

GP Practice

A ( ) 안에서 알맞은 것을 고르시오.

1 The movie will start (on, at) 3:30 p.m.

2 The great musician was born (at, in) 1756.

3 The contest will be held (on, at) May 5.

4 What do you eat (on, at) Christmas Day?

5 The grass starts growing (at, in) spring.

6 He likes swimming in the lake (at, in) the morning.

B 빈칸에 for 또는 during 중 알맞은 것을 쓰시오.

1 Boil the eggs ____________ 15 minutes.

2 You grew taller ____________ the winter vacation.

3 Brian fell asleep ____________ class again.

4 He traveled around Africa ____________ 30 days.

C 우리말과 의미가 같도록 ( ) 안의 말을 이용하여 문장을 완성하시오.

1 밤에는 별들이 밝게 빛난다. (night)

→ Stars shine brightly ____________ ____________.

2 점심식사 후에 산책을 가자. (lunch)

→ Let's take a walk ____________ ____________.

3 그 페스티벌은 5월 5일에서 9일까지 지속되었다. (May 5, May 9)

→ The festival ran ____________ ____________ ____________ ____________.

D 밑줄 친 부분에 대한 설명을 하고 틀린 경우엔 바르게 고치시오. (맞으면 'O' 표시) 

1	The ship will arrive <u>on</u> 8:00 p.m. → ( )	(on, at, in) + 구체적인 시간
2	He learned boxing <u>during</u> two years. → ( )	(during, for) + (특정한 때, 숫자 포함 기간)
3	The Olympics were held <u>on</u> 2008. → ( )	(on, at, in) + 연도
4	The bakery is closed <u>at</u> Mondays. → ( )	(on, at, in) + 요일

장소를 나타내는 전치사 I

GP 50

at
at home
at school
at the airport
at the party
비교적 좁은 장소나 지점 (~에)
on
on the sofa
on the table
on the wall
on the ground
표면에 접촉한 (~ 위에)
in
in the box
in the room
in Korea
in New York
공간의 내부 (~ 안에)
마을, 도시, 국가 (~에)

☆ I lost my backpack **at** the airport.
☆ Look at the pictures **on** the wall.
☆ Jasmine has some coins **in** her pocket.

장소를 나타내는 전치사 II

GP 51

over	(접촉 없이) ~ 위에	under	(접촉 없이) ~ 아래에
in front of	~ 앞에	behind	~ 뒤에
next to	~ 옆에	near	~ 근처에
across	~을 가로질러	across from	~ 맞은편에
between A and B	A와 B 사이에	from A to B	A부터 B까지

There was a rainbow **over** the hill.
You can find shade **under** a tree.

Emma feels shy **in front of** many people.
My house is **behind** the park.

A bodyguard stood **next to** the singer.

The train runs **across** the desert.
The café is **across from** the gas station.
Korea is **between** Japan **and** China.
☆ This plane flies **from** Seoul **to** Busan.

GP Practice

A ( ) 안에서 알맞은 것을 고르시오.

1 Nicole lives (at, in) New Zealand.

2 He left his bicycle (at, in) home.

3 Do you put sugar (on, in) your coffee?

4 There was dust (on, in) the books.

5 She is wearing a ring (at, on) her middle finger.

B 그림을 보고 보기의 전치사를 한 번씩만 이용하여 문장을 완성하시오.

보기	next to	behind	over

1 There is a tree ____________ the bench.

2 A blue bird is flying ____________ the tree.

3 A big dog is sitting ____________ the bench.

C 우리말과 의미가 같도록 ( ) 안의 말을 이용하여 문장을 완성하시오.

1 보트 한 대가 그 다리 아래를 지나고 있었다. (the bridge)

→ A boat was passing ____________ ____________ ____________.

2 그 암석은 화성에서 지구까지 이동해 온 거야. (Mars, Earth)

→ The rock traveled ____________ ____________ ____________ ____________.

3 저 산 위에 보름달 좀 봐. (the mountain)

→ Look at the full moon ____________ ____________ ____________.

4 그는 거울 앞에서 재킷을 입어 봤어. (the mirror)

→ He tried on a jacket __________ __________ __________ __________ __________.

D 밑줄 친 부분에 대한 설명을 하고 틀린 경우엔 바르게 고치시오. (맞으면 'O' 표시)

1	Kyle dropped a cup <u>in</u> the floor. → ( )	(표면 위에, 안에) (on, in) + the floor
2	He sat between Sue <u>or</u> me. → ( )	(A 와 B, A 또는 B) 사이에 between A (or, and) B
3	Her family lives <u>at</u> Seoul. → ( )	(도시에, 비교적 좁은 지점에) (at, on, in) + Seoul
4	I met my friends <u>in</u> the party. → ( )	(공간의 내부에, 비교적 좁은 지점에) (at, on, in) + the party

기타 전치사

GP 52

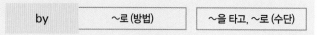

by | ~로 (방법) | ~을 타고, ~로 (수단)

May I pay **by** credit card?

We crossed the river **by** boat.

• Upgrade •

by + 교통수단	by + 통신수단
by car / airplane / bicycle	**by** e-mail / text message / the Internet

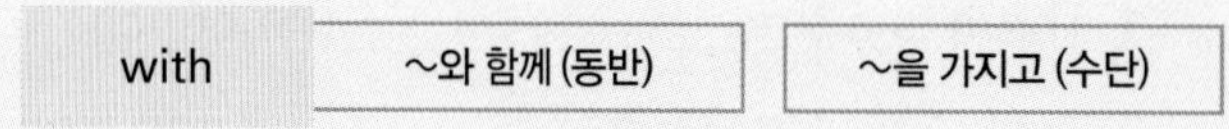

I carried the box **with** George.

Wash your hands **with** soap.

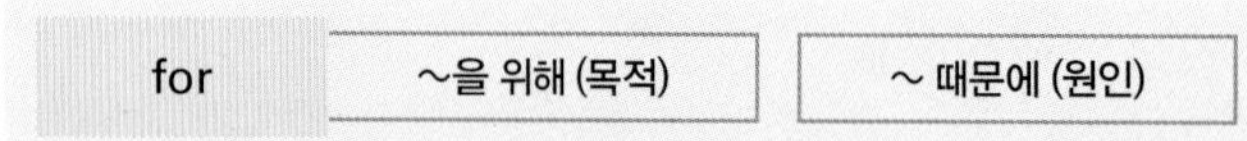

I bought some flowers **for** my mom.

Thank you **for** your advice.

We went **to** the museum yesterday.

Ken sent a text message **to** me.

> **Tip**
> 전치사 뒤에 대명사가 오면 목적격으로 쓴다.
> This gift is **for** ~~he~~. (×)
> → him.(o)

I have some questions **about** grammar.

Greg dressed **like** a zombie at the Halloween party.

GP Practice

A ( ) 안에서 알맞은 것을 고르시오.

1 He lied (about, by) his age.

2 This shampoo smells (like, with) fruit.

3 The painter showed her feelings (for, with) colors.

4 We will visit the moon (for, by) space shuttle.

B 공통으로 들어갈 알맞은 전치사를 보기에서 골라 문장을 완성하시오.

보기 |	with	by	for	to

1 I am sorry ____________ my mistake.
I made some cookies ____________ you.

2 She cut the bread ____________ a knife.
He watched the movie ____________ his mom.

3 My dad goes to work ____________ subway.
Could you send me the file ____________ e-mail?

4 We are moving ____________ a new house next month.
Sally brought flowers ____________ her mom.

C 우리말과 의미가 같도록 ( ) 안의 말을 이용하여 문장을 완성하시오.

1 그 까마귀는 그녀에게 몇 개의 단추를 가져다주었다. (she)
→ The crow brought some buttons ____________ ____________.

2 Susan은 그녀의 꿈에 관해 글을 썼다. (dream)
→ Susan wrote ____________ ____________ ____________.

3 모든 일은 어떤 이유 때문에 생긴다. (a reason)
→ Everything happens ____________ ____________ ____________.

D 밑줄 친 부분에 대한 설명을 하고 틀린 경우엔 바르게 고치시오. (맞으면 'O' 표시)

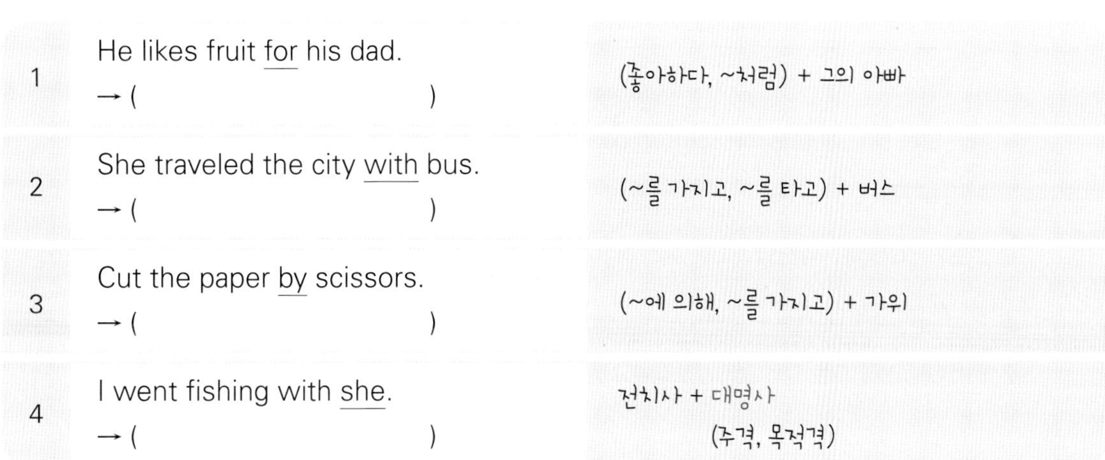

1	He likes fruit <u>for</u> his dad. → ( )	(좋아하다, ~처럼) + 그의 아빠
2	She traveled the city <u>with</u> bus. → ( )	(~를 가지고, ~를 타고) + 버스
3	Cut the paper <u>by</u> scissors. → ( )	(~에 의해, ~를 가지고) + 가위
4	I went fishing with <u>she</u>. → ( )	전치사 + 대명사 (주격, 목적격)

Grammar & Writing

A **우리말과 의미가 같도록 ( ) 안의 말을 배열하시오.**

1 그는 그의 좌석 아래 가방을 두었다. (his bag, put, his seat, under)

→ He ______________________________.

2 그는 나에게 팩스로 사진을 보냈다. (a, fax, by, picture)

→ He sent me ______________________________.

3 우리 가족은 일요일마다 쇼핑을 간다. (goes, on, shopping, Sundays)

→ My family ______________________________.

4 그 베이커리는 카페 맞은편에 있다. (is, a café, from, across)

→ The bakery ______________________________.

5 나는 주로 저녁에 샤워를 해. (the evening, take, in, a shower)

→ I usually ______________________________.

6 에스키모들은 머리에서 발까지 그들의 몸을 감싼다. (to, toe, their, from, bodies, head)

→ Eskimos cover ______________________________.

B **우리말과 의미가 같도록 ( ) 안의 말을 이용하여 문장을 완성하시오.**

1 작년에는 5월에 눈이 내렸어. (snow, May)

→ Last year, it ________ ________ ________.

2 그녀는 1월 1일에 태어났다. (January 1)

→ She was born ________ ________.

3 그 노신사는 지팡이를 짚고 걸었다. (walk, a cane)

→ The old gentleman ________ ________ ________ ________.

4 빈센트는 빵 위에 땅콩버터를 발랐어. (the bread, butter)

→ Vincent spread ________ ________ ________ ________.

5 저 구름은 솜사탕처럼 생겼어. (cotton candy)

→ The cloud looks ________ ________ ________.

6 소포가 월요일에서 수요일 사이에 도착할 것입니다. (Monday, Wednesday)

→ A package will arrive ________ ________ ________ ________.

7 콘서트 동안에, 그는 그의 팬들과 노래하고 춤을 추었다. (the concert)

→ ________ ________ ________, he sang and danced with his fans.

C Evan의 방에서 보이는 것이다. 전치사를 이용하여 문장을 완성하시오.

1 Evan is staying ________________ his room.

2 There is a table ________________ the tree.

3 There is some juice ________________ the table.

4 His sister is standing ________________ to the table.

5 His dog is hiding ________________ the tree.

D Anna가 보낸 생일초대 카드이다. 카드 내용에 알맞도록 보기에서 전치사를 골라 문장을 완성하시오.

보기 |	on	in	to	from	at

It's Anna's
10th birthday!
Join our celebration

Place : Sea World Park
273 East Road
Time : May 5, 2018
2 p.m.~4 p.m.

RSVP to me 123-456-789

*RSVP: 참여 여부를 알려 주세요.

1 Ana is inviting me ________________ her birthday party.

2 The party will be ________________ May 5.

3 Ana was born ________________ 2008.

4 Ana will hold the party ________________ Sea World Park.

5 They will have the party ________________ 2 p.m. to 4 p.m.

6 I will call her ________________ 123-456-789 and say, "Yes."

Actual Test

(1-4) 빈칸에 들어갈 알맞은 말을 고르시오.

1

A butterfly sat __________ my shoulder.

① on ② above
③ over ⑤ to
④ for

2

The next train will arrive __________ 8:30 a.m.

① on ② in
③ at ④ during
⑤ for

3

Please turn off your cell phone __________ the movie.

① by ② on
③ for ④ during
⑤ with

4

Only goalkeepers can catch the ball __________ their hands.

① with ② by
③ on ④ at
⑤ over

(5-6) 다음 중 어법상 어색한 것을 고르시오.

5 ① The train runs on railroads.
② He traveled around the world by ship.
③ A hair shop is next to the bus stop.
④ Henry jumped over the fence.
⑤ She met Roy at Japan.

6 ① It is very cold on December.
② She took this picture in 2016.
③ I'll call you after school.
④ Roses bloom from May to June.
⑤ He lived in London until last year.

7 밑줄 친 말의 쓰임이 다른 것을 고르시오.

① You have blond hair like William.
② The swimmer looks like a dolphin.
③ The puppy is like a cute doll.
④ The pandas like bamboo.
⑤ You have a soft voice like your dad.

(8-10) 빈칸에 공통으로 들어갈 말을 고르시오.

8

· I meet all my cousins ___________ New Year's Day. · He was lying ___________ the beach.

① on　② in
③ at　④ during
⑤ after

9

· She sent a letter ___________ me. · Does this express bus go ___________ Daegu?

① at　② with
③ to　④ over
⑤ between

10

· I filled the bathtub ___________ hot water. · Who is the man talking ___________ Jane?

① with　② to
③ at　④ next to
⑤ like

11 빈칸에 알맞지 않은 것을 고르시오.

A cat is sleeping ___________ a big box.

① behind　② on
③ next to　④ in
⑤ to

(12-14) 주어진 문장과 의미가 같도록 알맞은 전치사로 빈칸을 채우시오.

12 Jane began to watch a movie at 9 a.m. She watched it until 11 a.m.

⇨ Jane watched a movie ___________ 9 ___________ 11 a.m.

13 My first class is history. My second class is science.

⇨ I learn history ___________ science.

14 Rick and I are standing in line. I am standing in front of Rick.

⇨ Rick is standing ___________ me.

15 다음 우리말을 영어로 바르게 옮긴 것은?

노란선 뒤에서 기다려 주시기 바랍니다.

① Please stay next to the yellow line.
② Please stay by the yellow line.
③ Please stay on the yellow line.
④ Please stay behind the yellow line.
⑤ Please stay near the yellow line.

16 어법상 올바른 것으로 짝지어진 것은?

ⓐ Put the forks and knives on the table.
ⓑ He goes swimming in Sundays.
ⓒ The car was covered with snow.
ⓓ She brought some pie to he.
ⓔ Lunchtime is from 1 p.m. and 2 p.m.

① ⓐ, ⓑ　　② ⓐ, ⓒ
③ ⓑ, ⓓ　　④ ⓒ, ⓓ
⑤ ⓓ, ⓔ

(17-19) 다음 그림을 보고 알맞은 전치사로 빈칸을 채우시오.

17 My puppy and my baby brother are sitting ________ ________ ________ the TV.

18 My baby brother was sitting ________ ________ my puppy.

19 They are sitting ________ the floor.

(20-21) 빈칸에 들어갈 말이 순서대로 짝지어진 것을 고르시오.

20
· Please return the book ________ next Friday.
· Alvin slept ________ noon.

① by - by　　② by - until
③ until - by　　④ until - until
⑤ by - in

21
· The park is open ________ the daytime.
· It rained ________ three hours yesterday.

① for, for　　② for, in
③ during, in　　④ during, for
⑤ in, in

(22-23) 빈칸에 들어갈 말이 나머지와 다른 것은?

22 ① The concert will start ________ 7 p.m.
② I met Tom ________ the school festival.
③ She often drinks coffee ________ night.
④ We had an early dinner ________ home.
⑤ What happened ________ July 10 last year?

23 ① She puts the books ________ the shelves.
② The dentist is ________ the 5th floor.
③ I got a present ________ my birthday.
④ We feel tired easily ________ spring.
⑤ What does she do ________ Sundays?

24 다음 중 어법상 올바른 것을 두 개 고르시오.

① Fill at the blank.
② This movie is about space.
③ There is a bridge on the river.
④ He studied bugs during two years.
⑤ Put this box under the bed.

(25–26) 우리말과 의미가 같도록 빈칸을 채우시오.

25 영어 알파벳에서 C는 B와 D 사이에 온다.

⇨ C comes ________ B ________ D in the English alphabet.

26 크리스마스트리 아래 선물들이 있었어.

⇨ There were presents ________ the Christmas tree.

(27–28) 우리말과 의미가 같도록 ( ) 안의 말을 배열하시오.

27 나는 여름방학까지 기다릴 수가 없어.
(until, wait, summer vacation)

⇨ I can't ________________
________________.

28 그 소식은 입에서 입으로 퍼져나갔어.
(spread, from, mouth, mouth, to)

⇨ The news ________________
________________.

(29–30) 다음 문장에서 어색한 부분을 찾아 바르게 고치고 알맞은 이유를 고르시오.

29 Peter wrote his name over his books.

고치기: ________ ⇨ ________
이유: (접촉한 표면, 접촉 안 한 표면) 위는 (on, over) + 명사

30 Bears sleep for the winter.

고치기: ________ ⇨ ________
이유: '~동안'은 (during, for) + (특정한 기간명사, 숫자 포함 기간)

31 다음 조건을 이용하여 알맞게 영작하시오.

Paula와 나 사이에는 비밀이 없어.
조건 1: no, there are
조건 2: 8단어

⇨ ________________
________________.

한눈에 정리하는 Grammar Mapping

빈칸에 알맞은 답을 보기에서 골라 넣어 grammar mapping 완성하기

시간 전치사

① ________	+ 구체적 시각, 시점	**at** night, **at** nine o'clock, **at** 2 p.m.
on	+ ② ________, 특정한 날	**on** May 5, **on** April Fool's Day
in	+ ③ ________ 등	**in** December, **in** spring, **in** 2018
④ ________	~ 이전에	**before** 6 a.m., **before** noon
after	~ 이후에	**after** school, **after** work
for	~ 동안 (+ ⑤ ________)	**for** one hour, **for** two weeks
during	~ 동안 (+ ⑥ ________)	**during** the movie, **during** the day
⑦ ________	~와 ~ 사이에	**between** March **and** June
from ~ to	~부터 ~까지	**from** Monday **to** Friday

보기 | · 특정한 기간명사 · 요일, 날짜 · 숫자 포함 기간 · 월, 계절, 연도 · at · between ~ and · before

장소 전치사

at	~에 (비교적 좁은 장소, 지점)	**at** home, **at** the bus stop
⑧ ________	(표면에 접촉) ~ 위에	**on** the table, **on** your head
⑨ ________	~ 안에	**in** the pocket, **in** her room
⑩ ________	(접촉 없이) ~ 위에	a rainbow **over** the mountain
under	(접촉 없이) ~ 아래에	a ball **under** the tree
⑪ ________	~ 앞에	a dog **in front of** a box
behind	⑫ ________	a dog **behind** a box
next to	⑬ ________	a dog **next to** a box
near	~ 근처에	a park **near** my house
across	~을 가로질러	**across** the street
across from	맞은편에	**across from** the park
between ~ and	A와 B 사이에	**between** Peter **and** me
from ~ to	A부터 B까지	**from** here **to** the station

보기 | · ~ 옆에 · ~ 뒤에 · in front of · in · on · over

Grammar ViSTA Study!

Date	Memo
001	
002	
003	
004	
005	
006	
007	
008	
009	
010	
011	
012	
013	
014	
015	

016	
017	
018	
019	
020	
021	
022	
023	
024	
025	
026	
027	
028	
029	
030	
031	

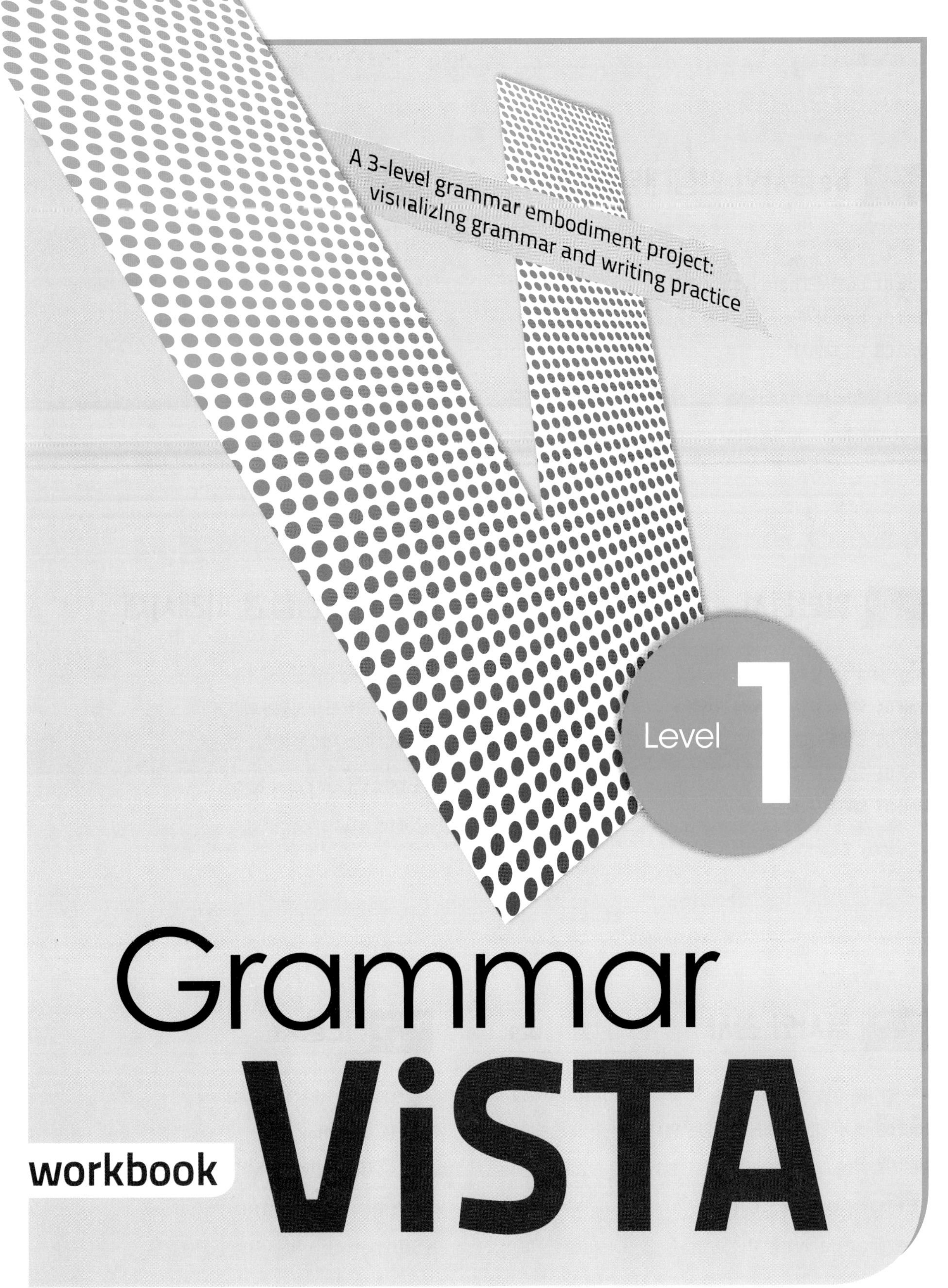

Grammar ViSTA

workbook

DARAKWON

목차

문법패턴 빈칸 채우기

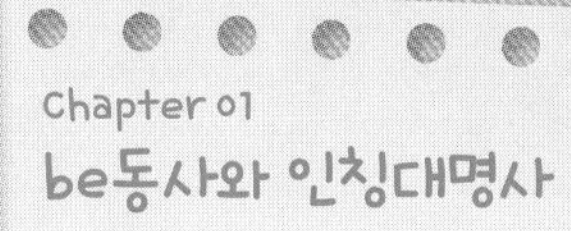

GP 01 be동사

* 본 교재 GP 참조

be동사는 주어와 시제에 따라 형태가 변하고 뒤에 명사, 형용사, 장소 표현 등이 온다.

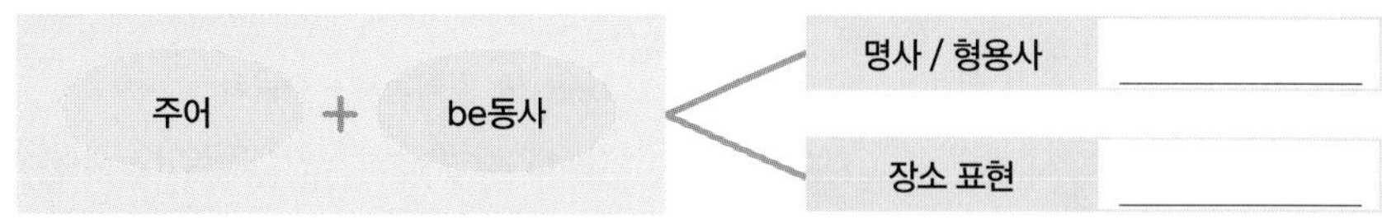

주어			be동사 현재형	줄임말	be동사 과거형
1인칭	단수	I	________	I'm	________
	복수	We	________	We're	________
2인칭	단수 / 복수	You	________	You're	________
3인칭	단수	He / She / It	________	He's / She's / It's	________
	복수	They	________	They're	________

❶ **be동사 현재형**

She **is** a designer. (~이다)

They **are** at school now. (~에 있다)

❷ **be동사 과거형**

The test **was** very difficult. (~이었다)

Many boys **were** on the playground. (~에 있었다)

Tip

인칭대명사와 be동사의 과거형은 축약하지 않는다.

· She is a pianist. → She's a pianist.

· She was a pianist then. → ~~She's~~ a pianist then. (X)

GP 02 There is / are 구문

[There is (are) + 명사]는 '~(들)이 있다'의 의미이고 there은 따로 해석하지 않는다.

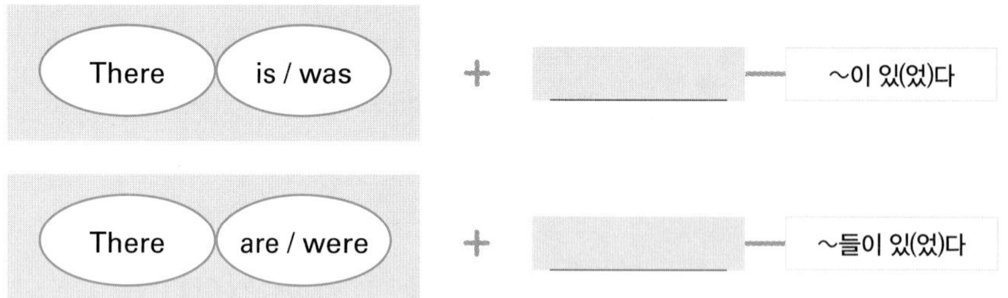

There is a book in my bag.

There are some birds in the tree.

There was a full moon in the sky.

GP 03 be동사 부정문

be동사 부정문은 be동사 다음에 not을 붙인다.

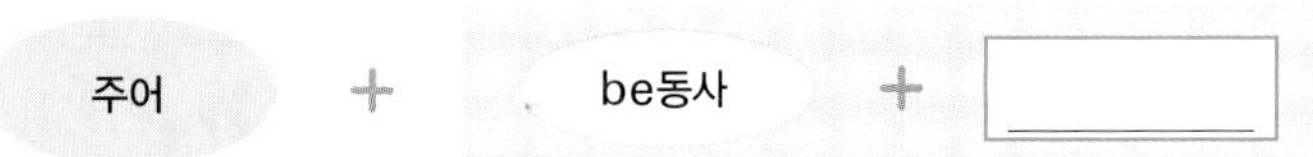

주어		be + not	줄임말	
현재형	I	______	I'm not	
	He / She / It	______	He's / She's / It's not	He / She / It isn't
	You / We / They	______	You're / We're / They're not	You / We / They aren't
과거형	I / He / She / It	______		I / He / She / It wasn't
	You / We / They	______		You / We / They weren't

I **am not** a bad student.
He **is not (isn't)** at home now.
Mary **was not (wasn't)** sleepy.
They **were not (weren't)** in the living room.

GP 04 be동사 의문문

be동사 의문문은 주어와 be동사의 순서를 바꾼다.

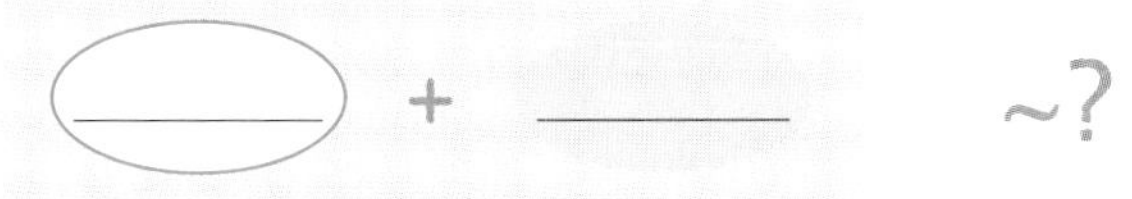

Be동사 + 주어 ~?	Yes, 주어 + be동사	No, 주어 + be동사n't
Am [Was] I ~?	Yes, you are [were].	No, you aren't [weren't].
Are [Were] you ~?	Yes, I am [was].	No, I'm not [wasn't].
Is [Was] he / she / it ~?	Yes, he / she / it is [was].	No, he / she / it isn't [wasn't].
Are [Were] we / you / they ~?	Yes, you / we / they are [were].	No, you / we / they / aren't [weren't].

A: **Are you** a middle school student? B: **Yes, I am. / No, I'm not.**
A: **Is Amy** ten years old? B: **Yes, she is. / No, she isn't.**
A: **Were they** in America last week? B: **Yes, they were. / No, they weren't.**

• Upgrade •

[There is / are] 부정문 **There is not** a book in my bag.
[There is / are] 의문문 **Are there** any birds in the tree? - **Yes, there are.**
- **No, there aren't.**

GP 05 인칭대명사

인칭대명사는 사람이나 사물을 대신 가리키는 말로 인칭, 수, 격에 따라 형태가 달라진다.

인칭	수	주격	소유격	목적격	소유대명사
		~은, 는 / ~이, 가	~의	~을 / 를	~의 것
1인칭	단수	I	________	________	________
	복수	we	________	________	________
2인칭	단수 (복수)	you	________	________	________
3인칭	단수	he	________	________	________
		she	________	________	________
		it	________	________	-
	복수	they	________	________	________

❶ **주격:** '~은, 는 / ~이, 가'로 해석하며, 문장에서 주어 역할을 한다.

She is an only daughter.

They are interested in cooking.

> **Tip**
> it's vs. its
> · It's cute. (It is의 줄임말)
> · We like its color. (it의 소유격)

❷ **소유격:** '~의'로 해석하며, [소유격 + 명사] 형태로 쓴다.

His car is very fancy.

Their shoes are very cheap.

❸ **목적격:** '~을, ~를, ~에게'로 해석하며, 문장에서 동사 또는 전치사의 목적어 역할을 한다.

Her friends like **her** very much. (동사의 목적어)

They go cycling with **me** every Sunday. (전치사의 목적어)

❹ **소유대명사:** '~의 것'이라고 해석하며, [소유격 + 명사]를 대신한다.

This cell phone is **mine**. (mine = my cell phone)

The bike is **hers**. (hers = her bike)

• Upgrade •

명사의 소유격과 소유대명사는 형태가 같으며 [명사's]로 나타낸다.

This is Jane's pen. (소유격)

This pen is Jane's. (소유대명사)

Unit 01 be동사·There is / are 구문

A ( ) 안에서 알맞은 것을 고르시오.

1 We (is, are) in the same club.

2 Yuna Kim (is, are) a gold medalist.

3 She's at the mall (now, yesterday).

4 Brad and I (am, are) classmates.

5 My friends (was, were) at the theater.

6 (They're, They were) hockey players last year.

7 There (is, are) many footprints on the snow.

8 Carrots (are, is) good for your health.

B 밑줄 친 be동사의 의미를 보기에서 골라 번호를 쓰시오.

보기 | ① ~이다 ② ~에 있다 ③ ~이었다 ④ ~에 있었다

1 My friends are over there. ( )

2 Allen and Cathy are lovely kids. ( )

3 They were in the building. ( )

4 I was very lucky last weekend. ( )

C 빈칸에 알맞은 be동사를 넣어 문장을 완성하시오.

1 He __________ a pilot in 2017.

2 The travelers __________ tired now.

3 Bill __________ a middle school student now.

4 They __________ scientists ten years ago.

5 There __________ no clouds in the sky yesterday.

6 Theme parks __________ crowded on Children's Day.

7 Tom and his family __________ in Japan now.

8 I __________ in front of the aquarium now.

9 The weather __________ perfect for surfing last week.

10 He __________ at the beach. He picked up some seashells.

D 빈칸에 there is 또는 there are를 넣어 문장을 완성하시오.

1 ______________________ an orange on the kitchen table.

2 ______________________ many wild animals in the jungle.

3 ______________________ four seasons in Korea.

4 ______________________ a bakery around the corner.

5 ______________________ many deserts in Africa.

6 ______________________ a book about American history.

E 우리말과 의미가 같도록 ( ) 안의 말을 배열하시오.

1 밖은 매우 어둡다. (is, very, it, dark)

→ ______________________________ outside.

2 단것은 우리의 치아에 나쁘다. (are, bad, things, sweet)

→ ______________________________ for our teeth.

3 Maggie는 지난 주말에 몹시 아팠다. (was, sick, Maggie, very)

→ ______________________________ last weekend.

4 수영장에는 두 명이 있었다. (two, were, people, there)

→ ______________________________ in the pool.

F 우리말과 의미가 같도록 ( ) 안의 말을 이용하여 문장을 완성하시오.

1 그는 지금 중국에 있다. (in China)

→ ________ ________ ________ ________ now.

2 그녀의 안경은 멋지다. (glasses)

→ ________ ________ ________ fashionable.

3 냉장고 안에 케이크가 하나 있었어. (a cake)

→ ________ ________ ________ ________ in the refrigerator.

4 올해는 토끼의 해이다. (this year)

→ ________ ________ ________ the year of the rabbit.

Unit 02 be동사 부정문과 의문문

A ( ) 안에서 알맞은 것을 고르시오.

1 Dolphins (aren't, isn't) fish.

2 (Is, Are) you tired now?

3 (Is, Are) Mr. Kim a farmer?

4 My sister (not is, is not) a nurse.

5 (Is, Are) fruits good for health?

6 (Am, Is) I late for the meeting?

7 They (wasn't, weren't) at school yesterday.

B 주어진 말을 이용하여 의문문을 완성하시오.

1 A: ____________ late? (we) B: No, we aren't.

2 A: ____________ absent? (he) B: Yes, he was.

3 A: ____________ ready for the trip? (you) B: No, I am not.

4 A: ____________ in England last week? (they) B: Yes, they were.

5 A: ____________ delicious? (the pudding) B: No, it isn't.

6 A: ____________ a singer? (your mom) B: Yes, she was.

7 A: ____________ models? (the boys) B: Yes, they are.

8 A: ____________ in the tree? (the birds) B: No, they weren't.

C 빈칸에 알맞은 be동사의 부정형을 넣어 문장을 완성하시오. (줄임말로 쓰기)

1 He ____________ at the Internet café now.

2 These dishes ____________ new. They are old.

3 This scarf ____________ mine. I found it in the restroom.

4 We ____________ in the science club. We don't like science.

5 Alice ____________ the class president last semester.

6 They ____________ great painters at that time.

7 William and I ____________ friends last year.

8 Your parents ____________ angry. They are just worried.

D 우리말과 의미가 같도록 ( ) 안의 말을 배열하시오.

1 그는 게으른 사람이 아니다. (person, isn't, lazy, he, a)

→ ______________________________.

2 너의 아빠는 회사에서 바쁘시니? (your father, busy, is)

→ ______________________________ at work?

3 Andrew는 매점에 없었다. (was, Andrew, not, at the cafeteria)

→ ______________________________.

4 너의 여동생은 학교에 결석했었니? (your sister, was, absent)

→ ______________________________ from school?

5 이 산에는 큰 나무들이 없다. (are, there, not, any tall trees)

→ ______________________________ on this mountain.

6 그들은 전 세계적으로 매우 유명하니? (are, very famous, they)

→ ______________________________ around the world?

E 우리말과 의미가 같도록 ( ) 안의 말을 이용하여 문장을 완성하시오. (부정문은 줄임말로 쓰기)

1 그녀는 개를 두려워하지 않는다. (afraid)

→ __________ __________ __________ of the dog.

2 토마토는 야채인가요? (a tomato)

→ __________ __________ __________ a vegetable?

3 엄마의 스프는 짜지 않았다. (salty)

→ My mom's soup __________ __________.

4 너의 부모님은 정원에 계시니? (parents)

→ __________ __________ __________ in the garden?

5 포도가 너무 시지는 않다. (too sour)

→ The grapes __________ __________ __________.

6 그 과학자는 실험실에 있었나요? (the scientist)

→ __________ __________ __________ in the lab?

Unit 03 인칭대명사

A ( ) 안에서 알맞은 것을 고르시오.

1 I need (you, your) help.

2 (Her, Hers) is not expensive.

3 My friend waited for (I, me).

4 I will introduce my sister. (It, She, He) is Emma.

5 I saw a book on the desk. Is (it, they) yours?

6 The dog is waiting for (it't, its) owner.

7 Look at Jim and his brothers. (He, They) are baseball players.

8 This man is the best entertainer. (It, He, They) is very popular.

B 다음 문장의 밑줄 친 부분의 정확한 의미를 고르시오.

	의미
1 It's my computer.	(그것은 ~이다, 그것의)
2 The bird built its nest.	(그것은 ~이다, 그것의)
3 Arthur loves his cousins.	(그의, 그의 것)
4 These red socks are not his.	(그의, 그의 것)
5 You are very special students.	(너는, 너희들은)
6 You are my best friend.	(너는, 너희들은)

C 밑줄 친 부분을 대신하는 알맞은 대명사를 ( )에 쓰시오.

1 Judy lost ( ) car key.

2 Tom baked bread. I tasted ( ).

3 These oranges are good. I like ( ).

4 Noah has a nickname. ( ) nickname is Magic Hands.

5 Mark is an only son. But ( ) has many friends.

6 This is your book, and that book is also ( ).

7 Jessy and Sara are in my group. ( ) are great students.

D 우리말과 의미가 같도록 ( ) 안의 말을 배열하시오.

1 너의 모자는 파란색이니? (is, your, blue, hat)

→ ______________________________?

2 이 신발들은 그의 것이다. (shoes, his, are, these)

→ ______________________________.

3 그 배우는 우리에게 미소 지었다. (smiled, at, the actor, us)

→ ______________________________.

4 그녀가 가장 좋아하는 음악은 재즈이다. (music, jazz, her, is, favorite)

→ ______________________________.

5 저 하얀색 햄스터는 그녀의 것이다. (is, hers, the white hamster)

→ ______________________________.

6 그 선수들은 그들의 운동복을 갈아입었다. (changed, their, the players, uniforms)

→ ______________________________.

E 우리말과 의미가 같도록 ( ) 안의 말을 이용하여 문장을 완성하시오.

1 우리는 그것들을 옮길 수 없다. (can't carry)

→ ______ ______ ______ ______.

2 그녀의 얼굴은 정말 빨개. (face, really red)

→ ______ ______ ______ ______ ______.

3 이 노래는 너와 나를 위한 것이야. (this song, for)

→ ______ ______ ______ ______ ______

______ ______.

4 내 것은 사물함 안에 있다. (in the locker)

→ ______ ______ ______ ______ ______.

5 그들은 우리와 함께 수영하러 갔다. (with, went swimming)

→ ______ ______ ______ ______ ______.

6 이 장난감들은 그들의 것이 아니다. (these toys)

→ ______ ______ ______ ______ ______.

Error Correction

▪ 밑줄 친 부분에 대한 설명을 체크하고 틀린 경우엔 바르게 고치시오. (맞으면 'O' 표시)

1	She are a designer. (→)	(2인칭 단수, 3인칭 단수) 주어 + be동사 현재형 (am, are, is)
2	They is at school now. (→)	(3인칭 단수, 3인칭 복수) 주어 + be동사 현재형 (am, are, is)
3	The test were very difficult. (→)	(3인칭 단수, 3인칭 복수) 주어 + be동사 과거형 (was, were)
4	Many boys was on the playground. (→)	(3인칭 단수, 3인칭 복수) 주어 + be동사 과거형 (was, were)
5	There is a book in my bag. (→)	There (is, are) + (단수명사, 복수명사)
6	He not is at home now. (→)	be동사의 부정문은 주어 + (not + be동사, be동사 + not)
7	Mary weren't sleepy. (→)	(3인칭 단수, 3인칭 복수) 주어 + be동사 과거형 부정 (wasn't, weren't)
8	Amy is ten years old? (→)	be동사의 의문문은 (주어 + be동사 ~?, Be동사 + 주어 ~?)
9	Are they in America last week? (→)	last week은 (현재, 과거) 표현이므로 (Are they ~?, Were they ~?)
10	He's car is very fancy. (→)	'(그는 ~이다, 그의) 차'이므로 (주격, 소유격)인 (he's, his)
11	Her friends like she very much. (→)	'(그녀가, 그녀를) 좋아한다'이므로 (주격, 목적격)인 (she, her)
12	They go cycling with me every Sunday. (→)	전치사 + (주격, 목적격)이므로 with + (I, me)
13	The bike is her. (→)	(그녀의, 그녀를, 그녀의 것)이므로 소유대명사 (her, hers)

Sentence Writing

▪ 주어진 단어를 알맞게 이용하여 우리말과 의미가 같도록 영작하시오.

1	a designer	그녀는 ~이다 / 디자이너 →
2	at school, now	그들은 있다 / 학교에 / 지금 →
3	the test, difficult	그 시험은 ~이었다 / 매우 어려운 →
4	many, on the playground	많은 소년들이 있었다 / 운동장에 →
5	there, a book, in my bag	~이 있다 / 책 한 권 / 내 가방 안에 →
6	at home, now	그는 있지 않다 / 집에 / 지금 →
7	sleepy	Mary는 ~이지 않았다 / 졸린 →
8	ten years old	~이니 / Amy는 / 10살? →
9	in America, last week	~있었니 / 그들은 / 미국에 / 지난주에? →
10	very fancy	그의 차는 / ~이다 / 아주 멋진 →
11	like, very much	그녀의 친구들이 / 좋아한다 / 그녀를 / 아주 많이 →
12	go cycling, with, every Sunday	그들은 사이클링 하러 간다 / 나와 함께 / 일요일마다 →
13	the bike	그 자전거는 / 그녀의 것이다 →

문법패턴 빈칸 채우기

GP 06 일반동사

일반동사는 be동사와 조동사를 제외한 모든 동사로 주어의 동작이나 상태를 나타낸다.

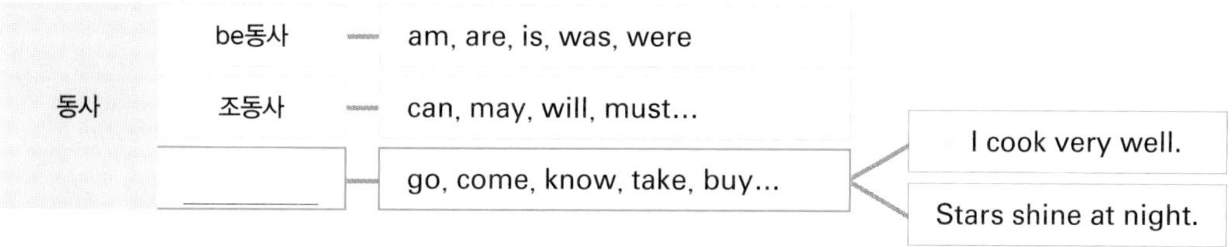

GP 07 일반동사 현재형

❶ 일반동사 현재형

3인칭 단수 주어를 제외하고는 동사원형을 쓰고 3인칭 단수 주어는 [동사원형 + -(e)s] 등의 형태로 쓴다.

1인칭 / 2인칭 / 복수 주어
주어
일반동사
I / We
You / They
일반동사 원형

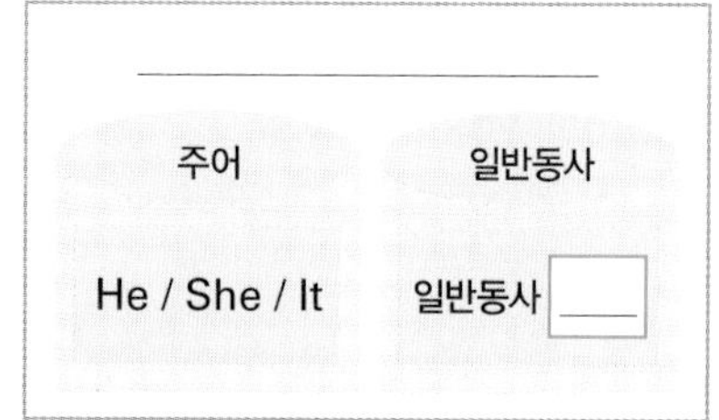

❷ 3인칭 단수 현재형 만드는 방법

규칙 변화	대부분의 동사	동사원형 + -s	walk → ________ love → ________	know → ________ make → ________
	-s, -ch, -sh, -o, -x로 끝나는 동사	동사원형 + -es	pass → ________ wash → ________	teach → ________ go → ________
	[자음 + y]로 끝나는 동사	y를 i로 바꾸고 + -es	study → ________ cry → ________	try → ________ copy → ________
불규칙 변화	have → has			

We **study** computer science at college.
He **watches** baseball games on TV.
The boy always **tries** his best.
Chris **has** many nicknames.

❸ 일반동사 현재형의 쓰임

현재의 사실, 반복적 습관, ____________ 등을 나타낸다.

My uncle **designs** cars. (현재의 사실)
I usually **go** to bed after eleven. (습관)
The sun **rises** in the east. (일반적 사실)

> **Tip**
> 현재형과 주로 쓰이는 부사(구)
> now, today, every day, every Sunday, on Sundays, once a week...

GP 08 일반동사 과거형

❶ 일반동사 과거형

주어의 인칭이나 수에 상관없이 동일한 형태로 쓰고 규칙 변화 동사(-ed)와 불규칙 변화 동사가 있다.

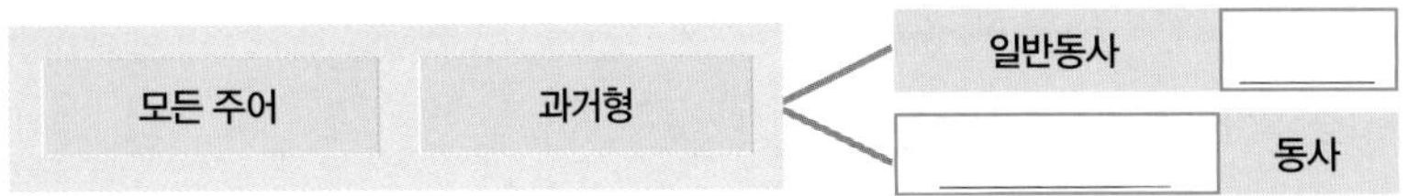

❷ 과거형 만드는 방법

ⓐ 규칙 변화

규칙 변화				
규칙 변화	대부분의 동사	동사원형 + -ed	walk → ______	help → ______
	e로 끝나는 동사	동사원형 + -d	love → ______	live → ______
	[자음 + y]로 끝나는 동사	y를 i로 바꾸고 + -ed	study → ______ cry → ______	try → ______ worry → ______
	[단모음 + 단자음]으로 끝나는 동사	자음을 한 번 더 쓰고 + -ed	stop → ______ drop → ______	plan → ______ clap → ______

Mammoths **lived** a long time ago.

We **played** basketball yesterday.

ⓑ 불규칙 변화

불규칙 변화				
불규칙 변화	형태가 다른 경우	begin → ______ find → ______ grow → ______ make → ______ speak → ______	come → ______ get → ______ have → ______ say → ______ tell → ______	do → ______ give → ______ hear → ______ sleep → ______ think → ______
	형태가 같은 경우	cut → **cut**	put → **put**	read → **read**

The festival **began** an hour ago.

We **heard** the news on the radio.

❸ 일반동사 과거형의 쓰임

과거의 동작이나 상태, 과거의 습관, ______________ 등을 나타낸다.

She **knew** David very well. (과거의 상태)

I **helped** Dad in the garden this morning. (과거의 동작)

Edison **invented** the light bulb in 1879. (역사적 사실)

> **Tip**
> 과거형과 주로 쓰이는 부사(구)
> yesterday, at that time, last night (week, year), [~ ago], [in + 과거 연도]...

GP 09 일반동사 부정문

일반동사 부정문은 [주어 + do / does / did + not + 동사원형] 형태이다.

❶ 일반동사 현재형 부정문

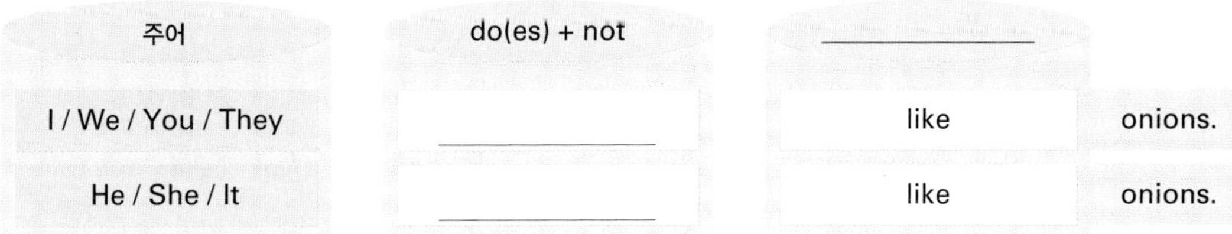

주어	do(es) + not	________	
I / We / You / They	________	like	onions.
He / She / It	________	like	onions.

I **do not study** on weekends.
Penguins **don't live** at the North Pole.
They **don't wear** blue jeans.

He **does not come** from Canada.
This plant **doesn't need** much sunlight.
Sam **doesn't like** black coffee.

❷ 일반동사 과거형 부정문

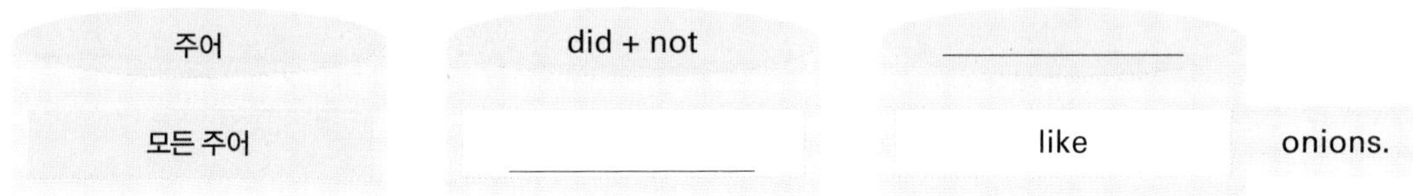

주어	did + not	________	
모든 주어	________	like	onions.

I **did not go** to his concert.
Olivia **did not take** the school bus.
It **didn't rain** heavily yesterday.
They **didn't use** the compass.
The boys **did not arrive** late.

• Upgrade •

동사 do의 부정문은 [주어 + do / does / did + not + do] 형태이다.
She **does** the dishes after dinner.
→ She **doesn't** the dishes after dinner. (X)
→ She ______________ the dishes after dinner. (O)

GP 10 일반동사 의문문

일반동사 의문문은 [Do / Does / Did + 주어 + 동사원형 ~?] 형태이다.

❶ 일반동사 현재형 의문문

의문문				대답			
	주어	일반동사		긍정 대답		부정 대답	
____	I / we / you / they	일반동사 ____	~?	Yes,	주어 + do.	No,	주어 + don't.
____	he / she / it	일반동사 ____	~?	Yes,	주어 + does.	No,	주어 + doesn't.

A: **Do you swim** well?

B: **Yes, I do.** / **No, I don't.**

A: **Do the stores close** on Sundays?

B: **Yes, they do.** / **No, they don't.**

A: **Does Michael walk** his dog every day?

B: **Yes,** ____________. / **No,** ____________.

❷ 일반동사 과거형 의문문

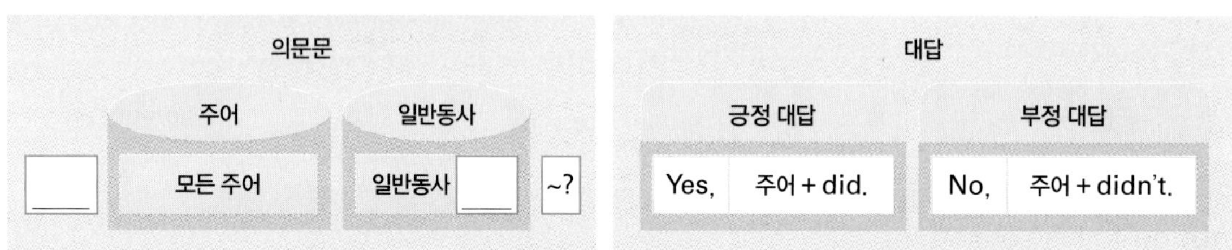

의문문				대답			
	주어	일반동사		긍정 대답		부정 대답	
____	모든 주어	일반동사 ____	~?	Yes,	주어 + did.	No,	주어 + didn't.

A: **Did your sister stay** in New York?

B: **Yes,** ____________. / **No,** ____________.

A: **Did Alex and you catch** a big fish?

B: **Yes, we did.** / **No, we didn't.**

• Upgrade •

[Do you ~?], [Do I ~?], [Do we ~?] 의문문의 대답은 주어의 형태가 바뀐다.

A: Do you have a pet? B: Yes, I (we) do. / No, I (we) don't.

A: Do I (we) walk to school? B: Yes, you (we) do. / No, you (we) don't.

Unit 04 일반동사와 일반동사 현재형

A ( ) 안에서 알맞은 것을 고르시오.

1 Bobby (eats, eat) lunch at two o'clock.

2 She often (forget, forgets) her address.

3 The soldiers (help, helps) the citizens.

4 John (washs, washes) his hands.

5 People (enjoy, enjoys) winter sports.

6 The river (pass, passes) under the bridge.

7 Mr. Morgan (visits, visites) Busan every summer.

8 The first class (finish, finishes) at 9:50 a.m.

B 주어진 동사의 현재형을 써서 문장을 완성하시오.

1 Sally and Jim ____________________ math. (like)

2 Some birds ____________________ south in winter. (fly)

3 The ladies often ____________________ tea together. (drink)

4 Korea ____________________ four seasons. (have)

5 James ____________________ his teeth hard. (brush)

6 He ____________________ the laundry every Saturday. (do)

7 We sometimes ____________________ the museum. (visit)

8 Lucy often ____________________ detective stories. (read)

C 보기에서 알맞은 동사를 골라 현재형으로 써서 문장을 완성하시오. (한 번씩만 사용)

보기 | do have set close dry

1 Every wall ____________________ an ear.

2 The sun ____________________ in the west.

3 Dan ____________________ his homework after dinner.

4 Becky ____________________ her hair after a shower.

5 The bank ____________________ at five o'clock.

D **우리말과 의미가 같도록 ( ) 안의 말을 배열하시오.**

1 그는 토요일마다 요리한다. (cooks, on, he, Saturdays)

→ ______________________________.

2 이 집은 창문이 많다. (many windows, this house, has)

→ ______________________________.

3 스코틀랜드에서는 남자들이 치마를 입는다. (skirts, wear, in, men, Scotland)

→ ______________________________.

4 그녀는 세 가지의 언어를 말한다. (three, speaks, languages, she)

→ ______________________________.

5 일찍 일어나는 새가 벌레를 잡는다. (catches, the early bird, the worm)

→ ______________________________.

6 나의 남동생은 하루에 12시간 잠잔다. (brother, sleeps, my, twelve hours)

→ ______________________________ a day.

E **우리말과 의미가 같도록 ( ) 안의 말을 이용하여 문장을 완성하시오**

1 나는 롤러스케이트를 원한다. (want roller skates)

→ ________ ________ ________ ________.

2 그들은 학교에 걸어간다. (walk to school)

→ ________ ________ ________ ________.

3 그녀는 매일 밤 음악을 듣는다. (listen to music)

→ ________ ________ ________ ________ every night.

4 Kevin은 많은 나라를 비행한다. (fly to)

→ ________ ________ ________ many countries.

5 나의 엄마는 매일 손빨래를 하신다. (wash clothes)

→ ________ ________ ________ ________ by hand every day.

6 동물원 동물들은 쉽게 먹이를 얻는다. (get food)

→ ________ ________ easily ________ ________.

Unit 05 일반동사 과거형

A ( ) 안에서 알맞은 것을 고르시오.

1 She (order, ordered) some pizza.

2 The hunters (caught, catched) a rabbit.

3 The sad news (breaked, broke) his heart.

4 The tourists (buyed, bought) oranges.

5 She (choosed, chose) this pink dress.

6 Jenny (red, read) the articles about him.

7 She (invitted, invited) me to the gallery.

8 Students (gave, gived) water to the flowers.

B 주어진 동사의 과거형을 써서 문장을 완성하시오.

1 It ____________________ to snow. (begin)

2 He ____________________ fast food often. (eat)

3 I ____________________ the audition. (pass)

4 We ____________________ a trip to Alaska. (plan)

5 She ____________________ a sandwich for dinner. (have)

6 We ____________________ school at three o'clock. (leave)

7 She ____________________ a movie last night. (watch)

8 Jane ____________________ the cake into four pieces. (cut)

C 보기에서 알맞은 동사를 골라 과거형으로 써서 문장을 완성하시오. (한 번씩만 사용)

보기 | take sell read sing put

1 I ____________________ a song for the baby.

2 We ____________________ our house last week.

3 Mike ____________________ the text message.

4 She ____________________ her hands into her pockets.

5 My family ____________________ our dog to the beach.

D

우리말과 의미가 같도록 ( ) 안의 말을 배열하시오.

1 우리 가족은 벼룩시장에서 쇼핑을 했다. (family, shopped, my)

→ ______________________________ at the flea market.

2 그녀는 2년 전에 대만에 갔었다. (she, to, Taiwan, went)

→ ______________________________ two years ago.

3 어젯밤에 비가 멈췄다. (it, raining, stopped)

→ ______________________________ last night.

4 그는 야생동물 사진을 찍었다. (pictures, he, took)

→ ______________________________ of wild animals.

5 나는 공항에서 엄마를 위해 향수를 샀다. (mom, for, bought, I, perfume, my)

→ ______________________________ at the airport.

6 우리는 여름휴가에 대해 이야기했다. (about, summer vacation, talked, we)

→ ______________________________.

E

우리말과 의미가 같도록 ( ) 안의 말을 이용하여 문장을 완성하시오.

1 그는 친구들에게 거짓말을 했다. (tell a lie)

→ ________ ________ ________ ________ to his friends.

2 그녀는 커피에 설탕을 조금 넣었다. (put some sugar)

→ ________ ________ ________ ________ in her coffee.

3 Danny는 6시에 알람을 맞추었다. (set the alarm)

→ ________ ________ ________ ________ for six o'clock.

4 나는 바닥에 포크를 떨어뜨렸다. (drop my fork)

→ ________ ________ ________ ________ on the floor.

5 내 친구는 어제 미국으로 떠났다. (leave for America)

→ ________ ________ ________ ________ ________ yesterday.

6 그녀는 발표 동안 많은 물을 마셨다. (drink a lot of water)

→ ________ ________ ________ ________ ________ ________ during the presentation.

Unit 06 일반동사 부정문

A ( ) 안에서 알맞은 것을 고르시오.

1 Brian doesn't (like, likes) cats.

2 She didn't (hit, hits) anyone.

3 We (don't, doesn't) want war.

4 My friend (doesn't, didn't) study Chinese last year.

5 They (aren't, don't) like horror movies.

6 My son (don't, doesn't) read books in English.

7 It (don't, doesn't) snow in New Zealand.

8 I didn't (know, knew) his phone number.

9 The ice cream (don't, doesn't) taste sweet.

10 The company (doesn't, didn't) send the package yesterday.

B 주어진 문장을 부정문으로 바꿔 문장을 완성하시오. (줄임말로 쓰기)

1 We enjoyed the musical.

→ ______________________________ the musical.

2 The students watch TV at school.

→ ______________________________ TV at school.

3 My daughter likes spicy food.

→ ______________________________ spicy food.

4 I do my homework at night.

→ ______________________________ my homework at night.

5 My mom did the laundry last night.

→ ______________________________ the laundry last night.

6 Sandra goes jogging in the morning.

→ ______________________________ in the morning.

7 Bill lives in New York.

→ ______________________________ in New York.

C 보기에서 동사를 골라 부정형을 써서 문장을 완성하시오. (한 번씩만 사용)

보기 |	rain	hear	do	like

1 Paula ________________ spicy food.

2 Michael ________________ the dishes last night.

3 My grandmother ________________ well. She needs help.

4 It ________________ but was sunny yesterday.

D 우리말과 의미가 같도록 ( ) 안의 말을 배열하시오.

1 그는 음악을 즐기지 않아. (music, he, enjoy, doesn't)

→ ________________________________.

2 그녀의 개는 짖지를 않아. (bark, her dog, doesn't)

→ ________________________________.

3 그들은 그 셔틀버스를 타고 학교에 가지 않아. (the shuttle bus, they, take, don't)

→ ________________________________ to school.

4 선생님은 오늘 문자 메시지를 확인하지 않으셨다. (check, text messages, didn't, his)

→ My teacher ________________________________ today.

E 우리말과 의미가 같도록 ( ) 안의 말을 이용하여 문장을 완성하시오.

1 그는 월요일에는 테니스를 치지 않는다. (play tennis)

→ ________ ________ ________ ________ on Mondays.

2 채식주의자들은 고기를 먹지 않는다. (eat meat)

→ Vegetarians ________ ________ ________.

3 그녀는 오늘 아침 주스를 마시지 않았다. (drink juice)

→ ________ ________ ________ ________ this morning.

4 나는 가게에서 아무것도 사지 않았다. (buy anything)

→ ________ ________ ________ ________ at the store.

Unit 07 일반동사 의문문

A ( ) 안에서 알맞은 것을 고르시오.

1 Did you (write, wrote) this book?

2 (Does, Do) Jacob play the flute?

3 (Does, Do) your brothers play soccer?

4 Did the boy (sets, set) up the tent?

5 (Do, Does) Justin and his cousin live together?

6 (Did, Does) the birds sing this morning?

7 (Do, Does) your sister walk to school?

B 주어진 대답에 알맞은 의문문을 완성하시오.

1 A: ______________ ______________ taste good?

B: No, it doesn't.

2 A: ______________ ______________ use sunblock?

B: Yes, they did.

3 A: ______________ ______________ love his mom's food?

B: Yes, he does.

4 A: ______________ ______________ exercise this morning?

B: No, they didn't.

C 주어진 동사를 이용하여 의문문을 완성하시오.

1 A: ______________ he ______________ fruit? (like)

B: Yes, he does.

2 A: ______________ we ______________ two exams? (have)

B: No, we don't.

3 A: ______________ you ______________ yoga today? (do)

B: Yes, I did.

4 A: ______________ your family ______________ to Spain? (travel)

B: No, we didn't.

D 우리말과 의미가 같도록 ( ) 안의 말을 배열하시오.

1 너는 너의 방을 청소했니? (room, did, clean, your, you)

→ ______________________________?

2 너는 자기 전에 샤워하니? (take, you, a shower, do)

→ ______________________________ before bed?

3 소포가 오늘 도착했나요? (arrive, did, the parcel)

→ ______________________________ today?

4 그녀는 내 이름을 기억하니? (she, does, my, name, remember)

→ ______________________________?

5 그가 이 학교를 디자인했나요? (design, he, did, this school)

→ ______________________________?

6 Diana는 빵을 버터와 같이 먹나요? (bread, have, Diana, does)

→ ______________________________ with butter?

E 우리말과 의미가 같도록 ( ) 안의 말을 이용하여 문장을 완성하시오.

1 너는 나를 신뢰하니? (trust)

→ ________ ________ ________ me?

2 너는 영어 알파벳을 외웠니? (memorize)

→ ________ ________ ________ the English alphabet?

3 Nick은 애완동물을 기르니? (have a pet)

→ ________ ________ ________ ________ ________?

4 그들은 일찍 자러 가니? (go to bed, early)

→ ________ ________ ________ ________ ________

________?

5 너는 너의 우산을 가져왔니? (bring, umbrella)

→ ________ ________ ________ ________ ________?

6 너의 오빠는 여자친구가 있니? (have)

→ ________ ________ ________ ________ a girlfriend?

Error Correction

Chapter 02
일반동사

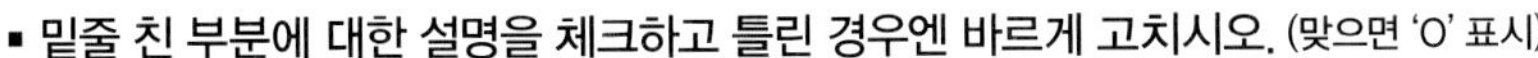

▪ 밑줄 친 부분에 대한 설명을 체크하고 틀린 경우엔 바르게 고치시오. (맞으면 'O' 표시)

1 I cooks very well.
(→)

주어 + 일반동사 현재형
(1인칭, 3인칭) 단수 (동사원형, 동사원형 + -(e)s)

2 He watchs baseball games on TV.
(→)

3인칭 단수 주어 + -ch로 끝나는 현재형 동사
(동사원형 + -s, 동사원형 + -es)

3 The boy always trys his best.
(→)

3인칭 단수 주어 + [자음 + y]로 끝나는 현재형 동사
(y 뒤에 -es, y 대신 -ies)

4 Chris has many nicknames.
(→)

주어 + 일반동사 현재형
(1인칭, 3인칭) 단수 + (haves, has)

5 We plaied basketball yesterday.
(→)

play의 과거형은 (규칙, 불규칙) 변화
[모음 + y]로 끝나므로 (y 뒤에 -ed, y 대신 -ied)

6 The festival begined an hour ago.
(→)

begin의 과거형은 (동사원형 + -ed, 불규칙 변화)

7 Edison invents the light bulb in 1879.
(→)

과거표현과 쓰면 동사 (현재형, 과거형)을 쓰고
invent의 과거형은 (동사원형 + -ed, 불규칙 변화)

8 They wear not blue jeans.
(→)

현재형 부정문은
(동사원형 + not, do(es)n't + 동사원형)

9 Sam don't like black coffee.
(→)

3인칭 단수 주어 + 현재형 부정문
(don't, doesn't) + 동사원형

10 It didn't rained heavily yesterday.
(→)

모든 인칭 주어 + 과거형 부정문
didn't + (과거형, 동사원형)

11 Swim you well? No, I don't.
(→)

현재형 의문문은
(일반동사 + 주어 ~?, Do(es) + 주어 + 동사원형 ~?)

12 Do Michael walk his dog every day?
(→)

3인칭 단수 주어 현재형 의문문은
(Do, Does) + 주어 + 동사원형 ~?

13 Did your sister stayed in New York?
(→)

과거형 의문문은
Did + 주어 + (동사 과거형, 동사원형) ~?

Sentence writing

▪ 주어진 단어를 알맞게 이용하여 우리말과 의미가 같도록 영작하시오.

1	cook, very well	나는 / 요리한다 / 매우 잘 →
2	watch, baseball games, on TV	그는 / 본다 / 야구경기를 / TV로 →
3	try, his best	그 소년은 / 언제나 애쓴다(다한다) / 그의 최선을 →
4	many nicknames	Chris는 / 가지고 있다 / 많은 별명을 →
5	play, basketball	우리는 / (놀이) 했다 / 농구를 / 어제 →
6	the festival, begin	축제는 / 시작했다 / 한 시간 전에 →
7	invent, the light bulb	Edison은 / 발명했다 / 전구를 / 1879년에 →
8	wear, blue jeans	그들은 / 입지 않는다 / 청바지를 →
9	like, black coffee	Sam은 / 좋아하지 않는다 / 블랙커피를 →
10	it, rain, heavily	비가 내리지 않았다 / 심하게 / 어제 →
11	swim, well	너는 ~하니 / 잘 수영하다? 아니 / 나는 못하다 →
12	walk, his dog	Michael은 ~하니 / 산책시키다 / 그의 개를 / 매일? →
13	your sister, stay	너의 언니는 ~했니 / 머무르다 / New York에? →

문법패턴 빈칸 채우기

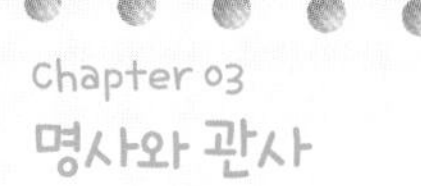

GP 11 셀 수 있는 명사

❶ **셀 수 있는 명사:** 단수형과 복수형이 있고, 단수형 앞에는 부정관사 a / an을 쓴다.

셀 수 있는 명사	단수형	________을 쓴다	a boy
	복수형	________를 붙인다	boys

She wants **a** new **bag**.　　She wants ten **bags**.

❷ 셀 수 있는 명사의 복수형

규칙 변화	대부분의 명사	명사 + -s	desks	trees	hours	apples
	-s, -sh, -ch, -x, -o로 끝나는 명사	명사 + -es	buses tomatoes	benches (예외) *photos	boxes	potatoes *pianos
	[자음 + y]로 끝나는 명사	y를 i로 바꾸고 + -es	city → ________ lady → ________		baby → ________ party → ________	
	-f, -fe로 끝나는 명사	f(e)를 v로 바꾸고 + -es	leaf → ________ wolf → ________		knife → ________ (예외) *roof → ________	
불규칙 변화	단수와 복수가 같은 경우	sheep → **sheep**	deer → **deer**		fish → **fish**	
	모음이 달라지는 경우	man → **men**	foot → ________		woman → **women**	
	그 외의 경우	child → **children**	mouse → ________			

GP 12 셀 수 없는 명사

❶ **셀 수 없는 명사:** 단수형만 있고 부정관사 a / an을 쓰지 않는다.

셀 수 없는 명사	단수형	________을 쓰지 않는다	~~a~~ sugar

She has very long **hair**.　　We had a lot of **fun** at the party.

❷ **물질명사의 수량 표현:** 물질명사는 단위 명사를 이용하여 양을 나타내고, 단위 명사는 복수형으로 쓸 수 있다.

	단위명사				단위명사		
a	________	of	water, juice, milk	a	cup	of	coffee, tea
a	________	of	paper, cake, pizza	a	slice	of	cheese, bread
a	________	of	water, juice, ink	a	loaf	of	bread

Can you bring me **a glass of water**?
They ordered **three cups of coffee**.

• Upgrade •

한 쌍을 이루는 명사(pants, shoes…)는 항상 복수형으로 쓰고, [____________] 형태로 수를 나타낸다.
I bought **a pair of / two pairs of shoes** yesterday.

GP 13 관사

관사는 명사 앞에서 명사의 의미와 성격을 나타내는 말로 부정관사와 정관사가 있다.

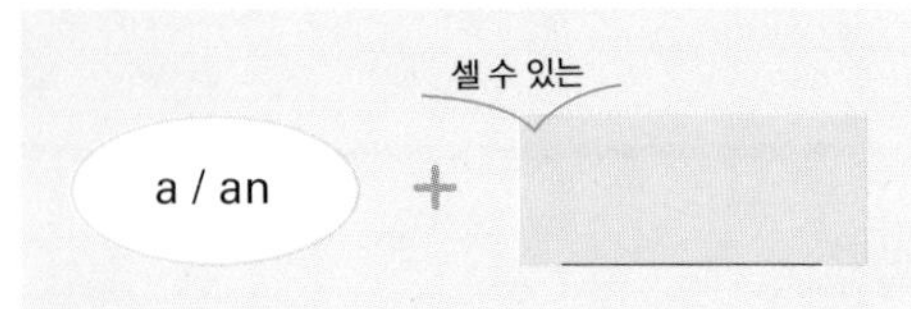

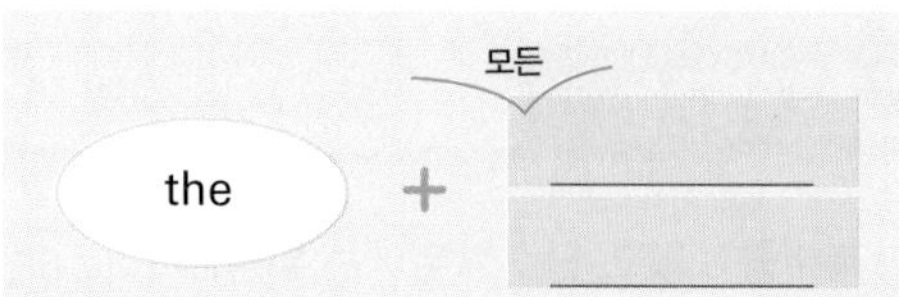

❶ 부정관사 a / an

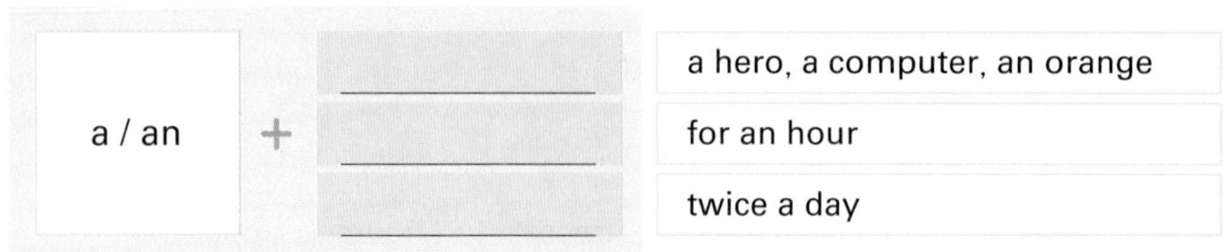

a / an
+
a hero, a computer, an orange
for an hour
twice a day

I usually eat **an apple** in the morning.
My sister reads two books **a week**.

> **Tip**
> a vs. an
> a는 자음으로 발음되는 단어 앞에 쓰고
> an은 모음으로 발음되는 단어 앞에 쓴다.
> · a university · an hour

❷ 정관사 the

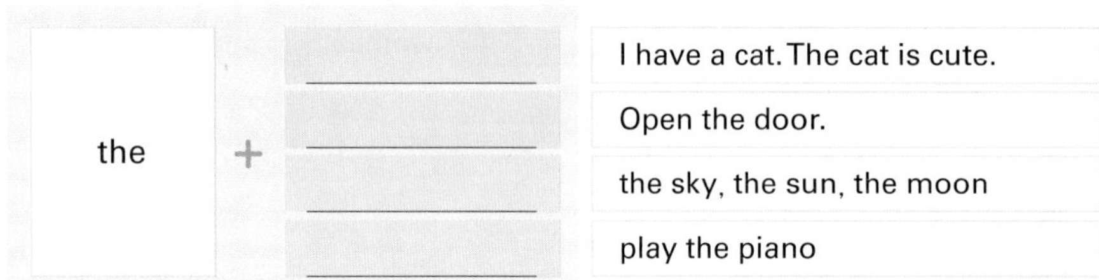

the
+
I have a cat. The cat is cute.
Open the door.
the sky, the sun, the moon
play the piano

She has a pen. **The pen** is very useful.
Can you pass me **the salt**?
The Earth is not a star but a planet.
I usually play **the violin** after school.

❸ 관사를 쓰지 않는 경우

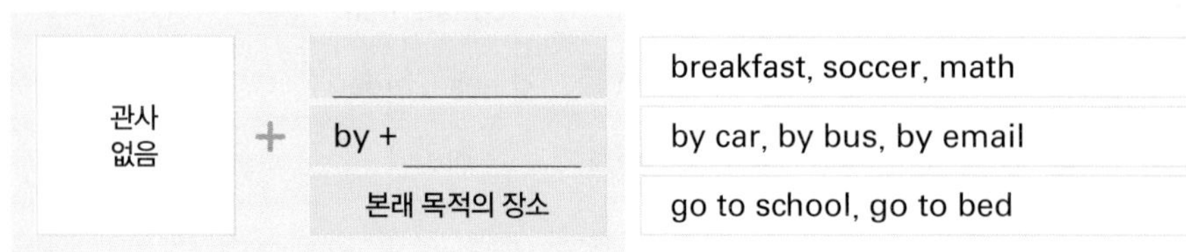

관사
없음
+
by +
본래 목적의 장소
breakfast, soccer, math
by car, by bus, by email
go to school, go to bed

John's favorite sport is **soccer**.
I traveled across Europe **by bus**.
My brother **goes to bed** before midnight.

Unit 08 셀 수 있는 명사와 셀 수 없는 명사

A 다음 명사의 복수형을 쓰시오.

1 bus → ____________

2 city → ____________

3 mouse → ____________

4 foot → ____________

5 tooth → ____________

6 watch → ____________

7 baby → ____________

8 woman → ____________

9 child → ____________

10 piano → ____________

11 potato → ____________

12 bench → ____________

13 roof → ____________

14 leaf → ____________

15 dish → ____________

16 thief → ____________

B ( ) 안에서 알맞은 것을 고르시오.

1 Are there (leafs, leaves) in the yard?

2 The children returned to (his, their) home.

3 I spilled some (milk, milks) on the floor.

4 My mom baked three loaves of (bread, breads).

5 The (waters are, water is) not clean in this river.

6 My teacher gives us a lot of (homework, homeworks).

7 Alice wrote some (stories, storys) about black people.

8 Mr. Smith bought two (wines, bottles of wine) for the Christmas party.

C ( ) 안의 말을 이용하여 빈칸을 채우시오.

1 Brush your ____________ after meals. (tooth)

2 He found two ____________ in the corner. (mouse)

3 There are many ____________ in the field. (sheep)

4 Bring me two ____________ and a frying pan. (knife)

5 The rose is a symbol of ____________. (love)

6 I don't have ____________ about the project. (information)

D 보기와 ( ) 안의 말을 이용하여 문장을 완성하시오. (한 번씩만 사용)

보기	loaf	piece	cup	bottle

1 ________ ________ ________ ________ ________ will be helpful. (a, hot tea)

2 She gave me ________ ________ ________ ________. (two, cake)

3 Ellen didn't buy ________ ________ ________ ________. (a, water)

4 I bought ________ ________ ________ ________ for breakfast. (three, bread)

E 우리말과 의미가 같도록 ( ) 안의 말을 배열하시오.

1 우리 가족들은 생선을 좋아하지 않는다. (my family, like, doesn't, fish)

→ ________________________________.

2 내 남동생은 멋진 바지를 원한다. (pants, nice, wants, my brother)

→ ________________________________.

3 공원에 많은 사람들이 있었다. (were, many, people, there)

→ ________________________________ at the park.

4 저는 종이 두 장이 필요합니다. (I, pieces, paper, two, of, need)

→ ________________________________.

5 아이들은 한국의 미래입니다. (are, the future, children, of Korea)

→ ________________________________.

F 우리말과 의미가 같도록 ( ) 안의 말을 이용하여 문장을 완성하시오.

1 신사 숙녀 여러분, 들어주셔서 감사합니다. (lady, gentleman)

→ ________ ________ ________, thank you for listening.

2 그 지붕들은 눈으로 덮여 있다. (the roof, be covered)

→ ________ ________ ________ ________ with snow.

3 나의 아빠는 운전할 때 선글라스를 쓴다. (wear, sunglasses)

→ ________ ________ ________ ________ when he drives.

4 볶음밥 위에 치즈 한 장을 올려 주세요. (put, cheese)

→ Please ________ ________ ________ ________ ________ on the fried rice.

5 우리에게 오렌지 주스 다섯 잔을 갖다 주시겠어요? (orange juice)

→ Could you bring us ________ ________ ________ ________ ________?

Unit 09 관사

A ( ) 안에서 알맞은 것을 고르시오. (x: 관사 필요 없음)

1 My favorite subject was (a, x) math.

2 He cleans his room once (a, the) day.

3 She goes to (a, the, x) school at 8:00.

4 I watched TV for (a, an) hour.

5 She will play (the, x) guitar at the school festival.

6 Dylan went to (a, the, x) bed early last night.

7 Neil Armstrong was the first man to land on (the, x) moon.

B 보기에서 알맞은 관사를 골라 ( ) 안에 쓰시오.

보기 |	a	an	the	x(관사 필요 없음)

1 I play ( ) soccer every day.

2 How many days are there in ( ) year?

3 Call 119 for ( ) ambulance.

4 It took 20 minutes by ( ) taxi.

5 I like ( ) English the most.

6 Washington, D.C. is ( ) capital of the United States.

C ( ) 안의 말을 이용하여 알맞은 대화를 완성하시오.

1 A: How long does it take?
B: It takes about ____________. (a, hour)

2 A: What do you do for exercise?
B: I do yoga ____________. (twice, week)

3 A: How do you go home?
B: I usually go home ____________. (by, subway)

4 A: Did you see a cat with yellow spots?
B: I saw ____________ in the garden. (cat)

D 우리말과 의미가 같도록 ( ) 안의 말을 배열하시오.

1 그 학생들은 쓰레기를 주웠다. (the, up, students, picked)

→ ______________________________ the trash.

2 지우개 하나 빌릴 수 있을까요? (eraser, borrow, an, I, can)

→ ______________________________?

3 바다에 큰 파도가 친다. (the, waves, sea, big, in)

→ There are ______________________________.

4 우리는 걸어서 학교에 다닌다. (on, school, we, to, foot, go)

→ ______________________________.

5 이 문서를 나에게 이메일로 보내 주세요. (by, send, the document, me, e-mail)

→ ______________________________.

6 Jim은 한 달에 4번 영화관에 간다. (goes, four times, a month, to the theater)

→ Jim ______________________________.

E 우리말과 의미가 같도록 ( ) 안의 말을 이용하여 문장을 완성하시오.

1 Tom은 어제 늦게 자러 갔다. (go)

→ Tom __________ __________ __________ late yesterday.

2 악어 한 마리가 바위 위에 있다. (there, alligator)

→ __________ __________ __________ __________ on the rock.

3 나는 그 손님들을 알지 못한다. (guest)

→ I don't know __________ __________.

4 그녀는 일 년에 한 번 Toronto를 방문했다. (once)

→ She visited Toronto __________ __________ __________.

5 내 여동생은 종종 플루트를 연주한다. (flute)

→ My sister often plays __________ __________.

6 그는 차가 한 대 있는데, 그 차는 매우 낡았다. (car)

→ He has __________ __________, and __________ __________ is very old.

Error Correction

▪ 밑줄 친 부분에 대한 설명을 체크하고 틀린 경우엔 바르게 고치시오. (맞으면 'O' 표시)

1 She wants new bag.
(→)
bag은 셀 수 (있는, 없는) 명사이고
앞에 a / an을 (쓴다, 쓰지 않는다)

2 She wants ten bags.
(→)
셀 수 있는 명사는 복수형이 (있고, 없고)
bag의 복수형은 (bags, bages)

3 We had a lot of funs at the party.
(→)
fun은 셀 수 (있는, 없는) 명사이고
복수형이 (있다, 없다)

4 Can you bring me a water?
(→)
물질명사 water는 셀 수 (있고, 없고)
수량 표현은 (a, a glass of) + water

5 They ordered three cup of coffee.
(→)
물질명사 coffee는 셀 수 (있고, 없고)
수량 표현은 (three, three cups of) + coffee

6 I usually eat a apple in the morning.
(→)
(a, an) + (자음 발음 단어, 모음 발음 단어)

7 My sister reads two books a week.
(→)
관사 + 명사
(a, the) (명사마다, 유일한 것)

8 She has a pen. A pen is very useful.
(→)
관사 + 명사
(a, the) (정해지지 않은 것, 이미 언급된 것)

9 Can you pass me a salt?
(→)
관사 + 명사
(a, the) (숫자 하나, 서로 알고 있는 것)

10 The Earth is not a star but a planet.
(→)
관사 + 명사
(a, the) (명사마다, 유일한 것)

11 I usually play violin after school.
(→)
관사 + 명사
(X, the) (운동 경기, 악기 이름)

12 John's favorite sport is the soccer.
(→)
관사 + 명사
(없음, the) (운동 경기, 악기 이름)

13 I traveled across Europe by the bus.
(→)
관사 + 명사
(없음, the) (교통수단, 본래 목적의 장소)

Sentence Writing

■ 주어진 단어를 알맞게 이용하여 우리말과 의미가 같도록 영작하시오.

1	want, new, bag	그녀는 / 원한다 / 새 가방을 →
2	want, bag	그녀는 / 원한다 / 가방 열 개를 →
3	have, a lot of, fun	우리는 / 가졌다 / 많은 즐거움을 / 파티에서 →
4	can, bring, glass	갖다 줄래요 / 나에게 / 물 한 잔을? →
5	order, cup, coffee	그들은 / 주문했다 / 커피 세 잔을 →
6	apple, morning	나는 / 보통 먹는다 / 사과 하나를 / 아침에 →
7	read, week	나의 여동생은 / 읽는다 / 책 두 권을 / 일주일에 →
8	pen, very useful	그녀는 / 가지고 있다 / 펜 하나를 / 그 펜은 ~이다 / 매우 유용한 →
9	can, pass, salt	건네줄래요 / 나에게 / 그 소금을? →
10	Earth, star, planet	지구는 / 항성이 아니다 / 그러나 행성이다 →
11	play, violin, after	나는 / 보통 연주한다 / 바이올린을 / 방과 후에 →
12	favorite, sport	John의 / 가장 좋아하는 스포츠는 / ~이다 / 축구 →
13	travel, across Europe	나는 / 여행했다 / 유럽을 / 버스로 →

문법패턴 빈칸 채우기

GP 14 this (these), that (those)

❶ this: 상대적으로 가까이 있는 사람이나 사물을 가리키고 복수형은 these이다.

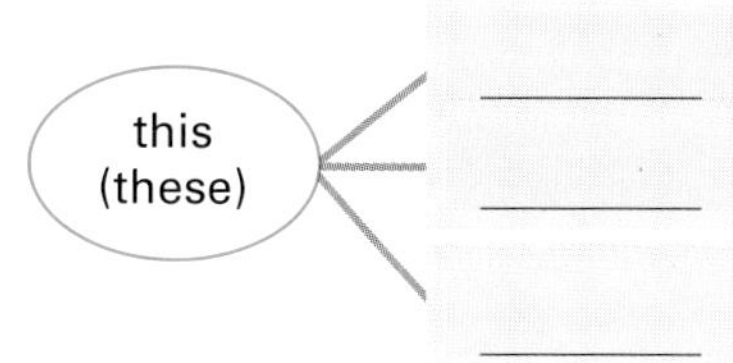

______ ☆ This is my favorite watch.

______ These are my new friends.

______ ☆ These houses are very old.

❷ that: 상대적으로 멀리 있는 사람이나 사물을 가리키고 복수형은 those이다.

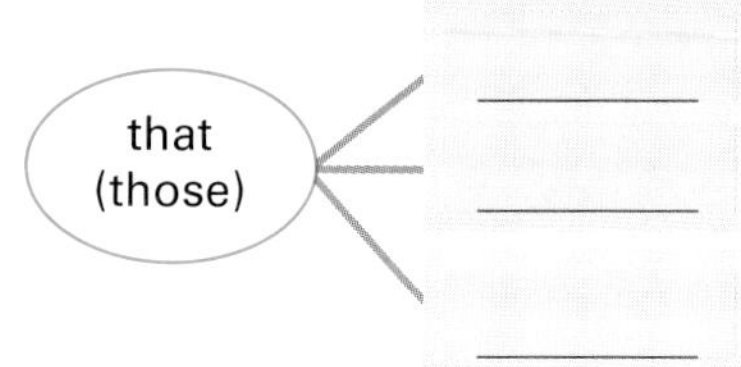

______ ☆ That is your birthday gift.

______ Are those your children?

______ ☆ Those trees don't have leaves.

• Upgrade •

this의 다른 쓰임

❶ 사람을 소개할 때

A: Allen, **this** is my sister Cathy. B: Nice to meet you, Cathy.

❷ 전화를 건 사람을 가리킬 때

Hi. **This** is Allen. Can I speak to Cathy?

GP 15 비인칭 주어 it

❶ 비인칭 주어 it: 시간, 요일, 날짜, 날씨, 거리, 명암 등을 나타낼 때 쓰는 it을 가리키고 '그것'이라고 해석하지 않는다.

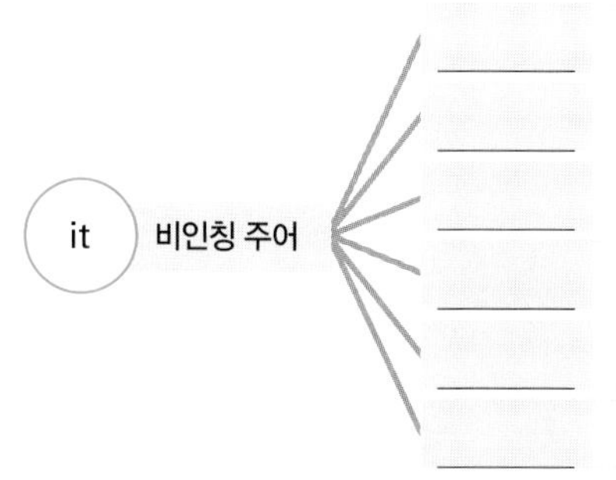

______ ☆ It's seven o'clock.

______ It is Friday.

______ It is August 3.

______ It is very hot outside.

______ It's about ten miles from here.

______ It is very bright out there.

❷ 대명사 it: 앞에 언급한 특정한 명사를 가리키며, '그것'으로 해석한다.

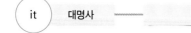

it 대명사 —— ______ ☆ She took this picture. I love it.

• Upgrade •

대명사 one: 앞에 언급한 명사와 같은 종류의 어떤 것을 가리킨다.

I need an eraser. Do you have **one**?

GP 16 some, any

some과 any는 '약간, 조금'의 의미로 사람이나 사물의 수와 양을 나타낸다.

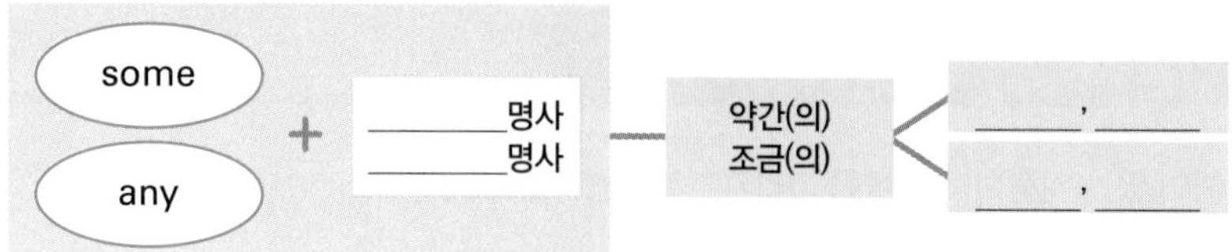

❶ some

I have **some** questions. (긍정문)

Will you have **some** chocolate? (권유문)

❷ any

I don't have **any** questions. (부정문)

Do you have **any** idea? (의문문)

GP 17 all, every, each

all과 every는 '모든'을 each는 '각각의'를 의미하고 막연한 전체를 대상으로 한다.

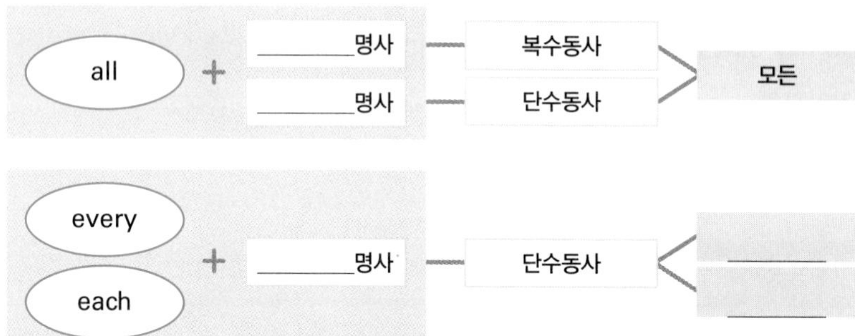

❶ all

All the boys *are* standing in the hall.

All the money *is* in a safe place.

❷ each

Each boy *has* his own cell phone.

❸ every

Every student *is* wearing shorts.

Unit 10 this (these), that (those)·비인칭 주어 it

A ( ) 안에서 알맞은 것을 고르시오.

1 Look! Is (that, those) your key?

2 James, (she, this, that) is my sister Lucy.

3 (This is, It's) April Fools' Day today.

4 (That, It) rains a lot in the summer in Korea.

5 I lost my book. I am looking for (it, this).

6 Did you make (this, these) hair bands?

7 I like (this, that) hat over there.

B 밑줄 친 it이 의미하는 것을 보기에서 찾아 쓰시오. (중복 사용 가능)

보기 | 대명사 날씨 시간 명암 거리 계절

1 How far is it to your school? ______________

2 It is windy on Jeju Island. ______________

3 This is a parrot. It can talk. ______________

4 Jessy made an apple pie. It tasted good. ______________

5 It was cold and snowing hard. ______________

6 It is dark in the kitchen. ______________

7 It is early winter in Korea. ______________

8 It's 5:40 p.m. ______________

C 보기에서 알맞은 대명사를 골라 빈칸을 채우시오. (한 번씩만 사용)

보기 | that those this these it

1 I made a mistake. But I corrected ______________.

2 These apples are bigger than ______________ over there.

3 What are ______________ in this box?

4 Hello. ______________ is James. Can I speak to Dylan?

5 Do you know ______________ man under the tree?

D **우리말과 의미가 같도록 ( ) 안의 말을 배열하시오.**

1 Jane, 이분이 우리 엄마야. (mom, is, this, my)

→ Jane, ______________________________.

2 저것이 너의 자전거니? (bike, is, your, that)

→ ______________________________?

3 벌써 8시야. (already, it, eight o'clock, is)

→ ______________________________.

4 저 장미들은 달콤한 향이 난다. (roses, sweet, smell, those)

→ ______________________________.

5 봄이다! 날씨가 따뜻해지고 있다. (getting, is, warm, it)

→ It is spring! ______________________________.

6 운이 좋으시네요. 이 신발들은 세일 중이에요. (on, are, these, sale, shoes)

→ You are lucky. ______________________________.

E **우리말과 의미가 같도록 ( ) 안의 말을 이용하여 문장을 완성하시오.**

1 이 여자들은 인도 출신이 아니다. (woman)

→ ________ ________ are not from India.

2 이 스프는 좋은 냄새가 나지는 않아. (soup)

→ ________ ________ doesn't smell good.

3 나는 저 남자를 TV에서 봤어. (see, man)

→ ________ ________ ________ ________ on TV.

4 거실이 너무 밝구나. (too bright)

→ ________ ________ ________ ________ in the living room.

5 사진 속의 이 소년들은 나의 학교 친구들이다. (my classmates)

→ ________ ________ in the picture ________ ________

________.

6 Jane의 고양이를 봤니? 그것은 너무 귀여워. (very cute)

→ Did you see Jane's cat? ________ ________ ________ ________.

Unit 11 some, any·all, every, each

A ( ) 안에서 알맞은 것을 고르시오.

1 He bought (any, some) books on sale.

2 I made chicken soup. Would you like (any, some)?

3 (Every, All) girl has something pink.

4 (Each, All) of the children are having fun.

5 (Each, Every) has a question.

6 They don't have (any, some) sharks in the aquarium.

B 보기에서 알맞은 대명사를 골라 빈칸을 채우시오. (중복 사용 가능)

보기 | each all some any

1 ____________ the customers are welcome.

2 ____________ student in my class has a nickname.

3 I didn't have ____________ bread today.

4 There is a lamp on ____________ side of the sofa.

5 She bought ____________ muffins on her way home.

6 He used ____________ the milk to make cheese.

7 Do you have ____________ information about the movie?

C 빈칸에 some 또는 any를 이용하여 대화를 완성하시오.

1 A: Would you like ____________ more tea?

B: No, thank you. I had a lot today.

2 A: Do you have ____________ questions?

B: Yes, I have ____________.

3 A: Did you go to the art museum?

B: Yes, I saw ____________ famous pictures.

4 A: Do you have ____________ plans for this weekend?

B: I don't have ____________ plans. Why?

D 우리말과 의미가 같도록 ( ) 안의 말을 배열하시오.

1 모든 음식은 냉장고에 있다. (all, is, of, the food)

→ ______________________________ in the fridge.

2 모든 새는 둥지로 다시 돌아온다. (every, comes, back, bird)

→ ______________________________ to its nest.

3 베짱이는 음식을 조금도 저장해 두지 않았다. (any, didn't, save, food)

→ The grasshopper ______________________________.

4 나는 열 개의 사과를 샀는데 일부는 썩었다. (rotten, some, are)

→ I bought ten apples, but ______________________________.

5 각각의 축구팀은 열한 명의 선수를 가진다. (each, has, soccer team)

→ ______________________________ eleven players.

6 아빠가 약간의 돈을 나에게 보내 주셨다. (my, some, dad, sent, money)

→ ______________________________ to me.

E 우리말과 의미가 같도록 ( ) 안의 말을 이용하여 문장을 완성하시오.

1 빵 좀 더 드실래요? (more bread)

→ Would you like __________ __________ __________?

2 그는 모든 접시를 싱크대에서 씻었다. (wash)

→ __________ __________ __________ dish in the sink.

3 나는 조금의 가족사진도 가지고 있지 않다. (family photos)

→ I don't have __________ __________ __________.

4 모든 멤버들은 제시간에 회의에 왔다. (be, the members)

→ __________ __________ __________ __________ on time for the meeting.

5 그녀는 돼지 저금통에 약간의 동전을 넣었다. (put, coin)

→ __________ __________ __________ __________ into a piggy bank.

6 각각의 아이돌 그룹은 여름마다 콘서트를 가진다. (hold, idol group)

→ __________ __________ __________ __________ a concert every summer.

Error Correction

▪ 밑줄 친 부분에 대한 설명을 체크하고 틀린 경우엔 바르게 고치시오. (맞으면 'O' 표시)

1	These is my favorite watch. (→)	가까이 있는 (단수, 복수)명사를 가리키며 (This, These) + 단수동사
2	This houses are very old. (→)	(This, These) + (복수명사, 단수명사)
3	That is your birthday gift. (→)	멀리 있는 (단수, 복수)명사를 가리키며 (That, Those) + 단수동사
4	That trees don't have leaves. (→)	(That, Those) + (복수명사, 단수명사)
5	This is seven o'clock. (→)	(이것, 시간)을 나타내는 (비인칭 주어, 대명사)
6	She took this picture. I love one. (→)	앞에 언급한 (특정한, 불특정한) 단수명사를 가리키는 대명사 (it, one)
7	I have any questions. (→)	(any, some)은·는 (긍정문, 부정문)에 사용
8	Will you have any chocolate? (→)	(any, some)은·는 (권유문, 의문문)에 사용
9	I don't have any questions. (→)	(any, some)은·는 (긍정문, 부정문)에 사용
10	All the boys is standing in the hall. (→)	all + (단수, 복수)명사 + (단수, 복수)동사
11	All the money are in a safe place. (→)	all + (단수, 복수)명사 + (단수, 복수)동사
12	Each boy have his own cell phone. (→)	each + (단수, 복수)명사 + (단수, 복수)동사
13	Every students is wearing shorts. (→)	every + (단수명사, 복수명사)

Sentence Writing

▪ 주어진 단어를 알맞게 이용하여 우리말과 의미가 같도록 영작하시오.

1	favorite, watch	이것은 / ~이다 / 내가 제일 좋아하는 시계 →
2	houses, old	이 집들은 / ~이다 / 매우 오래된 →
3	birthday gift	저것은 / ~이다 / 너의 생일 선물 →
4	have, leaves	저 나무들은 / 가지고 있지 않다 / 잎을 →
5	it, o'clock	7시다 →
6	took, picture, love	그녀는 / 찍었다 / 이 사진을 / 나는 좋아한다 / 그것을 →
7	have, questions	나는 / 가지고 있다 / 약간의 질문을 →
8	will, have, chocolate	~할래 / 너는 먹다 / 약간의 초코릿을? →
9	have, questions	나는 / 가지고 있지 않다 / 조금의 질문도 →
10	the boys, standing, the hall	모든 소년들이 / 서 있다 / 복도에 →
11	the money, a safe place	모든 돈은 / 있다 / 안전한 장소에 →
12	boy, own, cell phone	각각의 소년은 / 가지고 있다 / 자기 자신의 핸드폰을 →
13	student, wearing, shorts	모든 학생은 / 입고 있다 / 짧은 바지를 →

문법패턴 빈칸 채우기

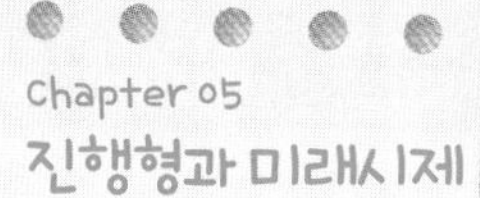

GP 18 진행형

❶ **현재진행형:** 지금 진행 중인 일을 나타낸다.

주어 + ________ + 동사원형 (____) ~하고 있는 중이다

He **is surfing** the Internet.
We **are studying** English grammar.

❷ **과거진행형:** 과거의 특정 시점에 진행 중인 일을 나타낸다.

주어 + ________ + 동사원형 (____) ~하고 있는 중이었다

They **were watching** a baseball game then.

• [동사원형 + -ing] 만들기

대부분의 동사	동사원형 + -ing	walk → walk**ing**	help → help**ing**
-e로 끝나는 동사	e를 빼고 + -ing	live → ________ come → ________	have → ________ make → ________
-ie로 끝나는 동사	ie를 y로 바꾸고 + -ing	die → ________	lie → ________
[단모음 + 단자음]으로 끝나는 동사	자음을 한 번 더 쓰고 + -ing	stop → ________ plan → ________	sit → ________ put → ________

GP 19 진행형 부정문과 의문문

❶ 진행형 부정문

주어 + ________ + [____] + 동사원형 (____)

I **am not joking**.
Andrew **was not listening** to the teacher.

❷ 진행형 의문문

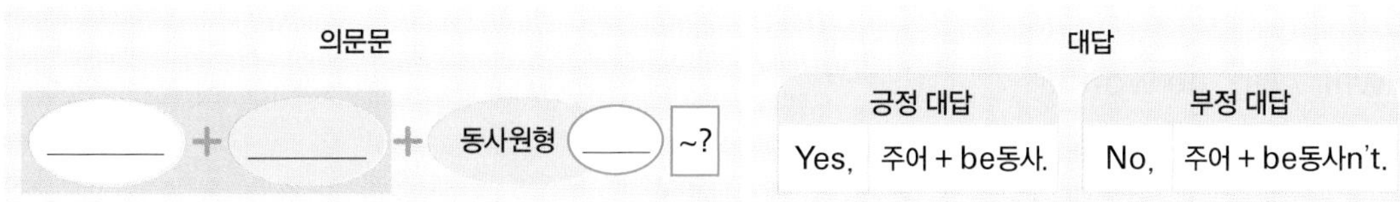

의문문
대답
________ + ________ + 동사원형 (____) ~?
긍정 대답
Yes, 주어 + be동사.
부정 대답
No, 주어 + be동사n't.

A: **Are you wearing** glasses? B: Yes, I am. / No, I'm not.
A: **Was Ann having** lunch then? B: Yes, she was. / No, she wasn't.

GP 20 미래시제

미래시제는 아직 일어나지 않은 미래의 동작이나 상태를 나타낸다.

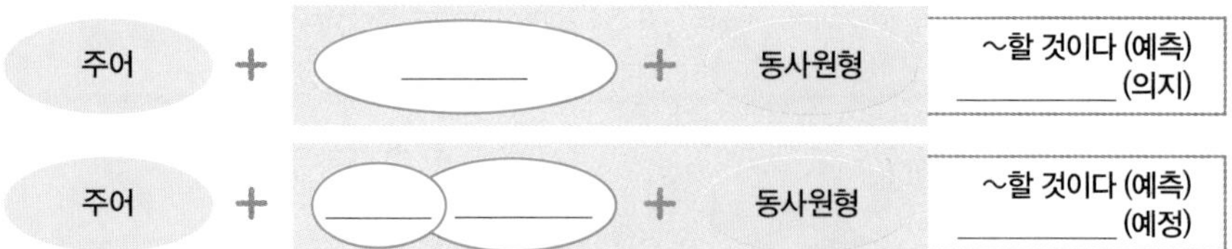

The game **will be** popular.

Mr. Johnson **will stay** at my house.

It **is going to rain** soon.

We **are going to have** a party.

Tip

미래시제와 주로 쓰는 부사(구)

tomorrow, soon, next week, next month, this Sunday, this weekend...

GP 21 미래시제 부정문과 의문문

❶ 미래시제 부정문

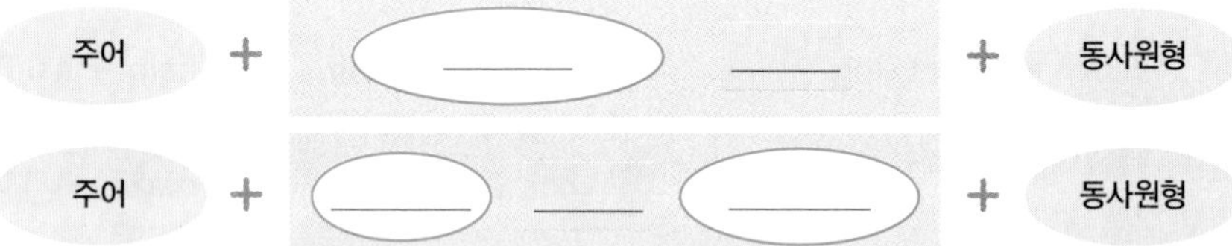

We **won't (will not) fight** again.

I **am not going to run** in the classroom.

❷ 미래시제 의문문

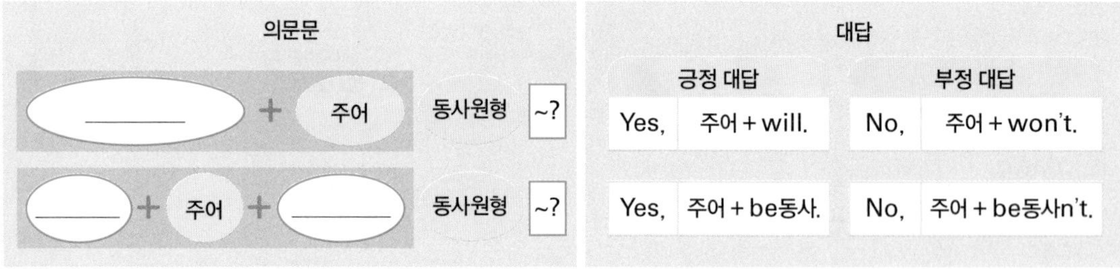

A: **Will the actor come** to Korea?

B: **Yes, he will. / No, he won't.**

A: **Are you going to invite** your friends?

B: **Yes, I am. / No, I'm not.**

Unit 12 진행형 부정문과 의문문

A ( ) 안에서 알맞은 것을 고르시오.

1 He is (waits, waiting) for the subway.

2 The boys (are, do) eating their snacks.

3 Kevin isn't (chats, chatting) on the phone.

4 Are the workers (build, building) a bridge?

5 I was (slept, sleeping) on the sofa.

6 She (wasn't, didn't) picking strawberries.

7 (Does, Is) my brother cleaning his desk?

8 Were Mary and you (took, taking) a walk?

9 We (wasn't, weren't) looking for a cat.

10 They (were, are) staying in Seoul last month.

B ( ) 안의 말을 이용하여 진행형 문장을 완성하시오. (부정문은 줄임말로 쓰기)

(1-4) 현재 진행형

1 It ____________ now. (rain)

2 I ____________ a horse. (ride)

3 ____________ the projector ____________? (work)

4 We ____________ the computer. (use / not)

(5-8) 과거 진행형

5 My sister ____________ a magazine. (read)

6 The kids ____________ in front of the TV. (dance)

7 ____________ my dad ____________ coffee? (drink)

8 They ____________ hats. (wear / not)

C ( ) 안의 동사를 이용하여 진행형 의문문을 만드시오.

1 A: __________ you __________ aerobics? (do) B: Yes, I am.

2 A: __________ your brother __________ the guitar? (play) B: No, he isn't.

3 A: __________ Jessica __________ lunch then? (have) B: No, she wasn't.

4 A: __________ you __________ the boxes? (carry) B: Yes, we were.

D **우리말과 의미가 같도록 ( ) 안의 말을 배열하시오.**

1 사장님은 요리사와 대화를 하고 있었다. (the cook, was, with, talking)

→ The boss ______________________________.

2 Matthew는 운전을 하는 중이 아니었다. (not, driving, was, a car)

→ Matthew______________________________.

3 그녀는 지금 문자를 보내고 있는 중이 아니다. (not, a text message, sending, is)

→ She ______________________________ now.

4 그들은 강을 따라 자전거를 타고 있었나요? (their bikes, were, they, riding)

→ ______________________________ along the river?

5 나의 친구들은 의자에 앉아 있다. (the chairs, in, sitting, are)

→ My friends ______________________________.

6 너의 오빠는 여행을 계획하는 중이니? (your, is, planning, brother)

→ ______________________________ a trip?

E **우리말과 의미가 같도록 ( ) 안의 말을 이용하여 문장을 완성하시오.**

1 저는 제 신발을 찾고 있어요. (look for)

→ ________ ________ ________ ________ my shoes.

2 Mike는 신문을 읽고 있었나요? (read)

→ ________ ________ ________ the newspapers?

3 어린 새끼 고양이가 우유를 더 달라고 울고 있다. (cry for)

→ The little kitten ________ ________ ________ more milk.

4 우리는 정원에서 장미를 키우고 있지 않다. (grow)

→ ________ ________ ________ ________ roses in the garden.

5 그들은 그때 농구를 하고 있지 않았다. (play)

→ ________ ________ ________ ________ basketball then.

6 마라톤 선수들은 지금 63빌딩을 지나가고 있나요? (pass, the marathon runners)

→ ________ ________ ________ ________ ________ by the 63 Building now?

Unit 13 미래시제 부정문과 의문문

A ( ) 안에서 알맞은 것을 고르시오.

1 It (won't, isn't) going to rain tonight.

2 (Are, Will) you bo my wife?

3 She's going to (has, have) a baby next month.

4 (Will, Is) he going to hear the alarm?

5 Harry won't (comes, come) to school today.

6 Are we going (to take, taking) a hot-air balloon trip?

7 (Does, Is) your brother going to wash the dishes?

8 I (won't change, will change not) my mind.

B ( ) 안의 말을 이용하여 문장을 완성하시오. (부정문은 줄임말로 쓰기)

1 James __________ __________ all the files. (will, download)

2 Evan __________ __________ __________ __________ his new jacket. (be going to, wear)

3 He __________ __________ his house. (will, design, not)

4 Suji __________ __________ __________ __________ at this hotel. (be going to, stay, not)

5 It __________ __________ cloudy tomorrow. (will, be)

6 She __________ __________ to my birthday party. (will, come, not)

7 I __________ __________ __________ __________ my homework soon.
(be going to, finish)

8 My children __________ __________ __________ __________ in the river.
(be going to, swim, not)

C ( ) 안의 말을 이용하여 미래시제 의문문을 완성하시오.

1 __________ Alex __________ us? (will, remember)

2 __________ he __________ __________ __________ tonight? (be going to, cook)

3 __________ this lesson __________ difficult? (will, be)

4 __________ he __________ __________ __________ the bag? (be going to, buy)

5 __________ Jack and you __________ __________ __________ her?
(be going to, meet)

D 우리말과 의미가 같도록 ( ) 안의 말을 배열하시오.

1 그는 피자를 더 이상 먹지 않을 거야. (pizza, eat, not, will, he)

→ ______________________________ anymore.

2 너는 과학 동아리에 가입할 거니? (join, you, will, the science club)

→ ______________________________?

3 그녀는 수영 수업을 수강할 것이다. (she, a swimming class, take, will)

→ ______________________________.

4 우리는 많은 사람을 초대하지는 않을 예정이다. (going, to, not, are, invite, we)

→ ______________________________ many people.

5 비행기는 곧 이륙할 것이다. (is, to, going, take off, the plane)

→ ______________________________ soon.

6 그 박물관은 다음주에 문을 여나요? (going, the museum, is, be, to, open)

→ ______________________________ next week?

E 우리말과 의미가 같도록 ( ) 안의 말을 이용하여 문장을 완성하시오

1 나의 개는 너에게 짖지 않을 거야. (will, bark)

→ ______ ______ ______ ______ ______ at you.

2 너는 스시를 주문할 거니? (going, order)

→ ______ ______ ______ ______ ______ sushi?

3 그녀는 다음주에 영국으로 떠날 것이다. (will, leave for)

→ ______ ______ ______ ______ England next week.

4 오늘은 덥지 않을 거야. (going, hot)

→ It ______ ______ ______ ______ ______ ______ today.

5 나는 일회용 젓가락을 사용하지 않을 것이다. (will, use)

→ ______ ______ ______ disposable chopsticks.

6 그녀가 다시 세상을 놀라게 할까? (will, surprise)

→ ______ ______ ______ ______ ______ again?

Error Correction

▪ 밑줄 친 부분에 대한 설명을 체크하고 틀린 경우엔 바르게 고치시오. (맞으면 'O' 표시)

1	He is surf the Internet. (→)	현재진행형은 am / are / is + (동사원형, 동사원형 + -ing)
2	We studying English grammar. (→)	현재진행형은 (동사원형 + -ing, be동사 + 동사원형 + -ing)
3	They are watching a baseball game then. (→)	과거진행형은 (are / were) + (동사원형, 동사원형 + -ing)
4	I am not joking. (→)	진행형 부정문은 (be동사, do) + not + (동사원형, 동사원형 + -ing)
5	Andrew did not listening to the teacher. (→)	진행형 부정문은 (be동사, do) + not + (동사원형, 동사원형 + -ing)
6	Are you wear glasses? (→)	진행형 의문문은 Be동사 + 주어 + (동사원형, 동사원형 + -ing) ~?
7	The game will is popular. (→)	미래시제는 will + (동사원형, 동사)
8	It is going rain soon. (→)	미래시제는 be동사 + (going to, going) + 동사원형
9	We going to have a party. (→)	미래시제는 (going to, be동사 + going to) + 동사원형
10	We not will fight again. (→)	will 포함한 부정문은 (not will, will not) + 동사원형
11	I am not going to run in the classroom. (→)	be going to 포함한 부정문은 (am not, not am) + going to + 동사원형
12	Will the actor comes to Korea? (→)	will 포함한 의문문은 Will + 주어 + (동사, 동사원형) ~?
13	Do you going to invite your friends? (→)	be going to 포함한 의문문은 (Do, Be동사) + 주어 + going to + 동사원형 ~?

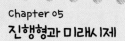

Sentence Writing

▪ 주어진 단어를 알맞게 이용하여 우리말과 의미가 같도록 영작하시오.

1	surf, the Internet	그는 / 서핑하는 중이다 / 인터넷을 →
2	study, English grammar	우리는 / 공부하는 중이다 / 영어 문법을 →
3	watch, then, a baseball game	그들은 / 관람하는 중이었다 / 야구 경기를 / 그때 →
4	joke	나는 / 농담하는 중이 아니다 →
5	listen to, the teacher	Andrew는 / 듣고 있지 않았다 / 선생님의 말씀을 →
6	wear, glasses	~이니 / 너는 / 착용하고 있는 중 / 안경을? →
7	will, popular	그 게임은 / ~일 거다 / 인기 있는 →
8	going, rain, soon	~할 거다 / 비 내리다 / 곧 →
9	going, have a party	우리는 / ~할 거다 / 가지다 / 파티를 →
10	will, fight	우리는 / ~않을 것이다 / 싸우다 / 다시 →
11	going, run	나는 / ~않을 것이다 / 뛰다 / 교실에서 →
12	will, actor, come	할 거니 / 그 배우가 / 오다 / 한국에? →
13	going, invite	~이니 / 너는 / ~할 거다 / 초대하다 / 너의 친구들을? →

문법패턴 빈칸 채우기

GP 22 can, may

❶ can + 동사원형

	can	
능력, 가능	________ (am / are / is able to)	She can play the violin. = She is able to play the violin.
허락	________	You can sit next to me.

(1) 능력·가능: ____________ (= be able to)

The robot **can** talk. (= is able to)

He **can't** ride a bicycle. (= is not able to)

The child **could** use chopsticks. (= was able to)

A: **Can** you fix the computer? B: Yes, I **can**. / No, I **can't**.

(2) 허락: ____________

You **can** come in.

Can (= Could) I use your pen?

• Upgrade •

조동사의 부정문과 의문문

평서문: 주어 + 조동사 + 동사원형	She **can read** Chinese.
부정문: 주어 + ________ + ________ + 동사원형	She **cannot read** Chinese.
의문문: ________ + ________ + 동사원형 ~?	**Can** she **read** Chinese?

❷ may + 동사원형

	may	
허락	________	You may go home now.
불확실한 추측	________	She may know you.

(1) 허락: ____________

You **may** leave your bag in the room.

You **may not** go out alone.

A: **May** (Can) I ask a question? B: Yes, you **may**. / No, you **may not**.

(2) 추측: ____________

She **may** be hungry.

Alex **may not** like the plan.

GP 23 must, have to, should

❶ must + 동사원형

	must	
의무	______	You must wear a seatbelt.
강한 추측	______	He must be tired.

(1) 의무: ____________ (= have to)

We **must (have to)** stop at red lights.

부정문: You **must not** give dogs ice cream.

의문문: A: **Must** I wear a seatbelt? B: Yes, you **must**. / No, you **don't have to**.

(2) 강한 추측: ____________

The cheesecake **must be** delicious. It is popular.

Anna always asks about you. She **must** like you.

❷ have to + 동사원형

	have to	
의무	______	You have to wait here.

She **has to** get some rest. She has a cold.

부정문: Phillip **doesn't have to** lose weight.

의문문: A: **Do** I **have to** wait? B: Yes, you **do**. / No, you **don't have to**.

• Upgrade •

평서문	He **must** go.	~해야 한다	He **has to** go.	~해야 한다
부정문	He **must not** go.	______	He **doesn't have to** go.	______
의문문	**Must** he go?	~해야 합니까?	**Does** he **have to** go?	~해야 합니까?

❸ should + 동사원형

	should	
충고, 조언	______	You should learn table manners.

Tom **should** eat more vegetables.

부정문: You **should not** tell a lie.

의문문: A: **Should** I call her tonight? B: Yes, you **should**. / No, you **don't have to**.

Unit 14 can, may

A ( ) 안에서 알맞은 것을 고르시오.

1 (May, Can) you help me?

2 You may (take, took) a seat.

3 (Do, Can) she speak Chinese?

4 Liz (can, could) play the piano then.

5 He could (travel, traveled) in Europe for one month.

6 A bat (can, is) able to sleep upside down.

7 I (can, can't) use my cell phone. It's broken.

8 Rebecca (not may, may not) come to the party.

9 (Are, Can) you able to reach the tree branch?

10 Some games may (be, are) helpful to you.

B 보기에서 알맞은 조동사를 골라 문장을 완성하시오.

보기 | can can't

1 Where is my dog? I ____________________ find it.

2 This box is too heavy. I ____________________ carry it.

3 Trust me. I ____________________ do that.

4 I ____________________ hear you well. Please speak louder.

5 Finish your meal first. Then, you ____________________ have dessert.

보기 | may may not

6 You ____________________ drive a car. You are too young.

7 ____________________ I order now?

8 You ____________________ believe it, but it is true.

9 Robin is smart. He ____________________ know the answer.

10 You are over 15 years old. So you ____________________ watch this movie.

C 밑줄 친 부분을 be able to를 이용하여 바꿔 쓰시오.

1 The bird can build a nest.

→ The bird ______________________ a nest.

2 We can swim with our pets here.

→ We ______________________ with our pets here.

3 I couldn't catch any fish in the river.

→ I ______________________ any fish in the river.

4 Can he climb the mountain?

→ ______________________ the mountain?

D 우리말과 의미가 같도록 ( ) 안의 말을 배열하시오.

1 그 비밀에 대해 나에게 말해 주시겠어요? (tell, me, you, can, about)

→ ______________________ the secret?

2 개는 빨간색을 볼 수 없어. (see, cannot, dogs)

→ ______________________ the color red.

3 우리 오늘은 어쩌면 무지개를 보게 될 수도 있어. (may, a rainbow, we, see)

→ ______________________ today.

4 너는 밤 10시 이후에 피아노를 치면 안 돼. (play, may, the piano, you, not)

→ ______________________ after 10 p.m.

E 우리말과 의미가 같도록 ( ) 안의 말을 이용하여 문장을 완성하시오

1 조심해. 손가락을 베일 수도 있어. (cut)

→ Be careful. ______ ______ ______ ______ ______.

2 여러분은 오늘 엘리베이터를 사용할 수 없습니다. (use, the elevator)

→ You ______ ______ ______ ______ ______ today.

3 Juliet은 Romeo와 결혼할 수 없었어. (marry)

→ Juliet ______ ______ ______ ______.

4 나는 비행기에서 화산을 볼 수 있었어. (see, the volcano)

→ I was ______ ______ ______ ______ ______ from the plane.

Unit 15 must, have to, should

A ( ) 안에서 알맞은 것을 고르시오.

1 We (must, has to) recycle bottles.

2 Do you (must, have to) walk the dog?

3 You (don't have to, not have to) hurry.

4 Students should not (cheat, cheated) on the exam.

5 Joe always sits next to you. He (must, must not) like you.

B 보기에서 알맞은 조동사를 골라 문장을 완성하시오.

보기 | must have to

1 ____________ I write with my right hand?

2 He doesn't ____________ go to the dentist.

3 You ____________ be joking. I can't believe it.

4 Do I ____________ keep a diary?

5 She ____________ not be tired. She had enough rest.

보기 | must not don't have to

6 It is Saturday. You ________________ get up early.

7 Graham knows the story. He ________________ read it again.

8 Pull the door open. You ________________ push the door open.

9 That is a bad word. You ________________ say that.

10 I was safe. You ________________ worry about me yesterday.

C 밑줄 친 부분의 쓰임을 보기에서 골라 쓰시오. (중복 사용 가능)

보기	ⓐ ~해야 한다 ⓑ ~임에 틀림없다 ⓒ ~하면 안 된다	쓰임
1 She should not speak so loudly.	
2 The baby must be hungry. He is crying.	
3 Should I take her advice?	
4 You must wash your hands.	

D 밑줄 친 부분을 have to를 이용하여 바꿔 쓰시오.

1 You must bring your passport.

→ You ______________________ your passport.

2 She must pack her school bag now.

→ She ______________________ her school bag now.

3 Leo must get off at the next station.

→ Leo ______________________ at the next station.

4 Tourists must listen to the guide.

→ Tourists ______________________ to the guide.

E 우리말과 의미가 같도록 ( ) 안의 말을 배열하시오.

1 제가 테이블을 차려야 하나요? (I, should, the table, set)

→ ______________________?

2 우리 구명조끼 착용해야 하나요? (wear, life jackets, have, to)

→ Do we ______________________?

3 저 선수들은 신호가 있기 전에 출발하면 안 돼. (not, start, must, the, players)

→ ______________________ before the signal.

4 축하해. 너는 분명 네 자신이 자랑스러울 거야. (must, be proud of, you)

→ Congratulations! ______________________ yourself.

F 우리말과 의미가 같도록 ( ) 안의 말을 이용하여 문장을 완성하시오.

1 Anna는 수영하는 방법을 배워야 해. (should, learn)

→ Anna ________ ________ how to swim.

2 그는 줄에 끼어들면 안 돼. (should, cut)

→ He ________ ________ ________ in line.

3 내가 동전을 먼저 넣어야 하나요? (insert, must)

→ ________ ________ ________ coins first?

4 이건 무인 자동차야. 나는 운전할 필요가 없어. (drive)

→ It is a self-driving car. I ________ ________ ________ ________.

Error Correction

Chapter 06
조동사

▪ 밑줄 친 부분에 대한 설명을 체크하고 틀린 경우엔 바르게 고치시오. (맞으면 'O' 표시)

1	The robot can talks. (→)	조동사 + (동사, 동사원형)
2	He not can ride a bicycle. (→)	조동사의 부정형 (not + 조동사, 조동사 + not)
3	Do you can fix the computer? (→)	조동사 의문문 어순 (Do + 주어 + 조동사, 조동사 + 주어) ~?
4	You may went home now. (→)	(약한 추측, 허락) 의미 조동사 + (동사, 동사원형)
5	May I asked a question? (→)	조동사 의문문 어순 조동사 + 주어 + (동사원형, 동사) ~?
6	She may is hungry. (→)	(약한 추측, 허락) 의미 조동사 + (동사, 동사원형)
7	We must stop at red lights. (→)	(~해야 한다, ~가 틀림없다) 의미 조동사 + (동사, 동사원형)
8	You don't must give dogs ice cream. (→)	'~하면 안 된다' 의미의 조동사 부정형은 (don't + 조동사, 조동사 + not)
9	The cheesecake must is delicious. It is popular. (→)	(~해야 한다, ~가 틀림없다) 의미 조동사 + (동사, 동사원형)
10	She have to get some rest. (→)	(~해야 한다, ~가 틀림없다) 의미 She + (have to, has to) + 동사원형
11	Phillip not have to lose weight. (→)	(~하면 안 된다, ~할 필요 없다) 의미 (doesn't, not) + have to
12	Do I must wait? (→)	'~해야 합니까?' 의미의 의문문 어순 (Do + 주어 + have to, Do + 주어 + must) ~?
13	Tom should eat more vegetables. (→)	(~해야 한다, ~해도 된다) 의미 조동사 + (동사, 동사원형)

Sentence Writing

Chapter 06
조동사

▪ 주어진 단어를 알맞게 이용하여 우리말과 의미가 같도록 영작하시오.

1	able, talk	그 로봇은 / 할 수 있다 / 말하다 →
2	can, bicycle	그는 / ~할 수 없다 / 타다 / 자전거를 →
3	can, fix	너는 할 수 있니 / 고치다 / 그 컴퓨터를? →
4	may, home	너는 / ~해도 된다 / 집으로 가다 / 지금 →
5	may, ask	제가 ~해도 될까요 / 물어보다 / 질문을? →
6	may, hungry	그녀는 / ~일지도 모른다 / 배고픈 →
7	must, at red lights	우리는 / ~해야 한다 / 멈추다 / 빨간불에 →
8	must, ice cream	너는 / ~하면 안 된다 / 주다 / 개들에게 / 아이스크림을 →
9	must, delicious	그 치즈케이크는 / ~임에 틀림없다 / 맛있는 →
10	have, get	그녀는 / ~해야 한다 / 갖다 / 약간의 휴식을 →
11	have, lose weight	Phillip은 / ~할 필요가 없다 / 줄이다 / 체중을 →
12	have, wait	내가 ~해야 할까 / 기다리다? →
13	should, vegetables	Tom은 / ~해야 한다 / 먹다 / 더 많은 야채를 →

문법패턴 빈칸 채우기

GP 24 who, what, which

who, what, which는 각각 사람, 사물, 정해진 대상의 선택을 물을 때 사용한다.

who — ______ / ______ / ______ / ______ + 명사

what — ______ / ______ / ______ / what + 명사

which — ______ / ______ / ______ / which + 명사

❶ who(m), whose: ________에 대해(이름이나 관계 등) 물을 때 사용

________ is your new teacher?
Who won the race?
Who(m) did you invite to the party?
____________ is barking outside?

> Tip
> 의문사가 주어일 때 어순
> [의문사 + ______ ~?]
> · Who saw the accident?

❷ what: ________에 대한 구체적인 정보를 물을 때 사용

________ is your favorite subject?
What did you buy for Jenny's birthday?
____________ is it now?

> Tip
> _____은 정해지지 않은 사물에 대한 정보를 묻는 말이고 _____는 정해진 대상에 대한 선택을 묻는 말이다.

❸ which: ________(A or B)에 대한 ________을 물을 때 사용

Which is cheaper, **pork or beef**?
________ do you want, **an orange** ________ **a kiwi**?
____________ do you like better, **baseball or volleyball**?

• Upgrade •

의문문의 대답 형태

❶ 의문사가 없는 의문문: Yes나 No로 대답한다.
Is your mom a teacher? - Yes, she is. / No, she isn't.

❷ 의문사가 없는 선택형 의문문: Yes나 No로 대답하지 않고 구체적인 정보로 대답한다.
Is it true or false? - It is true.

❸ 의문사가 있는 의문문: Yes나 No로 대답하지 않고 구체적인 정보로 대답한다.
What did you do yesterday? - I went to a concert.

GP 25 when, where, why, how

when, where, why, how는 각각 시간, 장소, 이유, 방법을 물을 때 사용한다.

when ______	where ______	why ______	how ______

❶ when: ______, ______, ______ 등을 물을 때 사용

When is the next holiday?

When does the movie start?

❷ where: ______와 ______를 물을 때 사용

Where is the restroom?

Where did you find this book?

❸ why: ______을 물을 때 사용하고 because로 대답

A: **Why** is Henry popular?

B: **Because** he has a sense of humor.

❹ how: ______, ______, ______ 등을 물을 때 사용

How did you know that?

How can I get to the airport?

Tip

why를 이용한 다양한 표현

① Why don't you ~?: 너 (너희들) ~하는 게 어때?

· Why don't you see a doctor?

② Why don't we ~?: 우리 ~하는 게 어때?

· Why don't we meet in the bookstore?

GP 26 how + 형용사 / 부사

[______________]는 '얼마나 ~한, 얼마나 ~하게'라는 의미로 정도를 나타낸다.

how	______	얼마나 키가 큰	how	______	얼마나 먼
how	______	몇 살의	how	______	얼마나 많이
how	______	얼마나 자주	how many	______	얼마나 많은 수의 ~
how	______	얼마나 긴	how much	______	얼마나 많은 양의 ~

How old is her baby?

How often do you work out?

How many students are there in the classroom?

GP 27 부정의문문

부정의문문은 동사의 부정형으로 시작하는 의문문으로 '~않니?'로 해석한다. 대답은, 질문이 긍정이든 부정이든 상관없이 대답하는 내용이 긍정이면 _______로 부정이면 _______로 쓴다.

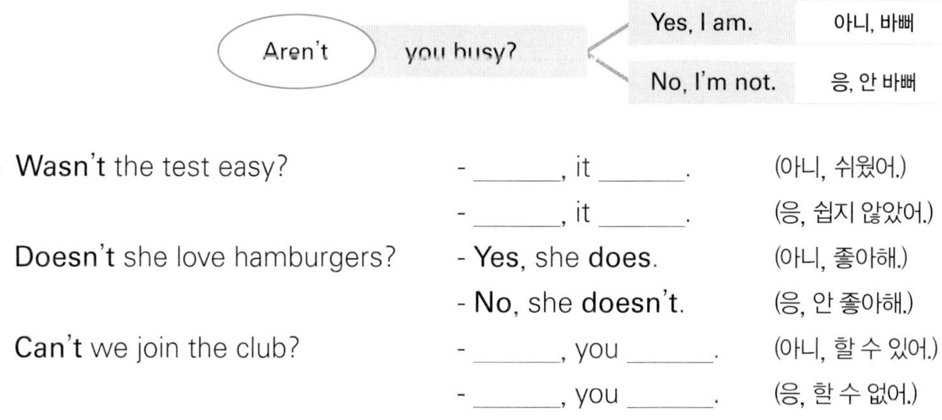

Wasn't the test easy? - _______, it _______. (아니, 쉬웠어.)
- _______, it _______. (응, 쉽지 않았어.)

Doesn't she love hamburgers? - **Yes**, she **does**. (아니, 좋아해.)
- **No**, she **doesn't**. (응, 안 좋아해.)

Can't we join the club? - _______, you _______. (아니, 할 수 있어.)
- _______, you _______. (응, 할 수 없어.)

GP 28 부가의문문

부가의문문은 상대방에게 확인이나 동의를 구하기 위해 평서문 뒤에 짧게 덧붙이는 의문문으로 '그렇지?', '그렇지 않니?'로 해석한다.

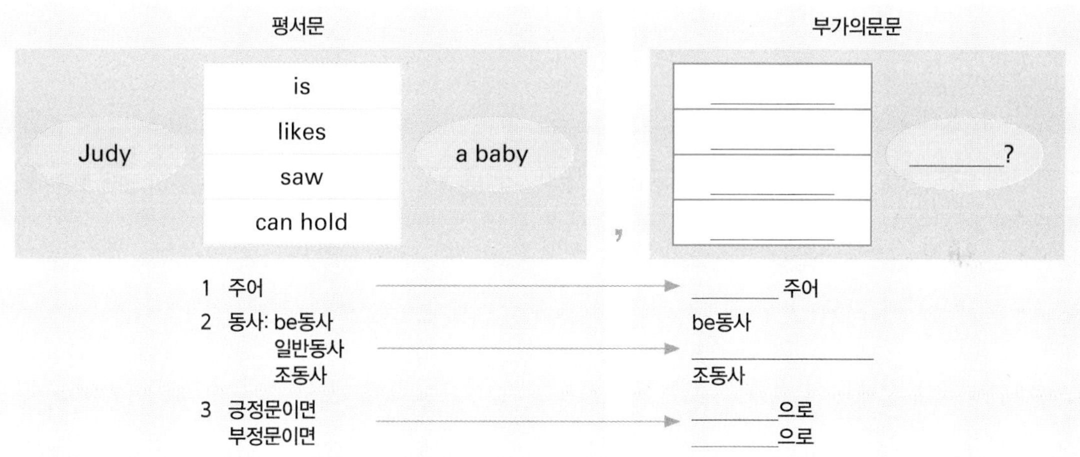

She has breakfast every morning, **doesn't she**?

You didn't see the polar bear, **did you**?

Cindy will move to the city, **won't she**?

• Upgrade •

부가의문문에 대한 대답은 부정의문문처럼 대답하는 내용이 긍정이면 _______로, 부정이면 _______로 한다.
이때 not은 항상 _______ 뒤에 써야 한다.

You have a pen, don't you? - **Yes**, I **do**. (아니, 있어.)

You will go to the theater, won't you? - **No**, I **won't**. (응, 안 갈 거야.)

GP 29 명령문과 제안문

명령문은 상대방에게 '~해라'라고 명령하거나 요청하는 문장이고 제안문은 '~하자'라고 권유하는 문장이다.

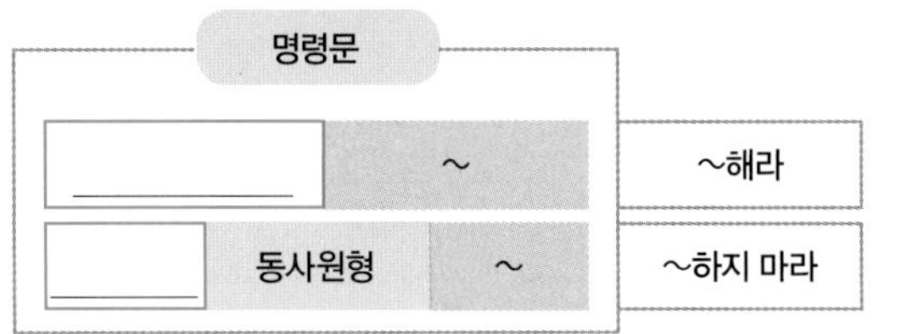

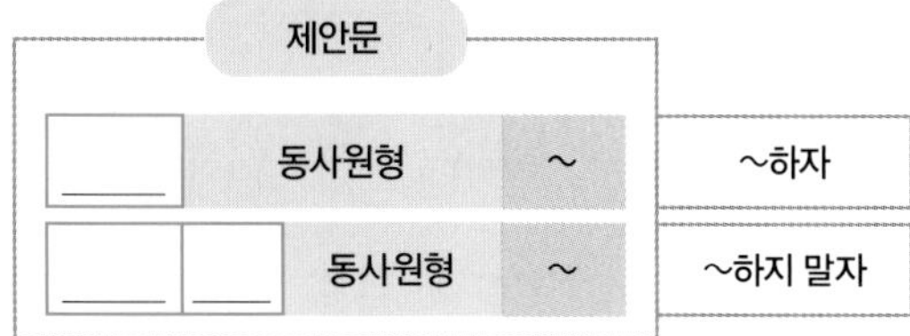

Dream big.
Don't be nervous.
Let's take a walk in the garden.
Let's not go out for dinner.

• Upgrade •

제안을 하는 여러 가지 표현 '~하는 것이 어때?'

❶ **How about taking** a break? [How / What about -ing ~?]
❷ **Shall we take** a break? [Shall we + 동사원형 ~?]
❸ **Why don't we take** a break? [Why don't we + 동사원형 ~?]

Tip

명령문의 부가의문문
[명령문 ~, will you?]
· Wash the dishes, will you?

제안문의 부가의문문
[Let's ~, shall we?]
· Let's go there, shall we?

GP 30 감탄문

감탄문은 놀람, 기쁨 등의 감정을 나타내는 문장으로 How로 시작하는 감탄문과 What으로 시작하는 감탄문이 있다. 보통 '정말(참) ~하구나'로 해석한다.

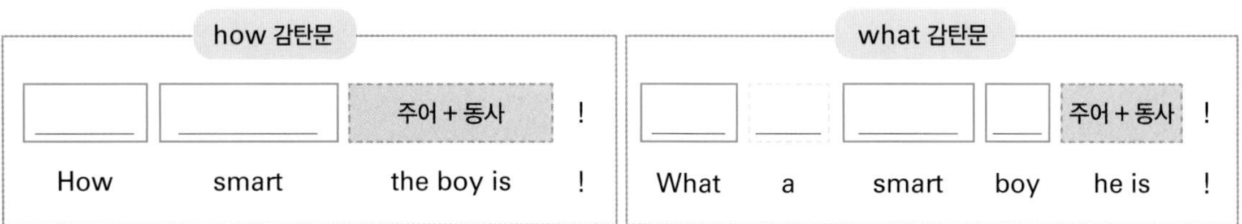

How popular the game is!
How slowly the turtle moves!

What a beautiful day (it is)!
What a great time (we had)!
What old buildings they are!

Tip

what 감탄문에서의 a / an 생략
명사가 _____이거나 _______ 명사일 때 a / an은 쓰지 않는다.

• Upgrade •

how 감탄문은 _______나 _______를 강조하고, what 감탄문은 _______가 포함된 어구를 강조한다.

Unit 16 who, what, which

A ( ) 안에서 알맞은 것을 고르시오.

1 A: (Which, What) are they? B: They are benches.

2 A: (Whose, Who) are they? B: My cousins.

3 A: (Who, Whose) bag is this? B: My mom's.

4 A: (Who, What) found the pen? B: My father did.

5 A: (What, Who) does she draw? B: She draws stars.

6 A: (What, Which) is better, math or science? B: Science.

B 보기에서 알맞은 의문사를 골라 대화를 완성하시오. (중복 사용 가능)

보기	which	who	what	whose

1 A: ______________ did you cook? B: I cooked spaghetti.

2 A: ______________ is he in the picture? B: He is Brian.

3 A: ______________ sweater is this? B: It is mine.

4 A: ______________ color is better, red or white? B: Red is better.

5 A: ______________ happened last night? B: Nothing special.

6 A: ______________ did you invite? B: I invited Jake.

C 대화의 밑줄 친 부분을 묻는 의문문을 완성하시오.

1 A: ____?

B: It is Mike's car.

2 A: ____, an apple or an orange?

B: An apple is cheaper.

3 A: ____?

B: My favorite subject is English.

4 A: ____?

B: My sister made this skirt.

5 A: ____?

B: Her name is Julia Kim.

D **우리말과 의미가 같도록 ( ) 안의 말을 배열하시오.**

1 이것은 누구의 강아지인가요? (puppy, is, whose, it)

→ ______________________________?

2 누가 이 음식을 주문하셨나요? (the food, ordered, who)

→ ______________________________?

3 추석에는 무엇을 먹니? (do, what, you, eat)

→ ______________________________ on Chuseok?

4 어느 책이 그녀의 것이니? (hers, which, is, book)

→ ______________________________?

5 어젯밤에 누구를 만났니? (last night, who, meet, you, did)

→ ______________________________?

6 그녀는 스커트와 바지 중 어느 것을 입었나요? (she, wear, did, which)

→ ______________________________, a skirt or pants?

E **우리말과 의미가 같도록 ( ) 안의 말을 이용하여 문장을 완성하시오.**

1 누가 이웃에 사나요? (live, next door)

→ ________ ________ ________ ________?

2 그것은 누구의 계획이었나요? (be, plan)

→ ________ ________ ________ ________?

3 그녀는 10년 전에 무엇을 가르쳤나요? (teach)

→ ________ ________ ________ ________ ten years ago?

4 이 프로그램의 감독이 누구니? (the director)

→ ________ ________ ________ ________ of this program?

5 학교 축제에 누구를 초대했니? (invite)

→ ________ ________ ________ ________ to the school festival?

6 미국과 영국 중 어느 나라를 가고 싶니? (want, country)

→ ________ ________ ________ ________ ________ to visit, America or England?

Unit 17 when, where, why, how·how + 형용사 / 부사

A 보기에서 알맞은 의문사를 골라 대화를 완성하시오.

보기	where	when	how	why

1 A: ______________ is my cell phone?

B: It's on the sofa.

2 A: ______________ did you go to the beach?

B: Two weeks ago.

3 A: ______________ did you call me?

B: Because I needed your computer.

4 A: ______________ will the weather be?

B: It will be sunny.

B 자연스러운 대화가 되도록 두 문장을 연결하시오.

1 Where is the mall? •　　• ⓐ It is at three o'clock.

2 When is the meeting? •　　• ⓑ Next to the hospital.

3 Why was your sister absent? •　　• ⓒ She went on vacation.

4 How old is the tree? •　　• ⓓ There are 5.

5 How many students are there? •　　• ⓔ It is 4 meters tall.

6 How tall is the tree? •　　• ⓕ About 1,100 years old.

C 대화의 밑줄 친 부분을 묻는 의문문을 완성하시오.

1 A: ____?

B: I ran away <u>because your dog barked at me</u>.

2 A: ____?

B: You can get to the zoo <u>by bus</u>.

3 A: ____?

B: She left China <u>two months ago</u>.

4 A: ____?

B: She studied English <u>in Canada</u>.

D 보기에서 알맞은 말을 골라 대화를 완성하시오.

보기 ㅣ	how long	how tall	how much	how often

1 A: ______________ did you pay? B: I paid 1,000 dollars.

2 A: ______________ is your brother? B: He is 175cm tall.

3 A: ______________ did it take to arrive here? B: It took two hours.

4 A: ______________ do you exercise? B: Three times a week.

E 우리말과 의미가 같도록 ( ) 안의 말을 배열하시오.

1 왜 그녀와 결혼했나요? (marry, why, her, you, did)

→ ______________________________?

2 언제 우리는 그를 만날 수 있나요? (him, when, meet, we, can)

→ ______________________________?

3 지난 주말 어땠나요? (weekend, how, was, last)

→ ______________________________?

4 너희는 어디에서 처음 만났니? (first meet, where, you, did)

→ ______________________________?

F 우리말과 의미가 같도록 ( ) 안의 말을 이용하여 문장을 완성하시오.

1 엄마, 제 양말들 어디 있어요? (my socks)

→ Mom, ________ ________ ________ ________?

2 그는 언제 영화 보러 갔나요? (go)

→ ________ ________ ________ ________ to the movies?

3 너의 할머니는 연세가 어떻게 되시니? (grandmother)

→ ________ ________ ________ ________ ________?

4 Kate는 어제 왜 피곤했니? (tired)

→ ________ ________ ________ ________ yesterday?

Unit 18 부정의문문·부가의문문

A ( ) 안에서 알맞은 것을 고르시오.

1 (Isn't, Doesn't) he Chinese?

2 (Aren't, Weren't) you at home yesterday?

3 Carrots are good for your eyes, (aren't, are) they?

4 Lucy has a twin sister, (hasn't, doesn't) she?

5 You weren't a teacher, (were, weren't) you?

6 (Wasn't, Didn't) Tom eat the onions?

7 Share the pizza with your sister, (don't, will) you?

8 Adam doesn't likc animated movies, does (Adam, he)?

B 다음 문장을 부정의문문으로 바꾸고, 알맞은 답을 고르시오.

1 You remembered me.

____________________________________? → No, I (did, didn't).

2 She is a pilot.

____________________________________? → Yes, she (is, isn't).

3 He looks like an actor?

____________________________________? → Yes, he (does, doesn't).

4 She was taller than you.

____________________________________? → No, she (was, wasn't).

C 빈칸에 알맞은 부가의문문을 쓰시오.

1 She sometimes visits her aunt, _______________?

2 The babies can't reach the shelf, _______________?

3 Bring me some water, _______________?

4 Elephants live long, _______________?

5 Your mom doesn't drink coffee, _______________?

6 The blue skirt is yours, _______________?

7 He was stung by a bee, _______________?

8 Daniel didn't watch the movie, _______________?

D 우리말과 의미가 같도록 ( ) 안의 말을 배열하시오.

1 학교에 갈 준비가 안 되었니? (ready, you, aren't)

→ ______________________ to go to school?

2 그의 아이디어는 나쁘지 않아, 그렇지? (idea, is, isn't, it, his, bad)

→ ______________________, __________?

3 그 새가 새장에 없었니? (the bird, in, wasn't, the cage)

→ ______________________?

4 그의 연설은 멋졌어, 그렇지 않니? (was, wasn't, his speech, it, great)

→ ______________________, __________?

5 이전에 미국에 살지 않았었나요? (in, live, you, didn't, America)

→ ______________________ before?

6 그녀가 피자를 데웠어, 그렇지 않니? (she, she, warmed, didn't, the pizza)

→ ______________________, __________?

E 우리말과 의미가 같도록 ( ) 안의 말을 이용하여 문장을 완성하시오.

1 당신은 나를 알지 않나요? (know)

→ ______ ______ ______ ______?

2 그녀는 너무 조심스럽지 않니? (too careful)

→ ______ ______ ______ ______?

3 이 방은 정말 깔끔하네, 안 그래? (really neat)

→ This room ______ ______ ______, ______ ______?

4 너는 어제 거기에 가지 않았니? (go there)

→ ______ ______ ______ ______ ______?

5 그 식물들은 곤충을 먹어, 안 그래? (eat, insects)

→ The plants ______ ______, ______ ______?

6 그는 아름다운 목소리를 가졌는걸, 안 그래? (have, beautiful voice)

→ He ______ ______ ______ ______, ______ ______?

Unit 19 명령문·제안문·감탄문

A ( ) 안에서 알맞은 것을 고르시오.

1 Don't (be, is) shy. Join us now.

2 (How, What) smart the dolphin is!

3 Let's (watch, watched) a horror movie together.

4 (How, What) an expensive stone it is!

5 Let's (don't, not) play the guitar at night.

6 (Visits, Visit) our website for more information.

7 (How, What) funny this video clip is!

B ( ) 안의 말을 이용하여 명령하는 문장을 만드시오.

1 ________ the stairs instead of the elevator. (take)

2 ________ ________ it with wet hands. (not, touch)

3 ________ careful. The lake is deep. (be)

4 ________ ________ on the bench. It is wet. (not, sit)

5 The road is slippery. ________ slowly. (walk)

6 ________ ________ afraid. I am your friend. (not, be)

7 ________ the baby with a blanket. (cover)

C ( ) 안의 말을 이용하여 제안하는 문장을 만드시오.

1 ________ ________ honest. (be)

2 ________ ________ the bags together. (carry)

3 ________ ________ talking. The teacher is looking at us. (stop)

4 ________ ________ ________ the window. Mosquitoes will come in. (not, open)

5 ________ ________ a break. I am getting tired. (take)

6 ________ ________ ________ any jokes to Jane. She doesn't like them. (not, tell)

7 ________ ________ ________ today. It was a great day. (not, forget)

D 다음 밑줄 친 부분을 강조하는 감탄문을 쓰시오.

1 It is a really great moment.

→ ______________________________!

2 His painting looks very real.

→ ______________________________!

3 We had a very exciting trip.

→ ______________________________!

4 The blanket is very soft.

→ ______________________________!

E 우리말과 의미가 같도록 ( ) 안의 말을 배열하시오.

1 얼마나 충격적인 소식인가! (shocking, the news, how, is)

→ ______________________________!

2 내일 늦지 마세요. (be, tomorrow, late, don't)

→ ______________________________.

3 얼마나 커다란 성인가! (a, big, what, it, castle, is)

→ ______________________________!

4 음식을 너무 많이 사지 말자. (buy, not, let's, food, too much)

→ ______________________________.

F 우리말과 의미가 같도록 ( ) 안의 말을 이용하여 문장을 완성하시오.

1 벽 위에 그림 그리지 마라. (draw)

→ ________ ________ on the wall.

2 여행을 위한 계획을 만들자. (make a plan)

→ ________ ________ ________ ________ for the trip.

3 너의 이웃들에게 친절하렴. (be, neighbors)

→ ________ ________ ________ ________ ________.

4 정말 멋진 퍼레이드였어! (the parade, amazing)

→ ________ ________ ________ ________ ________!

Error Correction

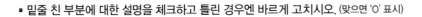

■ 밑줄 친 부분에 대한 설명을 체크하고 틀린 경우엔 바르게 고치시오. (맞으면 'O' 표시)

1	Who is your new teacher? (→)	(사람, 사물)에 대해 물을 때 (Who, What) 사용
2	Which is your favorite subject? (→)	정해진 범위 (없을 때, 있을 때) '무엇'의 의미는 (What, Which)
3	What do you want, an orange or a kiwi? (→)	정해진 범위 (없을 때, 있을 때) '어느 것'의 의미는 (What, Which)
4	A: When does the movie start? B: At six o'clock. (→)	(시간, 장소)를 물을 때 (When, Where)
5	A: Why did you find this book? B: In the box. (→)	(이유, 장소)를 물을 때 (Why, Where)
6	What can I get to the airport? (→)	방법(어떻게)을 물을 때 (How, What)
7	What often do you work out? (→)	'얼마나 자주'를 물을 때 (What often, How often)
8	Wasn't the test easy? Yes, it wasn't. (→)	부정의문문의 대답은 Yes, (긍정문, 부정문) / No, (긍정문, 부정문)
9	She has breakfast every morning, isn't she? (→)	긍정문의 부가의문문은 (긍정문, 부정문) 일반동사의 부가의문문은 (isn't, does't) she?
10	You didn't see the polar bear, did you? (→)	부정문의 부가의문문은 (긍정문, 부정문)
11	Not be nervous. (→)	(~해라, ~하지 마라) 부정 명령문은 (Not, Don't) + 동사원형
12	What popular the game is! (→)	(How, What) 감탄문은 뒤에 형용사 / 부사 + 주어 + 동사! 어순
13	How a beautiful day it is! (→)	(How, What) 감탄문은 뒤에 a(n) + 형용사 + 명사 + 주어 + 동사! 어순

▪ 주어진 단어를 알맞게 이용하여 우리말과 의미가 같도록 영작하시오.

1	new, teacher	누구니 / 너의 새 선생님은? →
2	favorite, subject	무엇이니 / 너의 가장 좋아하는 과목은? →
3	want, or, orange, kiwi	어느 것을 / 너는 원하니, / 오렌지 또는 키위? →
4	the movie, start	언제 / 영화는 시작하나요? →
5	this book, find	어디에서 / 너는 찾았니 / 이 책을? →
6	get to	어떻게 / 내가 갈 수 있을까요 / 공항에? →
7	often, work out	얼마나 자주 / 너는 운동하니? →
8	test, easy	~이지 않았니 / 그 시험은 / 쉬운? 아니, 쉬웠다 →
9	breakfast, have every morning	그녀는 / 아침을 먹는다 / 매일 아침, / 그렇지 않니? →
10	the polar bear, see	너는 / 못 봤다 / 북극곰을, / 그렇지? →
11	nervous	하지 마 / 긴장하다 →
12	the game, popular	정말 ~하구나 / 인기 있는 / 이 게임은! →
13	beautiful, it is	정말 ~하구나 / 아름다운 날! →

문법패턴 빈칸 채우기

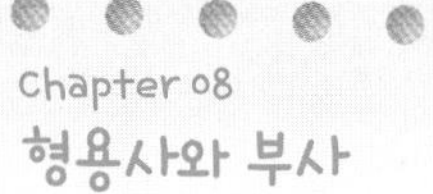

GP 31 형용사의 쓰임

❶ **명사 수식**: 대부분의 형용사는 명사 앞에서 _______를 _______하고 _______, _______, _______로 끝나는 대명사는 형용사가 _______에서 수식한다.

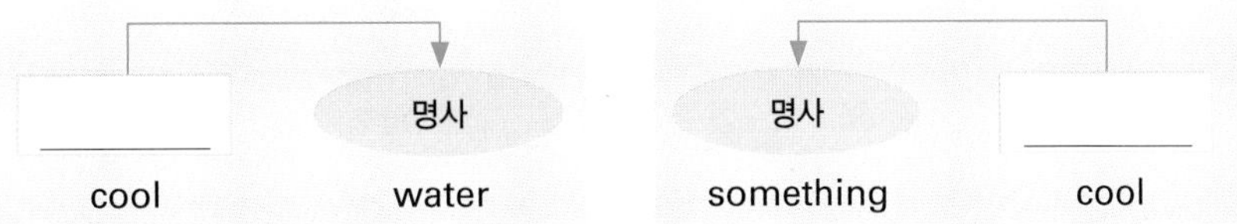

We are **close** *friends*.
I heard *something* **strange**.

❷ **보어**: 동사 또는 목적어 뒤에서 _______나 _______를 _______ 설명한다.

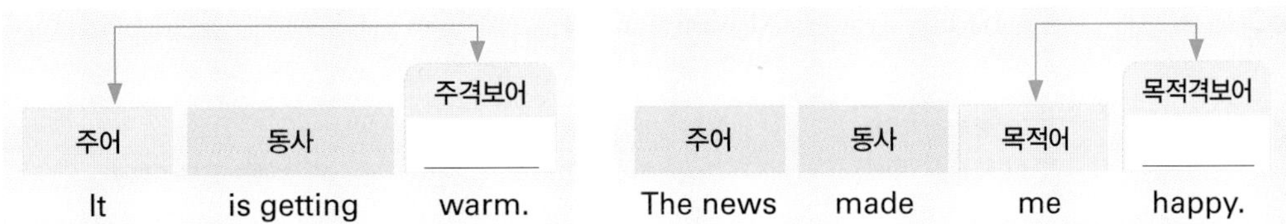

This movie was **interesting**.
I found *him* **honest**.

GP 32 수량 형용사

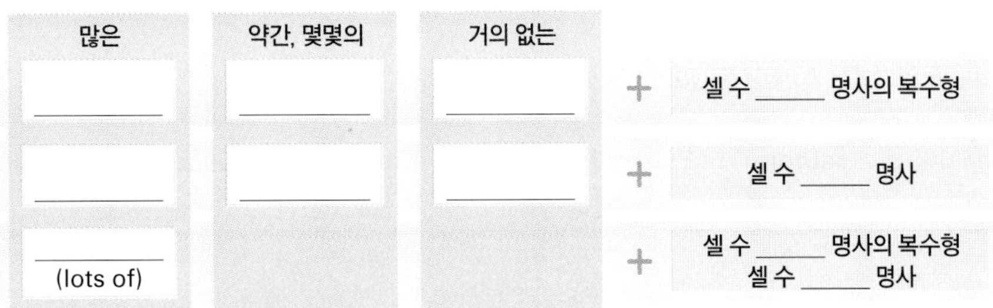

There are **many (= a lot of)** *holidays* in May.
Did you get **much (= a lot of)** *snow* last year?

He met Julie **a few** *days* ago.
She spread **a little** *jam* on the bread.
The actor is not famous. He has **few** *fans*.

GP 33 부사의 쓰임과 형태

❶ **부사의 쓰임:** 부사는 동사, 형용사, 다른 부사, 문장 전체를 수식하고 '~하게'로 해석한다.

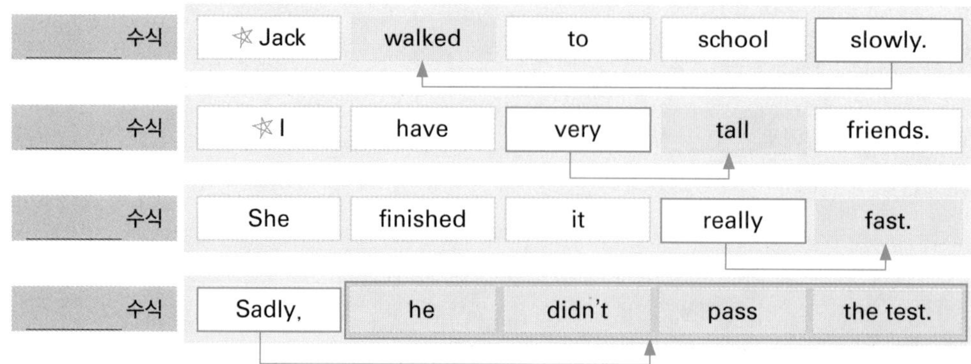

_____ 수식
Jack walked to school slowly.
_____ 수식
I have very tall friends.
_____ 수식
She finished it really fast.
_____ 수식
Sadly, he didn't pass the test.

❷ 부사의 형태

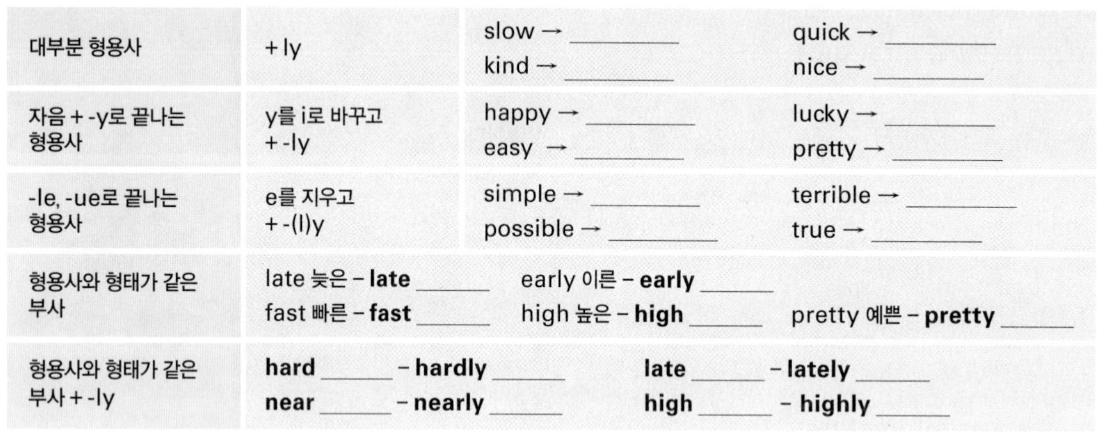

대부분 형용사	+ ly	slow → _____ kind → _____	quick → _____ nice → _____
자음 + -y로 끝나는 형용사	y를 i로 바꾸고 + -ly	happy → _____ easy → _____	lucky → _____ pretty → _____
-le, -ue로 끝나는 형용사	e를 지우고 + -(l)y	simple → _____ possible → _____	terrible → _____ true → _____
형용사와 형태가 같은 부사	late 늦은 - **late** _____ fast 빠른 - **fast** _____	early 이른 - **early** _____ high 높은 - **high** _____	pretty 예쁜 - **pretty** _____
형용사와 형태가 같은 부사 + -ly	**hard** _____ - **hardly** _____ **near** _____ - **nearly** _____	**late** _____ - **lately** _____ **high** _____ - **highly** _____	

Isabel is a **fast** learner. (형용사)
She learns things very **fast**. (부사)

> **Tip**
> 명사에 -ly를 붙이면 형용사가 된다.
> friend + ly → friendly (친근한) love + ly → lovely (사랑스러운)

GP 34 빈도부사

빈도부사는 반복의 정도를 나타내는 말로 조동사와 be동사 뒤, 일반동사 앞에 위치한다.

He may be wrong.

Tom is late for class.

GP 35 원급, 비교급, 최상급

❶ **원급을 이용한 비교**: 두 개 대상을 비교하여 그 정도가 같음을 의미한다.

A ______ ______ ______ B　A 가 B 만큼 ~한 (하게)

Sarah is **as busy as** a bee.
Chris can speak Korean **as well as** I.

❷ **비교급을 이용한 비교**: 두 개의 대상에 대한 정도를 비교한다.

A ______ ______ B　A 가 B 보다 ~한 (하게)

Cold air is **heavier than** hot air.
Apples are **cheaper than** strawberries today.

❸ **최상급을 이용한 비교**: 셋 이상의 대상에 대한 정도를 비교한다.

A ______ ______ ___/___ B　A 가 B 에서 가장 ~한 (하게)

This is **the biggest** orange **in** the store.
A whale is **the largest of** all animals.

❹ 비교급, 최상급 만드는 규칙

			원급	비교급	최상급
규칙 변화	대부분의 경우	+ -er / -est	long	______	______
	-e로 끝나는 경우	+ -r / -st	close	______	______
	[단모음 + 단자음]으로 끝나는 형용사 / 부사	자음 한 번 더 쓰고 + -er / -est	big	______	______
	자음 + -y로 끝나는 경우	y를 i로 고치고 + -er / -est	busy	______	______
	2, 3음절 이상 형용사 / 부사	more / most +	famous	______ famous	______ famous
	-ly로 끝나는 부사	more / most +	slowly	______ slowly	______ slowly
불규칙 변화			good / well	______	______
			bad / ill	______	______
			many / much	______	______
			little	______	______

Unit 20 형용사의 쓰임·수량 형용사

A ( ) 안에서 알맞은 것을 고르시오.

1 This sandwich tastes (salt, salty).

2 The news made him (angry, angrily).

3 I saved (lots of, many) money.

4 He is (friend, friendly) to the others.

5 Did you hear (new anything, anything new)?

6 Be (careful, carefully) about the bugs in the grass.

7 Fresh vegetables are (good, well) for your health.

8 The school has (a lot of, much) books in the library.

B 보기에서 알맞은 수량 형용사를 골라 문장을 완성하고, 수식을 받는 명사가 셀 수 있는지 여부를 체크하시오.

보기 | much many

1 ① I have too ______________ homework today. 셀 수 (있음, 없음)

② Do you have ______________ friends? 셀 수 (있음, 없음)

보기 | few little

2 ① The car uses ______________ gas. 셀 수 (있음, 없음)

② There were ______________ people at the park. 셀 수 (있음, 없음)

보기 | a few a little

3 ① She ate ______________ peanuts. 셀 수 (있음, 없음)

② There was ______________ snow on the road. 셀 수 (있음, 없음)

C 밑줄 친 형용사의 쓰임을 보기에서 고르시오. (중복 사용 가능)

보기 | ⓐ 명사수식 ⓑ 보어	쓰임
1 The baby's hair is <u>soft</u>.	
2 Brian tells <u>funny</u> jokes.	
3 The news made us <u>excited</u>.	
4 These shoes are <u>small</u> for me.	
5 There was a <u>pretty</u> rainbow in the sky.	

D 보기에서 알맞은 형용사를 골라 문장을 완성하시오. (한 번씩만 사용)

보기 | delicious wonderful dark used

1 Thank you for a __________ time.

2 He made an ugly cake. But it tasted __________.

3 It is getting __________ outside.

4 He bought a __________ car. But it looked new.

E 우리말과 의미가 같도록 ( ) 안의 말을 배열하시오.

1 나는 Jack이 정직하다는 것을 알게 되었어. (Jack, found, honest)

→ I __________.

2 우리는 집에서 편안함을 느껴. (comfortable, feel, home, at)

→ We __________.

3 위험한 어떤 것도 가지고 오면 안 됩니다. (anything, bring, can't, dangerous)

→ You __________.

4 그들은 결혼식에 몇 명 초대했어. (invited, few, people, a)

→ They __________ to their wedding.

5 매일 몇 시간 수면을 하나요? (hours, sleep, you, how many, do)

→ __________ every night?

F 우리말과 의미가 같도록 ( ) 안의 말을 이용하여 문장을 완성하시오.

1 저 아름다운 하늘을 봐. (beautiful, the)

→ Look at ______ ______ ______.

2 나는 약간의 종이가 필요해. (need)

→ I ______ ______ ______ paper.

3 동물원에 코끼리가 거의 없다. (elephants)

→ There are ______ ______ in the zoo.

4 겨울에는 눈이 많이 내리지 않는다. (have)

→ We don't ______ ______ snow in winter.

5 그는 차가운 어떤 것을 원한다. (want, cold)

→ He ______ ______ ______.

Unit 21 부사의 쓰임과 형태·빈도부사

A ( ) 안에서 알맞은 것을 고르시오.

1 He finished his meal (fast, fastly).

2 (Strange, Strangely), the cat likes baths.

3 It is getting warm. Spring is (near, nearly).

4 Jane is preparing for the contest (hard, hardly).

5 The gentleman (wears usually, usually wears) a suit.

6 The police caught the robber (brave, bravely).

7 We (never are, are never) lonely with each other.

B 보기와 같이 ( ) 안의 단어를 이용하여 문장을 완성하시오.

보기	(easy, easily)	He did his homework easily. The homework was not easy.

1 (honest, honestly) She answered me ________________.
She was very ________________.

2 (real, really) The news is ________________ shocking.
Is that ________________?

3 (nice, nicely) Be ________________ to your sister.
Talk to her ________________.

4 (simple, simply) Think about the question ________________.
The answer is ________________.

5 (late, lately) He was not ________________ for school today.
He comes to school early ________________.

C 밑줄 친 부사의 쓰임을 보기에서 골라 쓰고 부사가 수식하는 말에 동그라미 하시오.

보기 | ① 동사수식 ② 형용사 수식 ③ 부사 수식 ④ 문장 전체 수식	쓰임
1 They lived happily ever after.	
2 He washed the grapes quite carefully.	
3 This game is very interesting.	
4 Luckily, he found gold.	

D ( ) 안의 빈도부사를 알맞은 위치에 넣어 문장을 다시 쓰시오.

1 She buys things online. (often)

→ ____________________.

2 Kangaroos can walk backward. (never)

→ ____________________.

3 Mike was late for school. (usually)

→ ____________________.

4 He looks like a boy. (always)

→ ____________________.

E 우리말과 의미가 같도록 ( ) 안의 말을 배열하시오.

1 알바트로스는 높이 날아. (albatross, an, high, flies)

→ ____________________.

2 그 농구선수는 손이 매우 커. (really, has, big, hands)

→ The basketball player ____________________.

3 슬프게도, 우리 팀이 또 다른 게임도 졌어. (our, lost, team, sadly, another, game)

→ ____________________.

4 그는 주로 아침에 영화를 보러 가. (usually, to, the, movies, goes, he)

→ ____________________ in the morning.

F 우리말과 의미가 같도록 ( ) 안의 말을 이용하여 문장을 완성하시오.

1 그 시계는 정말로 싸다. (real)

→ The watch ________ ________ ________.

2 그녀는 조용히 그 문을 닫았다. (close, quiet)

→ She ________ ________ ________ ________.

3 그 기차는 항상 정시에 출발한다. (leave, on time)

→ The train ________ ________ ________ ________.

4 그 문제는 꽤 어려웠다. (hard, pretty)

→ The question ________ ________.

5 흥미롭게도, 문어는 파란색 피를 갖고 있어. (interesting)

→ ________, an octopus has blue blood.

Unit 22 원급, 비교급, 최상급

A ( ) 안에서 알맞은 것을 고르시오.

1 Seoul is not as (hot, hotter) as Busan.

2 My computer is (faster, fastest) than yours.

3 It is the (better, best) day of my life.

4 Cities are noisier (in, than) small towns.

5 Brad is the tallest (in, of) all the boys in his class.

6 You are (beautifuler, more beautiful) than a rose.

7 The Nile River is (a longest, the longest) river in the world.

B ( ) 안의 단어를 이용하여 비교급 문장을 완성하시오.

1 She can speak Spanish ______________________ me. (well)

2 Bears can run ______________________ humans. (fast)

3 Sound travels ______________________ light. (slowly)

4 My memory is ______________________ yours. (bad)

5 Peter practices the piano ______________________ me. (hard)

6 Sunlight is ______________________ moonlight. (bright)

7 These shoes are ______________________ mine. (comfortable)

C ( ) 안의 단어를 이용하여 최상급 문장을 완성하시오.

1 What is ______________________ planet in the solar system? (big)

2 That was ______________________ flood in history. (bad)

3 Today is ______________________ day of the year. (cold)

4 He is ______________________ member of the magic club. (young)

5 This orchestra is ______________________ in Korea. (famous)

6 ______________________ city in France is Paris. (large)

7 What is ______________________ bird in the world? (small)

D 다음 두 문장을 원급 문장으로 바꿔 쓰시오.

1 Tom is 16 years old. Emily is 16 years old, too.
→ Tom is ______________________________ Emily. (old)

2 Max arrived here at 7 a.m. You arrived here at the same time. (early)
→ Max arrived here ______________________________ you.

3 The red USB is $10. The white USB is also $10. (expensive)
→ The red USB is ______________________________ the white one.

4 He waters the plants every day. I water the plants every day, too. (often)
→ He waters the plants ______________________________ I.

E 우리말과 의미가 같도록 (　) 안의 말을 배열하시오.

1 피는 물보다 진하지. (blood, water, thicker, is, than)
→ ____.

2 우리 아빠가 나보다 더 잘생기셨어. (handsome, than, more, me, is)
→ My father ____.

3 그는 '가장 우수한 선수상'을 받았어. (most, the, valuable, player)
→ He won ____ award.

4 다이아몬드가 모든 돌 중에서 가장 단단해. (the, all, are, stones, hardest, of)
→ Diamonds ____.

F 우리말과 의미가 같도록 (　) 안의 말을 이용하여 문장을 완성하시오.

1 그녀는 새끼 고양이만큼 활달해. (playful)
→ She is ______________ ______________ ______________ a kitten.

2 Justin은 그의 엄마보다 요리를 더 잘해. (well)
→ Justin cooks ______________ ______________ his mom.

3 세계에서 가장 큰 새는 무엇이지? (big)
→ What is ______________ ______________ ______________ in the world?

4 그 책은 영화보다 더 재미있었어. (interesting)
→ The book is ______________ ______________ ______________ the movie.

Error Correction

▪ 밑줄 친 부분에 대한 설명을 체크하고 틀린 경우엔 바르게 고치시오. (맞으면 'O' 표시)

1	We are closely friends. (→)	(명사 수식, 보어) 쓰임의 (형용사, 부사)
2	This movie was interest. (→)	(명사 수식, 보어) 쓰임의 (형용사, 명사)
3	There are much holidays in May. (→)	(much, many) + (셀 수 없는 명사, 셀 수 있는 명사 복수형)
4	He met Julie a little days ago. (→)	(a few, a little) + 셀 수 있는 명사 복수형 (거의 없는, 약간은 있는) 의미
5	She spread a few jam on the bread. (→)	(a few, a little) + 셀 수 없는 명사 (거의 없는, 약간은 있는) 의미
6	Jack walked to school slow. (→)	(느린, 느리게) 걷다 (동사, 명사)를 수식하는 (부사, 형용사)
7	I have very tall friends. (→)	(명사, 형용사) 수식하는 (부사, 형용사)
8	He often may be wrong. (→)	빈도부사의 위치는 조동사의 (앞, 뒤)
9	Tom always is late for class. (→)	빈도부사의 위치는 be동사의 (앞, 뒤)
10	She never eats meat for dinner. (→)	빈도부사의 위치는 일반동사의 (앞, 뒤)
11	Sarah is as busier as a bee. (→)	~만큼 (바쁜, 더 바쁜) as + (원급, 비교급) + as
12	Cold air is heavy than hot air. (→)	~보다 (무거운, 더 무거운) (원급, 비교급) + than
13	The whale is the larger of all animals. (→)	~중에서 (더 큰, 가장 큰) the + (비교급, 최상급) + of 복수명사

Sentence Writing

▪ 주어진 단어를 알맞게 이용하여 우리말과 의미가 같도록 영작하시오.

1	close	우리는 / ~이다 / 가까운 친구들 →
2	interesting	이 영화는 / ~이었다 / 흥미로운 →
3	holidays, many, May	~들이 있다 / 많은 휴일들 / 5월에 →
4	meet, few	그는 / 만났다 / Julie를 / 며칠 전에 →
5	jam, spread, little	그녀는 / 발랐다 / 약간의 잼을 / 빵 위에 →
6	walk to school	Jack은 / 걸었다 / 학교로 / 천천히 →
7	tall, very	나는 / 갖고 있다 / 매우 키가 큰 / 친구들을 →
8	may, wrong	그는 / 종종 ~일 수도 있다 / 틀린 →
9	late, class	Tom은 / 언제나 늦다 / 수업에 →
10	meat, eat	그녀는 / 결코 먹지 않는다 / 고기를 / 저녁식사로 →
11	bee, busy	Sarah는 / ~만큼 바쁘다 / 벌 →
12	air, heavy	차가운 공기는 / 더 무겁다 / 뜨거운 공기보다 →
13	the whale, large	고래는 / 가장 크다 / 모든 동물들 중에서 →

문법패턴 빈칸 채우기

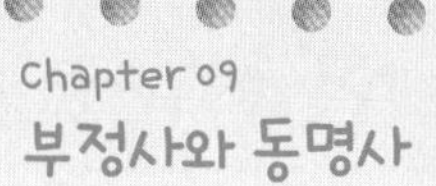

GP 36 to부정사의 명사적 쓰임

[to부정사의 의미]

to부정사는 [________________]의 형태로 동사의 성질을 가지며 ________, ________, ________ 역할을 한다.

eat 먹다 → to + 동사원형 → ______ (to 부정사) 먹는 것 / 먹을 / 는 / 먹기 위해서

[to부정사의 명사적 쓰임]

to부정사가 '________'의 의미로 명사처럼 문장에서 주어, 목적어, 보어 역할을 한다.

	주어	동사	목적어 / 보어
________	To make movies ______	is	fun.
________	I	want	to make movies. ______
________	My job	is	to make movies. ______

❶ ________ 역할: to부정사가 주어인 경우 보통 주어 자리에 ______을 사용하고 ___________는 뒤로 보낸다.

To read webtoons *is* fun.
= ______ *is* fun ___________ webtoons. (가주어 It)

❷ ________ 역할: 동사 ________, ________, ________, ________, ________, ________, ________ 등의 목적어로 쓰인다.

We *decided* **to visit** the zoo.
Jane *plans* **to raise** a dog.

> **Tip**
> to부정사의 부정문:
> ______ 또는 ______를 to부정사 바로 앞에 쓴다.
> I promised **not to be** late again.

❸ ________ 역할: 보통 be동사 뒤에서 주어의 상태, 성질 등을 나타낸다.

My dream *is* **to become** a game designer.
Their goal *was* **to find** gold.

• Upgrade •

[________ + ________]는 명사처럼 문장에서 주어, 목적어, 보어 역할을 한다.

Do you know **what to bring** to camp?
Tell me **where to go** next.

who(m) + to부정사	what + to부정사	when + to부정사	where + to부정사	how + to부정사
________	________	________	________	________

GP 37 to부정사의 형용사적 쓰임

to부정사가 '________'의 의미로 ________처럼 명사, 대명사를 수식한다. 이때 to부정사는 명사, 대명사 ______에서 수식한다.

He knows a special *way* **to cook** noodles.

Please give me *something cold* **to drink**.

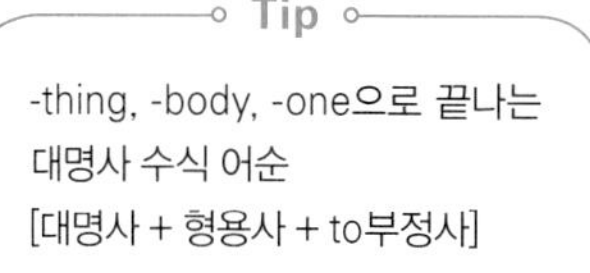

Tip
-thing, -body, -one으로 끝나는
대명사 수식 어순
[대명사 + 형용사 + to부정사]

GP 38 to부정사의 부사적 쓰임

to부정사가 '~하기 위해, ~해서, ~하기에' 등의 의미로 ________처럼 동사, 형용사 등을 수식한다.

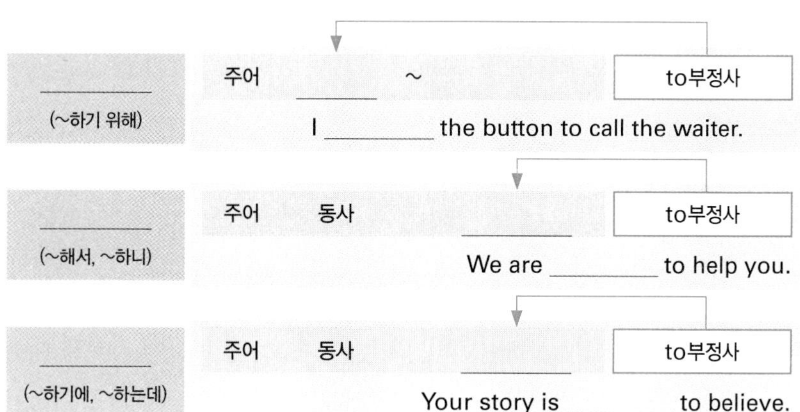

❶ ________________

They *used* robots **to make** ships.

❷ ________________

I am *sorry* **to hear** the news.

❸ ________________

His name is *easy* **to remember**.

Tip

여러 가지 감정을 나타내는 형용사

happy, glad, sorry, sad, surprised, shocked...

GP 39 동명사의 명사적 쓰임

[동명사의 의미]

동명사는 [________________]의 형태로 문장에서 동사의 성질을 가지면서 명사의 역할을 한다.

동명사

eat 먹다 → 동사원형 + -ing → eating 먹는 것

[동명사의 명사적 쓰임]

동명사가 '~하는 것'의 의미로 명사처럼 문장에서 주어, 목적어, 보어 역할을 한다.

	주어	동사	목적어 / 보어
________	Playing chess	is	his hobby.
________	He	enjoys	playing chess.
________	His hobby	is	playing chess.

❶ ________ 역할

Riding a roller coaster *is* scary.

Making movies *is* not easy.

❷ ________ 역할

________의 목적어: enjoy, ________, ________, ________, ________, ________ 등의 목적어로 쓰인다.

________의 목적어: in, about, for 등의 목적어로 쓰인다.

Do you *mind* **opening** the door for me?

Thank you *for* **listening**.

❸ ________ 역할

보통 be동사 뒤에서 주어의 상태, 성질 등을 나타낸다.

Her good habit *is* **getting up** early.

• Upgrade •

동명사의 부정문

________ 또는 ________를 동명사 바로 ________에 쓴다.

We are sorry for **not coming** earlier.

Unit 23 to부정사의 명사적 쓰임

A ( ) 안에서 알맞은 것을 고르시오.

1 (Have, To have) a pet snake is exciting.

2 (This, It) was great to travel the world by ship.

3 Do you want (to joins, to join) the drama club?

4 His goal is to (read, reads) 20 books this year.

5 Why did you decide (to bought, to buy) a big house?

6 (It, To) invent a flying car is her goal.

7 I forgot how (use, to use) the machine.

B 밑줄 친 부분의 해석을 쓰고, 보기에서 쓰임을 고르시오.

보기 | ① 주어 (~하는 것은) ② 목적어 (~하는 것을) ③ 보어 ('~하는 것'이다)		
1 She hopes to meet you again.	해석 ____________ 을	쓰임 ______
2 My wish is to see snow on my birthday.	해석 ____________ 이다	쓰임 ______
3 To say sorry is not easy.	해석 ____________ 은	쓰임 ______
4 The sailor decided to get a dog.	해석 ____________ 을	쓰임 ______
5 We need to call the police first.	해석 ____________ 을	쓰임 ______
6 It was wrong to tell lies.	해석 ____________ 은	쓰임 ______

C 보기에서 알맞은 단어를 골라 to부정사 형태로 바꿔 문장을 완성하시오.

보기 | sing cook drink find

1 ____________ on the stage was exciting.

2 His mission is ____________ water on the planet.

3 She wanted ____________ something cold.

4 It was easy ____________ instant noodles.

보기 | when / sleep how / go what / eat where / go

5 The tourist asked me ____________ to the train station.

6 She is thinking about ____________ for her vacation.

7 Please don't tell me ____________ tonight.

8 Let's decide ____________ for dinner.

D 우리말과 의미가 같도록 ( ) 안의 말을 배열하시오.

1 좋은 아들이 되는 것은 쉽다. (to, good, easy, son, a, be)

→ It is ______________________________.

2 수영하는 것을 언제 배웠니? (swim, learn, to, you, did)

→ When ______________________________?

3 Jane은 야채를 더 먹을 필요성이 있다. (eat, needs, more, to, vegetables)

→ Jane ______________________________.

4 그의 직업은 아픈 동물을 치료하는 것이다. (sick, treat, to, animals is)

→ His job ______________________________.

5 그녀는 어디에서 버스를 내려야 할지 알아. (where, knows, get off, the bus, to)

→ She ______________________________.

6 나는 이 셔츠를 입고 싶지 않아. (wear, to, skirt, this, want, don't)

→ I ______________________________.

7 영어를 말하는 것이 중요하다. (to, is, it, speak, English, important)

→ ______________________________.

E 우리말과 의미가 같도록 ( ) 안의 말을 이용하여 문장을 완성하시오.

1 그녀는 그 소설책을 사고 싶어 했다. (buy, want)

→ She ________ ________ ________ a novel.

2 운전하는 방법을 알고 있니? (drive, know)

→ Do you ________ ________ ________ ________?

3 그 규칙을 바꾸는 것은 매우 어려웠다. (change, the rule)

→ ________ ________ ________ ________ ________ very difficult.

4 나의 바람은 그랜드 캐니언에 방문하는 것이다. (visit)

→ My hope ________ ________ ________ the Grand Canyon.

5 네 음식을 가져오는 것은 괜찮아. (bring, own food)

→ It is okay ________ ________ ________ ________ ________.

6 산 속에 사는 것은 무서웠다. (on the mountain)

→ It was scary ________ ________ ________ ________ ________.

Unit 24 to부정사의 형용사적·부사적 쓰임

A 밑줄 친 부분의 해석을 쓰고, 보기에서 쓰임을 고르시오.

보기 | ⓐ 목적 (~하기 위해)	ⓑ 감정의 원인 (~해서)	ⓒ 형용사 수식 (~하기에)
1 I got up early to see the sunrise.	해석 ________	쓰임 ____
2 The kid was excited to see the pony.	해석 ________	쓰임 ____
3 The comic book is fun to read.	해석 ________	쓰임 ____
4 She was surprised to hear the truth.	해석 ________	쓰임 ____

B 보기에서 알맞은 말을 골라 형태를 바꿔 문장을 완성하시오.

보기			
	· something / wear	· time / go	· country / visit
	· two bags / carry	· three tests / take	· a plan / surprise

1 He looks cold. Get him ____________________.

2 Hurry! It is ____________________.

3 The doorman had ____________________.

4 Australia is a great ____________________.

5 Jane is busy. She has ____________________.

6 Tom has ____________________ her.

C 자연스러운 문장이 되도록 연결하시오.

1 She gave me something • • ⓐ to go to Busan.

2 He was sad • • ⓑ to eat.

3 Molly took the train • • ⓒ to lose his bag.

4 This book was boring • • ⓐ to read.

5 I am saving money • • ⓑ to open the door.

6 He stood up • • ⓒ to buy a bicycle.

D **우리말과 의미가 같도록 ( ) 안의 말을 배열하시오.**

1 이 노래는 부르기에 쉬워. (easy, sing, to, is).

→ This song ______________________________.

2 그녀는 금메달을 따게 되어 매우 기뻤다. (happy, win, to, a, was, gold medal)

→ She ______________________________.

3 나는 너에게 보여 줄 재미있는 것이 있다. (to, something, have, important, show)

→ I ______________________________ you.

4 그는 친구를 방문하기 위해 파리에 갔다. (went to, Paris, his friend, visit, to)

→ He ______________________________.

5 그 왕관은 쓰기에 매우 무거웠어. (heavy, wear, was, very, to)

→ The crown ______________________________.

6 그 선생님은 영어를 가르치는 최고의 방법을 알고 계셔. (the, way, best, teach, to, knows)

→ The teacher ______________________________ English.

E **우리말과 의미가 같도록 ( ) 안의 말을 이용하여 문장을 완성하시오.**

1 이 차는 운전하기에 안전해. (safe, drive)

→ This car is ________ ________ ________.

2 이 섬에는 볼 장소들이 많아. (see, places)

→ There are ________ ________ ________ ________ on this island.

3 그 보디가드는 그 가수를 보호하기 위해 왔어. (come, protect)

→ The bodyguard ________ ________ ________ ________ ________.

4 한국에 돌아오셔서 기쁘십니까? (come back, happy)

→ Are you ________ ________ ________ ________ ________

________?

5 너는 책을 읽을 충분한 시간이 있어. (enough, time, read)

→ You have ________ ________ ________ ________ ________.

6 그녀는 학교를 짓기 위해 아프리카로 갔어. (build schools, Africa)

→ She ________ ________ ________ ________ ________ ________.

Unit 25 동명사의 명사적 쓰임

A ( ) 안에서 알맞은 것을 고르시오.

1 (Flying, Fly) a kite is very fun.

2 Why did you give up (to read, reading) the book?

3 My hobby is (listening, listens) to classical music.

4 She was afraid of (touches, touching) the dragonfly.

5 I enjoyed (drawing, to draw) flowers on the wall.

6 The campaign is for (cleaned, cleaning) the Earth.

7 He quit (to drink, drinking) coffee.

8 How about (order, ordering) a pizza?

9 (To walking, Walking) fast is good exercise for me.

10 Avoid (go, going) out on dusty days.

B 보기에서 알맞은 단어를 골라 동명사를 이용한 문장으로 완성하시오.

보기	answer	paint	wait	act	travel

1 Do you enjoy ____________________ around the country?

2 She finished ____________________ the bench.

3 He practiced ____________________ for the play.

4 I am not in a hurry. I don't mind ____________________.

5 We are sorry for ____________________ your call late.

C 밑줄 친 부분의 해석을 쓰고, 보기에서 쓰임을 고르시오.

보기	ⓐ 주어 (~하는 것은)	ⓑ 동사의 목적어 (~하는 것을)
	ⓒ 전치사의 목적어 (~하는 것을)	ⓓ 보어 (~하는 것이다)

1 Thank you for <u>coming</u>.	해석 ______________을	쓰임 ______
2 I finished <u>cleaning</u> the room.	해석 ______________을	쓰임 ______
3 She stopped <u>singing</u>.	해석 ______________을	쓰임 ______
4 Her favorite activity is <u>reading</u> books.	해석 ______________이다	쓰임 ______
5 <u>Collecting</u> dolls was fun.	해석 ______________은	쓰임 ______

D 우리말과 의미가 같도록 ( ) 안의 말을 배열하시오.

1 왜 커피 마시는 것을 끊었나요? (you, drinking, quit, coffee)

→ Why did ______________________________?

2 나의 직업은 돌고래를 훈련시키는 것이야. (is, dolphins, training, my job)

→ ______________________________.

3 그 소년은 새로운 사람을 만나는 것을 즐겼어. (new, meeting, enjoyed, people)

→ The boy ______________________________.

4 충분한 물을 마시는 것이 중요해. (water, drinking, enough, important, is)

→ ______________________________.

5 그는 영화를 잘 만든다. (good, at, is, making, movies)

→ He ______________________________.

6 중국음식을 요리하는 것은 그녀의 취미이다. (Chinese food, cooking, her, is, hobby)

→ ______________________________.

E 우리말과 의미가 같도록 ( ) 안의 말을 이용하여 문장을 완성하시오.

1 그의 나쁜 습관은 너무 오래 이어폰을 사용하는 것이다. (use)

→ His bad habit ________ ________ earphones for too long.

2 저와 자리 바꿔 주셔도 괜찮을까요? (mind, change)

→ Would you ________ ________ seats with me?

3 그녀는 종이꽃을 접는 것을 잘해. (fold, be good at)

→ She ________ ________ ________ ________ paper flowers.

4 그들은 그 축구선수를 만나는 것에 대해 흥분되었어. (be excited about, meet)

→ They ________ ________ ________ ________ the soccer player.

5 그는 계속 재채기를 했다. (keep, sneeze)

→ The patient ________ ________.

6 그녀의 농담은 매우 재미있어서, 나는 웃는 것을 멈출 수 없었다. (stop, laugh)

→ Her joke was very funny, so I ________ ________ ________.

Error Correction

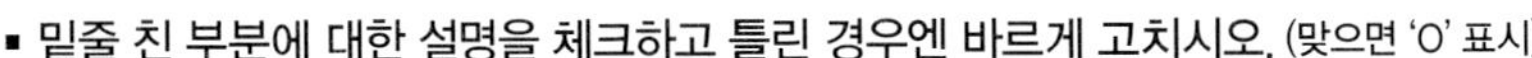

Chapter 09
부정사와 동명사

▪ 밑줄 친 부분에 대한 설명을 체크하고 틀린 경우엔 바르게 고치시오. (맞으면 'O' 표시)

1 Read webtoons is fun.
(→)
주어 + 동사 ~
(to부정사, 동사원형)

2 This is fun to read webtoons.
(→)
가주어 ~ 진주어
(This, It) (to부정사, 동사)

3 We decided visiting the zoo.
(→)
주어 + decide + 목적어
(동명사, to부정사)

4 My dream is become a game designer.
(→)
주어 + be동사 + 보어
(to부정사, 동사원형)

5 He knows a special way to cook noodles.
(→)
'(~ 요리해서, ~ 요리할) 방법' 의미의
(명사 + to부정사, to부정사 + 명사)

6 Please give me something cold drink.
(→)
'(마시다, 마실) 차가운 것' 의미의
something cold + (to부정사, 동사원형)

7 They used robots make ships.
(→)
'(~ 만들기에, ~ 만들기 위해) 사용하다' 의미의
동사 + (to부정사, 동사)

8 I am sorry to hear the news.
(→)
'(~ 듣게 되어, ~ 듣기 위해) 유감인' 의미의
(감정형용사, 부사) + to부정사

9 His name is easily to remember.
(→)
'(~ 기억해서, ~ 기억하기에) 쉬운' 의미의
(부사, 형용사) + to부정사

10 Ride a roller coaster is scary.
(→)
주어 + 동사 ~
(동사, 동명사)

11 Do you mind open the door for me?
(→)
주어 + mind + 목적어
(동사원형, 동명사)

12 Thank you for listen.
(→)
주어 + 동사 + 전치사 + 목적어
(동사원형, 동명사)

13 Her good habit is get up early.
(→)
주어 + 동사 + 보어
(동사원형, 동명사)

Sentence Writing

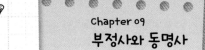

▪ 주어진 단어를 알맞게 이용하여 우리말과 의미가 같도록 영작하시오.

1	webtoons, fun	웹툰을 읽는 것은 / ~이다 / 재미있는 (5단어) →
2	it, webtoons, fun	재미있다 / 웹툰을 읽는 것은 (6단어) →
3	decide, the zoo	우리는 / 결정했다 / 동물원을 방문하는 것을 →
4	game designer, become	나의 꿈은 / ~이다 / 게임 디자이너가 되는 것 →
5	special way, noodles	그는 안다 / 특별한 방식 / 국수를 요리할 →
6	please, something, drink	제게 주세요 / 무언가 차가운 것을 / 마실 →
7	robots, ship	그들은 / 사용했다 / 로봇을 / 배를 만들기 위해 →
8	hear, sorry	나는 / 유감이다 / 그 소식을 듣게 되어 →
9	remember, easy	그의 이름은 / 쉽다 / 기억하기에 →
10	ride, scary, roller coaster	롤러코스터를 타는 것은 / ~이다 / 무서운 (6단어) →
11	mind, the door	당신은 꺼리시나요 / 문을 여는 것을 / 저를 위해? →
12	listen	고맙습니다 / ~때문에 / 들어 주는 것 →
13	good habit, get up	그녀의 좋은 습관은 / ~이다 / 일찍 일어나는 것 →

GP 40 감각동사 + 형용사

보고, 듣고, 느끼는 등 감각을 표현하는 동사를 감각동사라고 하며, 이 동사는 뒤에는 형용사를 쓴다.

주어	________	________	
S	look	happy	________
	feel	soft	________
	smell	nice	________
	sound	good	________
	taste	sweet	________

❶ ________ + ________

You **look** *young* in that blue shirt.

❷ ________ + ________

I **feel** *cold*. I need a blanket.

❸ ________ + ________

The sausage **smells** *delicious*.

❹ ________ + ________

Her voice **sounds** *beautiful*.

❺ ________ + ________

This juice **tastes** *sweet*.

Tip

감각동사 뒤에 ________를 쓰지 않는다.

· She looks happily. (X)

· She looks happy. (O)

• Upgrade •

[감각동사 + ________ + ________]

감각동사 뒤에 명사가 오면 명사 앞에 like를 쓴다.

My dog looks a bear. (X)

My dog ____________ *a bear*. (O)

GP 41 수여동사 + 간접목적어 + 직접목적어

수여동사는 ________의 목적어를 필요로 하고 '~에게(간접목적어) ~를(직접목적어) 해 주다'는 의미의 동사이다.

주어	수여동사	간접목적어	직접목적어
She	gave	me	a pencil.

↓ ________ ________

I **told** *him the reason*.

Andrew **teaches** *us English*.

He **bought** *his cat a toy*.

• Upgrade •

[주어 + 동사 + ________] → He **made** *a chair*. (의자를 ________)

[주어 + 동사 + ________목적어 + ________목적어] → He **made** *me a chair*. (나에게 의자를 ________)

GP 42 수여동사 + 직접목적어 + 전치사 + 간접목적어

[수여동사 + 간접목적어 + 직접목적어]는 [수여동사 + 직접목적어 + 전치사 + 간접목적어]로 바꿀 수 있다.
이때 전치사는 동사에 따라 전치사 to, for, of를 쓴다.

주어	수여동사	____목적어	____목적어
She	gave	me	a pencil.

주어	수여동사	____목적어	전치사	____목적어
She	gave	a pencil	to	me.

❶ ______를 사용하는 동사: ______, ______, ______, ______, ______, ______, ______…

He **showed** *us his puppy*.

→ He **showed** *his puppy* ______ *us*.

❷ ______를 사용하는 동사: ______, ______, ______, ______, ______…

She **bought** *me a flower*.

→ She **bought** *a flower* ______ *me*.

❸ ______를 사용하는 동사: ______…

Anna **asked** *him a favor*.

→ Anna **asked** *a favor* ______ *him*.

GP 43 목적격보어가 필요한 동사

일부 동사들은 목적어와 목적격보어를 필요로 한다. 목적격보어는 목적어의 상태, 성질 등을 설명하는 말이다.

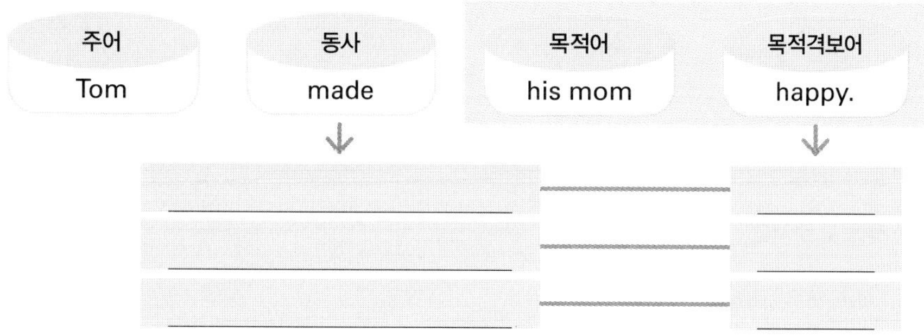

동사의 종류에 따라 명사, 형용사, to부정사 등이 목적격보어로 쓰인다.

주어	동사	목적어	목적격보어
Tom	made	his mom	happy.

❶ ___________로 _________를 쓰는 동사: make, call, name, elect, choose...

We **called** him an *iron man*.

They **named** the young lion *Simba*.

❷ ___________로 _________를 쓰는 동사: make, keep, find, leave...

The news **made** him *famous*.

I **found** Peter *smart*.

❸ ___________로 _________를 쓰는 동사: want, expect, tell, ask, advise, allow...

I **want** you *to like* my present.

The police **told** him *to stop*.

He **asked** us *to be* quiet.

Unit 26 감각동사 + 형용사

A ( ) 안에서 알맞은 것을 고르시오.

1 The tank looks (strong, strongly).

2 Does the soup smell (well, good)?

3 His plan (smells, sounds) strange.

4 The new teacher looks (a friend, friendly).

5 Did you (taste, feel) tired after work?

6 The muffin tastes (sweet, sweetly).

B ( ) 안에서 알맞은 것을 고르시오.

1 ⓐ She (felt, felt like) tired yesterday.

ⓑ She (felt, felt like) a superstar.

2 ⓐ The shampoo (smells, smells like) nice.

ⓑ The shampoo (smells, smells like) apples.

3 ⓐ The island (looks, looks like) a dragon.

ⓑ The island (looks, looks like) peaceful.

4 ⓐ The music (sounds, sounds like) thunder.

ⓑ The music (sounds, sounds like) powerful.

C 밑줄 친 동사의 알맞은 해석을 고르시오.

1 ⓐ I <u>felt</u> the wind on my cheeks. ⓑ The wind <u>felt</u> cool.	(느끼다, ~한 느낌이 나다) (느끼다, ~한 느낌이 나다)
2 ⓐ She <u>smelled</u> the peach. ⓑ The peach <u>smelled</u> fresh.	(냄새 맡다,~한 냄새가 나다) (냄새 맡다, ~한 냄새가 나다)
3 ⓐ He <u>looked</u> at the sky. ⓑ The sky <u>looked</u> beautiful.	(보다, ~하게 보이다) (보다, ~하게 보이다)
4 ⓐ Let me <u>taste</u> the pasta. ⓑ The pasta <u>tastes</u> great.	(맛을 보다,~한 맛이 나다) (맛을 보다, ~한 맛이 나다)

D **우리말과 의미가 같도록 ( ) 안의 말을 배열하시오.**

1 그 NASA 프로젝트는 신나게 들린다. (the NASA project, exciting, sounds)

→ ______________________________.

2 그 로션은 사과 냄새가 나. (the lotion, apples, smells, like)

→ ______________________________.

3 이 캔디는 신맛이 난다. (tastes, this, candy, sour)

→ ______________________________.

4 어떤 고양이들은 상자 안에서 안전하게 느껴. (feel, safe, some, cats, in a box)

→ ______________________________.

5 우리 엄마는 이 옛날 사진에서는 젊어 보이셔. (looks, young, my mom)

→ ______________________________ in this old photo.

6 그 소년은 슈퍼맨 같이 느꼈어. (felt, the boy, like, Superman)

→ ______________________________.

E **우리말과 의미가 같도록 ( ) 안의 말을 이용하여 문장을 완성하시오.**

1 이 버섯은 닭고기 맛이 난다. (taste, chicken)

→ This mushroom __________ __________ __________.

2 내 울 스웨터는 따스한 느낌이야. (feel, warm)

→ My wool sweater __________ __________.

3 우리는 모두 다르게 보인다. (look, different)

→ We all __________ __________.

4 이 생선은 냄새가 나빠. (smell, bad)

→ The fish __________ __________.

5 그의 꽃 그림은 진짜처럼 보여. (look, real)

→ His drawing of flowers __________ __________.

6 Alice는 오늘 아침 화난 것처럼 들렸다. (sound, angry)

→ Alice __________ __________ this morning.

7 왜 이 커피가 짠맛이 나지? (taste, salty)

→ Why does this coffee __________ __________?

Unit 27 수여동사+간접목적어+직접목적어·수여동사+직접목적어+전치사+간접목적어

A ( ) 안에서 알맞은 것을 고르시오.

1 He gave a rose (his wife, to his wife).

2 Did you send (to me, me) a text message?

3 I will write (him an e-mail, an e-mail him) today.

4 May I ask (a question you, you a question)?

5 We got movie tickets (of, for) our parents.

6 My grandma told a fairy tale (us, to us).

7 He taught (they, them) art.

B 밑줄 친 부분의 해석을 쓰고, 보기에서 쓰임을 고르시오. (중복 사용 가능)

보기 ㅣ ① 직접목적어 (~을, 를) ② 간접목적어 (~에게)		
1 Jason wrote <u>me</u> an e-mail.	해석 ________	쓰임 ____
2 He cooked <u>spaghetti</u> for his family.	해석 ________	쓰임 ____
3 Will you bring <u>us</u> good news next time?	해석 ________	쓰임 ____
4 She told <u>her secret</u> to Brian.	해석 ________	쓰임 ____
5 I will ask <u>her</u> the reason.	해석 ________	쓰임 ____

C 다음 두 문장의 의미가 갖도록 빈칸을 채우시오.

1 I will show you the way.

→ I will show ________ ________ ________ ________.

2 My uncle bought me nice shoes.

→ My uncle bought ________ ________ ________ ________.

3 She gave the waiter a tip.

→ She gave ________ ________ ________ ________ ________.

4 The dog found my missing key.

→ The dog found ________ ________ ________ ________ ________.

5 Please pass me the salad.

→ Please pass ________ ________ ________ ________.

D 우리말과 의미가 같도록 ( ) 안의 말을 배열하시오.

1 내가 네게 힌트를 하나 줄게. (give, to, a hint, you)

→ I will ______________________.

2 Kate가 우리에게 아이스크림을 사 줬어. (ice cream, us, bought)

→ Kate ______________________.

3 아빠가 우리에게 불고기를 요리해 주셨어. (cooked, bulgogi, us, for)

→ My dad ______________________.

4 너는 너의 엄마에게 저 예쁜 모자를 드렸니? (get, the pretty hat, your mom)

→ Did you ______________________?

5 그는 친구에게 작은 선물을 만들어 주었다. (a, gift, for, small, his friend, made)

→ He ______________________.

6 그는 나에게 직업을 찾아 주었다. (found, job, me, a)

→ He ______________________.

E 우리말과 의미가 같도록 ( ) 안의 말을 이용하여 문장을 완성하시오.

1 Julie는 나에게 초콜릿박스를 보냈어. (send, a box of chocolates)

→ Julie ______ ______ ______ ______ ______ ______.

2 Molly에게 장미를 주자. (get)

→ Let's ______ ______ ______ Molly.

3 내게 가위를 가져와 주겠니? (bring, the scissors)

→ Can ______ ______ ______ ______ ______?

4 그 기자는 그녀에게 질문을 했다. (ask)

→ The reporter ______ ______ ______ ______.

5 내게 2천원을 빌려줄 수 있니? (lend)

→ Can you ______ ______ ______ ______?

6 내가 너를 안아 줄게. (give, a hug)

→ Let me ______ ______ ______ ______.

Unit 28 목적격 보어가 필요한 동사

A ( ) 안에서 알맞은 것을 고르시오.

1 I found her advice (helpful, help).

2 She told him (water, to water) the plant.

3 This cream keeps the skin (soft, softly).

4 We elected (him, his) president of our school.

5 He ordered his dog (sit, to sit) down.

6 They asked us (wear, to wear) our seatbelts.

7 The war made them (strong, strongly).

8 These gloves will keep your hands (warm, warmly).

B ( ) 안의 말을 이용하여 우리말과 의미가 같도록 문장을 완성하시오.

1 나는 네가 행복하기를 원해. (want, you)

→ I ____________ ____________ ____________ ____________ happy.

2 너는 우리가 너를 믿기를 기대하니? (expect, we, believe)

→ Do you ____________ ____________ ____________ ____________ you?

3 그의 열정은 그를 특별하게 만들었다. (make, he, special)

→ His passion ____________ ____________ ____________.

4 우리는 칫솔을 건조하게 유지시켜야 한다. (keep, our toothbrushes, dry)

→ We have to ____________ ____________ ____________ ____________.

C 보기와 같이 목적격보어를 찾아 밑줄을 긋고, 목적격보어의 형태를 고르시오.

	목적격보어 형태
보기 I She found the box empty.	(명사 형용사 to부정사)
1 The hen keeps her eggs warm.	(명사 형용사 to부정사)
2 The adventure made him a real man.	(명사 형용사 to부정사)
3 They named the bird Dodo.	(명사 형용사 to부정사)
4 I want you to come.	(명사 형용사 to부정사)

D 우리말과 의미가 같도록 ( ) 안의 말을 배열하시오.

1 우리는 그 소문이 거짓임을 알았다. (the, false, rumor, found)

→ We ______________________________________.

2 내가 완벽할 것이라고 기대하지는 마. (to, me, expect, perfect, be)

→ Don't ______________________________________.

3 그는 그의 강아지에게 Superpower라고 이름 지었다. (his, dog, named, Superpower)

→ He ______________________________________.

4 늑대는 아기 돼지들에게 문을 열라고 말했다. (to, told, open, the baby pigs)

→ The wolf ______________________________________ the door.

5 언니는 내가 온라인으로 옷을 사기를 원한다. (to, me, buy, wants, clothes)

→ My sister ______________________________________ online.

6 그들의 털은 그들을 겨울에 따스하게 유지시켜 준다. (them, keeps, warm, in winter)

→ Their fur ______________________________________.

E 우리말과 의미가 같도록 ( ) 안의 말을 이용하여 문장을 완성하시오.

1 그들은 Tom을 책벌레라고 불렀다. (call, a bookworm)

→ They ________ ________ ________ ________.

2 달콤한 사탕은 사람들을 덜 피곤하게 만든다. (make, less tired)

→ Sweet candy ________ ________ ________ ________.

3 그녀는 경찰에게 그녀를 도와달라고 요청했다. (ask, the police)

→ She ________ ________ ________ ________ ________ ________.

4 아이들은 그 쿠키상자가 비었다는 것을 알았다. (find, empty, cookie jar)

→ The kids ________ ________ ________ ________ ________.

5 엄마는 내가 컴퓨터를 끄기를 원하셨다. (want, turn off)

→ Mom ________ ________ ________ ________ ________

the computer.

6 손을 깨끗하게 유지해라. (keep, clean)

→ ________ ________ ________ ________.

Error Correction

▪ 밑줄 친 부분에 대한 설명을 체크하고 틀린 경우엔 바르게 고치시오. (맞으면 'O' 표시)

1	You look young in that blue shirt. (→)	감각동사 look + (형용사, 부사) (보다, ~하게 보이다)
2	I feel coldly. I need a blanket. (→)	감각동사 feel + (형용사, 부사) (느끼다, ~하게 느끼다)
3	The sausage smells deliciously. (→)	감각동사 smell + (형용사, 부사) (냄새를 맡다, ~한 냄새가 나다)
4	Her voice sounds beauty. (→)	감각동사 sound + (형용사, 명사) (듣다, ~하게 들리다)
5	He showed to us his puppy. (→)	보여줬다 + (~를 ~에게, ~에게 ~를) 전치사 필요 (있음, 없음)
6	He showed his puppy for us. (→)	보여줬다 + (~를 ~에게, ~에게 ~를) 전치사 필요 (있음, 없음)
7	She bought for me a flower. (→)	사줬다 + (~를 ~에게, ~에게 ~를) 전치사 필요 (있음, 없음)
8	She bought a flower for me. (→)	샀다 + (~를 ~에게, ~에게 ~를) 전치사 필요 (있음, 없음)
9	Anna asked with him a favor. (→)	부탁했다 + (~를 ~에게, ~에게 ~를) 전치사 필요 (있음, 없음)
10	Anna asked a favor with him. (→)	부탁했다 + (~를 ~에게, ~에게 ~를) 전치사 필요 (있음, 없음)
11	We called him an iron man. (→)	주어 + call + 목적어 + 목적격보어 (형용사, 명사)
12	The news made him famously. (→)	주어 + make + 목적어 + 목적격보어 (형용사, 부사)
13	I want you like my present. (→)	주어 + want + 목적어 + 목적격보어 (동사, to부정사)

Sentence Writing

Chapter 10
동사의 종류

▪ 주어진 단어를 알맞게 이용하여 우리말과 의미가 같도록 영작하시오.

1	young, in that blue shirt	너는 / 어려 보인다 / 그 파란색 셔츠를 입으니 →
2	cold	나는 / 추운 느낌이 든다 →
3	sausage, delicious	그 소시지는 / 맛있는 냄새가 난다 →
4	voice, beautiful	그녀의 목소리는 / 아름답게 들린다 →
5	puppy, show	그는 / 보여 주었다 / 우리에게 / 그의 강아지를 →
6	puppy, show	그는 / 보여 주었다 / 그의 강아지를 / 우리에게 →
7	flower, buy	그녀는 / 사 주었다 / 나에게 / 꽃을 →
8	flower, buy	그녀는 / 샀다 / 꽃을 / 나를 위해 →
9	a favor, ask	Anna는 / 부탁했다 / 그에게 / 호의를 →
10	a favor, ask	Anna는 / 부탁했다 / 호의를 / 그에게 →
11	an iron man	우리는 / 불렀다 / 그를 / 아이언맨이라고 →
12	the news, famous	그 뉴스는 / 만들었다 / 그를 / 유명하게 →
13	present, like	나는 / 원한다 / 네가 / 내 선물을 좋아하기를 →

GP 44 and, but, or, so

등위접속사 ________, ________, ________은 대등한 관계에 있는 두 대상을 연결하고, ________는 원인과 결과를 나타내는 두 문장을 연결한다.

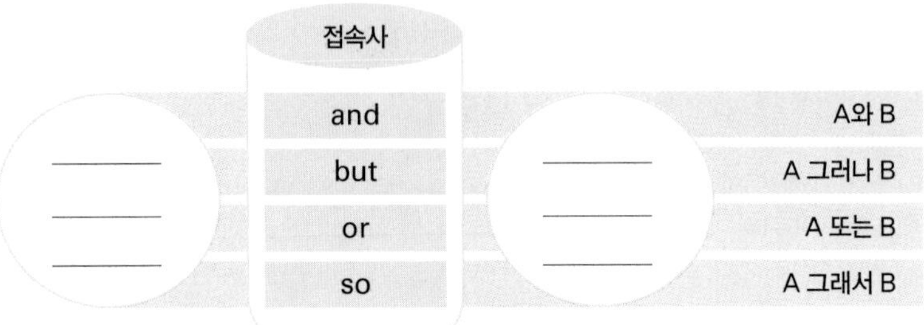

❶ and: 그리고, ~와

I think of you night **and** day.
The actor is married **and** has five sons.

❷ but: 그러나, 그런데

The soccer player is short **but** fast.
She heard the alarm, **but** she didn't get up.

❸ or: 또는, 혹은

Which subject do you like better, math **or** English?
You can visit the island by airplane **or** by ship.

❹ so: 그래서, 그러므로

Pandas are lazy, **so** they don't move a lot.
He missed the last bus, **so** he took a taxi.

Tip

접속사 so는 and, but, or과 달리 두 문장을 이어주는 역할만 할 수 있다.
Tom is kind so popular.(X)
Tom is kind, so **he is popular.**(O)

• Upgrade •

❶ [명령문, ________ ~]: ~해라, ________________________________
Open the window, **and** you will see the rainbow.

❷ [명령문, ________ ~]: ~해라, ________________________________
Open the window, **or** you won't see the rainbow.

GP 45 when, before, after

[주절과 부사절]

주절은 독립적으로 쓰일 수 있는 문장을 말하고 부사절은 [_______ + _______ + _______]의 형태로 시간, 조건, 이유 등을 나타내며 주절의 앞뒤에서 주절 전체를 수식한다.

[when, before, after]

when, before, after는 시간을 나타내는 접속사이다.

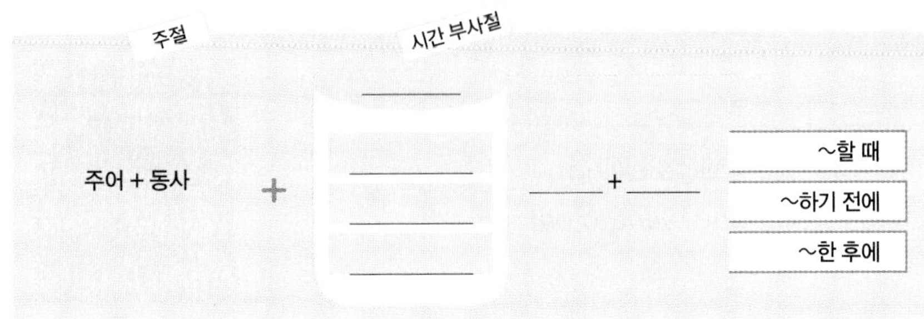

❶ ____________________

Give me a call **when** *you have time*.

When *Clara feels shy*, her face turns red.

❷ ____________________

Before *you pay for the candy*, you can't eat it.

Knock on the door **before** *you come in*.

❸ ____________________

After *he saw me*, he ran away.

Dry the dishes **after** *you wash them*.

• Upgrade •

____________에서는 ________시제 대신에 ________시제를 사용한다.

[I will bring a tent] [**when** / *go* (____________) *camping*.]
(주절) (부사절)

GP 46 because, if

because는 ______________을 나타내고, if는 ________을 나타내는 접속사이다.

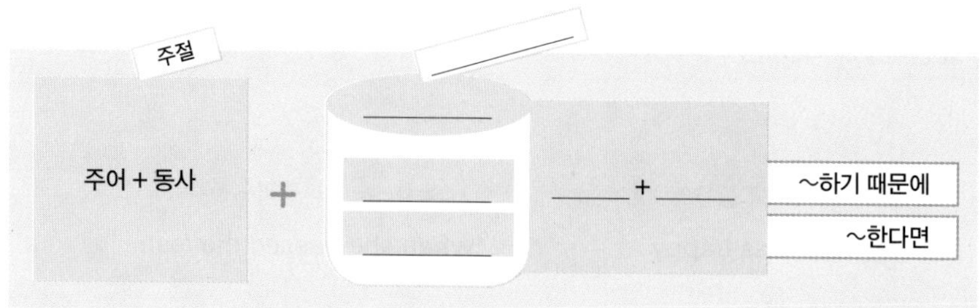

❶ ________________________

She likes the actor **because** *he is funny*.

Because *the movie is scary*, I won't watch it alone.

❷ ________________________

If *it snows tomorrow*, we will go skiing.

Pass me the cake **if** *you don't want to eat it*.

• Upgrade •

__________에서는 ________시제 대신에 ________시제를 사용한다.

[If *she* **wears** (~~will wear~~) *jeans*], [she will look younger.]

(부사절) (주절)

GP 47 that

[______________]는 '~하는 것(을)'로 해석하고, 명사처럼 주어, 목적어, 보어로 쓰인다.
한 묶음으로 특정 동사의 목적어로 쓰이며, 이때 that은 ________할 수 있다.

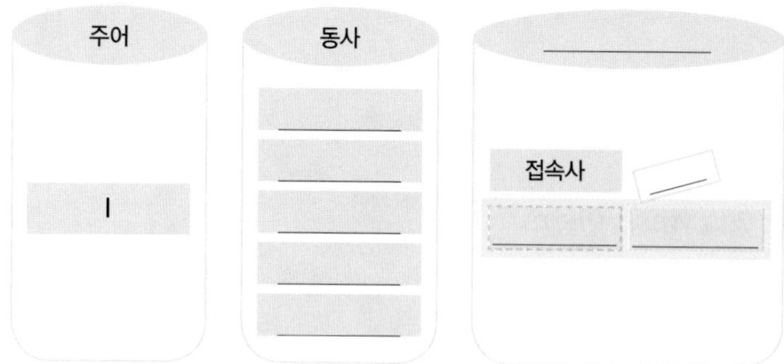

I can't believe **(that)** *my summer vacation is over*.

Some people say **(that)** *polar bears are left-handed*.

Do you think **(that)** *Emily is an angel*?

Unit 29 and, but, or, so

A ( ) 안에서 알맞은 것을 고르시오.

1 She invited me, (or, but) I can't go.

2 You may wait for him here (so, or) in the office.

3 I was wearing earphones, (so, but) I couldn't hear the bell.

4 He picked some flowers (or, and) gave them to Joan.

5 The soup was very salty, (so, but) I didn't finish it.

6 Jimmy is lazy (or, but) smart.

B 보기에서 알맞은 접속사를 골라 두 문장을 한 문장으로 완성하시오.

보기	and	but	or	so

1 I ate a sandwich. I am still hungry.

→ I ate a sandwich, ______________ I am still hungry.

2 In the fall, leaves turn red. Leaves turn yellow.

→ In the fall, leaves turn red ______________ yellow.

3 The weather was terrible. We had to stay home.

→ The weather was terrible, ______________ we had to stay home.

4 Would you like beef? Would you like chicken?

→ Would you like beef ______________ chicken?

C 보기에서 알맞은 표현을 골라 문장을 완성하시오.

보기		
	· and you will understand it.	· or you will catch a cold
	· so he got up late this morning	· but a pan pizza was delivered

1 I ordered a thin pizza, ____.

2 Wear a warm coat, ____.

3 He went to bed late, ____.

4 Read the book again, ____.

D 우리말과 의미가 같도록 ( ) 안의 말을 배열하시오.

1 우리 아빠는 일찍 일어나셔서 아침식사를 준비하셔. (breakfast, prepares, and)

→ My dad gets up early ______________________________.

2 나는 요리하는 것은 좋지만, 그 음식을 즐기지는 않아. (don't, but, enjoy, cooking, like)

→ I ______________________________ food.

3 서둘러, 그렇지 않으면 기차를 놓치게 될 거야. (will, miss, or, you)

→ Hurry up, ______________________________ the train.

4 우리는 우유와 버터를 그릇에서 섞었어. (milk, butter, and)

→ We mixed ______________________________ in the bowl.

5 너는 이 신발을 온라인 또는 오프라인 매장에서 살 수 있어. (offline, online, or)

→ You can buy the shoes from an ______________________________ store.

6 Clara는 왼손잡이야, 그래서 가위를 왼손으로 사용해. (she, the scissors, uses, so)

→ Clara is left-handed, ______________________________ with her left hand.

E 우리말과 의미가 같도록 ( ) 안의 말을 이용하여 문장을 완성하시오.

1 Jane이나 너 둘 중에 한 명이 대회의 승자가 될 거야. (you)

→ ________ ________ ________ will be the winner of the contest.

2 길이 미끄러워서 우리는 천천히 걸었어. (walk, slowly)

→ The street was slippery, ________ ________ ________ ________.

3 매일 과일을 많이 먹으렴, 그러면 건강해질 거야. (be healthy)

→ Eat a lot of fruit every day, ________ ________ ________ ________ ________.

4 당신은 언제라도 나에게 전화하거나 찾아와도 좋아요. (call, visit)

→ You can ________ ________ ________ ________ any time.

5 이 약은 고약한 맛이 나지만 너의 건강에 좋아. (be good for, health)

→ This medicine tastes bad ________ ________ ________ ________ ________ ________.

6 밖에 먼지가 많아서 우리는 마스크를 착용해야만 해. (must, wear, masks)

→ It is dusty outside, ________ ________ ________ ________ ________.

Unit 30 when, before, after

A ( ) 안에서 알맞은 것을 고르시오.

1 (When, Before) she was young, she was poor.

2 I go to bed (before, after) I brush my teeth.

3 Will you wake me up when Santa (comes, will come) tonight?

4 He winked at me (before, when) he saw me.

5 She warmed the pizza up (before, after) she ate it.

6 They shook hands (when, before) they met.

7 (After, Before) he dropped his fork, he asked for a new one.

B 접속사의 뜻에 주의하여 밑줄 친 부분을 해석하시오.

1 When she is tired, she takes a bath. 해석 ______________________

2 Get dressed after you take a shower. 해석 ______________________

3 After he won the prize, he became famous. 해석 ______________________

4 I make a plan before I begin to work. 해석 ______________________

5 You will get a discount when you visit us again. 해석 ______________________

6 Before I go out, I look in a mirror. 해석 ______________________

C 보기에서 알맞은 표현을 골라 문장을 완성하시오.

보기	
· after I made a shopping list	· before he leaves the hotel
· before you buy the pencil	· when I listen to music

1 He will pack his bag ______________________.

2 ______________________, all my stress goes away.

3 ______________________, I went to the market.

4 Check the price ______________________.

D **우리말과 의미가 같도록 ( ) 안의 말을 배열하시오.**

1 국수를 먹을 때, 그들은 젓가락을 사용한다. (noodles, they, when, eat)

→ They use chopsticks ______________________________.

2 어두워지기 전에 아이들은 집으로 돌아갈 거야. (it, dark, before, gets)

→ The children will go back home ______________________________.

3 그가 손을 씻은 후에, 그는 요리를 시작했어. (his hands, after, washed, he)

→ ______________________________, he started cooking.

4 봄이 오기 전에, 우리는 교실을 청소할 것이다. (comes, before, spring)

→ ______________________________, we will clean our classroom.

5 살을 약간 뺀 후에, 내 예전 바지를 다시 입을 거야. (some weight, after, lose, I)

→ ______________________________, I will wear my old pants again.

6 비가 올 때, 우리는 운동장에서 놀 수 없다. (it, when, rains)

→ ______________________________, we can't play on the playground.

E **우리말과 의미가 같도록 ( ) 안의 말을 이용하여 문장을 완성하시오.**

1 유성을 보았을 때, 나는 소원을 빌었다. (a shooting star)

→ ______ ______ ______ ______ ______ ______,

I made a wish.

2 그녀는 말하기 전에 항상 먼저 들어 준다. (talk)

→ She always listens first ______ ______ ______.

3 가스를 사용한 후에는 가스를 끌게요. (use)

→ I will turn off the gas ______ ______ ______ ______.

4 내가 집에 오기 전에, 남동생이 케이크를 다 먹을 것이다. (come home)

→ ______ ______ ______ ______, my brother will eat the whole cake.

5 그는 내가 그의 도움이 필요할 때 나를 도와줄까? (need, help)

→ Will he help me ______ ______ ______ ______ ______?

6 그가 마음을 바꾸기 전에 서둘자. (change, mind)

→ Let's hurry ______ ______ ______ ______ ______.

Unit 31 because, if, that

A ( ) 안에서 알맞은 것을 고르시오.

1 Do you know (because, that) carrots are grown in the ground?

2 We won't wait for you (that, if) you are late again.

3 Your dream will come true (that, because) you work hard.

4 If she (will get, gets) some rest, she will feel better.

5 Do you think (if, that) this dress looks good on me?

6 (That, If) you want, you can have this hat.

7 I couldn't use the computer (because, that) it was broken.

B 보기에서 알맞은 접속사를 골라 두 문장을 한 문장으로 완성하시오.

보기 | if because that

1 People say so. I look like my father.

→ People say ______________ I look like my father.

2 Tom is kind to everyone. He is popular.

→ ______________ Tom is kind to everyone, he is popular.

3 Be nice to your sister. Then she will like you.

→ ______________ you are nice to your sister, she will like you.

4 I didn't know it. She has a twin sister.

→ I didn't know ______________ she has a twin sister.

C 보기에서 알맞은 표현을 골라 문장을 완성하시오.

보기 | · if you add more salt · she can save the birds · because they smell bad · it feels cool

1 I like the color blue because ______________________________.

2 ______________________________, the spaghetti will taste better.

3 I don't like koalas ______________________________.

4 She hopes ______________________________.

D 우리말과 의미가 같도록 ( ) 안의 말을 배열하시오.

1 나는 낙타가 혹에 물을 저장하지 않는 것을 알아. (camels, water, don't store, that)

→ I know ______________________________ in their humps.

2 만약 당신이 19세면, 투표를 할 수 있어요. (you, if, 19 years old, are, over)

→ You can vote ______________________________.

3 호수가 깊기 때문에, 너는 여기서 수영할 수 없어. (the lake, deep, is, because)

→ ______________________________, you can't swim here.

4 이 게임을 이긴다면, 너는 트로피를 받게 될 거야. (you, if, game, this, win)

→ ______________________________, you will get a trophy.

5 나는 그가 아름다운 목소리를 갖고 있다고 생각해. (beautiful, that, he, a, has, voice)

→ I think ______________________________.

6 그녀가 열쇠를 잃어버려서 그녀는 상자를 열 수 없었어. (lost, she, because, the key)

→ She couldn't open the box ______________________________.

E 우리말과 의미가 같도록 ( ) 안의 말을 이용하여 문장을 완성하시오.

1 그 리포터가 내일 비가 올 거라고 말했어. (say, it)

→ The reporter ______ ______ ______ ______ ______ tomorrow.

2 내가 달에 가면, 내 몸무게는 8kg 일 거야. (go, the moon)

→ ______ ______ ______ ______ ______ ______,
my weight will be eight kilograms.

3 날씨가 더워서 우리는 수영하러 갔다. (it, hot)

→ We went swimming ______ ______ ______ ______.

4 물을 마시지 않으면, 음식을 소화시킬 수 없어. (drink water)

→ ______ ______ ______ ______ ______, you can't digest food.

5 밖이 먼지투성이어서, 나는 마스크를 썼다. (it, dusty, outside)

→ ______ ______ ______ ______ ______, I wore a mask.

6 나는 Dylan이 남자형제가 2명 있다는 것을 알아. (know, have)

→ I ______ ______ ______ ______ ______ ______.

Error Correction

▪ 밑줄 친 부분에 대한 설명을 체크하고 틀린 경우엔 바르게 고치시오. (맞으면 'O' 표시)

1	I think of you night but day. (→)	낮 (그리고, 그러나) 밤에
2	The soccer player is short or fast. (→)	키가 작은 (또는, 그러나) 빠른
3	Which subject do you like better, math and English? (→)	어느 것이 더 좋니, 수학 (그리고, 또는) 영어?
4	He missed the last bus, or he took a taxi. (→)	버스를 놓쳤어 + (또는, 그래서) 택시를 탔어
5	Open the window, or you will see the rainbow. (→)	창문을 열어 + (그렇지 않으면, 그러면) 너는 무지개를 볼 거야
6	Open the window, and you won't see the rainbow. (→)	창문을 열어 + (그러면, 그렇지 않으면) 너는 무지개를 못 볼 거야
7	Before Clara feels shy, her face turns red. (→)	얼굴이 빨개져 + 부끄러움을 (느낄 때, 느끼기 전에)
8	After you pay for the candy, you can't eat it. (→)	계산하기 (전에, 후에) + 그것을 먹을 수 없어
9	I will bring a tent when I will go camping. (→)	시간 부사절에서는 미래를 나타낼 때 (현재, 미래)시제 사용
10	She likes the actor that he is funny. (→)	그 배우가 좋아 + 재미있(는 것을, 기 때문에)
11	If it will snow tomorrow, we will go skiing. (→)	조건 부사절에서는 미래를 나타낼 때 (현재, 미래)시제 사용
12	Pass me the cake because you don't want to eat it. (→)	내게 줘 + 먹고 싶지 않(기 때문에, 다면)
13	Do you think if Emily is an angel? (→)	너는 생각하니 + Emily가 천사(라면, 라는 것을)?

Sentence Writing

▪ 주어진 단어를 알맞게 이용하여 우리말과 의미가 같도록 영작하시오.

1	think of	나는 너를 생각한다 / 낮과 밤에 →
2	short, fast	그 축구 선수는 ~이다 / 키가 작지만 빠른 →
3	which subject	어떤 과목을 / 더 좋아하니, / 수학 또는 영어? →
4	miss, take	그는 마지막 버스를 놓쳤다, / 그래서 / 택시를 탔다 →
5	the rainbow, see	창문을 열어라, / 그러면 / 너는 무지개를 볼 거다 →
6	the rainbow, see	창문을 열어라, / 그렇지 않으면 / 무지개를 못 볼 거다 →
7	feel shy, turn red	~할 때 + Clara가 부끄러움을 느끼다, / 그녀의 얼굴은 빨개진다 →
8	pay for, candy	~하기 전에 + 네가 사탕 값을 지불하다, / 그것을 먹을 수 없다 →
9	bring, go camping	나는 그 텐트를 가져 갈 거다 / ~할 때 + 내가 캠핑가다 →
10	the actor, funny	그녀는 그 남자배우를 좋아한다 / ~하기 때문에 + 그는 웃기다 →
11	it, snow, go skiing	~한다면 + 내일 눈이 온다, / 우리는 스키 타러 갈 것이다 →
12	the cake, pass	내게 케이크를 건네줘 / ~한다면 + 넌 이것을 먹고 싶지 않다 →
13	think, an angel	너는 생각하니 / ~라는 것을 + Emily가 천사다 →

GP 48 시간을 나타내는 전치사 I

______	______	______
at 2 o'clock	on Sunday	in September
at noon	on June 2	in summer
at night	on Halloween	in 2018
at dawn	on my birthday	in the morning
__________이나 ______	__________	__________ 등 비교적 긴 시간

My school starts ______ 8:30 a.m.
Alex was born ______ May 7.
People enjoy skiing ______ the winter.

GP 49 시간을 나타내는 전치사 II

__________	~ 전에	__________	~ 후에
__________	~ 동안	__________	~ 동안
__________	~까지 (동작 완료)	__________	~까지 (동작의 계속)
__________	A와 B 사이에	__________	A부터 B까지

The actor became famous **after** the movie.
I don't eat snacks **before** dinner.

Some koalas sleep **for** 17 hours a day.
Hamsters are underground **during** the day.

• Upgrade •

for + __________	during + __________
______ 20 minutes / five weeks	______ class / vacation

I must finish the report ______ tomorrow.
You can download the file ______ next month.

The beach is open ______ June ______ August.
He works **from** Monday **to** Friday.

GP 50 장소를 나타내는 전치사 I

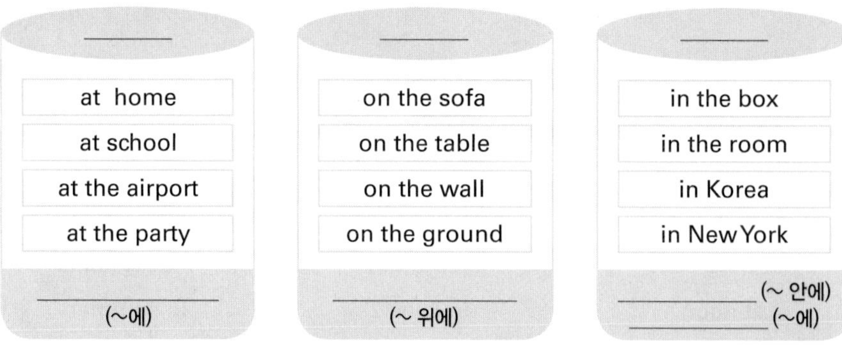

at home
at school
at the airport
at the party
__________ (~에)
on the sofa
on the table
on the wall
on the ground
__________ (~ 위에)
in the box
in the room
in Korea
in New York
__________ (~ 안에)
__________ (~에)

I lost my backpack **at** the airport.
Look at the pictures **on** the wall.
Jasmine has some coins **in** her pocket.

GP 51 장소를 나타내는 전치사 II

____________	(접촉 없이) ~ 위에	____________	(접촉 없이) ~ 아래에
____________	~ 앞에	____________	~ 뒤에
____________	~ 옆에	____________	~ 근처에
____________	~을 가로질러	____________	~ 맞은편에
____________	A와 B 사이에	____________	A부터 B까지

There was a rainbow **over** the hill.
You can find shade **under** a tree.

Emma feels shy **in front of** many people.
My house is **behind** the park.

A bodyguard stood **next to** the singer.

The train runs **across** the desert.
The café is **across from** the gas station.
Korea is **between** Japan **and** China.
This plane flies **from** Seoul **to** Busan.

GP 52 기타 전치사

by	______	______

May I pay **by** credit card?
We crossed the river **by** boat.

• Upgrade •

by + ______	by + ______
______ car / airplane / bicycle	______ e-mail / text message / the Internet

with	______	______

I carried the box **with** George.
Wash your hands **with** soap.

for	______	______

I bought some flowers **for** my mom.
Thank you **for** your advice.

to	______	______

We went **to** the museum yesterday.
Ken sent a text message **to** me.

Tip
전치사 뒤에 대명사가 오면 ______으로 쓴다.
This gift is **for** ~~he~~. (×)
→ him.(o)

about	______	like	______

I have some questions **about** grammar.
Greg dressed **like** a zombie at the Halloween party.

Unit 32 시간을 나타내는 전치사 I • II

A ( ) 안에서 알맞은 것을 고르시오.

1 Bats are active (at, in) night.

2 They stayed at home (at, on) a rainy day.

3 Come home early (before, after) school.

4 We have a midterm exam (in, on) October 11.

5 The king ruled Shilla from 654 (and, to) 661.

6 She will hold a concert (in, on) August.

7 What do you do (in, on) Halloween?

8 The drugstore is open (to, until) midnight.

9 We have a 10-minute break (during, between) classes.

10 The department store was crowded (for, during) the big sale.

B 보기에서 알맞은 전치사를 골라 문장을 완성하시오.

보기	in	on	at

1 Did you have lunch ______________ noon?

2 All my brothers were born ______________ winter.

3 My mom usually gets up ______________ 6 o'clock.

4 Birds sang loudly ______________ the early morning.

5 Did Christopher Columbus find America ______________ 1492?

6 Koreans usually eat seaweed soup ______________ their birthday.

C 빈칸에 for 또는 during 중 알맞은 것을 쓰시오.

1 I want to sleep ________________ two days.

2 We talked about the idea ________________ the meeting.

3 Chris will stay in Paris ________________ three months.

4 Bake the cookies in an oven ________________ 12 minutes.

5 Some animals mostly sleep ________________ the day.

6 He drew these pictures ________________ his trip to Africa.

D **우리말과 의미가 같도록 ( ) 안의 말을 배열하시오.**

1 가격이 8월 이후에 내려갔어. (after, went down, August)

→ The price ______________________________.

2 그들의 다음 앨범이 올해 7월에 나온다. (July, comes, out, in)

→ Their next album ______________________________ this year.

3 Jane은 자신의 순서 전에 긴장했어. (nervous, felt, her turn, before)

→ Jane ______________________________.

4 봄 세일은 2월 14일부터 28일까지이다. (February 14, 28, to, from, is)

→ The spring sale ______________________________.

5 우리는 새해 첫날에 일출을 보았어. (on, watched, the sunrise, New Year's Day)

→ We ______________________________.

6 우리에게 이 소포를 이번 주 목요일까지 보내세요. (the package, this, by, Thursday)

→ Send us ______________________________.

E **우리말과 의미가 같도록 ( ) 안의 말을 이용하여 문장을 완성하시오.**

1 이 우물은 여름에는 마른다. (summer)

→ The well goes dry __________ __________.

2 우리는 이번 주 일요일까지 여기에 머무를 거야. (this Sunday)

→ We will stay here __________ __________ __________.

3 그 지진은 오늘 오후 2시 27분에 발생했습니다. (2:27 p.m.)

→ The earthquake occurred __________ __________ __________ today.

4 클럽회원들은 수요일마다 만난다. (Wednesdays)

→ The club members get together __________ __________.

5 이 시간대 동안에는 햇볕을 피하세요. (these hours)

→ Stay out of the sun __________ __________ __________.

6 그 호텔은 조식을 아침 6시와 10시 사이에 제공한다. (10 a.m.)

→ The hotel serves breakfast __________ 6 __________ 10 a.m.

A ( ) 안에서 알맞은 것을 고르시오.

1 My mom works (at, on) a school.

2 The plane flew (over, on) the Alps.

3 They swam (between, across) the river.

4 Is there a bus stop (near, in) your school?

5 There are many stores (in, on) the market.

6 How far is it (from, between) the sun to the Earth?

B 보기에서 알맞은 전치사를 골라 문장을 완성하시오. (중복 사용 가능)

보기	in	on	at

1 Mr. Smith put his key ______________ the table.

2 There were two birds ______________ the cage.

3 You can find the hair shop ______________ the third floor.

4 What do you have ______________ your pocket?

5 My uncle looked happy ______________ the party.

6 She visited many places ______________ Europe.

C 보기에서 알맞은 전치사를 골라 문장을 완성하시오. (한 번씩만 사용)

보기	near	under	behind	over

1 You can find shade __________________ a tree.

2 The dog likes to hide __________________ the door.

3 My grandparents live __________________ my family.

4 Becky holds an umbrella __________________ her friend.

보기	across from	front	between	from

5 The park is __________________ the school.

6 I dropped a coin __________________ the wall and the bed.

7 There is a lake in __________________ of the park.

8 It takes 10 minutes __________________ the station to my house.

D **우리말과 의미가 같도록 ( ) 안의 말을 배열하시오.**

1 그들은 땅 아래에 터널을 지었다. (a tunnel, the ground, built, under)

→ They ________________________________.

2 우리는 다음 정거장에서 내릴 거예요. (the next stop, get off, at)

→ We will ________________________________.

3 달에 생명체가 있나요? (any life, the moon, on)

→ Is there ________________________________?

4 그 오리는 닭 두 마리 사이에서 자고 있더군. (two, between, sleeping, chickens)

→ The duck was ________________________________.

5 컵에 우유가 거의 없네. (in, milk, little, the glass)

→ There is ________________________________.

6 공이 네트 위로 튀었어. (the net, bounced, over)

→ The ball ________________________________.

7 그 소식은 나라 전역의 사람들에게 충격을 주었어. (across, people, shocked, the country)

→ The news ________________________________.

E **우리말과 의미가 같도록 ( ) 안의 말을 이용하여 문장을 완성하시오.**

1 나는 그녀 옆에 앉기를 원했다. (sit)

→ I wanted to ________ ________ ________ ________.

2 그는 아홉 시부터 다섯 시까지 근무하셔. (nine, five)

→ He works ________ ________ ________ ________.

3 나는 이 책 안에서 10달러 지폐를 한 장 찾았어. (the book)

→ She found a ten-dollar bill ________ ________ ________.

4 그 강아지는 등에 검은 점이 하나 있어. (its back)

→ The puppy has a black spot ________ ________ ________.

5 해가 구름 뒤에서 밝게 비추고 있다. (the clouds)

→ The sun is shining brightly ________ ________ ________.

6 우리는 뮤직페스티벌에서 즐거운 시간을 보냈어. (the music festival)

→ We had a great time ________ ________ ________ ________.

Unit 34 기타 전치사

A ( ) 안에서 알맞은 것을 고르시오.

1 She never writes her name (by, with) a red pen.

2 What did you give (at, to) your mom?

3 The soldiers fought (to, for) their country.

4 Christopher acted (like, at) my brother.

5 The teacher knows a lot (like, about) her students.

6 The country is famous (for, with) tulips.

7 Did you come here (like, by) subway?

B 보기에서 알맞은 전치사를 골라 문장을 완성하시오.

보기	by	about	to	like

1 Could you bring this ______________ my house?

2 You can order the food ______________ phone.

3 You look ______________ a musical actor.

4 Lucy told me ______________ her plan.

C 빈칸에 공통으로 들어갈 전치사를 보기에서 골라 쓰시오.

보기	with	by	for	to

1 He worked hard ______________ his family.
Samantha stayed at home ______________ rest.

2 Cut the watermelon ______________ a knife.
You can go shopping ______________ us.

3 Did you give food ______________ the dog?
Let's go ______________ the concert together.

4 Traveling ______________ plane is comfortable.
I will send you the file ______________ e-mail.

D 밑줄 친 전치사의 의미를 보기에서 고르시오.

보기 | ① ~을 가지고 ② ~와 함께 ③ ~를 위해 ④ ~ 때문에	의미
1 The boys played with the puppy.	
2 I am sorry for the mistake.	
3 We covered our faces with masks.	
4 Is milk really good for our health?	

E 우리말과 의미가 같도록 ( ) 안의 말을 배열하시오.

1 오늘의 주제는 해양 동물에 관한 것입니다. (sea, about, animals)

→ Today's topic is ______________________________.

2 나는 그 상자를 초록색 종이로 포장했어. (with, the box, green paper)

→ I wrapped ______________________________.

3 그녀는 안전을 위해 헬멧을 착용한다. (for, a helmet, safety)

→ She wears ______________________________.

4 그는 나에게 이메일로 초대장을 보냈다. (an, by, invitation, e-mail)

→ He sent me ______________________________.

5 나는 경찰에게 사실을 말할 거야. (the truth, the police, tell, to)

→ I will ______________________________.

F 우리말과 의미가 같도록 ( ) 안의 말을 이용하여 문장을 완성하시오.

1 당신과 얘기할 수 있을까요? (talk)

→ Can I __________ __________ __________?

2 Sandra는 전화로 티켓을 예약했어. (phone)

→ Sandra booked the ticket __________ __________.

3 올빼미처럼, 어떤 동물들은 밤에 사냥을 해. (owls)

→ __________ __________, some animals hunt at night.

4 나는 내 헤어스타일에 대한 너의 조언이 필요해. (hairstyle)

→ I need your advice __________ __________ __________.

5 Fred는 그의 친구들에게 자신의 게임 기술을 보여 줬어. (friends)

→ Fred showed his game skills __________ __________ __________.

Error Correction

▪ 밑줄 친 부분에 대한 설명을 체크하고 틀린 경우엔 바르게 고치시오. (맞으면 'O' 표시)

1	My school starts <u>on</u> 8:30 a.m. (→)	(on, at, in) + 구체적인 시간
2	Alex was born <u>at</u> May 7. (→)	(on, at, in) + 특정한 날
3	People enjoy skiing <u>on</u> the winter. (→)	(on, at, in) + 계절
4	Some koalas sleep <u>during</u> 17 hours a day. (→)	(during, for) + (특정한 기간명사, 숫자 포함 기간)
5	Hamsters are underground <u>for</u> the day. (→)	(during, for) + (특정한 기간명사, 숫자 포함 기간)
6	I lost my backpack <u>on</u> the airport. (→)	(표면 위에, 비교적 좁은 지점에) (at, on, in) + the airport
7	Look at the pictures <u>in</u> the wall. (→)	(표면 위에, 안에) (on, in) + the wall
8	Jasmine has some coins <u>at</u> her pocket (→)	(비교적 좁은 지점에, 안에) (on, in) + her pocket
9	This plane flies from Seoul <u>and</u> Busan. (→)	(A부터 B까지, A와 B 사이에) from A (and, to) B
10	We crossed the river <u>by</u> boat. (→)	(~을 가지고, ~을 타고) + boat
11	Wash your hands <u>by</u> soap. (→)	(~에 의해, ~을 가지고) + soap
12	Ken sent a text message to <u>I</u>. (→)	전치사 + (주격, 목적격) 대명사
13	Greg dressed <u>like</u> a zombie at the Halloween party. (→)	(좋아하다, ~처럼) + a zombie

Sentence Writing

Chapter 12
전치사

■ 주어진 단어를 알맞게 이용하여 우리말과 의미가 같도록 영작하시오.

1	start, 8:30 a.m.	나의 학교는 / 시작한다 / 아침 8시 30분에 →
2	was born	Alex는 / 태어났다 / 5월 7일에 →
3	enjoy skiing	사람들은 / 스키 타는 것을 즐긴다 / 겨울에 →
4	koalas, a day	일부 코알라들은 / 잠을 잔다 / 17시간 동안 / 하루에 →
5	hamsters, be underground	햄스터는 / 땅속에서 있다 / 낮 동안 →
6	backpack	나는 / 가방을 잃어버렸다 / 공항에서 →
7	look at	봐라 / 저 그림을 / 벽 위에 →
8	coins, pocket	Jasmine은 / 약간의 동전을 가지고 있다 / 그녀의 주머니 안에 →
9	fly	이 비행기는 / 날아간다 / 서울에서 부산까지 →
10	cross	우리는 / 강을 건넜다 / 보트로 →
11	soap	씻어라 / 너의 손을 / 비누를 가지고 →
12	text message	Ken은 / 문자 메시지를 보냈다 / 나에게 →
13	zombie Halloween party	Greg는 / 옷을 입었다 / 좀비처럼 / 핼러윈 파티에서 →

도전! 필수구문 156

Chapter 01 be동사와 인칭대명사 통문장 영작

001	그녀는 디자이너이다.	→
002	그들은 지금 학교에 있다.	→
003	그 시험은 매우 어려웠다.	→
004	많은 소년들이 운동장에 있었다.	→
005	내 가방 안에 책이 한 권 있다.	→
006	그는 지금 집에 있지 않다.	→
007	Mary는 졸리지 않았었다.	→
008	Amy는 10살이니?	→
009	그들은 지난주에 미국에 있었니?	→
010	그의 차는 아주 멋지다.	→
011	그녀의 친구들이 그녀를 아주 많이 좋아한다.	→
012	그들은 나와 함께 일요일마다 사이클링 하러 간다.	→
013	그 자전거는 그녀의 것이다.	→

도전! 필수구문 156

Chapter 02 일반동사 통문장 영작

014	나는 요리를 매우 잘한다.	→
015	그는 TV로 야구경기를 본다.	→
016	그 소년은 언제나 최선을 다한다.	→
017	Chris는 많은 별명을 가지고 있다.	→
018	우리는 어제 농구를 했다.	→
019	축제는 한 시간 전에 시작했다.	→
020	Edison은 1879년에 전구를 발명했다.	→
021	그들은 청바지를 입지 않는다.	→
022	Sam은 블랙커피를 좋아하지 않는다.	→
023	어제 비가 심하게 내리지는 않았다.	→
024	너는 수영 잘하니? 아니, 못해.	→
025	Michael은 매일 그의 개를 산책시키니?	→
026	너의 언니는 New York에 머물렀었니?	→

도전! 필수구문 156

Chapter 03 명사와 관사 통문장 영작

027	그녀는 새 가방을 원한다.	→
028	그녀는 가방 열 개를 원한다.	→
029	우리는 파티에서 아주 재미있게 보냈다.	→
030	나에게 물 한 잔 갖다 줄래요?	→
031	그들은 커피 세 잔을 주문했다.	→
032	나는 보통 아침에 사과 하나를 먹는다.	→
033	나의 여동생은 일주일에 책 두 권을 읽는다.	→
034	그녀는 펜이 하나 있다. 그 펜은 매우 유용하다.	→
035	그 소금 좀 나에게 건네줄래요?	→
036	지구는 항성이 아니라 행성이다.	→
037	나는 보통 방과 후에 바이올린을 연주한다.	→
038	John의 가장 좋아하는 스포츠는 축구이다.	→
039	나는 버스로 유럽을 여행했다.	→

도전! 필수구문 156

Chapter 04 대명사 통문장 영작

040	이것은 내가 제일 좋아하는 시계야.	→
041	이 집들은 매우 오래되었다.	→
042	저것은 너의 생일 선물이야.	→
043	저 나무들은 잎이 없어.	→
044	7시다.	→
045	그녀는 이 사진을 찍었어. 나는 그게 마음에 들어.	→
046	나는 약간의 질문이 있어.	→
047	초콜릿 조금 먹을래?	→
048	나는 어떤 질문도 없어.	→
049	모든 소년들이 복도에 서 있다.	→
050	모든 돈은 안전한 장소에 있다.	→
051	각각의 소년은 자기 자신의 핸드폰을 가지고 있다.	→
052	모든 학생은 짧은 바지를 입고 있다.	→

도전! 필수구문 156

Chapter 05 진행형과 미래시제 통문장 영작

053	그는 인터넷 서핑을 하는 중이다.	→
054	우리는 영어 문법을 공부하는 중이다.	→
055	그들은 그때 야구 경기를 관람하는 중이었다.	→
056	나는 농담하고 있는 중이 아니다.	→
057	Andrew는 선생님의 말씀을 듣고 있지 않았다.	→
058	너는 안경을 착용하고 있는 중이니?	→
059	게임은 인기 있을 거야.	→
060	곧 비가 올 거야.	→
061	우리는 파티를 열 예정이야.	→
062	우리는 다시 싸우지 않을 거예요.	→
063	저는 교실에서 뛰어다니지 않을 거예요.	→
064	그 배우가 한국에 올까요?	→
065	너는 너의 친구들을 초대할 예정이니?	→

도전! 필수구문 156

Chapter 06 조동사 통문장 영작

066	그 로봇은 말을 할 수 있다. (able)	→
067	그는 자전거를 탈 수 없다.	→
068	너는 그 컴퓨터를 고칠 수 있니?	→
069	너는 지금 집으로 가도 된다.	→
070	제가 질문을 물어봐도 될까요?	→
071	그녀는 배가 고플지도 몰라.	→
072	우리는 빨간 불에 멈춰야 한다.	→
073	너는 개들에게 아이스크림을 주면 안 된다.	→
074	그 치즈케이크는 맛있는 것이 분명해.	→
075	그녀는 약간의 휴식을 가져야 한다.	→
076	Phillip은 체중을 줄일 필요가 없다.	→
077	내가 기다려야 할까?	→
078	Tom은 더 많은 야채를 먹어야 한다.	→

도전! 필수구문 156

Chapter 07 의문사와 여러 가지 문장 통문장 영작

079	너의 새 선생님은 누구시니?	→
080	네가 제일 좋아하는 과목은 무엇이니?	→
081	너는 어느 것을 원하니, 오렌지 또는 키위?	→
082	영화는 언제 시작하나요?	→
083	너는 이 책을 어디에서 찾았니?	→
084	나는 공항에 어떻게 갈 수 있을까요?	→
085	너는 얼마나 자주 운동하니?	→
086	시험이 쉽지 않았니? 아니, 쉬웠어.	→
087	그녀는 매일 아침 아침식사를 해, 그렇지 않니?	→
088	너는 북극곰을 못 봤어, 그렇지?	→
089	긴장하지 마.	→
090	이 게임은 정말 인기가 있구나!	→
091	정말 아름다운 날이구나!	→

도전! 필수구문 156

Chapter 08 형용사와 부사 통문장 영작

092	우리는 가까운 친구들이다.	→
093	이 영화는 흥미로웠다.	→
094	많은 휴일들이 5월에 있다.	→
095	그는 Julie를 며칠 전에 만났다.	→
096	그녀는 빵 위에 약간의 잼을 발랐다.	→
097	Jack은 천천히 학교로 걸어갔다.	→
098	나는 매우 키가 큰 친구들을 갖고 있다.	→
099	그는 종종 틀릴 수도 있다.	→
100	Tom은 언제나 수업에 늦는다.	→
101	그녀는 결코 저녁식사로 고기를 먹지 않는다.	→
102	Sarah는 벌 만큼 바쁘다.	→
103	차가운 공기는 뜨거운 공기보다 무겁다.	→
104	고래는 모든 동물들 중에서 가장 크다.	→

도전! 필수구문 156

Chapter 09 부정사와 동명사 통문장 영작

105	웹툰을 읽는 것은 재미있다. (5단어)	→
106	웹툰을 읽는 것은 재미있다. (6단어)	→
107	우리는 동물원 방문하는 것을 결정했다.	→
108	나의 꿈은 게임 디자이너가 되는 것이다.	→
109	그는 국수를 요리할 특별한 방법을 알고 있다.	→
110	제게 무언가 차가운 마실 것을 주세요.	→
111	그들은 배를 만들기 위해 로봇을 사용했다.	→
112	나는 그 소식을 듣게 되어 유감이다.	→
113	그의 이름은 기억하기에 쉽다.	→
114	롤러코스터를 타는 것은 무섭다. (6단어)	→
115	당신은 저를 위해 문을 여는 것을 꺼려하시나요?	→
116	들어 주셔서 고맙습니다.	→
117	그녀의 좋은 습관은 일찍 일어나는 것이다.	→

도전! 필수구문 156

Chapter 10 동사의 종류 통문장 영작

118	너는 그 파란색 셔츠를 입으니 어려 보인다.	→
119	나는 추운 느낌이 든다.	→
120	그 소시지는 맛있는 냄새가 난다.	→
121	그녀의 목소리는 아름답게 들린다.	→
122	그는 우리에게 그의 강아지를 보여 주었다. (~에게 ~를)	→
123	그는 그의 강아지를 우리에게 보여 주었다. (~를 ~에게)	→
124	그녀는 나에게 꽃을 사 주었다. (~에게 ~를)	→
125	그녀는 꽃을 나를 위해 샀다. (~를 ~에게)	→
126	Anna는 그에게 부탁을 했다. (~에게 ~를)	→
127	Anna는 부탁을 그에게 했다. (~를 ~에게)	→
128	우리는 그를 아이언맨이라고 불렀다.	→
129	그 뉴스는 그를 유명하게 만들었다.	→
130	나는 네가 내 선물을 좋아하기를 원한다.	→

도전! 필수구문 156

Chapter 11 접속사 통문장 영작

131	나는 너를 낮과 밤에 (밤낮으로) 생각해.	→
132	그 축구 선수는 키가 작지만 빠르지.	→
133	어떤 과목을 더 좋아하니, 수학 또는 영어?	→
134	그는 마지막 버스를 놓쳤어, 그래서 택시를 탔어.	→
135	창문을 열어, 그러면 너는 무지개를 볼 거야.	→
136	창문을 열어, 그렇지 않으면 무지개를 못 볼 거야.	→
137	Clara가 부끄러움을 느낄 때, 그녀의 얼굴은 빨개져.	→
138	네가 사탕 값을 지불하기 전에, 너는 이것을 먹을 수 없어.	→
139	내가 캠핑을 갈 때, 나는 그 텐트를 가져갈 거야.	→
140	그녀는 그가 웃기기 때문에, 그 배우를 좋아한다.	→
141	내일 눈이 온다면, 우리는 스키를 타러 갈 것이다.	→
142	네가 케이크를 먹고 싶지 않다면, 내게 이것을 건네줘.	→
143	너는 Emily가 천사라고(라는 것을) 생각하니?	→

도전! 필수구문 156

Chapter 12 전치사 통문장 영작

144	나의 학교는 아침 8시 30분에 시작한다.	→
145	Alex는 5월 7일에 태어났다.	→
146	사람들은 겨울에 스키 타는 것을 즐긴다.	→
147	일부 코알라들은 하루에 17시간 동안 잠을 잔다.	→
148	햄스터는 낮 동안 땅속에서 있다.	→
149	나는 공항에서 가방을 잃어버렸다.	→
150	벽 위에 저 그림을 봐라.	→
151	Jasmine은 그녀의 주머니 안에 약간의 동전을 가지고 있다.	→
152	이 비행기는 서울에서 부산까지 날아간다.	→
153	우리는 보트로 강을 건넜다.	→
154	비누를 가지고 너의 손을 씻어라.	→
155	Ken은 나에게 문자 메시지를 보냈다.	→
156	Greg는 핼러윈 파티에서 좀비처럼 옷을 입었다.	→

불규칙 변화 동사 70

▪ 다음 동사의 과거형과 과거분사를 쓰시오.

	동사원형	의미	과거형	과거분사
01	bear	견디다, 낳다	bore	born
02	begin	시작하다		
03	bite	물다		
04	blow	불다		
05	break	깨다, 부수다		
06	bring	가져오다, 데려오다		
07	build	짓다		
08	burn	불타다		
09	buy	사다		
10	catch	붙들다		
11	choose	고르다		
12	come	오다		
13	cut	베다, 자르다		
14	drink	마시다		
15	drive	운전하다		
16	eat	먹다		
17	fall	떨어지다		
18	feel	느낌이 들다, 느끼다		
19	fight	싸우다		
20	find	발견하다		
21	forgive	용서하다		
22	get	얻다, 사다		

▪ 다음 동사의 과거형과 과거분사를 쓰시오.

	동사원형	의미	과거형	과거분사
23	give	주다		
24	go	가다		
25	grow	자라다, 기르다		
26	hear	듣다		
27	hide	감추다, 숨다		
28	hit	때리다, 치다		
29	hold	들다, 잡다		
30	keep	보유하다, 계속하다		
31	know	알다, 알고 있다		
32	lay	놓다		
33	leave	떠나다, 그만두다		
34	lend	빌려주다, 빌리다		
35	lie	눕다		
36	lose	잃다		
37	make	만들다		
38	meet	만나다		
39	pay	지불하다		
40	put	놓다, 두다		
41	read	읽다		
42	ride	타다		
43	rise	오르다, 뜨다		
44	run	달리다		
45	say	말하다		
46	see	보다		

▪ 다음 동사의 과거형과 과거분사를 쓰시오.

	동사원형	의미	과거형	과거분사
47	sell	팔다		
48	send	보내다, 부치다		
49	set	놓다		
50	shake	흔들다		
51	show	보여주다, 나타내다		
52	shut	닫다		
53	sing	노래하다		
54	sit	앉다		
55	sleep	잠자다		
56	speak	말을 하다		
57	spend	쓰다, 소비하다		
58	stand	서다, 일어서다		
59	steal	훔치다		
60	strike	치다, 때리다		
61	swim	헤엄치다, 수영하다		
62	take	잡다, 획득하다		
63	teach	가르치다		
64	tell	말하다, 알리다		
65	think	생각하다		
66	throw	던지다		
67	understand	이해하다, 알다		
68	wear	입고 있다		
69	win	이기다		
70	write	쓰다		

눈에 보이는 문법!
능동적인 자기주도 학습!

많은 문법 문제를 풀어 보고 알고 있다고 생각해도 비슷한 문제를 틀리고 실수하는 것은 정확한 문법 체계를 이해하고 있지 못하기 때문입니다. Grammar Vista Series는 문법 개념의 이해를 돕기 위해 체계적인 문법도식을 고안하여 시각적으로 학습할 수 있게 하였습니다. 또한 문법 개념을 명확하게 이해했는지를 학생 스스로 반복 확인할 수 있게 기획하여 자기주도 학습능력을 향상시킬 수 있도록 하였습니다.

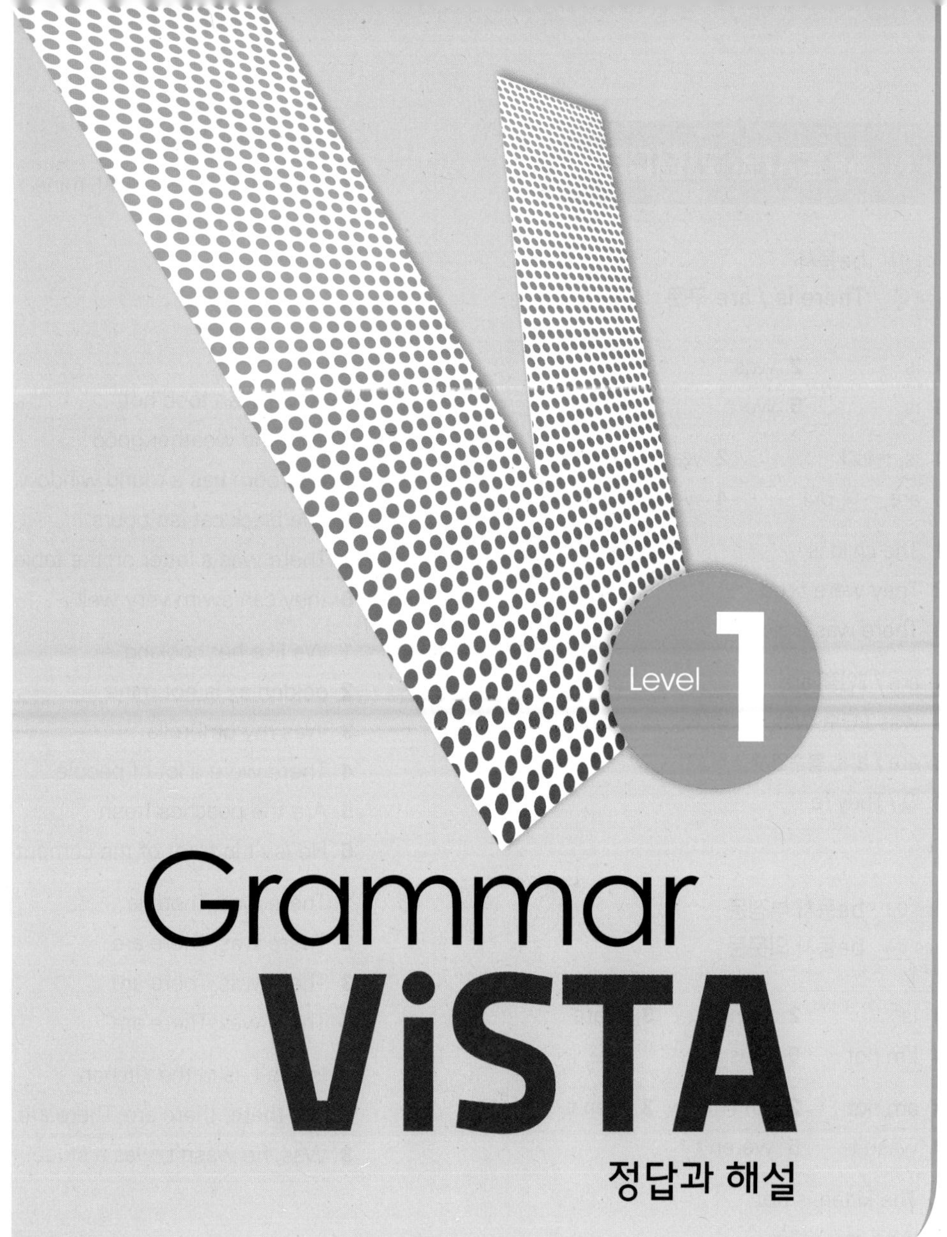

● 본 교재　　● workbook

Chapter 01 be동사와 인칭대명사

GP Practice 01 be동사
GP Practice 02 There is / are 구문 p. 13

A 1 is 2 was 3 are
4 is 5 were

B 1 is, ~이다 2 was, ~이었다
3 are, ~에 있다 4 were, ~에 있었다

C 1 The child is
2 They were tired
3 There was a clock

D 1 are / 2인칭, are
2 was / 단수, was
3 are / are, 복수명사
4 O / They're

GP Practice 03 be동사 부정문
GP Practice 04 be동사 의문문 p. 15

A 1 Is 2 aren't 3 Were
4 I'm not 5 Was

B 1 am not 2 isn't 3 aren't
4 wasn't 5 weren't

C 1 The kitten is not
2 Was my wallet
3 Is your room, isn't

D 1 are not, aren't / be동사 + not
2 Was it / Be동사 + 주어 ~?
3 he / 대명사
4 Is / Is

GP Practice 05 인칭대명사 p. 17

A 1 yours 2 Its 3 us
4 her 5 She

B 1 them 2 it
3 We 4 His

C 1 are mine
2 His cell phone
3 their nests

D 1 I / 나는, 주격, I
2 her / 그녀의, 소유격, her
3 mine / 나의 것, 소유대명사, mine
4 O / 목적격, them

Grammar & Writing p. 18

A 1 Is Mexican food hot
2 Was the weather good
3 His room has a round window
4 The black cat isn't ours
5 There was a letter on the table
6 they can swim very well

B 1 We like her cooking
2 golden ax is not mine
3 Was my umbrella
4 There were a lot of people
5 Are the peaches fresh
6 He isn't in front of the computer

C 1 There was, There is
2 There was, There are
3 There was, There are
4 There was, There are

D 1 Is, isn't, is in the kitchen
2 Are there, there are, There are
3 Was, he wasn't, was a student

Actual Test p. 20

1 ③ **2** ④ **3** ② **4** ① **5** ④ **6** ⑤ **7** ④
8 ④ **9** ② **10** ② **11** ① **12** They were at the bus stop **13** I am not good at **14** his, his, it
15 your pen **16** ⑤ **17** ③ **18** ② **19** ③
20 Am **21** weren't **22** Were your cousins at the party **23** There is not a big zoo **24** ⓑ, ⓒ
25 Is the chicken salad delicious **26** Minji and I were not (weren't) in Seoul last week
27 Are there two cushions on the sofa **28** is
29 Is → Was, 과거, 과거형 **30** I → me, 목적격, you and me **31** The cook wasn't popular then

1 주어가 3인칭 단수이고 now는 현재시제를 의미하므로 is를 씀.

2 주어가 1인칭 단수이고 last week은 과거시제를 의미하므로 was를 씀.

3 Tom and I는 1인칭 복수(we)이므로 are나 were가 가능함.

4 전치사 to(~에게) 뒤에 목적격을 사용함.

5 be동사 의문문이고 be동사가 were일 때 주어는 2인칭 단복수와 모든 복수 주어를 사용함.

6 '누구의 것'을 의미하는 소유대명사를 사용해야 하는데 us는 we의 목적격임.

7 Minju's book은 '민주의 책'이므로 her book을 의미함.

8 ④는 주어가 3인칭 단수(your mom)이므로 Is, 나머지는 Are (are)이다.

9 3인칭 단수(the cotton candy) 주어는 is / was를 사용함. [there are / were + 복수명사]

10 '그 색'은 '지갑의 색'을 의미하므로 지갑(a wallet)의 소유격 its를 사용함.

11 am not은 줄임말이 없고 I am not을 I'm not으로 줄이는 것은 가능함.

12 [3인칭 복수 주어 + were + 장소 표현]은 '~에 있었다'이다.

13 be동사 부정문 [주어 + be동사 + not]

14 '그의 컴퓨터' → his computer, '그의 것' → his, '그것을' → it(computer)

15 소유대명사는 [소유격 + 명사]로 바꿔 쓸 수 있다. [yours = your pen]

16 주어가 3인칭 복수(Sam and Suji)이므로 were가 맞음.

17 ① Was → Were ② No, Ann isn't. → No, she isn't. ④ Were → Was ⑤ Is → Are

18 ② You and I was → You and I were

19 be동사 부정문 [주어 + be동사 + not]

20 현재시제 be동사의 의문문은 [Be동사(Am, Are, Is) + 주어 ~?]이고 주어가 I이므로 be동사는 Am을 씀.

21 be동사 과거형(were)으로 질문하면 [Yes, 주어 + were.] 또는 [No, 주어 + weren't.]로 대답함.

22 과거시제 be동사의 의문문은 [Be동사(Was, Were) + 주어 ~?]이고 주어가 your cousins이므로 be동사는 were를 씀.

23 [There isn't + 단수명사]는 '~가 없다'이다.

24 ⓑ he was → they were, ⓒ they are → we are

25 be동사 의문문 [Be동사 + 주어 ~?]

26 be동사 부정문 [주어 + be동사 + not]

27 [There + is / are] 의문문은 [Is / Are + there ~?]이다.

28 모든 주어가 3인칭 단수이고 now는 현재시제를 의미하므로 공통으로 들어갈 말은 is이다.

29 last year은 과거를 나타내므로 be동사의 과거형을 사용함.

30 '너와 나를'은 목적격이므로 you and me를 써야 함.

31 과거시제 be동사의 부정문 [주어 + was / were + not]

Grammar Mapping

p. 24

① am (was) ② are (were) ③ is (was)
④ are (were) ⑤ not ⑥ Be동사 ⑦ his
⑧ its ⑨ us ⑩ you ⑪ her ⑫ them
⑬ mine ⑭ hers ⑮ theirs ⑯ 단수
⑰ 복수

Chapter 02 일반동사

GP Practice 06 일반동사
GP Practice 07 일반동사 현재형

p. 27

A **1** sleep **2** comes **3** buys **4** does **5** get

B **1** eat **2** has **3** brushes **4** picks up **5** plants

C **1** has many beaches **2** goes jogging **3** plays chess

D **1** visits / 단수, 동사원형(e)s **2** O / 복수, 동사원형 **3** finishes / 동사원형es **4** cries / y 대신 ies

GP Practice 08 일반동사 과거형

p. 29

A **1** read **2** thought **3** put **4** left **5** saw

B **1** rained **2** sent **3** practiced **4** lost **5** had

C **1** stopped **2** slept **3** grew

D **1** bought / 불규칙 변화 **2** lived / 과거형, 동사원형 + -d **3** cut / 과거형, 불규칙 변화 **4** studied / 규칙, y 대신 ied

GP Practice 09 일반동사 부정문

p. 31

A **1** doesn't **2** don't **3** didn't

4 didn't 5 like

B 1 doesn't like 2 didn't wear
3 didn't play 4 don't sleep
5 doesn't ride

C 1 don't laugh 2 doesn't eat
3 didn't go

D 1 don't write / don't
2 doesn't drink / doesn't
3 didn't drive / didn't
4 didn't get / 동사원형

GP Practice 10 일반동사 의문문

p. 33

A 1 Does 2 Do 3 Did
4 Do 5 like

B 1 Did, make, it did
2 Does, read, she does
3 Do, play, they don't

C 1 Does he snore
2 Do they live
3 Did the train arrive

D 1 Do you know / Do(es) + 주어 + 동사원형 ~?
2 Does / Does
3 Did / Did
4 need / 원형

Grammar & Writing

p. 34

A 1 Daniel made sandwiches
2 Did you see my painting
3 I didn't miss the plane for
4 Does she practice the violin
5 A shark lays her eggs
6 doesn't drink cold water

B 1 doesn't eat carrots
2 Did they learn yoga
3 I prepared a party
4 brushes his teeth
5 He didn't choose Mary
6 Does your mom have a job

C 1 didn't know
2 don't breathe
3 doesn't wear

D 1 Did, visit
2 didn't, caught
3 go, didn't, went
4 No, didn't, ate
5 Yes, did, arrived

Actual Test

p. 36

1 ⑤ **2** ① **3** ③ **4** ④ **5** ③ **6** ② **7** ① **8** ③ **9** ④ **10** ③ **11** we do **12** I didn't **13** ⑤ **14** ③ **15** ④ **16** Do, cook **17** didn't take **18** Did, did **19** goes around **20** didn't watch the TV show **21** ⑤ **22** ② **23** ③ **24** it doesn't rain in winter **25** Did you buy a Halloween costume **26** didn't cry **27** left, leaves **28** ② **29** read → reads, 단수, 동사원형(e)s **30** saved → save, 동사원형 **31** Does Sam drink milk every morning

1 drink의 3인칭 단수형은 drinks이다.

2 read[ri:d]의 과거형은 read[red]로 스펠링은 같지만 발음이 달라진다.

3 동사가 takes이므로 주어는 3인칭 단수이다.

4 일반동사 과거형의 부정문 [didn't + 동사원형]

5 일반동사 현재형 의문문 중 주어가 3인칭 단수일 경우 [Does + 주어 + 동사원형 ~?]이다.

6 [Do + 주어 + 동사원형 ~?] 의문문에서 3인칭 단수 주어는 불가하다.

7 일반동사 과거형 의문문 [Did + 주어 + 동사원형 ~?]

8 Peter and Jack은 3인칭 복수이므로 대답은 Yes, they do. / No, they don't.

9 ④는 Does로 [Does + 3인칭 단수 + 동사원형 ~?]의 형식을 취하고 나머지는 Do이다.

10 two hours ago는 과거형과 쓰는 표현이고 every day는 현재형과 쓰는 표현임.

11 your aunt and you는 2인칭 복수이고 현재형 의문문이므로 대답은 Yes, we do. / No, we don't.

12 you는 2인칭 단수이고 과거형 의문문이므로 대답은 Yes, I did. / No, I didn't.

13 주어가 3인칭 단수인 일반동사 현재형 부정문은 [doesn't + 동사원형]이다.

14 일반동사 과거형 의문문 [Did + 주어 + 동사원형 ~?]

15 ④ 주어가 3인칭 단수인 일반동사 현재형 부정문 [doesn't + 동사원형], goes → go로 바꿔야 함.

16 every Sunday는 현재형과 쓰는 표현임. 주어가 3인칭 복수인 일반동사 현재형 의문문은 [Do + 주어 + 동사원형 ~?]이다.

17 yesterday는 과거형과 쓰는 표현이고, 일반동사 과거형 부정문은 [didn't + 동사원형]이다.

18 last winter는 과거형과 쓰는 표현이고 일반동사 과거형 의문문은 [Did + 주어 + 동사원형 ~?]이다. 3인칭 단수가 주어인 과거형 부정문은 [did + not + 동사원형]이다.

19 지구가 태양을 도는 것은 일반적 사실이므로 현재형을 씀. [3인칭 단수 주어 + 동사원형(e)s]

20 last night는 과거형과 쓰는 표현임. 일반동사 과거형 부정문은 [didn't + 동사원형]이다.

21 yesterday는 과거형과 쓰는 표현임. 일반동사 과거형 의문문 [Did + 주어 + 동사원형 ~?], Does → Did로 바뀌어야 함.

22 ① went → go ③ wasn't → didn't ④ didn't → wasn't ⑤ swim → swims or swam

23 ③은 '~하다'의 일반동사이고 나머지는 일반동사 부정문이나 의문문 만들 때 사용하는 조동사 do이다.

24 주어가 3인칭 단수인 일반동사 현재형 부정문 [doesn't + 동사원형]

25 일반동사 과거형 의문문 [Did + 주어 + 동사원형 ~?]

26 last night은 과거형과 사용함. 일반동사 과거형 부정문 [didn't + 동사원형]

27 this morning은 과거형과 사용하고 usually는 현재형과 사용함.

28 ⓐ는 chat → chatted ⓑ는 asks → ask ⓓ는 loses → lose이다.

29 주어가 3인칭 단수이므로 일반동사 현재형 동사원형(e)s을 씀.

30 일반동사 과거형 부정문 [didn't + 동사원형]

31 주어가 3인칭 단수인 일반동사 현재형 의문문은 [Does + 주어 + 동사원형 ~?]이다.

Grammar Mapping
p. 40

① 3인칭 단수 주어 ② 복수 주어 / 1, 2인칭 단수 주어 ③ washes ④ y 대신 ies ⑤ has ⑥ y 대신 ied ⑦ do / does / did + not ⑧ Do / Does / Did ⑨ 동사원형

Chapter 03 명사와 관사

GP Practice 11 셀 수 있는 명사
GP Practice 12 셀 수 없는 명사
p. 43

A **1** dishes **2** knives **3** oranges **4** roofs **5** pianos **6** potatoes **7** parties **8** teeth **9** photos **10** deer

B **1** classes **2** a photo **3** babies **4** happiness **5** two cups of tea

C **1** sugar **2** Potatoes **3** three bottles of water

D
1 leaves / 있고, leaves
2 a box / 있는, 쓴다
3 Air / 없는, 쓰지 않는다
4 a piece of paper / 없고, a piece of

GP Practice 13 관사
p. 45

A **1** a **2** the **3** the **4** a **5** an

B **1** The **2** x **3** The **4** an **5** x

C **1** the cello **2** An umbrella **3** a week

D
1 the / the, 서로 알고 있는 것
2 O / the, 이미 언급된 것
3 a / a, ~마다
4 삭제 / 없음

Grammar & Writing
p. 46

A
1 I need a chair
2 He ate two bowls of rice
3 My brother bought a pair of pants
4 Call your mom once a day
5 The students go to school by bus
6 There were two benches in her garden

B
1 a great cook
2 Two women
3 a glass of juice
4 a uniform
5 The roofs
6 three slices of cheese

C
1 a glass of, two pieces of
2 a piece of, a bottle of
3 two cups of, three pieces of

D	1 X	2 X	3 an
	4 a	5 the	

Actual Test

p. 48

1 ④ 2 ① 3 ① 4 ② 5 ③ 6 ③ 7 ④
8 ④ 9 ④ 10 ⑤ 11 ③ 12 ② 13 ③
14 We found the star in the night sky
15 David played the drum with his friends
16 x, x 17 the 18 a 19 An 20 ② 21 ③
22 ⑤ 23 ② 24 ① 25 dishes 26 the table
27 leaves 28 Two mice 29 sheeps → sheep, 같음 30 Potatos → Potatoes, es 31 I need two loaves of bread 32 She has blue eyes and long hair

1 piano의 복수형은 pianos이다.
2 foot의 복수형은 feet이다.
3 동사 are가 있으므로 셀 수 있는 명사의 복수형이 알맞고, deer은 단수와 복수의 형태가 같음.
4 셀 수 있는 명사 photo는 복수형이 있지만, 셀 수 없는 명사 fun, water, bread, knowledge는 복수형이 없음.
5 주스 두 잔은 two glasses of juice이다.
6 셀 수 없는 명사는 앞에 부정관사 a / an을 쓸 수 없음.
7 동사 is가 있으므로 단수 명사가 와야 하는데 women은 woman의 복수형임.
8 보기와 ④번은 '~마다'를 의미함.
9 한 명의 대학생이라는 의미이므로 부정관사를 써야 하고, university의 발음이 자음으로 시작하므로 a가 와야 함. 식사 이름 앞에는 관사를 쓰지 않음.
10 ⑤의 by e-mail은 통신수단을 나타내므로 관사를 쓰지 않고, 나머지는 모두 정관사 the를 씀.
11 ③은 자음 발음이므로 a를 쓰고, 나머지는 모두 모음 발음이므로 an을 써야 함.
12 tooth의 복수형은 teeth이다.
13 커피 두 잔: two cups of coffee
14 하늘은 유일한 것이므로 the sky이고, '그 별'도 수많은 별 중 특정한 별을 지칭하는 것이므로 the star를 씀.
15 악기 이름 앞에는 정관사 the를 씀.
16 셀 수 없는 명사(물질명사) water는 a를 쓰지 않고, 특정한 사물이 아니므로 the도 쓰지 않음. 잠자기 위한 용도의 bed 역시 관사를 쓰지 않음.
17 이미 언급된 명사이므로 the를 씀.
18 '~ 마다'의 의미이므로 a를 씀.
19 특정되지 않은 어떤 한 명의 사람을 나타내고 모음 발음 단어 앞이므로 An을 씀.
20 빵 두 조각: two slices of bread, 치즈 두 조각: two slices of cheese
21 특정한 사물을 지칭하거나 지구나 달과 같이 유일한 것 앞에는 정관사 the를 씀.
22 ① teas → tea ② homeworks → homework
③ advices → advice ④ Mouses → Mice
23 ② 서로 알고 있는 것이므로 [a → the]로 써야 함.
24 ① paper는 셀 수 없는 명사이므로 two pieces of paper이다.
25 -sh로 끝나는 명사의 복수형은 [-sh + es]이다.
26 서로 알고 있는 식탁이므로 the table을 씀.
27 -f로 끝나는 명사의 복수형은 f를 v로 바꾸고 es를 붙임.
28 mouse의 복수형은 mice다.
29 sheep은 단수형과 복수형이 같음.
30 -o로 끝나는 명사의 복수형은 [-o + es]이다.
31 빵은 셀 수 없는 명사이므로 a loaf of를 이용하여 수량을 표시함. 빵 두 덩어리: two loaves of bread
32 눈은 셀 수 있는 명사이므로 복수형 eyes로 쓰고, hair는 셀 수 없는 명사이므로 단수형 hair를 씀.

Grammar Mapping

p. 52

① tomatoes ② ladies ③ 단위명사 ④ slices
⑤ bottles ⑥ 정해지지 않은 하나 ⑦ ~마다
⑧ 악기 이름 ⑨ 식사, 운동, 과목 이름

Chapter 04 대명사

GP Practice 14 this (these), that (those)
GP Practice 15 비인칭 주어 it

p. 55

A 1 This 2 those 3 These
4 those 5 It, It

B 1 해석 안 함 (O) 2 해석 안 함 (O)
3 그것 (O) 4 해석 안 함 (O)
5 그것 (O)

C 1 That hat
2 It is summer
3 These pandas

D 1 That / 단수, That

2 These / 복수, These
3 O / 특정한, it
4 It / 날씨, 비인칭 주어

GP Practice 16 some, any
GP Practice 17 all, every, each

p. 57

A
1 All　2 any　3 day
4 any　5 some

B
1 any　2 some　3 any
4 some　5 some

C
1 Every child　2 any air
3 All the players

D
1 any / any, 부정문
2 the apples / 복수
3 student / 단수명사
4 some / some, 권유문

Grammar & Writing

p. 58

A
1 I saved all my money
2 It is not far from my house
3 These people were very kind
4 She called me for some advice
5 Do you know that woman
6 He didn't eat any snacks

B
1 These are my classmates
2 put any ice
3 It rained a lot
4 Listen to those sounds
5 Every student has special talents
6 This is Mary

C
1 this　2 It　3 this

D
1 Each　2 some, all
3 any　4 some

Actual Test

p. 60

1 ③ **2** ① **3** ④ **4** ① **5** ④ **6** ⑤ **7** ④ **8** ② **9** that **10** Every **11** some **12** ③ **13** it, It **14** this, This **15** any **16** ② **17** some **18** It **19** ⑤ **20** ⑤ **21** ③ **22** some caffeine in green tea **23** it is dark **24** my every word **25** ⑤ **26** ④ **27** ① **28** ② **29** some → any, any **30** This → These, these **31** Each team has five players

1 멀리 떨어져 있는 '저 사람들'을 가리킬 때 those를 사용함.
2 시간을 나타내는 비인칭 주어 it을 씀.
3 전화 통화 중 전화 건 사람을 가리킬 때 This를 사용함.
4 앞에 이미 언급된 단수명사는 it을 씀.
5 날짜를 나타내는 비인칭 주어 it을 사용함.
6 these나 those로 질문하면 they로 대답함.
7 ④는 [this + 명사]로 '이 ~'의 쓰임이고, 나머지 this는 '이것 / 이 사람'을 가리킴.
8 ②는 앞에 언급한 특정한 명사를 가리키는 대명사이고 나머지는 비인칭 주어다.
9 멀리 떨어져 있는 '저것, 저 사람'을 가리킬 때 that을 씀.
10 [every(모든) + 단수명사 + 단수동사]
11 긍정문에서 '약간, 조금'의 뜻일 때 some을 사용함.
12 단수명사가 복수명사로 바뀐 것이므로 a를 삭제하고 That 대신 Those를 씀.
13 열쇠를 나타내는 대명사 it(그것), 거리, 시간을 나타내는 비인칭 주어 It을 사용함.
14 다른 사람을 소개할 때 쓰는 '이 분은'이라는 표현에 this를 쓰고 '이 소년'이라고 표현할 때도 This를 사용함.
15 의문문이나 부정문에서 '약간, 조금'의 뜻일 때 any를 씀.
16 ②는 제안, 요청을 나타내는 의문문이므로 some을 쓰고 나머지는 부정문, 의문문이므로 any를 사용함.
17 제안이나 요청을 하는 의문문에서 '어떤, 조금'은 some을 씀.
18 날씨를 나타내는 비인칭 주어 it을 사용한다.
19 '경찰들'이 복수이므로 This의 복수형 These를 씀.
20 시간, 거리, 날짜를 나타내는 비인칭 주어 It을 사용함.
21 ③ man이 단수이므로 [Those → That]이 되어야 함.
22 긍정문에서 '어떤, 조금'은 some을 사용함.
23 명암을 나타내는 비인칭 주어 it을 사용함.
24 [every + 단수명사]의 형태가 와야 함.
25 ⑤ '이 분은, 이 사람은'으로 사람을 소개할 때 this를 씀.
26 의문문에서 '약간, 조금'의 뜻일 때 any를 쓰고 긍정문에서는 '약간, 조금'의 뜻일 때 some을 사용함.
27 [each(각각의) + 단수명사], [all(모든) + (셀 수 있는) 복수명사]
28 [this / that + 단수명사]는 '이 ~', '저 ~'의 뜻이고, it은 앞에 언급한 특정한 명사를 가리킴.
29 '약간'을 의미하는 any는 부정문에 사용함.
30 [these + 복수명사]
31 [each(각각의) + 단수명사 + 단수동사]

Grammar Mapping

p. 64

① 멀리 있는 것(들) ② those ③ 대명사
④ 비인칭 주어 ⑤ 시간 ⑥ 날짜 ⑦ 명암
⑧ 부정문, 의문문 ⑨ 약간의, 조금의 ⑩ 모든

Chapter 05 진행형과 미래시제

GP Practice 18 진행형
GP Practice 19 진행형 부정문과 의문문

p. 67

A 1 am walking 2 waiting
3 is not 4 cleaning
5 Are, am

B 1 am going
2 Is, reading
3 isn't using
4 Was, painting
5 weren't looking

C 1 Ryan is searching
2 Is someone knocking
3 He wasn't watching

D 1 flying / 동사원형ing
2 was swimming / was, 동사원형ing
3 not studying / not
4 using / 동사원형ing

GP Practice 20 미래시제
GP Practice 21 미래시제 부정문과 의문문

p. 69

A 1 give 2 to join
3 am not 4 Will he be
5 Are

B 1 will finish
2 won't make
3 Will, have
4 isn't going to have
5 Are, going to borrow

C 1 I will not break
2 is going to fix
3 Will Nick come

D 1 I am going to / be going to
2 Will he move / 동사원형
3 Is she going / Be동사
4 will not / will not

Grammar & Writing

p. 70

A 1 My brother is playing the guitar
2 Are the students reading newspapers
3 The child is going to wash her hands
4 The school festival will be very fun
5 Bill is not making his bed
6 They aren't going to leave Seoul

B 1 Will the birds eat
2 They were holding
3 will not be late
4 Is she mopping
5 I am not going to wear
6 Were you taking out

C 1 he is, is going to play
2 Will he water
3 you going to get

D 1 is looking out
2 I'm not, am resting
3 they aren't, are reading
4 she wasn't, was watching
5 were talking on the phone

Actual Test

p. 72

1 ④ **2** ① **3** ④ **4** ⑤ **5** ① **6** ③ **7** ④ **8** ③ **9** ① **10** ⑤ **11** ④ **12** ③ **13** ① **14** be sick **15** not sleeping **16** she is not going to wear it **17** Are you listening to me now **18** will not tell a lie **19** ⑤ **20** Are, chatting **21** is going to start **22** he won't **23** he was **24** ⑤ **25** ③ **26** get → getting, 동사원형ing **27** does → is, is not **28** Is she going to **29** We will not join **30** He won't change his mind

1 plan의 진행형은 planning이다.

2 tomorrow는 미래 표현이므로 will meet이나 is going to meet을 씀.

3 미래시제 부정문 [be동사 + not + going to + 동사원형] 또는 [will + not + 동사원형]이다.

4 진행형 [주어 + be동사 + 동사원형ing]

5 현재진행형 의문문은 [am / are / is + 주어 + 동사원형ing], 미래시제는 [be동사 + going to + 동사원형]이므로 둘 다 is를 사용함.

6 미래시제 의문문은 [Be동사 + 주어 + going to + 동사원형 ~?], 과거진행시제는 [was / were + 동사원형ing]이므로 둘 다 going을 사용함.

7 과거진행시제는 [was / were + 동사원형ing]이고 주어가 복수이므로 were climbing을 씀.

8 will은 미래를 나타내는 시간 표현 부사(구)와 함께 사용함.

9 진행형 의문문에 대한 대답 [Yes, 주어 + be동사.]나 [No, 주어 + be동사n't.]이다.

10 미래시제 [be동사 + going to + 동사원형]이나 [will + 동사원형]이다.

11 미래시제 의문문 [Be동사 + 주어 + going to + 동사원형 ~?]이나 [Will + 주어 + 동사원형 ~?]이다.

12 진행형 부정문 [be동사 + not + 동사원형ing], ③ swim → swimming

13 현재진행형 부정문 [am / are / is + not + 동사원형ing], ① is not snow → is not snowing

14 [be going to + 동사원형]이 와야 하므로 형용사 sick은 be동사가 필요함.

15 현재진행형 부정 [be동사 + not + 동사원형ing]

16 미래시제 부정형 [be동사 + not + going to + 동사원형]

17 진행형 의문문 [Be동사 + 주어 + 동사원형ing ~?]

18 미래시제 부정형 [will + not + 동사원형]

19 ⑤는 동사원형 앞에 조동사 will이 와야 하고, 나머지는 be동사 is이다.

20 현재진행형 의문문 [Am / Are / Is + 주어 + 동사원형ing ~?]

21 예정된 가까운 미래의 일은 [주어 + be동사 + going to + 동사원형]이다.

22 미래시제 의문문에 대한 대답은 [Yes, + 주어 + will.]이나 [No, + 주어 + won't.]이다.

23 진행형 의문문에 대한 대답은 [Yes, + 주어 + be동사.]나 [No, + 주어 + be동사n't.]이다.

24 과거진행형 [was / were + 동사원형ing]

25 ⓐ lie의 진행형은 lying ⓒ 미래시제 의문문은 [Will + 주어 + 동사원형 ~?]이므로 help ⓓ 진행형 부정은 [be동사 + not + 동사원형ing]이므로 was not using이다.

26 진행형 의문문은 [Be동사 + 주어 +동사원형ing ~?]이다.

27 미래시제 부정문은 [be동사 + not + going to + 동사원형]이다.

28 미래시제 의문문 [Will + 주어 + 동사원형 ~?]이나 [Be동사 + 주어 + going to + 동사원형 ~?]이다.

29 미래시제 부정문 [be동사 + not + going to + 동사원형]이나 [will + not + 동사원형]이다.

30 미래시제 부정형 [will + not + 동사원형]

Grammar Mapping p. 76

① be동사 ② 동사원형ing ③ not ④ Be동사 ⑤ Is ⑥ live ⑦ die ⑧ be동사 + going to ⑨ be동사 + not + going to ⑩ Be동사 + 주어 + going to ⑪ Will ⑫ Are

Chapter 06 조동사

GP Practice 22 can, may p. 79

A
1 ⓐ, 풀 수 있다
2 ⓑ, 먹어도 된다
3 ⓒ, 비가 올 수도 있다
4 ⓑ, 전화해도 된다

B
1 can't 2 can't
3 Can 4 can

C
1 can't breathe
2 Can (May) I take
3 able to read
4 may be

D
1 can sit / 허락, 동사원형
2 could / 할 수 있었다, 과거형
3 may be / 약한 추측, 동사원형
4 Will you / 조동사 + 주어

GP Practice 23 must, have to, should p. 81

A
1 must 2 must not
3 get 4 must not
5 Must

B
1 must 2 have to
3 must 4 have to

C
1 should not exercise
2 don't have to wear
3 must be

D	1 O / ~가 틀림없다, 동사원형
	2 had to / ~해야 했다, had to
	3 should not / 조동사 + not
	4 don't / ~할 필요 없다, don't

Grammar & Writing

p. 82

A
1 have to set the alarm
2 May I have your name
3 must not water the cactus
4 is able to imitate her brother
5 must be hungry
6 can find kangaroos in Australia

B
1 must be twins
2 may not remember me
3 don't have to go outside
4 can walk on water
5 can lay sixty eggs a year
6 may (can) keep the change

C
1 cannot take pictures
2 can turn left
3 cannot swim
4 can use the free Wi-Fi
5 cannot eat food

D
1 May 2 should
3 have to 4 must

Actual Test

p. 84

1 ⑤ **2** ① **3** ② **4** ④ **5** ④ **6** ③ **7** ④ **8** ④ **9** ③ **10** ③ **11** ⑤ **12** have to **13** can **14** must not **15** must **16** could **17** ④ **18** ② **19** ③ **20** can **21** May **22** has to **23** don't have to lose weight **24** should not rub your eyes **25** ⑤ **26** ⑤ **27** ⑤ **28** was able to keep **29** may not like **30** are → be, ~해야 한다, 동사원형 **31** don't can → cannot, 뒤, not **32** He doesn't have to buy a new car

1 can't: ~하면 안 된다
2 must: ~임에 틀림없다(강한 추측)
3 [May + 주어 + 동사원형 ~?]: ~해도 될까요?(허락)
4 must, have to: ~해야 한다(의무)
5 [be동사 과거형 + able to] = [could]로 '~할 수 있었다'를 의미함.
6 나무가 백 년이 넘은 것이 '틀림없다'(강한 추측), '머리를 말려야 한다'(의무) 의미를 갖는 조동사가 와야 함.
7 '~해도 될까요?'(허락), '~일지도 모른다'(추측) 의미를 갖는 조동사가 와야 함.
8 조동사 의문문 [Should + 주어 + 동사원형 ~?]
9 보기의 should와 ③의 must는 '의무' ②는 '강한 추측' ①의 can과 ④의 [be동사 + able to]는 '능력' ⑤는 '약한 추측'으로 쓰임.
10 보기의 can과 ③의 may는 '허락' ①, ④, ⑤의 must, should, have to는 '의무' ② can은 '능력'을 의미함.
11 ① be → is ② [조동사 + 동사원형] plays → play ③ 조동사 의문문 Must you follow ~? ④ 조동사 부정문 should not
12 춥지 않아서 히터를 '켤 필요가 없다'를 의미함.
13 can: ~해도 된다(허락)
14 must not: ~하면 안 된다(금지)
15 [must + 동사원형]: ~임에 틀림없다(추측)
16 '~할 수 있었다'는 can의 과거형임.
17 ⓐ [조동사 + 주어 + 동사원형 ~?] helped → help ⓑ 조동사 의문문 [Must you move ~?] ⓓ 과거시제 have to → had to
18 ②는 강한 추측으로 '~임에 틀림없다'를 의미하고 나머지는 '의무 / 금지'를 의미함.
19 ③은 허락으로 '사용해도 된다'를 나타내며 나머지는 능력으로 '~할 수 있다'를 의미함.
20 [can] = [be동사 + able to]: ~할 수 있다(능력)
21 Can (May) I ~?: 제가 ~해도 될까요?
22 [must] = [have (has) to]: ~해야 한다
23 [don't have to]: ~할 필요 없다
24 [should not]: ~하면 안 된다(충고)
25 ⑤는 '~할 필요 없다'이며 나머지는 '~하면 안 된다'를 의미함.
26 [must + 동사원형]: ~임에 틀림없다(추측)
27 [A: 시험에 응시해야만 하니? B: 아니, 그럴 필요 없어.]가 문맥에 맞으므로 don't have to가 어울림.
28 [be동사 과거형 + able to]: ~할 수 있었다
29 [may not + 동사원형]: ~안 할 수도 있다(추측)
30 '~해야 한다' 의미는 [조동사 must + 동사원형]이다.
31 '~할 수 없다'를 의미하는 부정형은 조동사 can 뒤에 not을 붙여 cannot으로 씀.
32 [don't (doesn't) have to]: ~할 필요 없다

Grammar Mapping

p. 88

① 동사원형 ② not ③ be able to ④ ~해도 된다 ⑤ ~일지도 모른다 ⑥ ~임에 틀림없다 ⑦ don't have to ⑧ ~해야 한다

Chapter 07 의문사와 여러 가지 문장

GP Practice 24 who, what, which

p. 91

A
1 Who 2 What 3 What
4 Who 5 Which

B
1 ⓒ 2 ⓓ 3 ⓐ
4 ⓔ 5 ⓑ

C
1 Who(m) did you meet
2 What do Americans eat
3 Which was more delicious

D
1 What / 사물, What
2 Whose / 누구의, Whose + 명사
3 Which / 있을 때, Which
4 O / 주어, 의문사 + 동사

GP Practice 25 when, where, why, how
GP Practice 26 how + 형용사 / 부사

p. 93

A
1 Where 2 When
3 Why 4 How tall

B
1 ⓐ 2 ⓔ 3 ⓓ
4 ⓑ 5 ⓒ

C
1 Where did he live
2 How did you get
3 When does, close

D
1 Where / 장소, Where
2 How / 상태, How
3 How old / How + 형용사
4 Why / 원인, Why

GP Practice 27 부정의문문
GP Practice 28 부가의문문

p. 95

A
1 Doesn't 2 Didn't
3 Wasn't 4 won't
5 are

B
1 don't you 2 aren't they
3 does he 4 can't she
5 didn't she

C
1 Didn't you hear
2 isn't it
3 doesn't it

D
1 didn't / 긍정문, 부정문
2 is / 긍정문
3 don't / 부정문, don't
4 she / 대명사

GP Practice 29 명령문과 제안문
GP Practice 30 감탄문

p. 97

A
1 Be 2 How 3 What
4 Don't 5 give

B
1 How lucky I am
2 What a brave soldier he was
3 Be quiet in the library
4 Let's not stay up too late

C
1 Let's be honest
2 Don't throw away
3 What a scary story

D
1 Go / ~해라, 동사원형
2 not / 하지 말자, not
3 How / How
4 What / What

Grammar & Writing

p. 98

A
1 How big is the sun
2 When will they meet again
3 Who opened this box
4 Why did they go to the North Pole
5 What does your brother study
6 Don't take photos in the museum
7 You will buy a new bicycle, won't you

B
1 Whose phone rang
2 Doesn't she look
3 Where did you find my dog
4 How lovely the kittens
5 How much milk does he drink
6 Which do you like better

C
1 When 2 Where
3 What 4 Where
5 How old 6 How tall
7 How much

D
1 Turn off
2 Don't walk around
3 Don't leave

4 Lower

Actual Test p. 100

1 ④ **2** ④ **3** ③ **4** ① **5** ③ **6** ② **7** ⑤ **8** ④ **9** ① **10** ③ **11** ⑤ **12** Don't **13** What **14** How **15** ③ **16** ③ **17** ③ **18** ② **19** What **20** No **21** Who knows the answer **22** What a small world **23** How big is the glacier **24** ⑤ **25** Let's not tell **26** Which do you like better **27** How cold it was **28** Cindy → she, 부정문, 대명사 주어 **29** gives up → give up, Don't, 동사원형 **30** What an amazing eagle it is **31** No, they don't

1 앞문장이 긍정문이고 일반동사 과거형일 때 부가의문문은 [didn't + 대명사 주어?]이다.

2 what 감탄문 [What + a + 형용사 + 명사 + (주어 + 동사)!]

3 부정명령문 [Don't + 동사원형], 부정제안문 [Let's not + 동사원형]

4 수단과 방법을 물을 때 how를 씀.

5 '누가'라고 물을 때 who를 씀.

6 부정의문문에 대한 부정의 대답은 [No + 부정문], be동사 과거형으로 물었으므로 [be동사 과거형 + not]으로 대답함.

7 '누구의 것'이라고 물을 때 whose를 씀.

8 정해진 범위 없이 '무엇'이라고 물을 때 what을 씀.

9 사람에 관해 물을 때 who를 씀.

10 앞문장이 조동사 현재형(can)일 때 부가의문문은 [can't + 대명사주어?]이다.

11 의문사가 있는 의문문은 [의문사 + 동사 + 주어 ~?]이다.

12 부정명령문 [Don't + 동사원형], 부정의문문 [Don't + you +동사원형 ~?]

13 '무엇'이나 '무슨'을 물을 때 what을 씀.

14 how 감탄문은 [How + 형용사 / 부사 + 주어 + 동사!], '어떻게'를 물을 때 How를 씀.

15 '우리 ~하자'고 제안하는 표현으로 [Why don't we + 동사원형 ~?]과 [Let's + 동사원형 ~]을 사용함.

16 ⓐ Don't noisy. → Don't be noisy. ⓑ Warms → Warm ⓔ Let's don't → Let's not

17 부가의문문에서 앞문장이 긍정문이면 부정문으로 하는데 ③은 일반동사 과거시제이므로 [didn't + 주어]이다.

18 '얼마나 많은'을 물을 때 [how much + 단수명사], [how many + 복수명사]를 씀.

19 '무엇을'을 물을 때 what을 씀.

20 '~할 수 없니?'와 같은 부정의문문에 대한 대답은 [Yes, 긍정문]이나 [No, 부정문]을 씀.

21 '누구, 누가'를 뜻하는 의문사는 who이다.

22 what 감탄문 [What + a(n) + 형용사 / 부사 + 명사 (주어 + 동사)!]

23 [정도를 나타내는 의문사 how + 형용사 / 부사]: 얼마나 ~한 / ~하게

24 what 감탄문 [What + (a) + 형용사 + 명사 + (주어 + 동사)!], how 감탄문 [How + 형용사 / 부사 + 주어 + 동사!]

25 부정제안문 [Let's not + 동사원형]

26 정해진 범위 내에서 선택을 물을 때 which를 씀.

27 how 감탄문 [How + 형용사 + 주어 + 동사!]

28 긍정문의 부가의문문은 부정문을 써야 하고 어순은 [동사 + not + 대명사 주어]이다.

29 '~하지 마라' 의미의 부정 명령문은 [Don't + 동사원형]이다.

30 what 감탄문 [What + a / an + 형용사 + 명사!]

31 부정의문문에 부정의 대답은 [No + 부정문]이다. 일반동사 현재형으로 물었으므로 don't / doesn't로 대답함.

Grammar Mapping p. 104

① (~ 중에) 어떤 ② 언제 ③ 어떻게 ④ 얼마나 ~한 / 하게 ⑤ Doesn't ⑥ isn't she ⑦ did she ⑧ Don't ⑨ Let's not eat ⑩ 형용사 / 부사 ⑪ a / an + 형용사 + 명사

Chapter 08 형용사와 부사

GP Practice 31 형용사의 쓰임
GP Practice 32 수량 형용사 p. 107

A
1 sweet
2 a few
3 famous
4 much
5 something great

B
1 a lot of
2 little
3 few
4 a little

C
1 was useful
2 little interest
3 nothing delicious

D
1 lovely / 명사 수식, 형용사
2 little / little, 거의 없는
3 many / many, 많은
4 clean / 보어, 형용사

GP Practice 33 부사의 쓰임과 형태
GP Practice 34 빈도부사

p. 109

A **1** hard **2** carefully **3** Interestingly **4** usually rides

B **1** good, well **2** easily, easy **3** slowly, slow

C **1** walked fast
2 rained heavily
3 will never forget

D **1** quietly / 조용히, 동사, 부사
2 really / 정말로, 부사, 부사
3 is often / 뒤
4 O / 매우, highly

GP Practice 35 원급, 비교급, 최상급

p. 111

A **1** clear **2** most popular **3** stronger **4** largest

B **1** cold **2** higher **3** best **4** more exciting

C **1** as sour as
2 better than
3 brighter than
4 the biggest bird

D **1** tallest / 가장 큰, 최상급
2 hard / 딱딱한, 원급
3 faster / 더 빠른, 비교급
4 most famous / most + 원급

Grammar & Writing

p. 112

A **1** a little sand in my shoes
2 never misses a chance
3 landed the airplane safely
4 can always use my computer
5 The hens are laying few eggs
6 could seldom read the road signs
7 is more powerful than the old one

B **1** curly hair
2 the greatest moment
3 as slow as
4 a lot of buildings
5 always writes
6 more comfortable than

C **1** - ⓐ **2** - ⓐ **3** - ⓑ **4** - ⓐ

D **1** heavier than
2 taller than
3 as expensive as
4 the shortest of

Actual Test

p. 114

1 ⑤ **2** ② **3** ② **4** ② **5** ③ **6** ④ **7** ③ **8** ② **9** ①, ④ **10** ④ **11** ⑤ **12** hard **13** well **14** ⑤ **15** ⑤ **16** ② **17** ② **18** as heavy as **19** the worst movie **20** ⑤ **21** We are planning something special **22** often cooks dinner for us **23** Few people knew about his private life **24** ② **25** ④ **26** popular, the most popular **27** ③ **28** ① **29** a little → a few, a few, 복수 **30** lately → late, 늦게 **31** Time is more important than money

1 [few + 셀 수 있는 명사의 복수형]은 '~가 거의 없는'의 의미이고 나머지는 셀 수 없는 명사를 수식함.

2 [the + 최상급 + of ~]: ~중에서 가장 ~한

3 [more + 3음절 이상 형용사] + than: ~보다 더 ~한

4 '~하게 짓다' 동사를 수식하는 부사가 필요하며, fast는 형용사(빠른)와 부사(빠르게)가 같은 형태임.

5 [many + 셀 수 있는 명사의 복수형]

6 friendly는 형용사로 '친근한'이고 나머지는 부사이다.

7 비교 대상은 같아야 하므로 소유대명사가 와야 한다. '나의 손'과 비교하는 것이므로 your와 같은 소유격은 불가함.

8 빈도부사는 조동사 뒤에 위치함.

9 pretty가 부사로 쓰일 땐 '매우'이므로 '매우 친절한'으로 해석해야 하고, hardly는 '거의 ~하지 않는다'로 해석해야 함.

10 ④ [little + 셀 수 없는 명사(숙제)]이므로 맞고 나머지는 ① little rain ② many pictures ③ a little gasoline ⑤ talk much로 고쳐야 함.

11 ⑤ [비교급 + than]: ~보다 더 ~한, 나머지는 ① more ② the oldest ③ the smartest ④ as tall as로 고쳐야 함.

12 [열심히 일한다] = [열심히 일하는 직원]

13 [훌륭한 수영 선수] = [수영을 잘한다]

14 [a lot of + 셀 수 있는 명사 / 셀 수 없는 명사]

15 [명사 + -ly]는 형용사로 [lovely = 사랑스러운]을 의미함.

16 형용사 heavy는 '푸짐한'이고 부사 heavily는 '심하게'이다.

17 원급비교 [as + 형용사 + as]: ~만큼 ~한

18 [as + 형용사나 부사 원급 + as]: ~만큼 ~한

19 [the + 최상급 + of ~]

20 ⑤와 같이 명사를 수식하는 형용사일 때는 '이른'이고 나머지는 부사 '일찍'이다.

21 -thing으로 끝나는 대명사는 형용사가 뒤에서 수식함.

22 빈도부사는 일반동사 앞에 위치함.

23 수량형용사 [few + 복수명사]는 '거의 없는'을 의미함.

24 ⓑ 빈도부사는 조동사 뒤에 위치 should never ⓓ [as 원급 as]이므로 fast ⓔ -thing으로 끝나는 대명사는 형용사가 뒤에서 수식하므로 anything sweet이다.

25 3음절 이상 단어의 비교급 형태는 [more + 원급 + than]이다.

26 원급비교는 [as + 형용사 + as]로 '~만큼 ~한'을 의미하고 3음절 이상 단어의 최상급 형태는 [the most + 원급]이다.

27 -thing으로 끝나는 대명사를 수식하는 형용사는 뒤에 위치함.

28 빈도부사는 일반동사 앞에 위치함.

29 '몇몇의' 의미의 수량형용사는 [a few + 복수명사]이다.

30 '늦게' 의미의 부사는 late이다.

31 3음절 이상 단어의 비교급 형태는 [more + 원급 + than]이다.

Grammar Mapping
p. 118

① 명사 수식 ② much / a lot of ③ a little ④ 거의 없는 ⑤ little ⑥ 형용사 + -ly ⑦ often, always ⑧ 일반동사 ⑨ as 원급 as ⑩ than ⑪ 가장 ~한

Chapter 09 부정사와 동명사

GP Practice 36 to부정사의 명사적 쓰임
p. 121

A 1 To watch 2 to make 3 It 4 to climb

B 1 to drive 2 to become 3 to wash 4 to live

C
1 want to paint
2 is to make honey
3 It, to watch
4 promised to help

D
1 It / It, to부정사
2 O / to부정사
3 to visit / to부정사
4 to meet / to + 동사원형

GP Practice 37 to부정사의 형용사적 쓰임
GP Practice 38 to부정사의 부사적 쓰임
p. 123

A
1 to drink, 마실
2 to go home, 집에 갈
3 to do, 할
4 to buy, 살

B 1 ⓒ 2 ⓓ 3 ⓐ 4 ⓑ

C
1 sorry to hear
2 fancy skirts to wear
3 to look old
4 my turn to do the dishes

D
1 to meet / ~ 만나기 위해, to부정사
2 happy to see / ~ 봐서, 감정형용사
3 easy to cook / ~ 요리하기에, 형용사
4 anything to sell / ~ 판매할, to부정사

GP Practice 39 동명사의 명사적 쓰임
p. 125

A 1 Using 2 becoming 3 drawing 4 building

B 1 ⓒ 2 ⓐ 3 ⓓ 4 ⓑ

C
1 enjoys trying
2 is making a plan
3 kept waiting for
4 Finding a planet is

D
1 protecting / 동명사
2 closing / 동명사
3 Eating / 동명사
4 cooking / 동명사

Grammar & Writing
p. 126

A
1 finish cleaning the bathroom
2 lost a chance to attack
3 wanted to enter the cave
4 nothing interesting to watch
5 was afraid of catching a cold
6 enjoyed throwing tomatoes
7 is to become a makeup artist

B 1 need to practice
2 Raising a pet is
3 jumped to pick
4 It, to role-play
5 to buy new shoes
6 what to eat for dinner

C 1 to save 2 to buy
3 to burn 4 to lend

D 1 to become a cook
2 to order pizza
3 surfing
4 doing the dishes

Actual Test

p. 128

1 ④ **2** ① **3** ④ **4** ③ **5** ③ **6** ② **7** ④ **8** ③ **9** ③ **10** ③ **11** ③ **12** to do **13** swimming **14** to ask **15** ② **16** ④ **17** ③ **18** ① **19** It, to walk **20** believing **21** I am glad to meet you **22** Her hobby is reading detective novels **23** ④ **24** time to waste **25** promised to arrive **26** give up learning **27** to succeed **28** catch → to catch, ~하기 위해, to + 동사원형 **29** turn → turning, 목적어, 동사원형 + -ing **30** It was difficult to find your house

1 to부정사는 [to + 동사원형]의 형태이고, '~하기 위하여'란 부사적 용법의 '목적'으로 쓰임.

2 to부정사의 형용사용법은 '~할' 의미로 명사 뒤에서 수식함.

3 [mind + 목적어(동명사)]는 '~하는 것을 꺼리다'란 의미인데 이때 mind는 동명사를 목적어로 갖는 동사임.

4 [It ~ to부정사]의 형식으로 가주어 It을 문장 앞에 쓰고 뒤에 진주어인 to부정사를 씀.

5 [hope + 목적어(to부정사)]는 '~하는 것을 희망하다'란 의미인데 이때 hope는 to부정사를 목적어로 갖는 동사임.

6 ② [It ~ to부정사]이므로 가주어 It이 문장 앞에 오고 진주어 to부정사가 뒤에 와야 함.

7 expect와 like는 목적어로 to부정사를 갖는 동사임.

8 [decide + 목적어(to부정사)]이고, 나머지는 목적어로 동명사를 가짐.

9 [give up + 목적어(동명사)]이고 나머지는 목적어로 to부정사를 가짐.

10 '~하는 것'이란 표현은 주어 쓰임의 to부정사 또는 동명사로 나타내므로 'Decorating' 또는 'To decorate'가 맞다.

11 [주어 + 동사 + 형용사 + to부정사]: ~하기에 ~한

12 to부정사의 형용사 용법은 '~할'의 의미로 명사 뒤에서 수식함.

13 [enjoy + 목적어(동명사)]는 '~하는 것을 즐기다'란 의미임.

14 '~하기 위하여'란 의미로 to부정사의 부사적 용법이다.

15 [감정형용사 + to부정사], [전치사 for + 동명사] 어순이다.

16 ④는 [전치사 to + 명사]이고, 나머지는 [to + 동사원형]인 to부정사이다.

17 ③ [want + 목적어(to부정사)]는 명사적 용법이고, 나머지는 명사를 뒤에서 수식하는 형용사 용법임.

18 ①은 주격보어로 쓰인 동명사이고, 나머지는 동사 또는 전치사 뒤에 목적어로 쓰임.

19 가주어 It을 문장 앞에 쓰고 뒤에 진주어 to부정사를 쓰는 [It ~ to부정사]

20 주격보어로 쓰인 동명사이다.

21 [감정형용사 + to부정사]: ~해서 ~한 감정이 들다

22 주격보어로 쓰인 동명사이다.

23 ⓐ to부정사의 형태는 [to + 동사원형] ⓑ want는 목적어로 to부정사를 쓰고 ⓔ finish는 목적어로 동명사를 사용함.

24 to부정사 형용사 용법으로 '~할' 의미로 명사 뒤에서 수식함.

25 [promise + 목적어(to부정사)]: ~하는 것을 약속하다

26 [give up + 목적어(동명사)]: ~하는 것을 포기하다

27 to부정사의 부사적 용법(목적)은 '~하기 위해'이다.

28 '~하기 위해' 의미의 [to + 동사원형]이다.

29 [주어 + mind + 목적어(동사원형ing)]

30 [It ~ to부정사] 문장은 가주어 It을 문장 앞에 쓰고 뒤에 진주어 to부정사를 쓴다.

Grammar Mapping

p. 132

① to + 동사원형 ② 주어 ③ 명사 수식 ④ 목적 ⑤ 감정의 원인 ⑥ happy ⑦ difficult ⑧ 동사원형 + -ing ⑨ ~하는 것 ⑩ 명사 ⑪ 주어 ⑫ 목적어

Chapter 10 동사의 종류

GP Practice 40 감각동사 + 형용사

p. 135

A 1 good 2 sweet 3 look like
4 sounds 5 safe

B 1 tastes 2 looks
3 feels 4 sounds

C 1 looks great
2 smells fresh
3 taste sour
4 feel comfortable

D 1 looks sad / 형용사, ~하게 보이다
2 sounds good / 형용사, ~하게 들리다
3 O / 형용사, ~하게 느끼다
4 smells like lemons / smell like, ~처럼

GP Practice 41 수여동사 + 간접목적어 + 직접목적어
GP Practice 42 수여동사 + 직접목적어 + 전치사 + 간접목적어

p. 137

A 1 for 2 me the salad
3 for 4 me his secret
5 of her

B 1 to 2 for 3 of

C 1 showed us card tricks
2 cooked us pork cutlets
3 sent a text message to her

D 1 O / ~에게 ~를, 없음
2 to us / ~를 ~에게, 있음
3 O / ~에게 ~를, 없음
4 for / ~를 ~에게, 있음

GP Practice 43 목적격보어가 필요한 동사

p. 139

A 1 fresh 2 to get
3 to change 4 sleepy
5 a winner

B 1 class president
2 to sit
3 helpful
4 baby

C 1 call me Leo
2 keep the Earth warm
3 want my mom to understand

D 1 O / 명사
2 angry / 형용사
3 to wait / to부정사
4 to enjoy / to부정사

Grammar & Writing

p. 140

A 1 This carpet looks new
2 gave him a flu shot
3 make me a pumpkin pie
4 told the players to practice
5 showed his work to us
6 keeps the desert hot and dry

B 1 sounds perfect
2 named the cat Garfield
3 sent food to the poor country
4 passed me the ball
5 found the mud festival exciting
6 made this Christmas special

C 1 wrote, a card
2 gave, carnations
3 made, a cake
4 bought, gloves

D 1 look like stars
2 tastes bitter
3 sounds great
4 smell sweet

Actual Test

p. 142

1 ② **2** ④ **3** ④ **4** ③ **5** ② **6** ④ **7** ② **8** ② **9** ③ **10** ① **11** ② **12** to me **13** for you **14** of you **15** ③ **16** ② **17** ④ **18** ③ **19** The snow looks like a blanket **20** We want you to enjoy **21** ① **22** ③ **23** ④ **24** ② **25** tastes fresh **26** found his story true **27** of → for, for **28** heavily → heavy, 형용사, ~하게 보이다 **29** speak → to speak, to부정사 **30** I gave some seeds to my hamster

1 [look + 형용사]는 '~하게 보인다'이며 smartly는 형용사가 아닌 부사이다.
2 [make + 직접목적어 + for + 간접목적어]
3 [taste + 형용사]나 [taste like + 명사]: ~한 맛이 나다
4 [keep + 목적어 + 목적격보어(명사 / 형용사)]
5 [sound + 형용사]는 '~하게 들리다'이며 sadly는 형용사가 아닌 부사이다.
6 [make + 직접목적어 + for + 간접목적어]는 '~를 ~에게 만들어 주다'이므로 my dog 앞에 전치사 for가 필요함.
7 '다리가 ~해 보이다', '목소리가 ~하게 들리다', '피자가 ~한

냄새가 나다'란 의미로 감각동사 looks, sounds, smells가 필요함.

8 [cook + 직접목적어 + for + 간접목적어]: ~을 ~에게 요리해 주다

9 [look + 형용사]: ~해 보이다

10 목적격보어로 형용사를 갖는 동사로 [keep + 목적어 + 목적격보어(형용사)] 형식으로 씀.

11 [find + 직접목적어 + for + 간접목적어]: ~를 ~에게 찾아 주다

12 [show + 간접목적어 + 직접목적어] = [show + 직접목적어 + to + 간접목적어]

13 [get + 간접목적어 + 직접목적어] = [get + 직접목적어 + for + 간접목적어]

14 [ask + 간접목적어 + 직접목적어] = [ask + 직접목적어 + of + 간접목적어]

15 [send + 직접목적어(~을 / 를)]이고 나머지는 [수여동사 + 간접목적어(~에게)]이다.

16 ⓐ는 call him a liar ⓑ는 made me cold noodles ⓒ는 smells like an orange ⓓ는 told me to run ⓔ는 keep your teeth clean이다.

17 [ask + 목적어 + 목적격보어(to부정사)]: ~에게 ~하라고 요청하다

18 [make + 목적어 + 목적격보어(형용사)]: ~를 ~상태로 만들다

19 [look like + 명사]: ~처럼 보이다

20 [want + 목적어 + 목적격보어(to 부정사)]: ~가 ~하기를 원하다

21 [show + 직접목적어 + to + 간접목적어]와 [ask + 목적어 + 목적격보어(to부정사)]

22 [make + 직접목적어 + for + 간접목적어]와 [make + 목적어 + 목적격보어(형용사)]

23 [4형식 동사 + 간접목적어 + 직접목적어]: ~에게 ~를 ~해 주다

24 ⓐ [ask + 목적어 + 목적격보어(to부정사)] ⓑ [sound + 형용사] ⓔ [give + 직접목적어 + to + 간접목적어]

25 [taste + 형용사]: ~한 맛이 나다

26 [find + 목적어 + 목적격보어(형용사)]

27 '~를 ~에게 만들어 주다'는 [make + 직접목적어 + for + 간접목적어]이다.

28 [감각동사 look + 형용사]는 '~하게 보이다' 의미임.

29 '~에게 ~하라고 충고하다'는 [advise + 목적어 + 목적격보어(to부정사)]이다.

30 [give + 직접목적어 + to + 간접목적어]

Grammar Mapping

p. 146

① 형용사 ② 간접목적어, ~에게 ③ 직접목적어, ~을 / 를 ④ 전치사 ⑤ to ⑥ for ⑦ of ⑧ 목적어 ⑨ 목적격보어 ⑩ 명사 ⑪ excited ⑫ to study

Chapter 11 접속사

GP Practice 44 and, but, or, so

p. 149

A
1 or **2** but
3 so **4** and

B
1 so **2** and
3 or **4** but

C
1 but she is slim
2 agree or disagree
3 picked an apple and ate
4 so he went

D
1 so / 그래서
2 but / 그러나
3 and / 그리고
4 O / 그렇지 않으면

GP Practice 45 when, before, after

p. 151

A
1 when **2** before
3 after **4** arrives

B
1 ⓓ **2** ⓐ **3** ⓑ **4** ⓒ

C
1 After the rain stops
2 When she is nervous
3 when it rains
4 before you eat dinner

D
1 after / 한 후
2 O / 현재
3 When / 봤을 때
4 before / 전에

GP Practice 46 because, if
GP Practice 47 that

p. 153

A
1 If **2** are
3 because **4** that

B
1 If **2** that
3 if **4** because

C
1 If you add
2 Because it was hot
3 that we like her
4 if you are late

D
1 O / 것을
2 because / 커서
3 because / 더웠기 때문에
4 if / 한다면

Grammar & Writing

p. 154

A
1 after he washed it
2 because the chair was wet
3 and turned on the TV
4 that baseball is boring
5 if I have enough money
6 so teenagers listen to it a lot

B
1 but he hates snow
2 before he drives
3 because I had a toothache
4 when she visits England
5 or you will catch a cold
6 that English grammar is important

C
1 was taking a shower when the phone rang
2 went to the hospital because he broke his arm
3 must warm up before you go into the water

D
1 after he talked with Paul
2 when I come back home
3 so I won't read it
4 If you wear the sunglasses
5 because it gives us a lot of information

Actual Test

p. 156

1 ② **2** ④ **3** ① **4** ④ **5** ① **6** before **7** or **8** because **9** ④ **10** ② **11** ① **12** ④ **13** ⑤ **14** ④ **15** ③ **16** ② **17** so **18** that **19** ④ **20** (that) William is a good singer **21** when she drives in a school zone **22** and you will grow tall **23** ④ **24** ① **25** If you press the button **26** when I work on the computer **27** so it showed its teeth **28** will move → moves, 미래, 현재 **29** so → because, 이유, because **30** I know that oil doesn't mix with water

1 but은 '그러나'의 의미로 앞 문장의 내용과 다른 내용의 뒤 문장을 이어 말할 때 쓰는 접속사이다.

2 or은 '또는'의 의미로 쓰이는 접속사이다.

3 and는 '그리고'의 의미로 앞뒤 내용을 나란히 연결해 줄 때 쓰는 접속사이다.

4 because는 '~하기 때문에'란 의미로 이유, 원인 등을 말할 때 쓰는 접속사이다.

5 when은 '~할 때'라는 의미의 접속사로 때나 시기를 나타냄.

6 before: ~하기 전에

7 or: 또는

8 because: ~하기 때문에

9 ④ '동물을 사랑하다'와 '요리사가 되고 싶다'를 so(그래서)로 연결하는 것은 어색함.

10 ②의 경우 우리가 안에 머물렀을 때 비가 내렸다는 의미이므로 when이 적절함.

11 ① '만약 ~한다면' 조건 부사절에서는 미래시제 대신에 현재시제를 사용함.

12 ④ 내가 그를 아는 것은 가까이 살았기 때문이므로 이유를 나타내는 because이고 나머지는 hope, think, hear, know의 목적어로 쓰인 [that + 주어 + 동사]로 '~하는 것을' 의미함.

13 동사 think의 목적어로 쓰인 [that + 주어 + 동사]는 '~하는 것을' 생각하다로 해석함.

14 '열심히 한다면, 잘할 것이다' 의미이므로 조건 접속사 If를 씀.

15 '쿠키를 태웠지만 맛있다'가 자연스러운 흐름이므로 접속사 but이 필요하고, [명령문 + or]은 '~해라, 그렇지 않으면 ~할 것이다'란 의미임.

16 '산타가 올 때 일어날 것이다'이므로 when, '책을 읽는다면 답을 알게 될 것이다'이므로 If를 씀.

17 원인을 나타내는 문장과 결과를 나타내는 문장을 연결하는 접속사는 so이다.

18 know의 목적어로 쓰인 [that + 주어 + 동사]: ~하는 것을

19 ⓐ '오늘 또는 내일 떠날 것이다'이므로 or ⓑ 조건 부사절에서는 미래시제 대신에 현재시제를 사용하므로 will을 삭제 ⓔ '화가 나서 아무 말도 하지 않았다'이므로 so이다.

20 think의 목적어로 쓰인 [that + 주어 + 동사]: ~하는 것을

21 '스쿨존에서 운전할 때는 천천히 운전한다'의 의미이므로 접속사 when을 사용함.

22 '일찍 자라, 그러면 키가 클 것이다'이므로 [명령문 + and]이다.

23 잠옷을 입은 후에 잠자리에 드는 것이므로 after를 사용함.

24 '버스를 놓쳤기 때문에 다음 버스를 기다리다'이므로 이유 접속사인 because를 씀.

25 if: ~한다면

26 when: ~할 때

27 화가 나서 그 결과 이빨을 드러내는 것이므로 접속사 so(그래서)를 사용함.

28 시간 부사절에서는 미래시제 대신 현재시제를 사용함.

29 잠을 잘 수 없는 이유를 이끄는 접속사이므로 because를 사용함.

30 know의 목적어로 쓰인 [that + 주어 + 동사]: ~하는 것을

Grammar Mapping p. 160

① and ② 그러나 ③ 또는 ④ so ⑤ because
⑥ ~할 때 ⑦ ~한 후에 ⑧ before ⑨ ~한다면

Chapter 12 전치사

GP Practice 48 시간을 나타내는 전치사 I
GP Practice 49 시간을 나타내는 전치사 II p. 163

A **1** at **2** in **3** on
4 on **5** in **6** in

B **1** for **2** during
3 during **4** for

C **1** at night
2 after lunch
3 from May 5 to May 9

D **1** at / at
2 for / for, 숫자 포함 기간
3 in / in
4 on / on

GP Practice 50 장소를 나타내는 전치사 I
GP Practice 51 장소를 나타내는 전치사 II p. 165

A **1** in **2** at **3** in
4 on **5** on

B **1** behind **2** over
3 next to

C **1** under the bridge
2 from Mars to Earth
3 over the mountain
4 in front of the mirror

D **1** on / 표면 위에, on
2 and / A 와 B, and
3 in / 도시에, in
4 at / 비교적 좁은 지점에, at

GP Practice 20 기타 전치사 p. 167

A **1** about **2** like
3 with **4** by

B **1** for, for **2** with, with
3 by, by **4** to, to

C **1** to her
2 about her dream
3 for a reason

D **1** like / ~처럼
2 by / ~를 타고
3 with / ~를 가지고
4 her / 목적격

Grammar & Writing p. 168

A **1** put his bag under his seat
2 a picture by fax
3 goes shopping on Sundays
4 is across from a café
5 take a shower in the evening
6 their bodies from head to toe

B **1** snowed in May
2 on January 1
3 walked with a cane
4 butter on the bread
5 like cotton candy
6 between Monday and Wednesday
7 During the concert

C **1** in **2** under **3** on
4 next **5** behind

D **1** to **2** on **3** in
4 at **5** from **6** at

Actual Test p. 170

1 ① **2** ③ **3** ④ **4** ① **5** ⑤ **6** ① **7** ④ **8** ① **9** ③ **10** ① **11** ⑤ **12** from, to **13** before **14** behind **15** ④ **16** ② **17** in front of **18** next to **19** on **20** ② **21** ④ **22** ⑤ **23** ④ **24** ②, ⑤ **25** between, and **26** under **27** wait until summer vacation **28** spread from mouth to mouth **29** over → on, 접촉한 표

면, on **30** for → during, during, 특정한 기간명사
31 There are no secrets between Paula and me

1 [on + 명사]: (표면에 접촉하여) ~ 위에
2 [at + 특정한 시점(시각)]: ~에
3 [during + 특정한 기간]: ~ 동안
4 [with + 도구]: ~를 가지고
5 [in + 장소(도시나 국가)]
6 [in + 월]
7 ④ like는 '좋아하다'의미의 동사이며, 나머지는 '~처럼'의미의 전치사이다.
8 [on + 장소]: (접촉한 표면의) ~ 위에
9 to: ~에게, ~로
10 with: ~를 가지고, ~와 함께
11 [to + 명사]는 '~에게', '~로'이므로 상황에 맞지 않다.
12 시간 전치사 [from A to B]: A에서 B까지
13 before: ~ 이전에
14 behind: ~ 뒤에
15 behind: ~ 뒤에
16 ⓑ [on + 요일]이므로 on Sundays ⓓ 전치사 뒤의 대명사는 목적격을 쓰므로 to him ⓔ A부터 B까지는 from A to B이므로 and를 to로 바꿔야 함.
17 in front of: ~ 앞에
18 next to: ~ 옆에
19 on: (접촉한 표면) 위에
20 금요일까지 반납이 완료되어야 하는 기한이므로 by '까지'(완료시점), 정오까지 수면을 계속하는 것이므로 until '까지'(계속)이다.
21 [during + 특정한 기간], [for + 숫자 포함한 기간]
22 ⑤ [on + 날짜]이고 나머지는 at을 씀.
23 ④ [in + 계절]이고 나머지는 on을 씀.
24 ① '~ 안을 채우는 것'이므로 fill in ③ '접촉 없이 ~ 위로'이므로 over the river ④ 숫자를 포함한 기간 앞에서 '~ 동안'을 의미하므로 for two years이다.
25 [between A and B]: A와 B 사이에
26 under: ~ 아래에
27 [until + 명사]: ~까지 계속
28 [from A to B]: A에서 B까지
29 [on + 명사]: 접촉한 표면 위
30 [during + 특정한 때]: ~ 동안
31 [between A and B]: A와 B 사이에

Grammar Mapping p. 174

① at ② 요일, 날짜 ③ 월, 계절, 연도 ④ before ⑤ 숫자 포함 기간 ⑥ 특정한 기간명사 ⑦ between ~ and ⑧ on ⑨ in ⑩ over ⑪ in front of ⑫ ~ 뒤에 ⑬ ~ 옆에

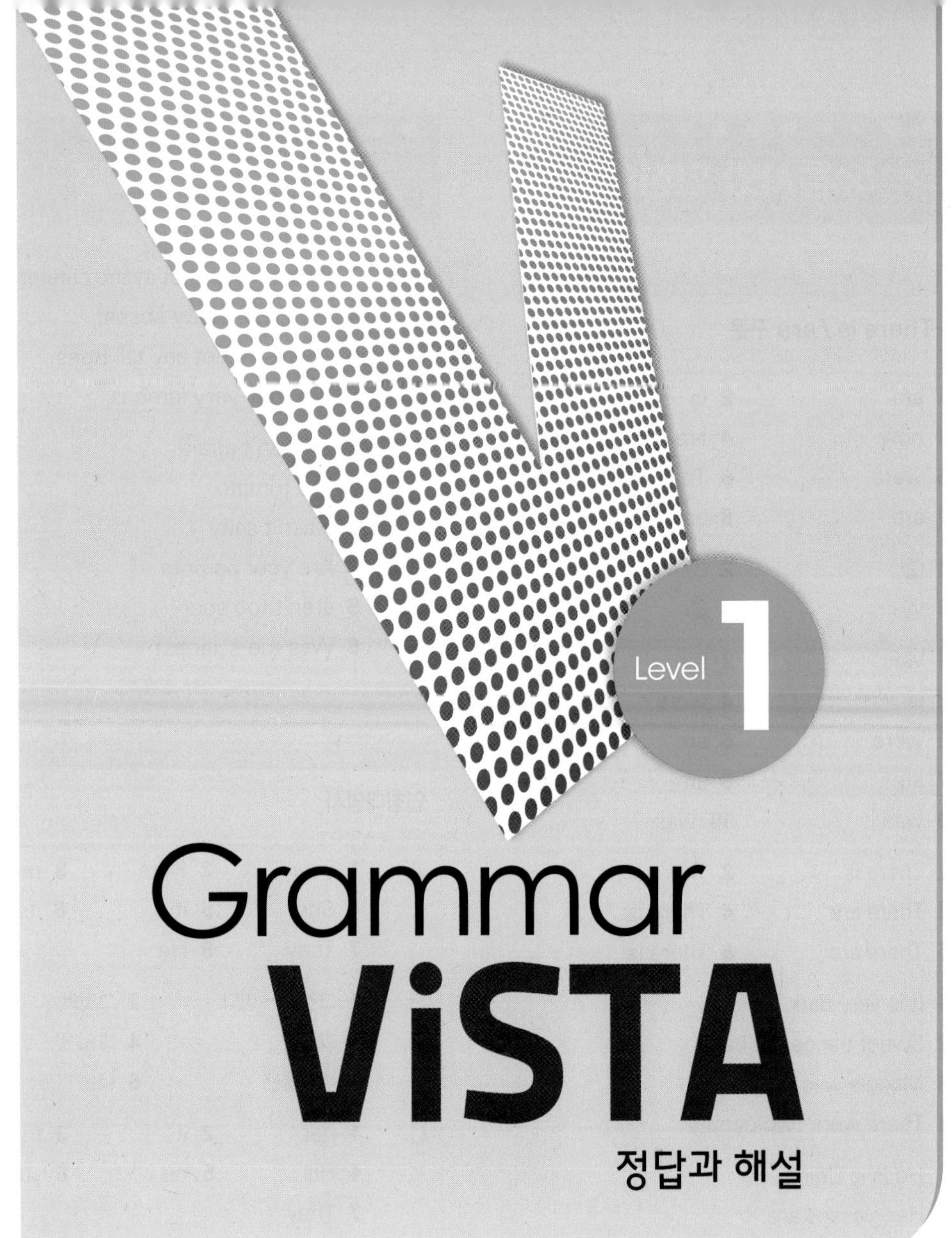

• 본 교재 • workbook

Chapter 01 be동사와 인칭대명사

Unit 01 p. 7

be동사·There is / are 구문

A
1 are 2 is
3 now 4 are
5 were 6 They were
7 are 8 are

B
1 ② 2 ①
3 ④ 4 ③

C
1 was 2 are
3 is 4 were
5 were 6 are
7 are 8 am
9 was 10 was

D
1 There is 2 There are
3 There are 4 There is
5 There are 6 There is

E
1 It is very dark
2 Sweet things are bad
3 Maggie was very sick
4 There were two people

F
1 He is in China
2 Her glasses are
3 There was a cake
4 This year is

Unit 02 p. 9

be동사 부정문과 의문문

A
1 aren't 2 Are
3 Is 4 is not
5 Are 6 Am
7 weren't

B
1 Are we 2 Was he
3 Are you 4 Were they
5 Is the pudding 6 Was your mom
7 Are the boys 8 Were the birds

C
1 isn't 2 aren't
3 isn't 4 aren't
5 wasn't 6 weren't
7 weren't 8 aren't

D
1 He isn't a lazy person
2 Is your father busy
3 Andrew was not at the cafeteria
4 Was your sister absent
5 There are not any tall trees
6 Are they very famous

E
1 She isn't afraid
2 Is a tomato
3 wasn't salty
4 Are your parents
5 aren't too sour
6 Was the scientist

Unit 03 p. 11

인칭대명사

A
1 your 2 Hers 3 me
4 She 5 it 6 its
7 They 8 He

B
1 그것은 ~이다 2 그것의
3 그의 4 그의 것
5 너희들은 6 너는

C
1 her 2 it 3 them
4 His 5 he 6 yours
7 They

D
1 Is your hat blue
2 These shoes are his
3 The actor smiled at us
4 Her favorite music is jazz
5 The white hamster is hers
6 The players changed their uniforms

E
1 We can't carry them
2 Her face is really red
3 This song is for you and me
4 Mine is in the locker
5 They went swimming with us
6 These toys are not theirs

Error Correction p. 13

1	is	3인칭 단수, is
2	are	3인칭 복수, are

3	was	3인칭 단수, was
4	were	3인칭 복수, were
5	O	is, 단수명사
6	is not / isn't	be동사 + not
7	was not / wasn't	3인칭 단수, wasn't
8	Is Amy	Be동사 + 주어 ~?
9	Were they	과거, Were they ~?
10	His	그의, 소유격, his
11	her	그녀를, 목적격, her
12	O	목적격, me
13	hers	그녀의 것, hers

Sentence Writing p. 14

도전! 필수구문 156 p. 130

1 **001** She is a designer.

2 **002** They are at school now.

3 **003** The test was very difficult.

4 **004** Many boys were on the playground.

5 **005** There is a book in my bag.

6 **006** He is not (isn't) at home now.

7 **007** Mary was not (wasn't) sleepy.

8 **008** Is Amy ten years old?

9 **009** Were they in America last week?

10 **010** His car is very fancy.

11 **011** Her friends like her very much.

12 **012** They go cycling with me every Sunday.

13 **013** The bike is hers.

Chapter 02 | 일반동사

Unit 04 p. 19

일반동사와 일반동사 현재형

A
1 eats **2** forgets
3 help **4** washes
5 enjoy **6** passes
7 visits **8** finishes

B
1 like **2** fly
3 drink **4** has
5 brushes **6** does
7 visit **8** reads

C
1 has **2** sets
3 does **4** dries
5 closes

D
1 He cooks on Saturdays
2 This house has many windows
3 Men wear skirts in Scotland
4 She speaks three languages
5 The early bird catches the worm
6 My brother sleeps twelve hours

E
1 I want roller skates
2 They walk to school
3 She listens to music
4 Kevin flies to
5 My mom washes clothes
6 Zoo animals, get food

Unit 05 p. 21

일반동사 과거형

A
1 ordered **2** caught
3 broke **4** bought
5 chose **6** read
7 invited **8** gave

B
1 began **2** ate
3 passed **4** planned
5 had **6** left
7 watched **8** cut

C
1 sang **2** sold
3 read **4** put

5 took

D
1 My family shopped
2 She went to Taiwan
3 It stopped raining
4 He took pictures
5 I bought perfume for my mom
6 We talked about summer vacation

E
1 He told a lie
2 She put some sugar
3 Danny set the alarm
4 I dropped my fork
5 My friend left for America
6 She drank a lot of water

Unit 06 p. 23

일반동사 부정문

A
1 like
2 hit
3 don't
4 didn't
5 don't
6 doesn't
7 doesn't
8 know
9 doesn't
10 didn't

B
1 We didn't enjoy
2 The students don't watch
3 My daughter doesn't like
4 I don't do
5 My mom didn't do
6 Sandra doesn't go jogging
7 Bill doesn't live

C
1 doesn't like
2 didn't do
3 doesn't hear
4 didn't rain

D
1 He doesn't enjoy music
2 Her dog doesn't bark
3 They don't take the shuttle bus
4 didn't check his text messages

E
1 He doesn't play tennis
2 don't eat meat
3 She didn't drink juice
4 I didn't buy anything

Unit 07 p. 25

일반동사 의문문

A
1 write
2 Does
3 Do
4 set
5 Do
6 Did
7 Does

B
1 Does it
2 Did they
3 Does he
4 Did they

C
1 Does, like
2 Do, have
3 Did, do
4 Did, travel

D
1 Did you clean your room
2 Do you take a shower
3 Did the parcel arrive
4 Does she remember my name
5 Did he design this school
6 Does Diana have bread

E
1 Do you trust
2 Did you memorize
3 Does Nick have a pet
4 Do they go to bed early
5 Did you bring your umbrella
6 Does your brother have

Error Correction p. 27

1	cook	1인칭, 동사원형
2	watches	동사원형 + -es
3	tries	y 대신 -ies
4	O	3인칭, has
5	played	규칙, y 뒤에 -ed
6	began	불규칙 변화
7	invented	과거형, 동사원형 + -ed
8	don't wear	do(es)n't + 동사원형
9	doesn't	doesn't
10	rain	동사원형
11	Do you swim	Do(es) + 주어 + 동사원형 ~?
12	Does	Does
13	stay	동사원형

Sentence Writing p. 28

도전! 필수구문 156 p. 131

1 014	I cook very well.
2 015	He watches baseball games on TV.
3 016	The boy always tries his best.
4 017	Chris has many nicknames.
5 018	We played basketball yesterday.
6 019	The festival began an hour ago.
7 020	Edison invented the light bulb in 1879.
8 021	They don't wear blue jeans.
9 022	Sam doesn't like black coffee.
10 023	It didn't rain heavily yesterday.
11 024	Do you swim well? No, I don't.
12 025	Does Michael walk his dog every day?
13 026	Did your sister stay in New York?

Chapter 03 명사와 관사

Unit 08 p. 31

셀 수 있는 명사와 셀 수 없는 명사

A
1 buses 2 cities
3 mice 4 feet
5 teeth 6 watches
7 babies 8 women
9 children 10 pianos
11 potatoes 12 benches
13 roofs 14 leaves
15 dishes 16 thieves

B
1 leaves 2 their
3 milk 4 bread
5 water is 6 homework
7 stories 8 bottles of wine

C
1 teeth 2 mice
3 sheep 4 knives
5 love 6 information

D
1 A cup of hot tea
2 two pieces of cake
3 a bottle of water
4 three loaves of bread

E
1 My family doesn't like fish
2 My brother wants nice pants
3 There were many people
4 I need two pieces of paper
5 Children are the future of Korea

F
1 Ladies and gentlemen
2 The roofs are covered
3 My dad wears sunglasses
4 put a slice of cheese
5 five glasses of orange juice

Unit 09 p. 33

관사

A
1 x 2 a
3 x 4 an
5 the 6 x
7 the

B
1 x 2 a
3 an 4 x
5 x 6 the

C
1 an hour 2 twice a week
3 by subway 4 the cat

D
1 The students picked up
2 Can I borrow an eraser
3 big waves in the sea
4 We go to school on foot
5 Send me the document by e-mail
6 goes to the theater four times a month

E
1 went to bed
2 There is an alligator
3 the guests

4 once a year
5 the flute
6 a car, the car

Error Correction p. 35

1	a new bag	있는, 쓴다
2	O	있고, bags
3	fun	없는, 없다
4	a glass of water	없고, a glass of
5	cups	없고, three cups of
6	an	an, 모음 발음 단어
7	O	a, 명사마다
8	The	the, 이미 언급된 것
9	the	the, 서로 알고 있는 것
10	O	the, 유일한 것
11	the violin	the, 악기 이름
12	삭제	없음, 운동 경기
13	삭제	없음, 교통수단

Sentence Writing p. 36
도전! 필수구문 156 p. 132

1 027	She wants a new bag.
2 028	She wants ten bags.
3 029	We had a lot of fun at the party.
4 030	Can you bring me a glass of water?
5 031	They ordered three cups of coffee.
6 032	I usually eat an apple in the morning.
7 033	My sister reads two books a week.
8 034	She has a pen. The pen is very useful.
9 035	Can you pass me the salt?
10 036	The Earth is not a star but a planet.
11 037	I usually play the violin after school.
12 038	John's favorite sport is soccer.
13 039	I traveled across Europe by bus.

Chapter 04 | 대명사

Unit 10 p. 39

this (these), that (those)·비인칭 주어 it

A
1 that 2 this
3 It's 4 It
5 it 6 these
7 that

B
1 거리 2 날씨
3 대명사 4 대명사
5 날씨 6 명암
7 계절 8 시간

C
1 it 2 those
3 these 4 This
5 that

D
1 this is my mom
2 Is that your bike
3 It is already eight o'clock
4 Those roses smell sweet
5 It is getting warm
6 These shoes are on sale

E
1 These women
2 This soup
3 I saw that man
4 It is too bright
5 These boys, are my classmates
6 It is very cute

Unit 11 p. 41

some, any·all, every, each

A 1 some 2 some 3 Every
4 All 5 Each 6 any

B 1 All 2 Each 3 any
4 each 5 some 6 all
7 any

C 1 some 2 any, some
3 some 4 any, any

D 1 All of the food is
2 Every bird comes back
3 didn't save any food
4 some are rotten
5 Each soccer team has
6 My dad sent some money

E 1 some more bread
2 He washed every
3 any family photos
4 All the members were
5 She put some coins
6 Each idol group holds

Error Correction p. 43

1	This	단수, This
2	These	These, 복수명사
3	O	단수, That
4	Those	Those, 복수명사
5	It	시간, 비인칭 주어
6	it	특정한, it
7	some	some, 긍정문
8	some	some, 권유문
9	O	any, 부정문
10	are	복수, 복수
11	is	단수, 단수
12	has	단수, 단수
13	student	단수명사

Sentence Writing p. 44

도전! 필수구문 156 p. 133

1 **040** This is my favorite watch.

2 **041** These houses are very old.

3 **042** That is your birthday gift.

4 **043** Those trees don't have leaves.

5 **044** It's seven o'clock.

6 **045** She took this picture. I love it.

7 **046** I have some questions.

8 **047** Will you have some chocolate?

9 **048** I don't have any questions.

10 **049** All the boys are standing in the hall.

11 **050** All the money is in a safe place.

12 **051** Each boy has his own cell phone.

13 **052** Every student is wearing shorts.

Chapter 05 | 진행형과 미래시제

Unit 12 p. 47

진행형 부정문과 의문문

A 1 waiting 2 are
3 chatting 4 building
5 sleeping 6 wasn't
7 Is 8 taking
9 weren't 10 were

B 1 is raining 2 am riding
3 Is, working 4 aren't using
5 was reading 6 were dancing
7 Was, drinking 8 weren't wearing

C
1 Are, doing
2 Is, playing
3 Was, having
4 Were, carrying

D
1 was talking with the cook
2 was not driving a car
3 is not sending a text message
4 Were they riding their bikes
5 are sitting in the chairs
6 Is your brother planning

E
1 I am looking for
2 Was Mike reading
3 is crying for
4 We are not growing
5 They were not playing
6 Are the marathon runners passing

Unit 13 p. 49

미래시제 부정문과 의문문

A
1 isn't 2 Will
3 have 4 Is
5 come 6 to take
7 Is 8 won't change

B
1 will download
2 is going to wear
3 won't design
4 isn't going to stay
5 will be
6 won't come
7 am going to finish
8 aren't going to swim

C
1 Will, remember
2 Is, going to cook
3 Will, be
4 Is, going to buy
5 Are, going to meet

D
1 He will not eat pizza
2 Will you join the science club
3 She will take a swimming class
4 We are not going to invite
5 The plane is going to take off
6 Is the museum going to be open

E
1 My dog will not bark
2 Are you going to order
3 She will leave for
4 is not going to be hot
5 I won't use
6 Will she surprise the world

Error Correction p. 51

1	surfing	동사원형 + -ing
2	are studying	be동사 + 동사원형 + -ing
3	were	were, 동사원형 + -ing
4	O	be동사, 동사원형 + -ing
5	was	be동사, 동사원형 + -ing
6	wearing	동사원형 + -ing
7	be	동사원형
8	to rain	going to
9	are going	be동사 + going to
10	will not	will not
11	O	am not
12	come	동사원형
13	Are	Be동사

Sentence Writing p. 52
도전! 필수구문 156 p. 134

1 053	He is surfing the Internet.
2 054	We are studying English grammar.
3 055	They were watching a baseball game then.
4 056	I am not joking.
5 057	Andrew was not listening to the teacher.
6 058	Are you wearing glasses?
7 059	The game will be popular.
8 060	It is going to rain soon.

9 061 We are going to have a party.

10 062 We won't (will not) fight again.

11 063 I am not going to run in the classroom.

12 064 Will the actor come to Korea?

13 065 Are you going to invite your friends?

Chapter 06 | 조동사

Unit 14 p. 55

can, may

A
1 Can 2 take
3 Can 4 could
5 travel 6 is
7 can't 8 may not
9 Are 10 be

B
1 can't 2 can't
3 can 4 can't
5 can 6 may not
7 May 8 may not
9 may 10 may

C
1 is able to build
2 are able to swim
3 was not able to catch
4 Is he able to climb

D
1 Can you tell me about
2 Dogs cannot see
3 We may see a rainbow
4 You may not play the piano

E
1 You may (can) cut your finger
2 may not use the elevator
3 could not marry Romeo
4 able to see the volcano

Unit 15 p. 57

must, have to, should

A
1 must 2 have to
3 don't have to 4 cheat
5 must

B
1 Must 2 have to
3 must 4 have to
5 must 6 don't have to
7 doesn't have to 8 must not
9 must not 10 didn't have to

C
1 ⓒ 2 ⓑ 3 ⓐ 4 ⓐ

D
1 have to bring 2 has to pack
3 has to get off 4 have to listen

E
1 Should I set the table
2 have to wear life jackets
3 The players must not start
4 You must be proud of

F
1 should learn
2 should not cut
3 Must I insert
4 don't have to drive

Error Correction p. 59

1	talk	동사원형
2	cannot / can't	조동사 + not
3	Can you fix	조동사 + 주어
4	may go	허락, 동사원형
5	May I ask	동사원형
6	may be	약한 추측, 동사원형
7	O	~해야 한다, 동사원형
8	must not	조동사 + not
9	must be	~가 틀림없다, 동사원형
10	has to	~해야 한다, has to
11	doesn't have to	~할 필요 없다, doesn't
12	have to	Do + 주어 + have to
13	O	~해야 한다, 동사원형

Sentence Writing p. 60

도전! 필수구문 156 p. 135

1 066	The robot is able to talk.
2 067	He can't ride a bicycle.
3 068	Can you fix the computer?
4 069	You may go home now.
5 070	May I ask a question?
6 071	She may be hungry.
7 072	We must stop at red lights.
8 073	You must not give dogs ice cream.
9 074	The cheesecake must be delicious.
10 075	She has to get some rest.
11 076	Phillip doesn't have to lose weight.
12 077	Do I have to wait?
13 078	Tom should eat more vegetables.

Chapter 07 의문사와 여러 가지 문장

Unit 16 p. 65

who, what, which

A **1** What **2** Who
3 Whose **4** Who
5 What **6** Which

B **1** What **2** Who
3 Whose **4** Which
5 What **6** Who

C **1** Whose car is it
2 Which is cheaper
3 What is your favorite subject
4 Who made this skirt
5 What is her name

D **1** Whose puppy is it
2 Who ordered the food
3 What do you eat
4 Which book is hers
5 Who did you meet last night
6 Which did she wear

E **1** Who lives next door
2 Whose plan was it (that)
3 What did she teach
4 Who is the director
5 Who(m) did you invite
6 Which country do you want

Unit 17 p. 67

when, where, why, how·how + 형용사 / 부사

A **1** Where **2** When
3 Why **4** How

B **1** ⓑ **2** ⓐ
3 ⓒ **4** ⓕ
5 ⓓ **6** ⓔ

C **1** Why did you run away
2 How can I get to the zoo
3 When did she leave China
4 Where did she study English

D **1** How much **2** How tall
3 How long **4** How often

E **1** Why did you marry her
2 When can we meet him
3 How was last weekend
4 Where did you first meet

F **1** where are my socks
2 When did he go
3 How old is your grandmother
4 Why was Kate tired

Unit 18 p. 69

부정의문문·부가의문문

A **1** Isn't **2** Weren't
3 aren't **4** doesn't

5 were
6 Didn't
7 will
8 he

B
1 Didn't you remember me, didn't
2 Isn't she a pilot, is
3 Doesn't he look like an actor, does
4 Wasn't she taller than you, wasn't

C
1 doesn't she
2 can they
3 will you
4 don't they
5 does she
6 isn't it
7 wasn't he
8 did he

D
1 Aren't you ready
2 His idea isn't bad, is it
3 Wasn't the bird in the cage
4 His speech was great, wasn't it
5 Didn't you live in America
6 She warmed the pizza, didn't she

E
1 Don't you know me
2 Isn't she too careful
3 is really neat, isn't it
4 Didn't you go there yesterday
5 eat insects, don't they
6 has a beautiful voice, doesn't he

Unit 19 p. 71

명령문, 제안문, 감탄문

A
1 be
2 How
3 watch
4 What
5 not
6 Visit
7 How

B
1 Take
2 Don't touch
3 Be
4 Don't sit
5 Walk
6 Don't be
7 Cover

C
1 Let's be
2 Let's carry
3 Let's stop
4 Let's not open
5 Let's take
6 Let's not tell
7 Let's not forget

D
1 What a great moment it is
2 How real his painting looks
3 What an exciting trip we had
4 How soft the blanket is

E
1 How shocking the news is
2 Don't be late tomorrow
3 What a big castle it is
4 Let's not buy too much food

F
1 Don't draw
2 Let's make a plan
3 Be nice (kind) to your neighbors
4 How amazing the parade was

Error Correction p. 73

1	O	사람, who
2	What	없을 때, What
3	Which	있을 때, Which
4	O	시간, When
5	Where	장소, Where
6	How	How
7	How often	How often
8	was	긍정문, 부정문
9	doesn't she	부정문, doesn't
10	O	긍정문
11	Don't be	~하지 마라, Don't
12	How	How
13	What	What

Sentence Writing p. 74

도전! 필수구문 156 p. 136

1 079	Who is your new teacher?
2 080	What is your favorite subject?
3 081	Which do you want, an orange or a kiwi?
4 082	When does the movie start?
5 083	Where did you find this book?
6 084	How can I get to the airport?
7 085	How often do you work out?

8 **086**	Wasn't the test easy? Yes, it was.
9 **087**	She has breakfast every morning, doesn't she?
10 **088**	You didn't see the polar bear, did you?
11 **089**	Don't be nervous.
12 **090**	How popular the game is!
13 **091**	What a beautiful day (it is)!

Chapter 08 형용사와 부사

Unit 20 p. 78

형용사의 쓰임·수량 형용사

A
1 salty **2** angry
3 lots of **4** friendly
5 anything new **6** careful
7 good **8** a lot of

B
1 ① much, 없음 ② many, 있음
2 ① little, 없음 ② few, 있음
3 ① a few, 있음 ② a little, 없음

C
1 ⓑ **2** ⓐ
3 ⓑ **4** ⓑ
5 ⓐ

D
1 wonderful **2** delicious
3 dark **4** used

E
1 found Jack honest
2 feel comfortable at home
3 can't bring anything dangerous
4 invited a few people
5 How many hours do you sleep

F
1 the beautiful sky
2 need a little
3 few elephants
4 have much
5 wants something cold

Unit 21 p. 80

부사의 쓰임과 형태·빈도부사

A
1 fast **2** Strangely
3 near **4** hard
5 usually wears **6** bravely
7 are never

B
1 honestly, honest
2 really, real
3 nice, nicely
4 simply, simple
5 late, lately

C
1 lived, ①
2 carefully, ③
3 interesting, ②
4 he found gold, ④

D
1 She often buys things online
2 Kangaroos can never walk backward
3 Mike was usually late for school
4 He always looks like a boy

E
1 An albatross flies high
2 has really big hands
3 Sadly, our team lost another game
4 He usually goes to the movies

F
1 is really cheap
2 closed the door quietly
3 always leaves on time
4 was pretty hard
5 Interestingly

Unit 22 p. 82

원급, 비교급, 최상급

A
1 hot **2** faster
3 best **4** than
5 of **6** more beautiful
7 the longest

B
1 better than
2 faster than
3 more slowly than
4 worse than
5 harder than
6 brighter than
7 more comfortable than

C
1 the biggest
2 the worst
3 the coldest
4 the youngest
5 the most famous
6 The largest
7 the smallest

D
1 as old as
2 as early as
3 as expensive as
4 as often as

E
1 Blood is thicker than water
2 is more handsome than me
3 the most valuable player
4 are the hardest of all stones

F
1 as playful as
2 better than
3 the biggest bird
4 more interesting than

Error Correction p. 84

1	close	명사 수식, 형용사
2	interesting	보어, 형용사
3	many	many, 셀 수 있는 명사 복수형
4	a few	a few, 약간은 있는
5	a little	a little, 약간은 있는
6	slowly	느리게, 동사, 부사
7	O	형용사, 부사
8	may often	뒤
9	is always	뒤
10	O	앞
11	busy	바쁜, 원급
12	heavier	더 무거운, 비교급
13	largest	가장 큰, 최상급

Sentence Writing p. 85

도전! 필수구문 156 p. 137

1 092 We are close friends.

2 093 This movie was interesting.

3 094 There are many holidays in May.

4 095 He met Julie a few days ago.

5 096 She spread a little jam on the bread.

6 097 Jack walked to school slowly.

7 098 I have very tall friends.

8 099 He may often be wrong.

9 100 Tom is always late for class.

10 101 She never eats meat for dinner.

11 102 Sarah is as busy as a bee.

12 103 Cold air is heavier than hot air.

13 104 The whale is the largest of all animals.

Chapter 09 | 부정사와 동명사

Unit 23 p. 89

to부정사의 명사적 쓰임

A
1 To have　　2 It
3 to join　　4 read
5 to buy　　6 To
7 to use

B
1 만나는 것, ②　　2 보는 것, ③
3 말하는 것, ①　　4 기르는 것 (갖는 것), ②
5 부르는 것, ②　　6 거짓말을 하는 것, ①

C
1 To sing　　2 to find
3 to drink　　4 to cook
5 how to go　　6 where to go
7 when to sleep　　8 what to eat

D
1 easy to be a good son
2 did you learn to swim

3 needs to eat more vegetables
4 is to treat sick animals
5 knows where to get off the bus
6 don't want to wear this shirt
7 It is important to speak English

E
1 wanted to buy
2 know how to drive
3 To change the rule was
4 is to visit
5 to bring your own food
6 to live on the mountain

Unit 24 p. 91

to부정사의 형용사적·부사적 쓰임

A
1 보기 위해, ⓐ
2 보게 되어서, ⓑ
3 읽기에, ⓒ
4 들어서, ⓑ

B
1 something to wear
2 time to go
3 two bags to carry
4 country to visit
5 three tests to take
6 a plan to surprise

C
1 ⓑ 2 ⓒ
3 ⓐ 4 ⓐ
5 ⓒ 6 ⓑ

D
1 is easy to sing
2 was happy to win a gold medal
3 have something important to show
4 went to Paris to visit his friend
5 was very heavy to wear
6 knows the best way to teach

E
1 safe to drive
2 many places to see
3 came to protect the singer
4 happy to come back to Korea
5 enough time to read books
6 went to Africa to build schools

Unit 25 p. 93

동명사의 명사적 쓰임

A
1 Flying 2 reading
3 listening 4 touching
5 drawing 6 cleaning
7 drinking 8 ordering
9 Walking 10 going

B
1 traveling 2 painting
3 acting 4 waiting
5 answering

C
1 온 것, ⓒ
2 청소하는 것, ⓑ
3 노래하는 것, ⓑ
4 읽는 것, ⓓ
5 모으는 것, ⓐ

D
1 you quit drinking coffee
2 My job is training dolphins
3 enjoyed meeting new people
4 Drinking enough water is important
5 is good at making movies
6 Cooking Chinese food is her hobby

E
1 is using
2 mind changing
3 is good at folding
4 are excited about meeting
5 kept sneezing
6 couldn't stop laughing

Error Correction p. 95

1	To read	to부정사
2	It	It, to부정사
3	to visit	to부정사
4	to become	to부정사
5	O	~ 요리할, 명사 + to부정사
6	something cold to drink	마실, to부정사
7	to make	~ 만들기 위해, to부정사
8	O	~ 듣게 되어, 감정형용사
9	easy to remember	~ 기억하기에, 형용사
10	Riding	동명사

11 opening 동명사

12 listening 동명사

13 getting up 동명사

Sentence Writing p. 96

도전! 필수구문 156 p. 138

1 105	To read webtoons is fun.
2 106	It is fun to read webtoons.
3 107	We decided to visit the zoo.
4 108	My dream is to become a game designer.
5 109	He knows a special way to cook noodles.
6 110	Please give me something cold to drink.
7 111	They used robots to make ships.
8 112	I am sorry to hear the news.
9 113	His name is easy to remember.
10 114	Riding a roller coaster is scary.
11 115	Do you mind opening the door for me?
12 116	Thank you for listening.
13 117	Her good habit is getting up early.

Chapter 10 | 동사의 종류

Unit 26 p. 100

감각동사 + 형용사

A
1 strong **2** good
3 sounds **4** friendly
5 feel **6** sweet

B
1 ⓐ felt, ⓑ felt like
2 ⓐ smells, ⓑ smells like
3 ⓐ looks like, ⓑ looks
4 ⓐ sounds like, ⓑ sounds

C
1 ⓐ 느끼다
ⓑ ~한 느낌이 나다
2 ⓐ 냄새 맡다
ⓑ ~한 냄새가 나다
3 ⓐ 보다
ⓑ ~하게 보이다
4 ⓐ 맛을 보다
ⓑ ~한 맛이 나다

D
1 The NASA project sounds exciting
2 The lotion smells like apples
3 This candy tastes sour
4 Some cats feel safe in a box
5 My mom looks young
6 The boy felt like Superman

E
1 tastes like chicken
2 feels warm
3 look different
4 smells bad
5 looks real
6 sounded angry
7 taste salty

Unit 27 p. 102

수여동사 + 간접목적어 + 직접목적어
수여동사 + 직접목적어 + 전치사 + 간접목적어

A
1 to his wife **2** me
3 him an e-mail **4** you a question
5 for **6** to us
7 them

B
1 나에게, ② **2** 스파게티를, ①
3 우리에게, ② **4** 그녀의 비밀을, ①
5 그녀에게, ②

C
1 the way to you
2 nice shoes for me
3 a tip to the waiter
4 my missing key for me
5 the salad to me

D
1 give a hint to you
2 bought us ice cream
3 cooked bulgogi for us

4 get your mom the pretty hat
5 made a small gift for his friend
6 found me a job

E
1 sent me a box of chocolates
2 get roses for
3 you bring me the scissors
4 asked her a question
5 lend me 2,000 won
6 give you a hug

Unit 28 p. 104

목적격 보어가 필요한 동사

A
1 helpful 2 to water
3 soft 4 him
5 to sit 6 to wear
7 strong 8 warm

B
1 want you to be
2 expect us to believe
3 made him special
4 keep our toothbrushes dry

C
1 warm, 형용사
2 a real man, 명사
3 Dodo, 명사
4 to come, to부정사

D
1 found the rumor false
2 expect me to be perfect
3 named his dog Superpower
4 told the baby pigs to open
5 wants me to buy clothes
6 keeps them warm in winter

E
1 called Tom a bookworm
2 makes people less tired
3 asked the police to help her
4 found the cookie jar empty
5 wanted me to turn off
6 Keep your hands clean

Error Correction p. 106

1	O	형용사, ~하게 보이다
2	cold	형용사, ~하게 느끼다
3	delicious	형용사, ~한 냄새가 나다
4	beautiful	형용사, ~하게 들리다
5	us	~에게 ~를, 없음
6	to us	~를 ~에게, 있음
7	me	~에게 ~를, 없음
8	O	~를 ~에게, 있음
9	him	~에게 ~를, 없음
10	of him	~를 ~에게, 있음
11	O	명사
12	famous	형용사
13	to like	to부정사

Sentence Writing p. 107

도전! 필수구문 156 p. 139

1 118	You look young in that blue shirt.
2 119	I feel cold.
3 120	The sausage smells delicious.
4 121	Her voice sounds beautiful.
5 122	He showed us his puppy.
6 123	He showed his puppy to us.
7 124	She bought me a flower.
8 125	She bought a flower for me.
9 126	Anna asked him a favor.
10 127	Anna asked a favor of him.
11 128	We called him an iron man.
12 129	The news made him famous.
13 130	I want you to like my present.

Chapter 11 접속사

Unit 29 p. 111

and, but, or, so

A
1 but
2 or
3 so
4 and
5 so
6 but

B
1 but
2 and
3 so
4 or

C
1 but a pan pizza was delivered
2 or you will catch a cold
3 so he got up late this morning
4 and you will understand it

D
1 and prepares breakfast
2 like cooking but don't enjoy
3 or you will miss
4 milk and butter
5 online or offline
6 so she uses the scissors

E
1 Jane or you
2 so we walked slowly
3 and you will be healthy
4 call or visit me
5 but is good for your health
6 so we should (must) wear masks

Unit 30 p. 113

when, before, after

A
1 When
2 after
3 comes
4 when
5 before
6 when
7 After

B
1 그녀가 피곤할 때
2 네가 샤워한 후에
3 그가 상을 탄 후에
4 내가 일을 시작하기 전에
5 네가 우리를 다시 찾아올 때
6 내가 나가기 전에

C
1 before he leaves the hotel
2 When I listen to music
3 After I made a shopping list
4 before you buy the pencil

D
1 when they eat noodles
2 before it gets dark
3 After he washed his hands
4 Before spring comes
5 After I lose some weight
6 When it rains

E
1 When I saw a shooting star
2 before she talks
3 after I use it
4 Before I come home
5 when I need his help
6 before he changes his mind

Unit 31 p. 115

because, if, that

A
1 that
2 if
3 because
4 gets
5 that
6 If
7 because

B
1 that
2 Because
3 If
4 that

C
1 it feels cool
2 If you add more salt
3 because they smell bad
4 that she can save the birds

D
1 that camels don't store water
2 if you are 19 years old
3 Because the lake is deep
4 If you win this game
5 that he has a beautiful voice
6 because she lost the key

E
1 said that it will rain
2 If I go to the moon
3 because it was hot
4 If you don't drink water
5 Because it was dusty outside
6 know that Dylan has two brothers

Error Correction p. 117

1	and	그리고
2	but	그러나
3	or	또는
4	so	그래서
5	and	그러면
6	or	그렇지 않으면
7	When	느낄 때
8	Before	전에
9	go	현재
10	because	기 때문에
11	snows	현재
12	if	다면
13	that	라는 것을

Sentence Writing p. 118

도전! 필수구문 156 p. 140

1 **131**	I think of you night and day.
2 **132**	The soccer player is short but fast.
3 **133**	Which subject do you like better, math or English?
4 **134**	He missed the last bus, so he took a taxi.
5 **135**	Open the window, and you will see the rainbow.
6 **136**	Open the window, or you won't see the rainbow.
7 **137**	When Clara feels shy, her face turns red.
8 **138**	Before you pay for the candy, you can't eat it.
9 **139**	I will bring a tent when I go camping.
10 **140**	She likes the actor because he is funny.
11 **141**	If it snows tomorrow, we will go skiing.
12 **142**	Pass me the cake if you don't want to eat it.
13 **143**	Do you think (that) Emily is an angel?

Chapter 12 전치사

Unit 32 p. 122

시간을 나타내는 전치사 I·II

A
1 at **2** on
3 after **4** on
5 to **6** in
7 on **8** until
9 between **10** during

B
1 at **2** in
3 at **4** in
5 in **6** on

C
1 for **2** during
3 for **4** for
5 during **6** during

D
1 went down after August
2 comes out in July
3 felt nervous before her turn
4 is from February 14 to 28
5 watched the sunrise on New Year's Day
6 the package by this Thursday

E
1 in summer
2 until this Sunday
3 at 2:27 p.m.
4 on Wednesdays
5 during these hours
6 between, and

Unit 33 p. 124

장소를 나타내는 전치사 I·II

A
1 at **2** over
3 across **4** near
5 in **6** from

B
1 on 2 in
3 on 4 in
5 at 6 in

C
1 under 2 behind
3 near 4 over
5 across from 6 between
7 front 8 from

D
1 built a tunnel under the ground
2 get off at the next stop
3 any life on the moon
4 sleeping between two chickens
5 little milk in the glass
6 bounced over the net
7 shocked people across the country

E
1 sit next to her
2 from nine to five
3 in the book
4 on its back
5 behind the clouds
6 at the music festival

Unit 34 p. 126

기타 전치사

A
1 with 2 to
3 for 4 like
5 about 6 for
7 by

B
1 to 2 by
3 like 4 about

C
1 for, for 2 with, with
3 to, to 4 by, by

D
1 ② 2 ④
3 ① 4 ③

E
1 about sea animals
2 the box with green paper
3 a helmet for safety
4 an invitation by e-mail
5 tell the truth to the police

F
1 talk with you
2 by phone
3 Like owls
4 about my hairstyle

5 to his friends

Error Correction p. 128

1	at	at
2	on	on
3	in	in
4	for	for, 숫자 포함 기간
5	during	during, 특정한 기간명사
6	at	비교적 좁은 지점에, at
7	on	표면 위에, on
8	in	안에, in
9	to	A부터 B까지, to
10	O	~을 타고
11	with	~을 가지고
12	me	목적격
13	O	~처럼

Sentence Writing p. 129
도전! 필수구문 156 p. 141

1 144	My school starts at 8:30 a.m.
2 145	Alex was born on May 7.
3 146	People enjoy skiing in the winter.
4 147	Some koalas sleep for 17 hours a day.
5 148	Hamsters are underground during the day.
6 149	I lost my backpack at the airport.
7 150	Look at the pictures on the wall.
8 151	Jasmine has some coins in her pocket.
9 152	This plane flies from Seoul to Busan.
10 153	We crossed the river by boat.
11 154	Wash your hands with soap.

12 155	Ken sent a text message to me.
13 156	Greg dressed like a zombie at the Halloween party.

불규칙 변화 동사 70

p. 142

01	bore	born
02	began	begun
03	bit	bitten
04	blew	blown
05	broke	broken
06	brought	brought
07	built	built
08	burnt	burnt
09	bought	bought
10	caught	caught
11	chose	chosen
12	came	come
13	cut	cut
14	drank	drunk
15	drove	driven
16	ate	eaten
17	fell	fallen
18	felt	felt
19	fought	fought
20	found	found
21	forgave	forgiven
22	got	got / gotten
23	gave	given
24	went	gone
25	grew	grown
26	heard	heard
27	hid	hidden
28	hit	hit
29	held	held
30	kept	kept
31	knew	known
32	laid	laid
33	left	left
34	lent	lent
35	lay	lain
36	lost	lost
37	made	made
38	met	met
39	paid	paid
40	put	put
41	read	read
42	rode	ridden
43	rose	risen
44	ran	run
45	said	said
46	saw	seen
47	sold	sold
48	sent	sent
49	set	set
50	shook	shaken
51	showed	shown
52	shut	shut
53	sang	sung
54	sat	sat
55	slept	slept
56	spoke	spoken
57	spent	spent
58	stood	stood
59	stole	stolen
60	struck	struck
61	swam	swum
62	took	taken
63	taught	taught
64	told	told
65	thought	thought
66	threw	thrown
67	understood	understood
68	wore	worn
69	won	won
70	wrote	written